Hiking Georgia

Third Edition

Donald W. Pfitzer

FALCONGUIDES ®

GUILFORD, CONNECTICUT
HELENA, MONTANA
AN IMPRINT OF THE GLOBE PEQUOT PRESS

FALCONGUIDES®

Copyright © 2000, 2006 by Morris Book Publishing, LLC
Previously published by Falcon Publishing, Inc.

FalconGuides is an imprint of The Globe Pequot Press.
Falcon and FalconGuides are registered trademarks of
Morris Book Publishing, LLC.

Maps by Trailhead Graphics © Morris Book Publishing, LLC

Spine photo © Michael DeYoung
All interior photographs are by the author unless otherwise
noted.

Library of Congress Cataloging-in-Publication Data
Pfitzer, Donald W.
   Hiking Georgia / Donald W. Pfitzer. —3rd ed.
      p. cm. — (A Falconguide)
   ISBN 978-0-7627-3642-3
   1. Hiking—Georgia—Guidebooks. 2. Family recreation—
Georgia—Guidebooks. 3. Backpacking—Georgia—
Guidebooks. 4. Georgia—Guidebooks. I. Title. II. Series.

GV199.42.G46P46 2006
796.5109758—dc22   2006015901

Manufactured in the United States of America
Third Edition/Second Printing

To buy books in quantity for corporate use
or incentives, call **(800) 962–0973**
or e-mail **premiums@GlobePequot.com**.

To Billie S. Pfitzer
and
Martha E. Pfitzer

Contents

Acknowledgments x

Introduction 1

    Physiographic Regions and Natural History 3

    Archaeology and History 3

    Zero Impact Hiking 4

    Be Prepared 4

    Insects, Snakes, and Other Concerns 8

    Navigation 10

    Planning Your Trip 12

    Weather 15

    Hiking with Children 15

    Hikers with Special Needs 17

    Volunteering 18

Using This Guide 19

    How to Use the Maps 20

Map Legend 21

The Hikes

Northwest Georgia: Cumberland Plateau and Ridge and Valley 23

National Forest Trails 24

    1. Chickamauga Creek Trail 24

    2. Keown Falls and Johns Mountain Trails 27

    3. The Pocket Recreation Area Trail 33

State Park and Wildlife Management Area Trails 35

    4. Cloudland Canyon State Park Trails 35

    5. Crockford–Pigeon Mountain Wildlife Management Area Trails 40

    6. Arrowhead Wildlife Interpretive Trail 46

    Honorable Mentions

    A. James H. (Sloppy) Floyd State Park 49

    B. Chickamauga Battlefield National Military Park 49

Northeast Georgia: Blue Ridge Mountains 51

National Forest Trails 52

    7. Lake Conasauga Recreation Area Trails 52

    8. DeSoto Falls Trail 57

    9. Cooper Creek Wildlife Management Area Trails 60

    10. Arkaquah and Brasstown Bald Trails 65

    11. Wagon Train Trail 69

    12. Jacks Knob Trail 73

    13. Lake Winfield Scott Recreation Area Trails 76

14. Sosebee Cove Trail 80

15. High Shoals Scenic Area and Falls Trail 82

16. Ellicott Rock Wilderness Trail 86

17. Rabun Beach Recreation Area: Angel Falls Trail 89

18. Warwoman Dell Nature Trail and Becky Branch Falls Trail 92

19. Three Forks Trail 95

20. Anna Ruby Falls and Lion's Eye Nature Trails 98

21. Smith Creek Trail 99

22. Andrews Cove Recreation Area Trail 103

23. Dukes Creek Trail 106

24. Raven Cliff Falls Trail 108

25. Lake Russell Recreation Area: Sourwood Trail 111

26. Panther Creek Trail 114

State Park and Wildlife Management Area Trails 119

27. Fort Mountain State Park Trails 119

28. Amicalola Falls State Park Trails 124

29. Leonard E. Foote Hike Inn Trail 127

30. Vogel State Park Trails 132

31. Unicoi State Park Trails 138

32. Smithgall Woods and Dukes Creek Conservation Area Trails 141

33. Moccasin Creek Wildlife Trail and Hemlock Falls Trail 145

34. Black Rock Mountain State Park Trails 149

35. Tallulah Gorge State Park Trails 154

36. Victoria Bryant State Park Trails 159

37. Lake Russell Wildlife Management Area: Broad River Trail 163

   Honorable Mentions

   C. Holcomb Creek Trail 167

   D. Aska Area Trails 167

   E. Duncan Ridge National Recreation Trail 168

   F. Lake Russell Recreation Area: Ladyslipper Trail 168

   G. Brasstown Valley and Mountain Park 169

   H. Tugaloo State Park 169

   I. Benton MacKaye Trail 170

   J. Cohutta Wilderness Area 170

Central Georgia: Piedmont and Fall Line Area 171

National Forest Trails 172

38. Oconee River Recreation Area Trails 172

39. Twin Bridges Trail 176

State Park Trails 179

40. Red Top Mountain State Park Trails 179

41. Richard B. Russell State Park Trails 183

42. Hard Labor Creek State Park Trails 186

43. Watson Mill Bridge State Park Trails 189

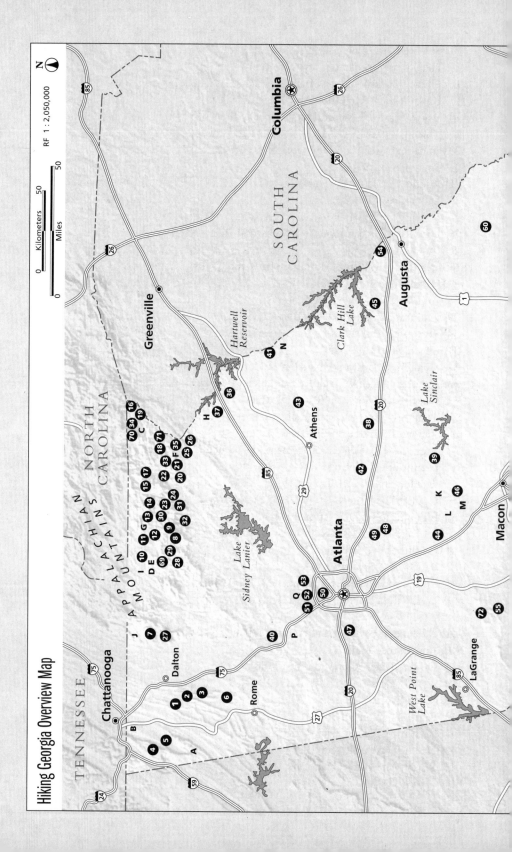

Hiking Georgia Overview Map

RF 1 : 2,050,000

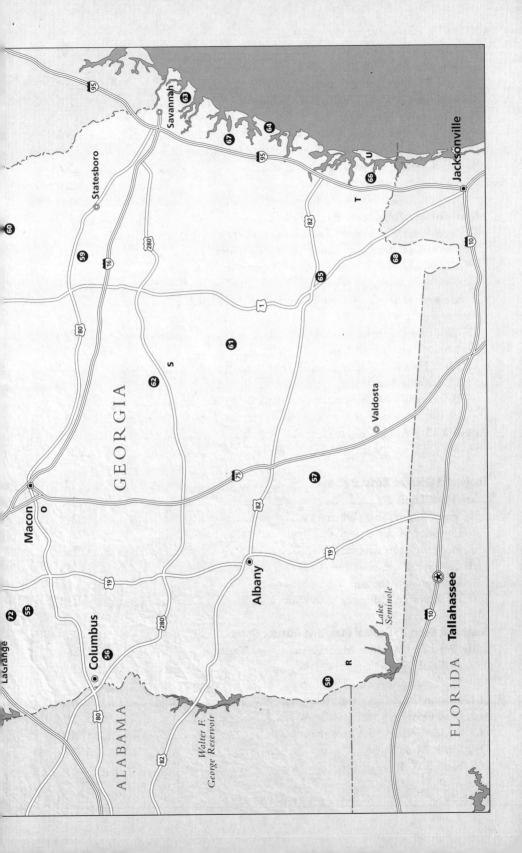

44. High Falls State Park Trails 193

45. Mistletoe State Park Trails 196

National Wildlife Refuge Trails 201

46. Piedmont National Wildlife Refuge Trails 201

   Honorable Mentions

   K.   Charlie Elliott Wildlife Center 205

   L.   Rum Creek Wildlife Management Area Nature Trail 205

   M. Ocmulgee River Trail 206

   N. Bobby Brown State Park 206

   O. Ocmulgee National Monument 207

Metro Atlanta Area State Park Trails 208

47. Sweetwater Creek State Conservation Park Trails 208

48. Panola Mountain State Conservation Park Trails 213

49. Davidson–Arabia Mountain Nature Preserve Trails with
    Arabia Mountain Trail 216

Chattahoochee River National Recreation Area 222

50. East Palisades Trail 223

51. West Palisades Trail 226

52. Johnson Ferry North Trail 229

53. Island Ford Trail 232

   Honorable Mentions

   P. Kennesaw Mountain National Battlefield Park 235

   Q. Chattahoochee River National Recreation Area: Cochran Shoals.........235

Augusta City Area 237

54. Augusta Canal National Heritage Area Trail 237

Southwest Georgia: Coastal Plain 241

State Park Trails 242

55. Sprewell Bluff State Park Trails 242

56. Providence Canyon State Park Trails 245

57. Reed Bingham State Park Trails 250

58. George T. Bagby State Park Trails 255

   Honorable Mention

   R. Kolomoki Mounds State Historic Park 258

Southeast Georgia: Coastal Plain and Atlantic Coast 259

State Park and Wildlife Management Area Trails 260

59. George L. Smith State Park Trails 260

60. Magnolia Springs State Park Trails 265

61. General Coffee State Park Trails 269

62. Little Ocmulgee State Park Trails 272

63. Skidaway Island State Park Trails 276

64. Sapelo Island Trails 280

65. Laura S. Walker State Park Trails 285

66. Crooked River State Park Trails 288

National Wildlife Refuges Trails 293

67. Harris Neck National Wildlife Refuge and Savannah Coastal
    Refuge Complex 293
68. Okefenokee National Wildlife Refuge Trails 298
    Honorable Mentions
    S. Big Hammock Natural Area 302
    T. Hofwyl–Broadfield Plantation Historic Site 302
    U. Cumberland Island National Seashore 303

Long Trails 305

69. Appalachian Trail in Georgia 306
70. Bartram National Heritage Trail 314
71. Chattooga National Wild and Scenic River Trail 321
72. F. D. Roosevelt State Park: Pine Mountain and Mountain Creek
    Nature Trails 326

Appendix A: Local Hiking Clubs and Conservation Organizations 333
Appendix B: Federal and State Land Management Agencies 334
Appendix C: Additional Resources 336
Appendix D: Other Georgia State Parks with Hiking Trails 338
Index 339
About the Author 341

Acknowledgments

Many people helped make this book possible. Thanks to the Department of Natural Resources, particularly Commissioner Noel Holcomb; Becky Kelly, Parks and Historic Sites Division Director; and former Director David Waller, Wildlife Resources Division, all of whom gave me much support and encouragement. I also appreciate the help that came from the USDA Forest Service, National Park Service, and U.S. Fish and Wildlife Service.

I am especially grateful to Henry Chambers, Geographical Information Systems (GIS) Analyst for the State Parks and Historic Sites Division, who helped in deciding which trails to include, walked with me on several hikes, and reviewed the descriptions of most of the trails. This guide is more accurate because of his help. Jim Robertson was especially helpful, both as a guide through problems with the computer and as a hiking companion. LeRoy Powell was of great editorial help as well as a hiking companion. Thanks to Dr. M. Virginia Tuggle and Annette Loudermilk, who graciously reviewed the sections dealing with personal health and safety.

Thanks also to those who were so generous in providing information and assistance: Erika Mavity, Larry Thomas, Sherry Payne, Mike Davis, Afton Martin, and Jeff McDonald from the USDA Forest Service; Alex Reynolds and Stephen Rudolph from the National Park Service; Bob Slack, David Foot, Gae Stovall, Danny Tatum, Chris Covington, Jennifer Glover, Kim Hatcher, and Cindy Rettinger from the State Parks and Historic Sites Division; Carroll Allen, Allen Padgett, and Don Wofford from the State Wildlife Resources Division; and Evelyn Azar, Jane Whaley, and Jerry Lord from the U.S. Fish and Wildlife Service. Mary Terry of the Dekalb County Parks Department also provided valuable information.

Special thanks to the Georgia Appalachian Trail Club, the Benton MacKaye Trail Association, and the Pine Mountain Trail Association, whose members have volunteered thousands of hours to build and maintain Georgia's trails. Thanks, too, to the ethical and considerate hikers and campers who spend time in the wilderness without leaving a trace of their passing.

Finally, I am most grateful and appreciative of the help and encouragement from Billie Pfitzer, who put up with all the hiking trips and my periodic frustration and who spent many hours editing this and earlier editions.

Introduction

Georgia has everything to delight the hiker. The largest state east of the Mississippi beckons to you with more than 1,000 miles of hiking trails. You can walk along wild mountain streams, through rolling foothills, among the towering pines of the coastal plain, or on a pristine beach of the Atlantic Coast barrier islands. Hundreds of species of animals and thousands of species of plants are waiting to be discovered and enjoyed along the trails of Georgia.

Trails vary in length and difficulty from an easy one-hour walk along a quiet nature trail in a state park to an 80-mile trek on the Appalachian National Scenic Trail; from a stroll along a sandy beach on an undeveloped island to hikes among the sheer sandstone cliffs of Cloudland Canyon. Because many of Georgia's trails are less than 5 miles long and its temperate climate permits hiking year-round, you can walk these shorter trails again and again throughout the year as each season exhibits its own special charm.

All of the more than 800 miles of trails discussed in this guide are on public land. Although most are in the mountains and hills of north Georgia, there are many interesting and challenging hikes in central and south Georgia as well as close to metropolitan centers.

Hiking is truly an activity for all ages and physical abilities. Men and women seventy or more years old have through-hiked the Appalachian Trail (AT). Wide-eyed children with their parents have watched a doe and her fawn cross their path in a state park's quiet woodlands. There are trails for people with special needs, including the sight impaired and wheelchair dependent.

Physicians, cardiologists, and other health and fitness professionals tell us that walking briskly for thirty minutes three times a week can do great things for the heart and that walking is the best form of exercise for people of many different physical abilities. Hiking in natural areas is more than physical therapy. Seeing a flower in bloom, watching a squirrel scamper up a tree or a deer bound away only to look back inquisitively, listening to a bird stake his claim for nesting territory, or pausing and absorbing the beauty of grand mountain scenery or the closeness of a cypress swamp is therapy for the mind.

Georgia's trails lead to areas rich in botanical, zoological, and geological lore. You may find a quiet beach or mountain overlook for sitting and reflecting, a cold mountain stream brimming with trout, or peaceful warm-water lakes. Trails in national forests and state wildlife management areas may lead to remote and secluded hunting grounds. Whatever your interests, there is probably a trail on Georgia public lands that will help you experience them.

Physiographic Regions and Natural History

Five major physiographic provinces span Georgia from south to north: Coastal Plain, Piedmont, Blue Ridge, Ridge and Valley, and Cumberland Plateau. The most extensive of these, the Coastal Plain, extends from numerous subtropical barrier islands of the Atlantic Coast north to the very irregular "fall line," which crosses the state from Augusta through Milledgeville and Macon to Columbus. Lying north of the fall line is the Piedmont Plateau, rolling foothills that rise gradually from 500 feet to about 1,700 feet where they meet the mountains about 50 miles north of Atlanta.

Three smaller regions lie north of the Piedmont: the Cumberland Plateau, the Ridge and Valley, and the Blue Ridge. The Blue Ridge region in Georgia's northeast is part of the Appalachian Mountain system, considered to be among the oldest mountains in the world. The mountains here rise to the greatest height in Georgia—4,783 feet at Brasstown Bald. The Cumberland Plateau is in the extreme northwest corner of the state. Part of the Allegheny Mountain system, it is represented by Lookout and Sand Mountains, which reach to 2,364 feet. Between these two regions lies the Ridge and Valley, which extends from the Georgia-Tennessee line southwest 75 miles toward Cedartown.

Georgia spans the continent in climate and plant and animal forms, giving you an almost unlimited range of experiences from which to choose. The coastal islands, bathed by the Gulf Stream's warm currents, have many subtropical affinities. The mountains over 4,000 feet elevation have strong similarities to Canadian forests.

Plant and animal diversity in the Blue Ridge is world renowned. More than 150 species of trees and more than 400 species of shrubs and vines grow in the state. Add an almost countless number of flowering herbaceous plants, ferns, mosses, liverworts, lichens, mushrooms and other fungi, and the sum equals a plant community as diverse as anywhere in the country. Also known to occur in Georgia are more than 65 species of mammals, more than 75 species of snakes and lizards, and more than 120 species of salamanders, toads, frogs, and turtles.

A number of good field guides are available to help you identify plants and animals you see on the trails, including *Native Trees of Georgia,* printed by the Georgia Forestry Commission; *Wildflowers of the Southeastern States* by Duncan and Foote; and any of the popular Peterson Field Guide series. See Appendix C: Additional Resources for a more comprehensive list.

Archaeology and History

The mark of humankind on Georgia extends from Ice Age Paleo-Indian culture predating 9000 B.C. through gatherers, mound builders, and more permanent villages of farmers who settled here in the early 1500s, when Hernando de Soto traveled the full

◀ *Paint marks on trees lead the way on the Chickamauga Creek Trail.*

length of Georgia in search of gold. Colonial history in Georgia predates the Revolutionary War, and the Civil War is recorded throughout the state. One of Georgia's earliest true trailblazers was botanist William Bartram, who traveled through Georgia extensively during the mid-1770s. The Bartram Trail bears his name today. In 1838 the U.S. government forced the strong democratic society of the Cherokee Indian Nation of north Georgia to resettle on a reservation west of the Mississippi River. Much of this history is found along the many miles of trails that lace the state.

Zero Impact Hiking

Reward the thousands of volunteers who create and help maintain the trails and allow those who follow your footsteps to enjoy their own wilderness experience by leaving an area as pristine as you found it—or better. The following guidelines can help ensure enjoyable hiking experiences for years to come:

- Be a conscientious camper. Do not camp close to streambanks or other natural water sources. Use camp stoves instead of wood fires for cooking. Bury human waste at least 6 to 8 inches deep and at least 100 feet from streams. A small shovel or spade should be standard part of any camper's equipment.

- Pack it in; pack it out. Few things are more irritating than finding aluminum cans, candy wrappers, and other litter along the trail. Pack out what you pack in—and carry an extra garbage bag on hikes for carting out litter left behind by others.

- Stay on the trail. Designated paths limit the impact on natural areas. Taking shortcuts or straying off the blazed trail can cause damage to sensitive areas that can take years to heal.

- Respect other trail users. If you are on a multiuse trail that allows horses, remember that they have the right-of-way. Step aside quietly, off the trail if necessary, and let horse and rider pass. Although hikers generally have right-of-way on trails shared with mountain bikers, it's probably best to yield for safety's sake—especially on narrow or steep trail sections. Only a few of the trails in this guide are multiple-use trails and are so designated.

Be Prepared

Getting in Shape

If you are out of shape, start a walking program early if you are planning a long, several-day hike. Walk every day. Take the stairs instead of the elevator; walk up hills to strengthen leg muscles. If outdoor walking is not feasible, go to a gym and use a treadmill and other strength- and endurance-building equipment. Hiking should be fun, and you will enjoy your hike much more if you are in reasonably good shape.

Erect trilllium is among the many flowers found on the Sosebee Cove Trail.

White-tailed deer fawns are very much at home throughout the state.

Know the terrain, and plan hikes that are within your physical ability. Do not attempt day hikes or backpacking segments that are more than you can accomplish in daylight. Hiking after dark is dangerous.

Should I Drink from That Stream?

In Georgia the answer is no—unless the water has been treated by boiling, filtered with a reliable filter/purifier, or treated with an effective chemical purifier.

From the mountains to the sea, there is no real shortage of water in Georgia. However, water quality can be a problem. Day hikers should bring sufficient water for drinking unless potable water is known to be available. All Georgia state parks and most USDA Forest Service campgrounds and recreation areas have potable running water. Only occasionally will you find yourself several miles from surface water from a spring, stream, or lake. On long trails like the Appalachian Trail, water sources are marked both by signs and on trail maps. Again, this water must be treated before it is considered safe to drink.

Giardiasis is the most common waterborne disease in Georgia. Symptoms include watery diarrhea, abdominal bloating, flatulence, abdominal tenderness, cramping pain, and weight loss. It is estimated that 4 percent of the population harbors *Giardia lamblia,* usually from drinking water or eating food contaminated with the protozoa. The parasites colonize in the upper small intestine, and cysts containing dormant giardia are passed in the stools of small mammals like raccoons and beavers. Larger mammals, including black bears, deer, wild pigs, cattle, horses, and dogs, can also spread the disease. Humans can and do spread the parasite to water sources through improper disposal of feces.

Do not drink water directly from streams, no matter how remote they are or how clean and pure they seem to be. If you need to use water from springs and streams, treat the water first. The simplest method is to boil the water for three or four minutes. Dr. William McKell, medical advisor for Southeastern Outdoor Press Association, recommends that water be boiled or treated with saturated potassium iodide or tetraglycine hydroperiodate (Globaline). Use only treated water to wash fruits, vegetables, or utensils.

Several types of light, portable water filters are available from outdoor supply stores. The filter you choose should be capable of filtering giardia and other bacteria, as well as suspended clays and other particles. Be sure to follow the directions and change the filter cartridge regularly.

First Aid

A first-aid kit should be part of every hiker's backpack, whether you're on a day hike or a longer trek. There are many good lightweight, compact kits on the market. Be sure the kit contains the following items, or make up your own following this list:

- Adhesive bandages
- Moleskin
- Sterile gauze and dressing
- White surgical tape
- Ace bandage
- Antihistamine
- Aspirin
- Antacid
- Betadine solution
- First-aid manual

- Tweezers
- Scissors
- Antibacterial wipes
- Triple-antibiotic ointment
- Plastic gloves
- Sterile cotton-tip applicators
- Syrup of ipecac (to induce vomiting)
- Thermometer
- Wire splint

Sunburn. Wear sunscreen (SPF 15 or higher), protective clothing, a wide-brimmed hat, and sunglasses when you are hiking. If you get sunburn, treat the area with aloe vera gel, and protect the area from further sun exposure. Don't let overcast skies fool you into thinking you're safe—you can burn even when you cannot see the sun.

Blisters. Be prepared to take care of these hike spoilers by carrying moleskin, gauze, and tape or adhesive bandages. An effective way to apply moleskin is to cut out a circle of moleskin and cut the center out of it—like a doughnut—and place it over the blister area, reducing the pressure to the sensitive skin. Other products that can help combat blisters are Bodyglide and Second Skin. Body Glide is applied to suspicious hot spots before a blister forms to help reduce friction to that area. Second Skin is applied to the blister after it has popped and helps prevent further irritation.

Insects, Snakes, and Other Concerns

Georgia has its share of fauna that could impact your hike if you're not prepared. Insects, including bees, wasps, hornets, and fire ants; spiders, chiggers, and ticks; snakes; and mammals like black bears, wild pigs, and skunks could make for an unpleasant encounter. But for most hikers, very few of these critters, except for stinging and biting bugs, are of any real concern. Encountering a wasp nest along a trail is much more likely than seeing a poisonous snake. Bear encounters are extremely rare, except at campsites where garbage has been allowed to accumulate. At some shelters along the Appalachian Trail, where hundreds of campers a year spend the night, bears may become night-visitors looking for food. To virtually eliminate all bear problems, hang all your food high in a tree when camping, and don't sleep with food in your tent or beside your sleeping bag. You will seldom if ever see black bears while walking trails. They will usually run before you get close enough to see them.

Biting and Stinging Insects

Stinging insects represent the greatest and most frequently encountered danger on Georgia's trails. Wasps build nests on bridge handrails or under benches. Running the hand against a wasp nest or brushing against a nest hanging on low vegetation can cause stings that are fortunately only temporarily painful for most people. However, for those few who are allergic to bee and wasp stings, the problem can be life threatening. Know your sensitivity—or the sensitivity of anyone in your hiking party—and prepare for it. Know what to do in the event of a sting, and carry the appropriate antihistamines or other medication in your first-aid kit to use immediately if stung.

Chiggers (red bugs), mosquitoes, biting flies, and gnats are common throughout the state. They are most annoying during the warmer months and during twilight and nighttime hours. In parts of southern Georgia and in the coastal counties, mosquitoes can be very annoying during the day. Be sure to use an effective all-around repellent. The most effective repellents contain at least 30 percent DEET. Other repellents are available for those who are sensitive to DEET, including young children.

Ticks

In Georgia there are two tick-borne diseases that are noteworthy: Lyme disease and Rocky Mountain spotted fever. Lyme disease occurs throughout Georgia but is most prevalent in the southern two-thirds of the state. It is transmitted by the deer, or black-legged, tick. This tick is much smaller than the wood, or dog, tick that can transmit spotted fever. A few spotted fever cases are reported each year. Lyme disease has become much more frequent.

The best way to avoid ticks on the trail is to use an effective repellent before you head out. DEET is effective against ticks. Another highly effective repellent, which also kills ticks, is Permanone. It should *not* be applied directly to the skin but is very effective when applied to clothes and footwear before going into tick-infested areas. Wear a long-sleeved shirt and long pants tucked into your footwear. Examine yourself carefully immediately after a day hike and once a day or more on longer hikes. The tiny deer tick nymphs, the most active carrier of the Lyme disease spirochete, may be picked up even during mild winter months in central and south Georgia.

Removing an attached tick in the first eight or ten hours is important. To remove the tick, use forceps to grasp the tick as close to the skin as possible; gently but firmly pull the tick away, trying not to leave its mouthparts in the skin. (**Caution:** Squeezing the tick's body can act like a syringe, forcing the tick's body fluids with the spirochetes into your body and increasing the potential for Lyme disease.) Pro-tick Remedy, manufactured by SCS LTD, is a handy and effective tool for removing an attached tick. It is available in outdoor sporting goods stores. Once the tick is removed, clean the bite with alcohol, apply an antibiotic, and observe the bite site for several days. In about half the cases of Lyme disease, redness occurs around the bite and may take on a bull's-eye appearance. This should be reported to a doctor as soon as possible. Treated early, Lyme disease is quickly cured.

Snakes

Poisonous snakes in Georgia run from the small, secretive coral snake to the eastern diamondback rattlesnake, our largest North American snake. The coral snake occurs in both dry and moist sandy-loam areas of the southern third of Georgia. The timber rattlesnake occurs throughout the state from the mountains through the Coastal Plain. (It may be called the canebrake rattlesnake in the southern part of the state.) Coral snakes and rattlesnakes are rarely seen.

Both the northern and southern copperheads occur in Georgia. The larger southern copperhead is found throughout the Piedmont, along the fall line, and in the Coastal Plain. The northern copperhead is generally found in the Piedmont and all the mountain regions. The cottonmouth, or water moccasin, is found from the fall line south throughout the Coastal Plain along streams, river swamps, and marshes.

Many new hikers in Georgia seem to fear snakes more than other hazards along the trail, carrying snakebite kits with little knowledge of how to use them. Most of these kits have blades to cut the fang puncture, a tourniquet, disinfectant, and other things—none of which are practical first aid for a poisonous snakebite. The best first aid for poisonous snakebite is get to medical help as soon as possible.

If you do carry a snakebite kit, it should be the type with a good syringe. Sawyer kits are equipped with syringes and are very light and easy to use. Keep in mind that using the syringe is only a first-aid measure to be used while getting to professional medical attention. The syringe is also very useful to relieve the effects of insect stings.

To reduce your risk of snakebite, don't put your foot or hand anywhere without looking first. Be cautious stepping over logs. Keep your hands and feet out of cavities around boulders. Since many snakes are nocturnal, carry and use a flashlight if you need to walk around the campsite or on trails at night during warm weather. Even nonvenomous snakebites can be painful and prone to infection.

Poison Ivy

Poison ivy is present on many trails in Georgia. It is most obvious in late spring and throughout the summer months. Learn to recognize it and avoid it: "Leaves of three, let it be." Washing exposed skin with soap and water as soon as possible after contact is the best way to prevent irritation.

Hypothermia

Hypothermia has been called the number-one killer of all outdoor injuries. The lowering of internal body temperature from exposure to cold, wind, rain, or immersion in cold water, hypothermia can occur even when outdoor temperatures are not very cold. Learn to recognize the symptoms and know that injuries increase the risk of hypothermia. First signs include shivering, followed by no shivering, disorientation, and confusion. Later the person may appear apathetic and moody. As hypothermia becomes more advanced, the victim may lapse into a coma.

The first step in treatment of hypothermia, after making all possible arrangements to get the person to expert medical attention, is to reduce heat loss. Get the victim out of the wind and into dry clothes and/or a windproof shell like a poncho or space blanket (a good addition to your first-aid kit). Pay special attention to covering the head and back of the neck, with a cap, hat, or anything windproof and warm. Next try to produce heat in the body core. If the victim can drink, give him/her warm, sweet fluids—not alcohol.

After applying dry clothing and a windproof outer covering, get the victim walking, with support if necessary. Exercise is the best way to improve internal organ heat. If you are alone and recognize hypothermia, drink hot fluids like sweet hot chocolate, get into dry clothes, protect yourself from the wind, and keep moving. Movement is crucial. Obviously, it's important to be able to recognize the condition before you become disoriented or confused.

Navigation

Maps

U.S. Geological Survey (USGS) 7.5-minute series topographic quadrangles, scale 1:24,000, referred to in the text for each hike, are the best and most dependable maps for long hikes and wilderness backpack trip planning. Learn how to read them, and then learn to rely on them for keeping oriented on the trail. This is especially important for any cross-country hikes requiring good orienteering techniques. These USGS quadrangles are available at most outdoor shops that cater to hikers' needs. They can be purchased from the Georgia Geologic Survey (19 Martin Luther King Jr. Drive, Maps and Publications Room, Suite 400, Atlanta, GA 30334; 404–656–3214) and the U.S. Geological Survey National Mapping Division (12201 Sunrise Valley Drive, Mail Stop 809, Reston, VA 22092; 703–648–7070).

The USDA Forest Service offers recreation maps, a trail guide, and booklets of the Chattahoochee and Oconee National Forests. A Forest Visitors Map, Appalachian Trail Map, Chattooga Wild and Scenic River Map, and Cohutta Wilderness Map are available for purchase. Visit www.fs.fed.us/conf for purchase information.

Page-size maps of the trails in most of the state parks can be obtained free of charge from the respective parks or downloaded from www.gastateparks.org. These maps may not be to scale, but they will keep you oriented. They also can help you take advantage of all the special natural and historical points of interest along the way.

The Georgia Appalachian Trail Club offers a small-scale map with helpful hints for hiking the AT. *Guide to the Appalachian Trail in North Carolina and Georgia* contains maps, trail mileages, water and shelter locations, and side trails; it can be purchased at hiking and backpacking outfitters and stores or from the Appalachian Trail Conference: www.georgia-atclub.org.

The comprehensive Web site of the Benton MacKaye Trail Association (www.bmta.org) contains excellent information on this newest of the long trails in Georgia and other trails throughout the mountains of northeast Georgia.

Compass

The compass is probably the most valuable tool you can have to stay properly oriented in unfamiliar terrain. Some characteristics to look for in a compass are a rectangular base with detailed scales, a liquid-filled protective housing, a sighting line on the mirror, and luminous arrows. Learn to use the compass so well that you don't even think about disbelieving it.

Global Positioning System (GPS)

This is possibly the most useful navigation gadget to come along for the serious hiker. As with all such tools, you must learn how to use a GPS accurately. Most brands are sold with good instructions that anyone with computer experience should be able to master. Practice with your GPS until you are comfortable with it before you go into the backcountry on an extended hike. Used with mapping programs, you can come home from a hike and download the GPS data into your PC for a permanent record of your hike.

All GPS products use the same satellite support base. The real difference among products is in the quality of satellite reception. All are limited when in mountainous terrain with deep valleys and under dense deciduous tree cover. (Deciduous tree leaves are notorious for diffusing radio signals.)

Great blue herons feed in the Chattahoochee River along the Johnson Ferry Trail.

Planning Your Trip

For safety's sake, always leave your hike itinerary with someone before you head out. It should include where you will be hiking, where you will park, your estimated time of completing the trip, and whom to contact if necessary. "Trail Contacts" for each trail description list phone numbers and Web sites that can be used to contact park personnel should emergencies arise. There are registers on the Appalachian Trail at the Springer Mountain trailhead and at many of the shelters. It is a good idea to leave pertinent information at these points.

For the AT and some other trails, you must register with the appropriate land-managing agencies. The Coosa Backcountry Trail, which originates at Vogel State Park; Tallulah Gorge State Park; and the Pine Mountain Trail at F. D. Roosevelt State Park are other trails requiring registration to obtain a free permit to camp along these trails. Advanced reservations (fee for ferry passage) are required to hike and camp at Cumberland Island National Seashore.

Clothing and Equipment

Comfortable clothing and footwear will do more to make a hike pleasant than almost anything else. The great variety of hiking and walking situations make it impossible to cover all personal needs, but here are a few suggestions:

- **Dress in layers.** The first is a light, inner layer made of material that will wick away moisture from the skin. Next is a warmer porous layer that can be removed if necessary. Over that wear an outside layer that is wind and/or rain proof. This permits you to regulate your temperature easily by adding or removing layers as the weather and exertion dictates. Because rain in Georgia is frequent and unpredictable, a good poncho/rain slicker should be standard backpacking equipment.

- **Dress for safety during hunting season.** Many of the trails in this guide are in national forests and state wildlife management areas where hunting is permitted in season. Although there is little risk in hiking during hunting season, it's a good idea to wear a bright, preferably blaze-orange, outer garment such as a jacket, vest, or cap. Don't flash a white handkerchief during deer season or a red or blue one during turkey season. Hunting is not permitted in most Georgia state parks, leaving hundreds of miles of excellent trails for those nervous about hiking elsewhere during hunting season.

Footwear. Everyone seems to have a different idea about what type of footwear to wear for hiking. Footwear boils down to personal preference, but it should be sturdy and supportive. Many people still wear good leather boots for serious hiking; others prefer lighter weight boots with breathable, water-resistant fabrics. The best advice for the beginner is to visit a good outdoor outfitter and try on several styles before finally deciding.

Backpacks. There are many types and styles of backpacks. For day hiking, the smaller day-pack type is all you need. It should fit and have padded shoulder and hip pads. Make sure they are wide enough to be comfortable. The pack should have external pockets for easy access to items like camera, water, and maps. External straps are handy to lash things like a jacket or poncho. The main bag should be large enough for lunch or other bulky things. Don't burden yourself with a day pack that is too large. You may find that a fanny pack or a photo vest will carry all you want or need.

For extended overnight hikes, you will need a luggage carrier on your back. Two basic types are the internal and external frame packs. No matter which you prefer, fit and balance when loaded are the most important features to consider. If you have not been exposed to wearing a larger backpack, go to a good outdoor shop with folks who know the equipment and see the various options. External-frame packs are easier to load and unload when you have stopped for a break or to set up camp for the night; they are also easier to adjust and balance. On the trail, however, the exposed frame is bulkier and can bump against thick brush and other trail hazards. If you'll be hiking through long stretches of laurel and rhododendron thickets or rocky overhangs on a one-night trip, you might want to opt for an internal-frame pack.

The most critical measurement for fitting a pack is torso length. The pack needs to rest evenly on your hips without sagging. A good pack will come in more than one size and have straps and hip belts that are adjustable to your body size and characteristics. Find an outdoor store with a salesperson who knows how to fit a pack properly. If the store rents equipment, rent before you buy, again with the help of that knowledgeable salesperson. This applies to tents and sleeping pads as well. Comfortable, well-fitted clothing and gear will enhance the pleasure and fun of your hiking and camping experience.

Sleeping Bags. Sleeping bags are rated by temperature. The bags are filled with two basic fibers: synthetic and goose down, and in both cases there is a wide range in quality and price. Good quality goose down is lighter and warmer per weight than synthetics, although there are some very good synthetic fibers that approach goose down. When you decide to buy a sleeping bag, be sure it is long enough for your body and covers the range of temperatures in which you are apt to use it.

You will need a sleeping pad for comfort and extra protection from the cold ground. There are inflatable mattresses and closed-cell foam pads. Inflatable pads are usually heavier and more cumbersome for backpacking. They are usually more comfortable than foam sleeping pads, although foam pads have improved significantly in recent years. As with sleeping bags, you get what you pay for. How much is a good night's sleep worth to you? Here, again, you may be able to rent pads for field tests before committing to the purchase.

Tents. Like backpacks and sleeping bags, tents are available in a wide variety of types, prices, and uses. For backpacking, weight and size control your choices. For a one- or two-person tent, size is even more important. Ease of setting the tent up is a primary concern. If possible, try to set up a tent before you buy. At least take the time to set up the tent at home before you head out to the campsite. This is also the time to put the sleeping pad and bag in place and try it out.

Since some stores rent equipment, this is a great way to find out what type of tent, backpack, or other camping equipment is best suited for you. Several good books on the subject are mentioned in Appendix C. Most are available in libraries. One of the best is Colin Fletcher's *The Complete Walker III*. Others are available in the better outdoor sporting goods stores.

Several of Georgia's state parks offer programs that cover outdoor equipment. Some have overnight camping trips conducted by experienced hikers and backpackers. Amicalola Falls State Park schedules four such programs each year. Other state parks have similar programs; most are posted by park at www.gastateparks.org.

Camp Stoves. Modern, lightweight camp stoves and lanterns eliminate the need for campfires and the unsightly stone fire rings left behind. Backpack stoves are ideal for wilderness camp cooking. If you must build a fire on the trail, use a shallow pit instead of a stone fire ring, and when you leave the campsite be sure the fire is completely out and covered over with soil. Ultra-light one- or two-burner liquid fuel stoves like Peak are popular. With the refillable lightweight fuel bottles, there is nothing to throw away. Enough extra fuel for a two- or three-night trip is little weight for the convenience.

Weather

Hiking in Georgia is a year-round activity, with many good hiking days in winter. Wintertime snow and cold or freezing rain in the mountains and spring and summer showers and thunderstorms throughout the state are about the only weather conditions that hamper your comfort on the trail. Fall weather is best, and September through November is the most popular time to hike.

Be aware of changing weather conditions. If thunderstorms are in the forecast, recognize that lightning in forest cover can be dangerous. Do not hike along ridgetops and on mountain crests with large exposed rock formations during electrical storms, especially with metal-frame backpacks.

Wintertime hikes can be especially beautiful in the limited snow that falls in the Georgia mountains. Plans for snow hiking should include adequate footwear and clothing to tolerate the cold, wet conditions in case an emergency occurs. Being wet and cold invites hypothermia, a potentially life-threatening condition.

Weather in the mountains can change rapidly from pleasant temperatures and clear skies to stormy, wet, and cold conditions in a matter of a few hours. The mountains receive an annual rainfall of 60 to 80 inches. The rest of the state averages 50 inches per year. Snowfall occurs in the mountains every year, while snowfall is rare in south Georgia.

Hiking with Children

Children learn by example. Hiking and camping trips are excellent opportunities to teach young ones to tread lightly and minimize their imprint upon the environment. Many state parks have nature trails ideal for beginning hikers and offer interpretive programs for children and adults conducted by park naturalists and program specialists.

Kids can enjoy the backcountry as much as their parents, but they see the world from a different perspective. It's the little things adults barely notice that are so special to children. Bugs scampering across the trail, spider webs dripping with morning dew, lizards doing pushups on a trail-side boulder, skipping rocks on a lake, watching sticks run the rapids of a mountain stream, exploring animal tracks in the sand—these are but a few of the natural wonders kids will enjoy while hiking backcountry trails.

To make the trip fun for the kids, let the young ones set the pace. Until they get older and are able to keep up with you, forget about that 30-mile trek to your

Bloodroot, one of the earliest to bloom at Sosebee—the wildflower mecca.

favorite backcountry campsite. Instead, plan a destination that is only a mile or two from the trailhead. Kids tire quickly and become easily sidetracked, so don't be surprised if you don't make it to your destination. Plan alternative campsites en route to your final camp.

Help children enjoy the hike and to learn about what they see. Point out special things along the trail. Help them anticipate what is around the next bend—perhaps a waterfall, or a pond filled with wiggling tadpoles. Make the hike fun and interesting, and kids will keep going.

Young skin is very sensitive to the sun, so be sure to carry an appropriate sunscreen and apply it to your kids before and frequently during the hike. If your camp will be next to a lake or large stream, consider bringing a life vest for your child.

Allow older children who are able to walk a mile or two to carry their own packs. Some kids will want to bring favorite toys or books along. They can carry these special things themselves, learning at an early age the advantages of packing light.

Kids may become bored more easily once you arrive in camp; a little extra effort may be required to keep them occupied. Imaginative games and special foods they don't get at home can make the camping trip a new and fun experience for kids and parents alike.

Careful planning that stresses safety will help make your trip an enjoyable one. Be prepared for mosquitoes and other biting insects with an effective repellent that you have tried on the kids ahead of time. On the trail is too late to find out that the repellent is more irritating than the bugs. DEET is the effective ingredient in most repellents; however, prolonged exposure to 30 percent DEET can cause adverse reactions in some children. Skedaddle (6.5 percent DEET) and Skintastic (7.5 percent) are less effective than stronger DEET concentrations, but they are less irritating to children.

Make sure your kids know what poison ivy looks like it—and know not to touch it. Long pants and sleeves will help prevent contact, but if it can't be avoided, wash the contact area with soap as soon as possible after exposure to help prevent skin rashes.

Be especially watchful for stinging insects, such as wasps, hornets, and bees. Your first-aid kit should contain an effective topical ointment to relieve the pain of stings. Examine children carefully and often for ticks. If a tick has become attached, remove it as described in the section dealing with ticks.

Children can be more sensitive to heat and cold than adults. Be prepared with appropriate clothing in layers that can be removed or added as necessary. Properly fitting footwear will help prevent blisters on young, tender feet.

State parks are great places for family hiking, with the added advantage of fully equipped comfort stations. National Park Service areas in Georgia have especially good trails for family day hiking. The Chattahoochee River National Recreation Area contains more than 40 miles of trails in the shadow of metropolitan Atlanta. Most are short trails that can be completed in one or two hours. The Ocmulgee National Monument is an outstanding archaeological and historical site, with 6 miles of easy trails, a picnic area, a fine museum, and a visitor center. Situated on the edge of Macon, it is ideal for family outings.

Hikers with Special Needs

State and federal land management agencies in Georgia are putting a great deal of effort into making their facilities accessible to visitors with special needs. Many state parks in the flat Coastal Plain or southern region of the state have trails that can be used by parents with children in strollers and by wheelchairs with some assistance. The land is relatively level, and the sandy-loam soil will support wheels with wide tires.

Visitors to George T. Bagby State Park in southwest Georgia have used wheelchairs specially equipped with balloon-type tires that make most of the 3.0-mile trail and the wildlife-viewing gazebo accessible. At Okefenokee National Wildlife Refuge, the entire length of the 4,000-foot boardwalk and its two photographic blinds can be traveled by wheelchair. There are no railings, making it possible for all visitors to feel much closer to the swamp. Ocmulgee National Monument near Macon has about 1,200 feet of paved trail. There are several short, paved trails in the Piedmont and mountain parks, and a trail at Anna Ruby Falls near Helen is designed for sight-impaired visitors.

Some trails in the following areas are wheelchair accessible or accessible with assistance:

Georgia Parks and Historic Sites
Hike 4: Cloudland Canyon State Park
Hike 28: Amicalola Falls State Park
Hike 36: Victoria Bryant State Park
Hike 40: Red Top Mountain State Park
Hike 56: Providence Canyon State Park
Hike 57: Reed Bingham State Park

National Parks
Honorable Mention O: Ocmulgee National Monument
Honorable Mention Q: Chattahoochee River National Recreation Area: Cochran Shoals Trails

USDA Forest Service
Hike 20: Anna Ruby Falls and Lion's Eye Nature Trails
Hike 23: Dukes Creek Trail

U.S. Fish and Wildlife Service
Hike 68: Okefenokee National Wildlife Refuge

There is some variation in the interpretation of accessible. This depends on the degree of affliction and the type of equipment used. The wide tires on some types of wheelchairs make many trails accessible that would not be for conventional narrow tires. In each description of the hikes mentioned above are listings for the land management offices, with addresses, phone numbers, and Web sites that can be contacted for more information about the current conditions of the trails.

Volunteering

Georgia is home to several hiking clubs and conservation organizations that are involved in hiking. Some devote a large amount of their time to trail maintenance. The Georgia Appalachian Trail Club, Benton MacKaye Trail Club, and the Pine Mountain Trail Association plan regular outings to work on these trails. The Georgia Department of Natural Resources, USDA Forest Service, National Park Service, and U.S. Fish and Wildlife Service also welcome volunteers who are willing to help maintain and mark trails. The Forest Service's "Adopt-A-Trail" program is especially suited to volunteer efforts. See Appendix B for agency contact information.

Using This Guide

Hiking Georgia is divided into five sections: Northwest Georgia: Cumberland Plateau and Ridge and Valley; Northeast Georgia: Blue Ridge Mountains; Central Georgia: Piedmont and Fall Line Area, including the Metro Atlanta Area; Southwest Georgia: Coastal Plain; and Southeast Georgia: Coastal Plain and Atlantic Coast. All the trails are on public land, including national forest and national park lands, State Department of Natural Resources: State Park and Historic Sites and Wildlife Resources Division lands, and other political groupings. As much as possible they are listed in these areas from west to east and north to south.

Easy, Moderate, Strenuous. Degrees of difficulty are based on the grade or incline of the trail. A flat trail with very little elevation change is designated easy whether it is 0.5 mile or 5.0 miles long. A moderate hike will have a moderately steep grade for extended distances. A strenuous trail may have steep grades for 0.5 mile or more. Degree of difficulty may be expressed with two or three ratings, as easy to moderate or moderate with strenuous stretches. Where a trail is uneven and footing is more difficult because of boulders or other obstacles, this will be discussed in the description of the hike.

What one person in excellent physical condition may call moderate may be strenuous to another in poor condition. Thus, the ratings are not precise. They are intended only to provide a simple method of planning a hike based on the terrain.

Trail surface is described to provide an idea of what to expect underfoot on the trail and what footwear might be appropriate.

Blazes and Other Trail Markers. All but a very few trails described in this guide are marked in some fashion. A paint mark (blaze) on a tree is the most frequent trail marker. One trail will be marked or blazed throughout with one color paint. In a state park with several different trails, a different color may be used for each trail. A few trails are marked with a white 3- or 4-inch diamond-shaped piece of metal nailed to trees and posts along the trail instead of paint blazes. The Chattooga River Trail is marked this way. Carsonite stakes, flat fiberglass posts about 4 inches wide and 4 or 5 feet tall are being used to mark some trailheads and occasionally along some trails. These are less vulnerable to vandalism and are marked with decals designating trail use and activities not permitted on the trail. In the Oconee National Forest, the USDA Forest Service has placed numbers on the posts to indicate the trail number.

It has become standard to mark sudden changes in direction of a trail with two blaze marks, one above the other on the same tree. Most trails are marked so that you should not travel more than 0.25 mile without seeing a blaze. Because of dense vegetation, state park and many USDA Forest Service trails are marked with paint blazes much more frequently. Where two trails occasionally join for a distance, two colors or types of blazes will be used until the trails separate again.

How to Use the Maps

Maps are included for the trail discussions. In most instances there is one map per discussion. When two sets of trails are combined on a single map, a notation in the text will point you to the appropriate page. These maps are of necessity small scale and are designed to provide basic information in finding the trailhead and planning the hike.

The maps in this book that depict a detailed close-up of an area use elevation tints, called hypsometry, to portray relief. Each gray tone represents a range of equal elevation, as shown in the scale key with the map. These maps will give you a good idea of elevation gain and loss. The darker tones are lower elevations and the lighter grays are higher elevations. The lighter the tone, the higher the elevation. Narrow bands of different gray tones spaced closely together indicate steep terrain, whereas wider bands indicate areas of more gradual slope.

Maps that show larger geographic areas use shaded, or shadow, relief. Shadow relief does not represent elevation; it demonstrates slope or relative steepness. This gives an almost 3-D perspective of the physiography of a region and will help you see where ranges and valleys are.

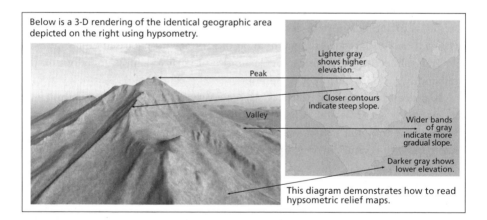

Below is a 3-D rendering of the identical geographic area depicted on the right using hypsometry.

Lighter gray shows higher elevation.

Peak

Closer contours indicate steep slope.

Valley

Wider bands of gray indicate more gradual slope.

Darker gray shows lower elevation.

This diagram demonstrates how to read hypsometric relief maps.

Map Legend

Transportation

Interstate Highway	75
U. S. Highway	27
State Highway	19
Primary Road	
Forest Road	138
Improved Road	
Unimproved Road	= = = = =
Featured Trail	▬ ▬ ▬ ▬
Other Trail	- - - - - - - -

Boundaries

National Park	
State Park	
National Forest	
National Wildlife Refuge	
Wilderness Area	

Hydrology

Lake/Reservoir	
River	
Creek	
Swamp	
Sand	

Physiography

Terrain (lighter shade indicates higher elevation)

Symbols

Trailhead	𝕏
Ranger Station/ Park Office	
Visitor Center/ Information	?
Parking	P
Point of Interest	▪
Campground	△
Campsite	▲
Picnic Area	
Shelter	
Boat Ramp/ Launch Site	
Overlook	👁
Dump Station	
Peak	▲ Grassy Mountain 3,692 ft.
Elevation Point	1,545 ft. ×
Bridge	
UTM Grid	3952000

Northwest Georgia:
Cumberland Plateau and
Ridge and Valley

Boardwalk along the Pocket Recreation Area Trail (Hike 3).

National Forest Trails

1 Chickamauga Creek Trail

The length and diversity of this trail makes for a nice half-day excursion as you hike up and down two ridges with moderately steep grades. There are no grand views, but there is plenty of wildlife, wildflowers, and forest types. The streams, hardwood forests mixed with pine and laurel thickets, ridgetops, and valleys make this trail an exceptionally good birding area. There's also a good population of deer, turkey, and other small game.

Start: From the Ponder Branch trailhead
Distance: 6.4-mile loop
Approximate hiking time: 3 to 4 hours
Difficulty: Moderate
Elevation gain/loss: 640 feet
Lay of the land: Ridges and valleys
Season: Year-round; wearing a blaze-orange cap or vest advised during deer and turkey season
Land status: Chattahoochee National Forest

Nearest town: LaFayette
Fees and permits: No fees or permits required
Maps: USGS Catlett; Trail Guide to the Chattahoochee-Oconee National Forests
Trail contacts: USDA Forest Service, Armuchee-Cohutta Ranger District, 3941 Highway 76, Chatsworth, GA 30705; (706) 695–6736; www.fs.fed.us/conf

Finding the trailhead: Go east from LaFayette on Highway 136 for 7 miles to the crest of Taylor Ridge at Maddox Gap. To get to the Ponder Branch trailhead, continue east from Maddox Gap on Highway 136 for another 1.6 miles to Ponder Branch Road. Turn north (left) and travel 0.6 mile on the paved road to Forest Road 219, an unpaved continuation of Ponder Branch Road. Go 1.7 miles to the end of the road; you will ford the small Ponder Branch on the way. FR 219 ends at a turnaround and primitive camping area.

For an alternate trailhead, at Maddox Gap go north on Forest Road 250 for 1.8 miles to Forest Road 250A. This is the point where the trail crosses the Tennessee Valley Divide. You can park off to the side of the road here to begin hiking the trail in either direction.

The Hike

The trail straddles the ridgeline that separates the Tennessee and Alabama River watersheds. Ponder Branch flows south to the Alabama River system. East Chickamauga Creek flows north before emptying into the Tennessee and Mississippi River system. The protected watersheds for these small permanent streams lie completely within the national forest. This is an exceptionally popular wildflower area.

The Chickamauga Creek loop trail can be hiked in either direction and from either trailhead. This hike starts at the Ponder Branch trailhead. A short path leads

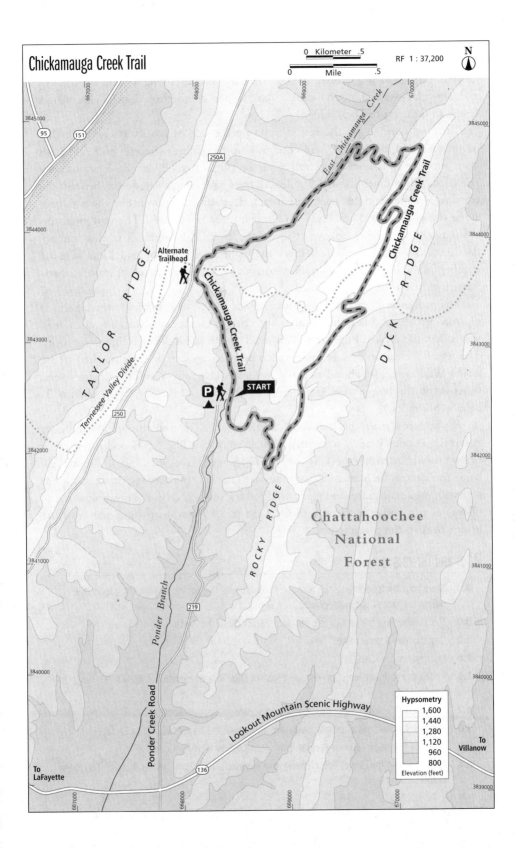

from the parking area across Ponder Branch on a footbridge to the loop trail. The powerline right-of-way crosses the trail near this point. Hiking around the loop in a counterclockwise direction avoids the steeper climb from East Chickamauga Creek to the crest of Dick Ridge.

Turn right and begin the gentle climb up the side of Rocky Ridge through a mountain laurel thicket. The trail continues up the ridge, switching back and forth from one cove to the next until you reach the ridge crest. Follow this crest until you cross under the power line at 1.2 miles. All trees have been cleared from beneath the transmission lines, and this open area attracts deer. After the power line, the path goes along the east side of Dick Ridge in a much more open forest. The trail intercepts a dirt road at 1.8 miles, follows it up to the crest, and continues to the drainage divide at 2.5 miles. At 1,620 feet, this is the highest point on the trail. From here the trail begins the descent to East Chickamauga Creek. A long stretch of exposed sandstone formations lie along the path.

The path then drops quickly through several switchbacks until you reach another old roadbed at 4.2 miles; this is the trail to the creek. At East Chickamauga Creek you follow the old road upstream. This small stream flows through limestone rocks. The water is clear, and many snails, called periwinkles, can be seen attached to the stones. Wildflowers are abundant along the creek. The path crosses the stream several times as you climb up to the Tennessee Valley Divide and FR 250A to the other trailhead at 5.6 miles.

At the forest road, the trail drops immediately back into the woods and goes down the Ponder Branch watershed to Baker Hollow. This hardwood forest comprises many large trees, especially the American beech trees growing on the streambank. You'll cross the branch several times in the course of dropping down to the flat area with mountain laurel and many wildflowers. You will cross the power line right-of-way as you come to the end of the loop at 6.4 miles. Turn right and cross the bridge back to the parking area.

Miles and Directions

0.0 Start from the parking area. Cross the footbridge to the trailhead where the loop trail meets the power line right-of-way; turn right.

0.9 The southernmost point of the trail turns abruptly to the north.

1.2 Cross under a power line.

1.8 Intercept a dirt road.

2.5 Reach the rounded crest on the west side of Dick Ridge (elevation 1,620 feet); begin to descend.

4.2 Reach East Chickamauga Creek and turn south, going upstream.

5.6 Reach FR 250A, the alternate trailhead, and revisit the Tennessee Valley Divide.

5.9 Come to the headwater of Ponder Branch and follow it downstream.

6.4 Arrive back at the power line clearing and the loop's end. Turn right and cross the bridge to the parking area.

2 Keown Falls and Johns Mountain Trails

Keown Falls, a 60-foot straight drop over a rock ledge, can be spectacular during the wet season. Two observation decks afford grand views of the Ridge and Valley. The Johns Mountain Overlook deck is wheelchair accessible. There are excellent wild-flower displays in spring and summer, with magnificent leaf colors in fall.

Start: End of Forest Road 208 for the Johns Mountain Trail; end of Forest Road 702 for Keown Falls Trail.

Distance: Keown Falls Trail, 1.4-mile loop; Johns Mountain Trail, 3.2-mile loop

Approximate hiking time: Keown Falls, about 1½ hours; Johns Mountain Trail, about 2½ hours

Difficulty: Moderate, with short stretches of steep grades; steep stone steps to the Keown Falls Overlook protected by railings

Elevation gain/loss: From Keown Falls Recreation Area to the observation deck above the falls, 415 feet climb; from this deck to the observation deck at the top of Johns Mountain, another 485 feet; total combined climb of 900 feet

Season: Year-round; Keown Falls Recreation Area open year-round; access road to Johns Mountain Overlook open March 18 to November 21

Land status: Chattahoochee-Oconee National Forests

Nearest town: LaFayette

Fees and permits: No fees or permits required

Maps: USGS Sugar Valley; Chattahoochee National Forest Map

Trail contacts: USDA Forest Service, Armuchee-Cohutta Ranger District, 3941 Highway 76, Chattsworth, GA 30705; (706) 695-6736; www.fs.fed.us/conf Georgia Wildlife Resources Division, Game Management, 2592 Floyd Springs Road, Armuchee, GA 30105; (706) 295-6041; www.gohuntgeorgia.com

Finding the trailhead: To get to Johns Mountain Overlook from LaFayette, take Highway 136 east 13 miles to Villanow. One-half mile past Villanow, turn right (south) on Pocket Road. Go 4 miles south to FR 208, a gated and graveled road. Go 2.1 miles to the parking area for the Johns Mountain Overlook. The trailhead for this loop trail is at the overlook parking area.

For Keown Falls Trail, follow the same directions as above but go 2 miles farther south on Pocket Road to FR 702. Turn right; the trailhead is at the parking and picnic area at the end of this 0.7-mile unpaved road.

The Hikes

The ideal day hike here is to start from the Keown Falls Recreation Area and hike to the falls overlook and then to the falls, going counterclockwise on this loop. The Johns Mountain Trail begins a few yards from the deck at the direction sign. Walk this trail clockwise. Hiked together, these two loop trails give you an excellent look at the unique Ridge and Valley Physiographic Province, which terminates just to the west in Alabama and the northeastern part of Georgia and extends northeastward

The Johns Mountain observation deck.

through Tennessee, Virginia, Maryland, Pennsylvania, and New York. (**Note:** Pay close attention to spring and summer thunderstorms on the mountain.)

Keown Falls Trail

The Keown Falls loop trail begins from the day-use area at the west end of the parking area and passes under an A-frame structure on a graveled path with a hand-placed rock border. This path continues until you reach the loop segment at 0.1 mile and the sign with arrows pointing to the left and right. For this hike, we will go to the right, which leads directly to the falls. You will go through a pleasant cove forest with many spring flowers and beautiful leaf colors in the fall.

The trail parallels the stream until it reaches the steeper part of the climb. The path crosses the stream and enters an area of massive boulders. Ferns and wildflowers are at their best in this east-facing cove in early spring. Trillium, toothwort, windflower, giant chickweed, azalea, mayapple, dwarf crested iris, Solomon's seal, false Solomon's seal, and many others bloom in spring. Flowering trees are just as colorful and include yellow poplar, dogwood, redbud, and serviceberry.

You now begin the climb to the falls as the path switches back and forth at a moderate grade until you near the sandstone cliff. Mountain laurel and Virginia pines form thickets through which the trail passes to the stone steps, at 0.5 mile, leading up to the observation deck. The elevation is 1,400 feet at the deck, and you have climbed 415 feet. You have an excellent view of the falls. In the distance to the east you will see Horn Mountain across Furness Valley. In the wet season, the falls are quite impressive as the stream drops 60 feet over the cliff overhang. The woolly lip fern, found in only a few very specific sites in the state, grows on the rock cliffs.

Go back down the stone steps and turn to the trail under the falls. If there is good water flow, this is a rare opportunity to actually walk between the falling water and the rock overhang. The trail follows the base of the bluff and is quite wet during the rainy season. The smaller waterfall comes through a cleft in the cliff. You must step over the small branch below the falls and among large boulders. Very shortly you pass the boulder field and the trail makes a couple of switchbacks down to more level walking to the end of the loop and the parking area at 1.4 miles.

Pinxter azalea blooms in April along the stream above the falls; mountain laurel puts on its show in May. Here the sign for the Johns Mountain Overlook and trail directs you to either the left or right. To the left (south), it is 2.5 miles to the overlook; to the right (north) is 1.0 mile. The trail is a much more gradual climb to the left. This loop is described below from the trailhead at the end of FR 208.

Miles and Directions

0.0 Start from the west end of the parking/picnic area; walk through an A-frame.

0.1 The trail forks here. Take the path to the right.

0.7 Arrive at the observation deck after climbing the steps.

1.2 Come to the end of the loop.

1.4 Arrive back at the parking area.

Johns Mountain Trail

Johns Mountain Trail begins at a well-designed observation deck on one of the highest points on this ridge. Great sunsets and sunrises are common from this splendid observation deck. The view extends to Taylor Ridge, Pigeon, and Lookout Mountains to the west across the Armuchee Valley. To the east is Furnace Valley and Horn Mountain. Visitors in wheelchairs can come to the parking area by vehicle and roll onto the observation deck.

Going south you pass the radio relay tower at 0.1 mile. Continue south along the ridge crest. The west brow of the mountain on your right is the steep sandstone bluffs. You are now on the flat plateau of the mountain in a parklike forest of smaller trees. Follow the trail among large boulders and twisted oaks, pines, and a few hickories. Occasional breaks in the trees allow peeks of the same view you get from the overlook.

Keown Falls and Johns Mountain Trails; The Pocket Recreation Area Trail

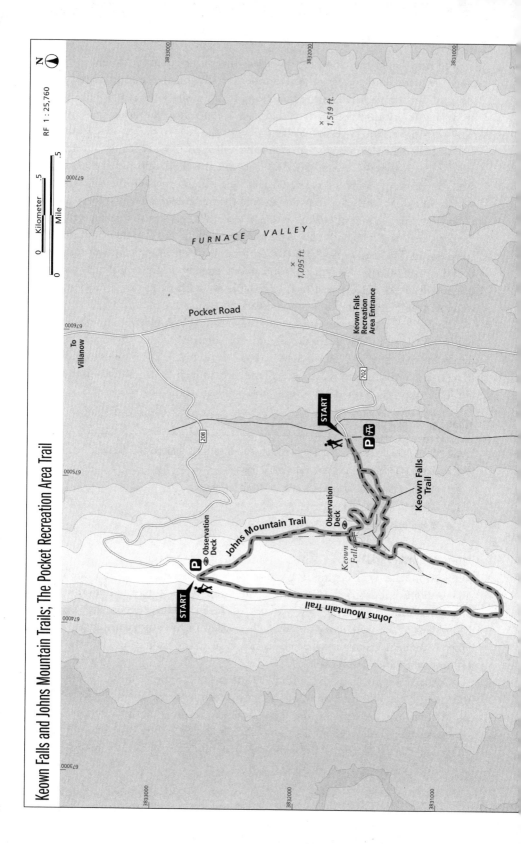

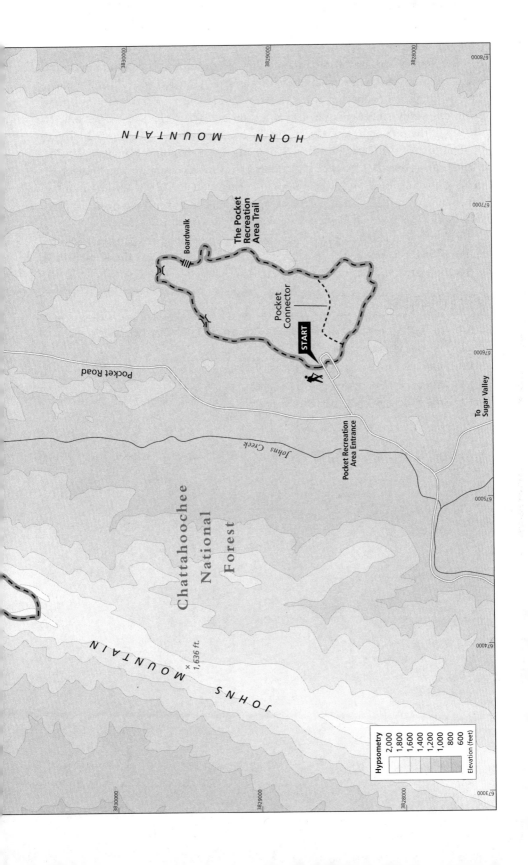

HORN MOUNTAIN

Boardwalk

The Pocket Recreation Area Trail

Pocket Connector

START

Pocket Road

Pocket Recreation Area Entrance

Johns Creek

To Sugar Valley

Chattahoochee National Forest

JOHNS MOUNTAIN

× 1,636 ft.

Hypsometry	
	2,000
	1,800
	1,600
	1,400
	1,200
	1,000
	800
	600
	Elevation (feet)

3830000

3829000

3828000

6780000

6777000

6776000

6775000

6774000

6773000

At 1.3 miles you turn to the east and then northeast as you descend toward the east escarpment of the mountain to the overlook deck for Keown Falls at 2.3 miles. The two trails are connected at the deck above the falls by a short path. You now begin the steady climb, going along the stream that forms the falls for 0.9 mile to the top of the mountain again at the overlook and parking area for the 3.2 loop.

This part of the Chattahoochee National Forest is the Johns Mountain Wildlife Management Area (WMA). There is a short fire-arms season for deer and black bear in late November and small game hunting during the fall and early winter months. When hiking during hunting season, stay on the trails and wear blaze-orange apparel such as a cap or jacket. (Check www.gohuntgeorgia.com for WMA seasons.)

A new long trail coming into Georgia, the Pinhoti Trail, joins the Johns Mountain Trail at the parking area and follows it down to the falls, to the Keown Falls Recreation Area, and on to Pocket Road.

Miles and Directions

0.0 Start at the parking area at the end of FR 208 and the observation deck, going south.

0.1 Pass the radio relay tower.

1.3 Reach the south end of trail as it loops to the left and heads north.

2.3 Arrive at the observation deck over Keown Falls.

3.2 Arrive back at the observation deck and parking area.

3 The Pocket Recreation Area Trail

A 2.7-mile mostly level, white-blazed loop trail in an area of unique geological and botanical significance, this hike is around a well-managed and regionally popular campground. The Pocket is a valley surrounded by the horseshoe-shaped formation of Mill and Horn Mountains. Boardwalks over the wet areas associated with springs permit a close-up view of wetland plants and animals.

See map on page 30–31
Start: Trail sign in parking area across from the comfort station
Distance: 2.7-mile loop
Approximate hiking time: 1½ hours
Difficulty: Easy
Elevation gain/loss: Negligible
Trail surface: Dirt; boardwalks over wet areas and springs
Lay of the land: Flat, with gentle grades along the base of a low ridge
Season: Trail year-round; campground closed November 15 to April 1

Land status: Chattahoochee-Oconee National Forests
Nearest towns: Sugar Valley, Calhoun
Fees and permits: No fees or permits required
Maps: USGS Sugar Valley; Chattahoochee National Forest map
Trail contacts: USDA Forest Service, Armuchee-Cohutta Ranger District, 3941 Highway 76, Chattsworth, GA 30705; (706) 695-6736; www.fs.fed.us/conf

Finding the trailhead: From La Fayette take Highway 136 east about 13 miles to Pocket Road, 0.5 mile past Villanow. Turn south (right) on Pocket Road and go 8 miles to the recreation area. One trailhead is across the road from the comfort station. The other is near Campsite 15. The trail can be hiked in either direction.

From Interstate 75 at Calhoun take exit 312. Go west on Highway 53/143 to Highway 143 to Calhoun. Take Highway 136 and go 5.5 miles to Sugar Valley, then follow Pocket Road (Lake Marvin Road) 8.9 miles to the entrance of the Pocket Recreation Area.

The Hike

The Pocket area suffered extensive damage from the Blizzard of 1993 and a tornado in 2000. Great numbers of large Virginia and loblolly pines, hardwood trees, and buildings fell throughout the Pocket. Many trees fell across the trail, and Forest Service personnel spent hours of back-breaking labor clearing the trail and campground.

For the first 0.5 mile, this delightful loop hike passes through pine woods and hardwoods and across one of the spring runs on convenient boardwalks. Other boardwalks cross some of the more permanently boggy areas. In a dominantly Virginia pine area about halfway around the loop, at 1.1 miles, a large patch of pink lady's slipper orchids begin blooming about April 20. If you look closely, you will see others among the pines at different places along the trail. Many other wildflowers bloom here in spring and throughout summer and fall, including toothworts, trilliums, mayapples, violets, and bluets. At 1.0 mile, the next and longest (200 feet) boardwalk crosses another of the crystal-clear brooks and a wet bog. This and other bogs along the trail have thick mats of sphagnum, a moss that grows only in very wet areas.

The trail moves from the wet areas to dry ridge sides where oaks, hickories, and pines dominate. Dogwoods, sourwoods, blueberry bushes, and wildflowers thrive beneath the forest canopy. Near the end of the loop you pass an amphitheater built on a quiet wooded slope. This open-air facility is wheelchair accessible, and programs are held here in season. The path to the amphitheater passes through a wooded area of large yellow poplars, maples, buckeyes, and other forest species along a pretty spring brook, enabling those in wheelchairs to enjoy part of the Pocket Trail. From here it is only a short distance back to the trailhead.

Mile and Directions

0.0 Start from the road opposite the comfort station and spring branch.

0.1 Leave the road and follow the earthen trail.

0.6 Cross the first boardwalk.

1.0 Cross the second and longest boardwalk.

1.4 Begin a gentle climb and walk along a low ridge.

1.9 Pass the connector trail that turns to the right.

2.7 Close the loop back at the parking area

Additional Trails

A nature trail at the south end of the loop trail is a must-do option. A spur path leads to an observation platform over an aquatic area.

4 Cloudland Canyon State Park Trails

Because so little of the Cumberland Plateau touches the state, Cloudland Canyon is a unique geological feature in Georgia. The canyons and waterfalls are beautiful. The flatter tops of the plateau provide sharp contrast to the sheer canyon walls, all softened by an almost complete cover of trees and shrubs that add color to the ancient sandstone cliffs. The myriad shades of green as the different species of trees begin to leaf out in spring is just as striking as the multicolor display when the same trees take on their autumn hues. In winter, the leafless trees expose the cliffs for a fresh and different look.

A 0.25-mile paved trail along the rim overlooking the canyon is completely wheelchair accessible. The featured West Rim and Cloudland Canyon Falls Trails form the main trail system along with the Backcountry Trail, a backpacking option.

Start: For both West Rim and Falls Trails, on the paved walkway leading from the day-use area/East Rim Overlook behind the cabins

Distance: West Rim Trail, 4.1-mile lollipop; Falls Trail, 0.3 mile one-way to the first falls; 0.5 mile one-way to the second falls, most of which is down the canyon wall on a wooden stairway; Backcountry Trail, 2.0-mile loop

Approximate hiking time: West Rim Trail, 2½ hours; Falls Trail, 1½ hours; Backcountry Trail, 1½ hours

Difficulty: West Rim Trail, moderate with a few short, steep, rocky places; trails down to the falls are short but strenuous; Backcountry Trail, moderate to strenuous

Elevation gain/loss: West Rim Trail, 50 feet; Falls Trails, 500 feet; Backcountry Trail, 65 feet

Trail surface: Mostly earthen, with some exposed stone; park paved road; wooden stairway to falls

Lay of the land: Rolling plateau surface and canyon walls

Season: Year-round

Land status: Georgia State Parks Division

Nearest towns: Trenton, Georgia; Lookout Mountain and Chattanooga, Tennessee

Fees and permits: Parking $3.00 per day

Maps: USGS Durham; page-size map, available in the park office or from the Web site

Trail contacts: Cloudland Canyon State Park, 122 Cloudland Canyon Park Road, Rising Fawn, GA 30738; (706) 657-4050; www.gasateparks.org

Finding the trailhead: From Trenton, Georgia, on Interstate 59, take exit 11 and go east 6.3 miles on Highway 136 to the park entrance. The park office is immediately on the right; continue 1.2 miles to East Rim Overlook parking area. The trailhead for the West Rim and Falls Trails is at the overlook parking area. The trailhead for the Backcountry Trail is on the road to the tennis courts, 0.25 mile past the courts.

From Lookout Mountain, Tennessee, take the Lookout Mountain Scenic Highway 14.5 miles to Highway 136. Turn right and go 0.9 mile to the park entrance. Follow directions above to trailhead.

The Hikes

The trail for both the waterfalls and the West Rim begins in the parking lot for the overlook and picnic area. The 0.25-mile path to the overlook is paved and wheelchair accessible. The trailhead is well marked. The West Rim Trail has white blazes, and the Falls Trail has yellow. You are cautioned to stay on the trail and not climb on rocks or around the waterfalls. The rocks can be very slippery and dangerous. Caution is also advised for people with heart problems and those in poor physical condition using the waterfalls stairway.

West Rim Trail

The West Rim Trail goes behind several cabins and begins the descent to Daniel Creek, which forms the waterfalls. In a short distance, 0.2 mile, the trail to the falls turns off to the right in a series of wooden steps. The West Rim Trail continues, reaching a picturesque footbridge over fast-flowing and cascading Daniel Creek at 0.25 mile. Catawba rhododendron and mountain laurel thickets interspersed with sourwood, dogwood, and larger oaks, hickories, hemlocks, and maples shade the trail. After crossing the bridge, which is only about 30 or 40 yards above the highest falls, you begin climbing up to the plateau top. Mosses, ferns, and many wildflowers line the trail in spring and summer. You travel through an area of large sandstone boulders and rock overhangs that form natural shelters. After some switchbacks and 0.4 mile into the trail, you will walk along the rim of the gulf, or canyon. From here you can look down from carefully placed overlooks.

You leave the canyon rim and come to a fork in the trail at 0.9 mile; this marks the point where the loop trail returns. Continuing to the left, in a clockwise direction, you hike through the oak-hickory forest of the Cumberland Plateau. There is very little change in elevation for the next mile. Blueberries, dogwood, and sourwood grow under the larger trees. Dwarf iris, pipsissewa, spring beauty, phlox, bird's-foot violets, and many other wildflowers grow in the well-drained sandy soil and along the small stream drainages. Two paths lead off the trail, providing access to the tent and trailer campgrounds. You cross the paved park road at 1.5 miles. From here you approach the western escarpment of Lookout Mountain; you can look down on the town of Trenton and Lookout Valley, a drop of more than 1,200 feet. The path goes north along this rim to stone steps and a spectacular rocky point overlook at 1.8 miles. On a clear day you can see to the Tennessee River, where it forms Moccasin Bend at Chattanooga, Tennessee.

Climb back up the rocky steps and continue back toward the western rim of Sitton Gulf. The path leads to several beautiful overlooks along the way. Almost

Sitton Gulf in summer from the overlook on the West Rim Trail.

anytime during the day you will see hawks or vultures soaring on the wind currents along the steep escarpments. You will pass several spur paths on the left that lead to cabins. Leaving the canyon bluff, you come to Whiteoak Spring Branch at 2.9 miles; cross the bridge and at 3.0 miles join the trail back to the bridge over Daniel Creek. Continue to the parking area trailhead for a hike of 4.1 miles.

Miles and Directions

0.0 Start from the parking area.

0.2 Come to the turnoff for the Falls Trail; stay on the white-blazed trail.

0.25 Cross a footbridge over Daniel Creek.

0.4 Enjoy your first view of the canyon from the west rim.

0.9 At forks in the trail, take the left path.

1.5 Cross the paved park road.

1.8 Arrive at a grand overlook to the north toward Chattanooga, Tennessee.

2.9 Cross bridge over Whiteoak Springs Branch.

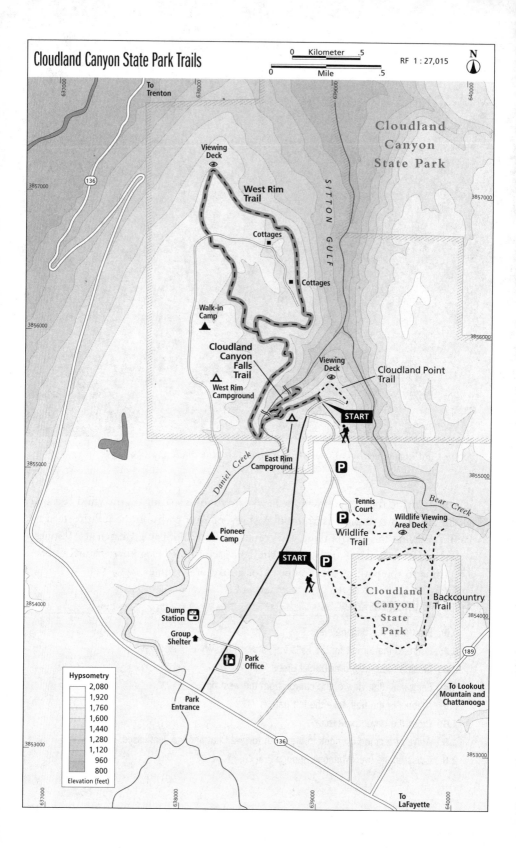

3.0   Return to the forks to complete the loop portion of the hike.

3.9   Returning to the trail on left that leads to the falls, continue on to parking area.

4.1   Arrive back at the parking area.

Cloudland Canyon Falls Trail

The Cloudland Canyon Falls Trail, accessed from the West Rim Trail, is a series of wooden steps and boardwalks. The flowers growing on the steep canyon face are outstanding. Jack-in-the-pulpit, windflower, hydrangea, foam flower, Solomon's seal, long-spurred violet, dwarf crested iris, bellwort, and great patches of trilliums are only a few of the flowers blooming in spring. Several species of ferns, including maidenhair and marginal, grow among the other lush vegetation. Magnificent yellow poplars, hemlocks, and buckeyes thrive on the lower levels of the gulch. The quantity of water over the falls varies greatly from season to season. The water falls into large splash pools and then continues to cascade down over the boulder-strewn streambed. Each of the falls has its own distinctive beauty, making the hike down and back over the face of the canyon wall on the well-built steps worth the effort.

Additional Trails

The **Backcountry Trail** begins at the parking area for the group camp. This red-blazed trail is designed for backpacking and camping. Eleven primitive campsites are situated along the 2.0-mile trail.

5 Crockford–Pigeon Mountain Wildlife Management Area Trails

The wheelchair-accessible Shirley Miller Wildflower Trail boardwalk is designed to permit viewing many species of flowers up close with the least impact. The South Pocket Trail, on the west side of the mountain, goes past unique geological formations, sandstone bluffs, and a picturesque waterfall in addition to wildflowers, some very rare. The unique sandstone formations are the special features on the Rocktown Trail, located 2 miles south of the mountaintop end of South Pocket Trail.

Start: Shirley Miller Wildflower and South Pocket Trails, parking area at the end of Pocket Road; Rocktown Trail, parking area at the end of Rocktown Road

Distance: Shirley Miller Wildflower Trail, 800-foot boardwalk; South Pocket Trail, 7.4 miles out and back, beginning at the lower parking area; Rocktown Trail, 2.0 miles out and back, plus another 0.5 mile walking among the rock formations

Approximate hiking time: Shirley Miller Wildflower Trail, 1 hour; South Pocket Trail, 5 hours; Rocktown Trail, 1 hour for the trail, plus another hour for exploring the interesting sandstone formations

Difficulty: Rocktown and Wildflower Trails, easy; South Pocket Trail, moderate

Elevation gain/loss: South Pocket Trail, 1,040 feet

Trail surface: Gravel at trailhead; sandy loam and exposed rocky areas

Season: Year-round; horse and bicycle trails and areas closed during firearms seasons and before 10:00 A.M. during archery and turkey seasons (for current hunting seasons: www.gohuntgeorgia.com)

Other trail users: Equestrians and cyclists on all but Wildflower and Rocktown Trails

Land status: DNR Wildlife Resources Division

Nearest towns: LaFayette

Fees and permits: No fees or permits required

Maps: USGS Cedar Grove and LaFayette; page-size map of the management area, available at the check station or from the Department of Natural Resources

Trail contacts: Office of Regional Supervisor, Department of Natural Resources, Wildlife Resources Division, 2592 Floyd Springs Road, Armuchee, GA 30105; (706) 295-6041 Department of Natural Resources, Wildlife Resources Division, 2070 U.S. Highway 278 Southeast, Social Circle, GA 30279; (770) 918-6416; www.gohuntgeorgia.com

Finding the trailhead: For Wildflower and South Pocket Trails, go west from LaFayette on Highway 193 for 5.5 miles to Hog Jowl Road. Turn south on Hog Jowl Road and drive 2.5 miles to Pocket Road. (Note: This turn is difficult to see; it is at the top of a rise just past the Mount Herman Baptist Church.) Pocket Road is a dead end; it is paved for about 0.5 mile and gravel for the next 0.8 mile. After fording a small branch, you come to a gravel parking area on the left. The trailhead is the gate on the gravel road.

For Rocktown Trail, take Highway 193 west from LaFayette for 2.5 miles to Chamberlain Road. Turn south (left) and go 3.3 miles to the Crockford-Pigeon Mountain Wildlife Management Area Check Station sign. Turn right on the paved road into the management area. The check station is on

Sessile trilliums on the Shirley Miller Wildflower Trail.

the left. Continue on the road past the check station, and go up the mountain for 4.6 miles to Rocktown Road. This gravel road ends in 0.7 mile at a parking area and turnaround. An information board here gives some of the history of the area. The trailhead is at this sign.

The Hikes

Most of Pigeon Mountain is in the Crockford–Pigeon Mountain Wildlife Management Area under the supervision of the Department of Natural Resources, Wildlife Resources Division. The name comes from the now-extinct passenger pigeon, which once roosted here in great numbers, and for Jack Crockford, former Director of the Wildlife Resources Division. The mountain is noted for its many extensive caves that honeycomb the limestone formations under the plateau. The best known of the caves is Ellison Cave, with exceptionally deep pits. (**Note:** Spelunking is by permit only.)

All hiking trails in this management area are blazed and, with the exception of Rocktown Trail, are used by equestrians and cyclists as well as hikers. Before hiking trails other than South Pocket and Rocktown, it is a good idea to pick up a man-

Crockford–Pigeon Mountain Wildlife Management Area Trails

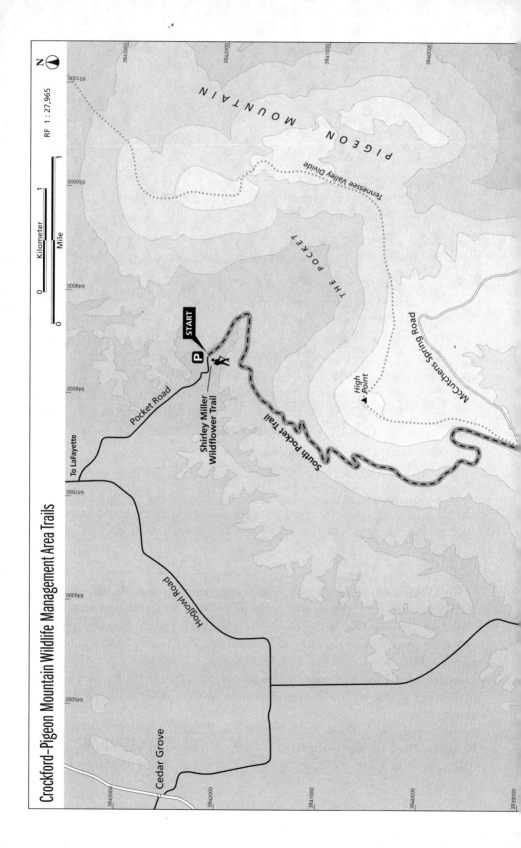

RF 1 : 27,965

N

START

P

Shirley Miller
Wildflower Trail

South Pocket Trail

Pocket Road

To LaFayette

Hoglowl Road

Cedar Grove

THE POCKET

PIGEON MOUNTAIN

Tennessee Valley Divide

McCutchens Spring Road

High
Point

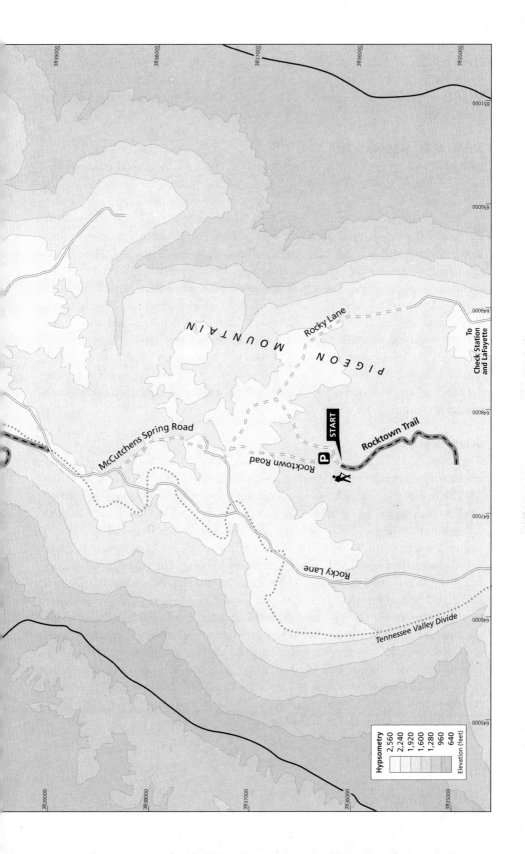

agement area map at the check station. There are many miles of marked and unmarked trails and old logging and jeep roads on and around the mountain. They make for interesting hiking, but it is easy to get lost on Pigeon Mountain if you are not careful.

Shirley Miller Wildflower Trail

Dedicated in 1999, the Shirley Miller Wildflower Trail is named for the wife of former U.S. Senator Zell Miller, both of whom are instrumental in preserving natural areas in the state.

The Wildflower Trail, an 800-foot wheelchair accessible boardwalk, begins at the plaque and information sign across the road from the parking area. Interpretive signs along the walk enhance the educational and natural history experience. The Georgia Conservancy's *Guide to the North Georgia Mountains* states, "Several rare and uncommon plant species have been recorded here, making it one of the most remarkable botanical areas in Georgia." At least eleven significant species found almost nowhere else in Georgia are present in the small mixed-hardwood forest below the wet-weather falls. These include celandine poppy, Ohio buckeye, bent trillium, nodding spurge, lance-leaf trillium, wild hyacinth, log fern, harbinger of spring, Virginia bluebell, hairy mock-orange, and blue ash. When the plants are in bloom, the forest below the waterfall near the start of the trail is truly remarkable, with some species occurring in thick beds.

South Pocket Trail

The South Pocket Trail begins at 920 feet elevation and climbs to 1,960 feet. It traverses an excellent wildlife and birding area with fine scenery, especially in winter.

The trail begins with a walk up the 0.4-mile jeep road beside and above Pocket Branch to a clearing above the falls. At this point the trail forks into a loop. For this hike, go to the right and hike only this south section. This blue-blazed trail crosses Pocket Branch. You pass through a hardwood forest of oaks, hickories, red cedars, yellow-poplars, buckeyes, mulberries, and other large trees. The undergrowth is dogwoods, redbuds, sourwoods, and lower shrubs, including mountain laurel, sweet shrub, wild hydrangea, spicebush, blueberry, and azalea. There are no steep grades; in fact, there are several flat and some downhill stretches. Switchbacks keep the climb moderate, although you gain more than 1,000 feet of elevation. You pass interesting rock outcrops with wet seeps supporting many flowers and ferns. At the top you intercept the West Brow Trail, marked with white blazes, at McCutchens Spring Road. You drop back down South Pocket Trail and backtrack to the parking area. (**Option:** Follow the West Brow Trail for about 1.0 mile to High Point, the highest point on Pigeon Mountain at 2,330 feet.)

Miles and Directions

0.0 Start from the parking area. Step around the bar gate in the jeep road.

0.4 Leave the roadway to the right and cross Pocket Branch.

1.0 Begin the gentle climb.

2.8 After several switchbacks, you're heading north.

3.0 Go east (left) and turn right to head south.

3.4 Reach McCutchens Spring Road, and begin backtracking to the trailhead. (**Option:** Hike northeast 1.0 mile to High Point before returning to South Pocket Trail, adding 2.0 miles to your hike.)

7.4 Arrive back at the trailhead.

Rocktown Trail

The Rocktown Trail is easy and flat. It begins at the well-developed gravel parking area, crosses the headwater branch of Allen Creek, and goes through a mixed forest of Virginia pines, oaks, and hickories. You pass a few large boulders before reaching the huge ones. Do not let the trail's short length lead you to think you should schedule only a few minutes for this hike. You can easily spend a day among the rock formations and not see everything. The brownish-red color of the rocks is caused by iron ore deposits, which were once mined extensively around Pigeon Mountain.

Miles and Directions

0.0 Start on the path at the parking area, crossing a small branch of Allen Creek.

0.4 You see the first sample of the large exposed rocks.

1.0 Reach the end of trail and discover why it was named Rocktown. Walk a little further to explore the formations off the marked trail and then return along the same trail.

2.0 Arrive back at the trailhead.

6 Arrowhead Wildlife Interpretive Trail

This easy, level hike winds in and out of a dozen or more different wildlife habitat types, including open fields, forest, forest edge, and water. This is one of the most interesting short trails in the state, providing a short course in wildlife management for both game and non-game animals. Interpretive signs strategically placed along the path explain what has been done to improve the diversity of animals and plants. The trail is short enough for a quick morning or evening walk and has enough variety to keep you busy for a day of watching and photography.

Start: At the parking area with an information board

Distance: 2.2-mile loop

Approximate hiking time: 1½ hours

Difficulty: Easy

Elevation gain/loss: Negligible

Trail surface: Earthen, with sod in places

Lay of the land: Gently rolling

Season: Year-round, with wildlife active throughout the year

Land status: DNR, Wildlife Resources Division

Nearest town: Rome

Fees and permits: No fees or permits required

Maps: USGS Armuchee; Wildlife Resources Division trail map, available in the headquarters office

Trail contacts: Regional Supervisor, Georgia Wildlife Resources Division, Game Management Section, 2592 Floyd Springs Road, Armuchee, GA 30105; (706) 295-6041 Department of Natural Resources, Wildlife Resources Division, 2070 U.S. Highway 278 Southeast, Social Circle, GA 30279; (770) 918-6400; www.gohuntgeorgia.com; www.gofishgeorgia.com

Finding the trailhead: From Rome go north about 10 miles on U.S. Highway 27 to Highway 156 (Floyd Spring Road). Turn right (east) and go 4.3 miles to a special parking area just before the main entrance to the DNR Wildlife Resources Division Northwest Regional Game Management Headquarters. The gravel parking area is the trailhead. A large sign with orientation information and a map of the trail directs you.

The Hike

This trail has much to offer, including opportunities for wildlife viewing and photography, songbirds and waterfowl, nesting Canada geese, an active beaver dam, and wildflowers spring through fall. Eighteen marked points on the trail are interpreted in a brochure available in the District Office.

The wide, easy-to-follow path begins at the corner of the parking area. You can look down on one of the old fish hatchery ponds as you begin walking through an open area to the first interpretive sign, with information about waterfowl and wading birds (the Canada geese nest in April). The next stop is at a platform overlooking a small pond. A wood duck nest box is mounted on a post in the willow- and alder-lined pool. A sign tells about this duck and the habitat it needs.

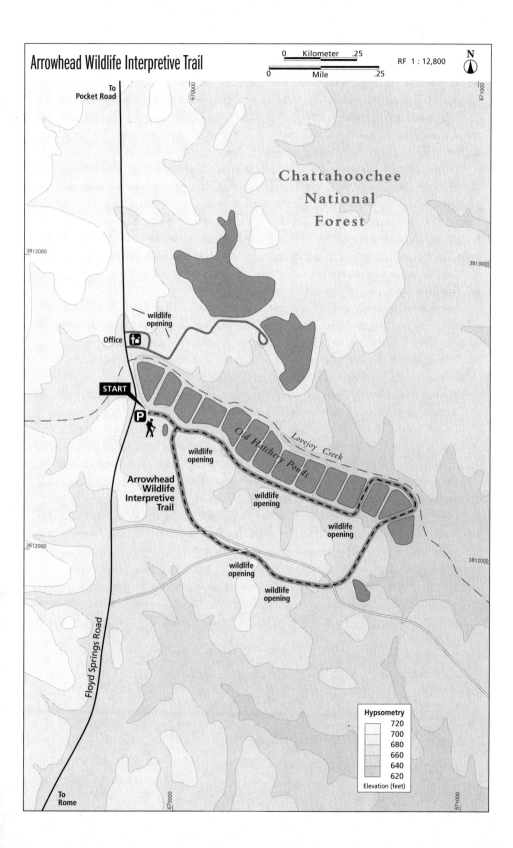

You pass a pole with gourds for martin nest boxes and into the wooded area, where the trail is marked with blue blazes. At first it is a pure pine stand, where dwarf iris blooms beside the path in April. This tract has a good white-tailed deer population that is described at the next sign. The trees have changed now to hardwood forest. You walk along a dirt roadbed cut for a firebreak. The importance of dead and hollow trees is described at the next sign, followed by a discussion of red oak and pignut hickory. Forestry management practices are described here. Blueberries are abundant where prescribed burns (described on a later sign) have encouraged their growth. The trail now passes through a small field of grasses, clover, and a few small shrubs. This is a planned opening in the forest to provide food for a number of different animals. The edge of the opening is important to many birds not otherwise found in the woods, and many other animals take advantage of these grassy openings.

The trail goes back into the woods, through a wet area, and to the sign discussing the important practice of prescribed burning.

Another open field with an attractive rectangular pond is next. Nest boxes for wood ducks are located here. Bluebirds also thrive in these old open fields, as described on the next sign, with a nest box nearby. Walking toward the larger ponds of the old hatchery, you pass a sign telling about the naturalized Japanese honeysuckle that is now used by many species of wildlife.

The trail crosses the dikes between the ponds. Watch for nesting platforms for Canada geese in most of the ponds. The geese readily adapt to them and also nest right on the ground on the banks of the ponds. Red-winged blackbirds nest in the willows and alders at the pond edge. Beyond the ponds, the trail follows along the spring creek that supplies water for the ponds. Beavers have built a large dam here, and their lodges can be seen in the backwater. Many other animals, both aquatic and terrestrial, use the beaver pond and its edges.

The trail markers lead you back to the south side of the ponds and back to the trailhead. There is much wildlife to be seen along these ponds, and the species vary from season to season. Reptiles and amphibians are abundant by the water's edge. At one time, an alligator took up residence in the old hatchery pools. The careful hiker can see and photograph many kinds of plants and animals on this trail.

Honorable Mentions

A James H. (Sloppy) Floyd State Park

Surrounded by countryside and the Chattahoochee National Forest, this state park makes an ideal day hike or weekend camping and hike opportunity. It is one of the few parks located in the Ridge and Valley physiographic province. Here the ridges are sharp and the valleys are wide where large springs like Marble Spring occur. Both ridges and valleys are covered with hardwood forest and pine where the land has been cleared in the past.

There are 3.0 miles of hiking trails in the park. You have your choice of a walk around the lake to gently rolling wooded paths to a steep climb up Taylor Ridge. A 1.6-mile spur connects the park trails with the 60-mile Pinhoti Trail, which runs from the national forest in Alabama to the Benton MacKaye and Appalachian Trails in the high-mountain Chattahoochee National Forest. Two lakes covering a total fifty-one acres provide excellent fishing. A boardwalk with one lake trail is popular with children and others who enjoy feeding large bluegills and catfish. Nearby are Cloudland Canyon State Park, Chickamauga Creek Trail, Rocky Mountain Public Fishing Area, and the Summerville Fish Hatchery.

For more information: James H. Floyd State Park, 2800 Sloppy Floyd Lake Road, Summerville, GA 30747; (706) 857–0826; www.gastateparks.org.

DeLorme: Georgia Atlas and Gazetteer: Page 18 A3

B Chickamauga Battlefield National Military Park

The park is in the northwest corner of Georgia, about 5 miles south of the Tennessee-Georgia state line. The National Park Service headquarters and visitor center for Chickamauga Battlefield is located at the north entrance on U.S. Highway 17. The park's six trails vary in length from 5 to 20 miles, totaling about 40 miles of overlapping trails—70 miles if each trail is hiked separately. Each trail is color blazed to follow a specific theme of the historical battles. Roads parallel parts of the battlefield trails so that much can be viewed from a vehicle. Most visitors choose points of interest to hike throughout the park.

The park is open year-round. Spring wildflowers are abundant and fall colors of the many hardwood trees can be spectacular. These trails provide a unique and enjoyable way to study Civil War history in a natural setting. The visitor center has outstanding exhibits and an extensive gun collection. An almost hour-by-hour account of the battles is described on plaques, interpretive signs, and great monuments along the trails. The land is almost the same as what the soldiers saw in September 1863.

For more information: Superintendent, Chickamauga and Chattanooga National Military Park, P.O. Box 2128, Fort Oglethorpe, GA 30742; (706) 866–9241, ext. 123; www.nps.gov\chch.

DeLorme: Georgia Atlas and Gazetteer: Page 12 B4

Northeast Georgia:
Blue Ridge Mountains

View from the Sourwood Trail at Lake Russell Recreation Area (Hike 25).

National Forest Trails

7 Lake Conasauga Recreation Area Trails

Three trails vary from a quiet walk around nineteen-acre Conasauga Lake, the highest in Georgia, to an easy hike through a songbird management area to a moderate hike up to Grassy Mountain fire tower, with views of the largest of the Chattahoochee Forest wilderness areas. The lowest elevation here is 3,140 feet; the highest is 3,692 feet, at the fire tower on Grassy Mountain.

Start: Songbird and Grassy Mountain Tower Trails, from the overflow parking area; also from the Lake Trail at the dam
Distance: Songbird Trail, 1.7-mile lollipop; Lake Trail, 1.0-mile loop; Tower Trail, 4.0 miles out and back from the campground connector (4.4 miles if starting at the shared Songbird trailhead)
Approximate hiking time: Songbird Trail, 1 hour; Lake Trail, 30 minutes; Tower Trail, 2 hours
Difficulty: Easy to moderate
Elevation gain/loss: 552 feet
Trail surface: Sandy loam with leaf litter; some grassy old roadbeds; gravel roads
Lay of the land: Rolling mountainous

Season: Hiking year-round; campground open April 15 to October 30
Land status: Chattahoochee-Oconee National Forests
Nearest towns: Eton, Chattsworth
Fees and permits: Day-use fee $3.00 per vehicle; other fees for camping
Maps: USGS Crandall; page-size map of the Songbird and Lake Trails with the beginning of the Tower Trail, available from the campground host
Trail contacts: USDA Forest Service, Armuchee-Cohutta Ranger District, 3941 Highway 76, Chatsworth, GA 30705; (706) 695-6736; www.fs.fed.us/conf; for fishing regulations and seasons: www.gofishgeorgia.com; for hunting seasons: www.gohuntgeorgia.com

Finding the trailhead: From Chatsworth go north 4 miles on U.S. Highway 411 to Eton. Turn right (east) at the traffic light and follow the paved CCC Camp Road until the pavement ends. At this point the road becomes Forest Road 18. Follow this gravel road to Forest Road 68. Turn left and go 9 miles to the end of FR 68 at the recreation area. On the way you will pass the Holly Creek Check Station and the large COHUTTA WILDLIFE MANAGEMENT AREA sign. This is a steep climb. At the top of the mountain, FR 68 turns left and Forest Road 64 turns right. These dirt roads form the boundary of the Cohutta Wilderness Area. Follow the signs 4.3 miles to Lake Conasauga Recreation Area. To reach the Songbird and Grassy Mountain Trails, continue 1.2 miles to the Overflow Campground. A day-use parking area is across the road from the campground. A songbird information board marks the trailhead for the two trails.

From Ellijay go west on Highway 52 for 9.5 miles to the LAKE CONASAUGA RECREATION AREA and WILDLIFE MANAGEMENT AREA signs. Turn right on a paved road, which becomes Forest Road 18 in about 1.0 mile. The road forks at the pavement's end. Continue 4.0 miles to FR 68. Turn hard right and follow the directions above.

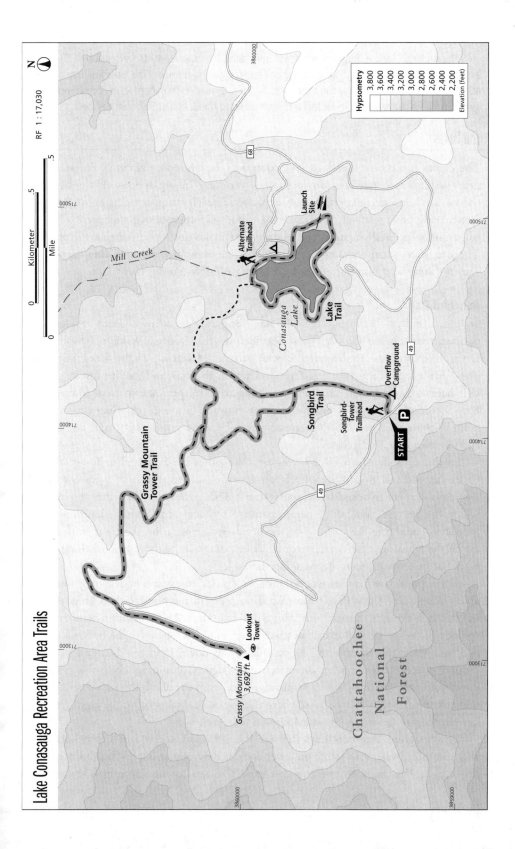

Lake Conasauga Recreation Area Trails

RF 1 : 17,030

N

Hypsometry

3,800
3,600
3,400
3,200
3,000
2,800
2,600
2,400
2,200

Elevation (feet)

Mill Creek

Alternate Trailhead

Launch Site

Conasauga Lake

Lake Trail

Grassy Mountain Tower Trail

Songbird Trail

Songbird-Tower Trailhead

Overflow Campground

START

P

49

49

68

Grassy Mountain 3,692 Ft.

Lookout Tower

Chattahoochee

National

Forest

0 Kilometer .5

0 Mile .5

The trailhead for the Songbird and Tower Trails is on Forest Road 49 (an extension of FR 68) across from the camping overflow area. A gravel parking area is provided. The Lake Trail can be accessed from several points around the lake: the campground, picnic areas, and boat launching ramp. Campers can start the Tower Trail and walk down to the Songbird Trail from the dam.

The Hikes

The Conasauga Recreation Area, located in the Chattahoochee National Forest very near the Tennessee state line, provides a wide variety of hiking opportunities for both the novice hiker and experienced backpacker. The elevation remains above 3,000 feet, making this a relatively cool place in summer. Campgrounds, picnic areas, a boat launching ramp, and beautiful mountain forests make this a popular getaway place. The area offers exceptional birding, wildflowers, mountain scenery, wildlife, lake and stream fishing, and hunting in nearby Cohutta Wildlife Management Area.

Songbird Trail

Songbird Trail passes through the 120-acre Songbird Management Tract developed cooperatively by the USDA Forest Service and the Georgia Wildlife Resources Division's Nongame–Endangered Species Program. Clearings in the forest kept in grass/shrub stands, a beaver pond, rhododendron thickets, and mature forests provide habitat diversity that attracts a wide range of bird species. Experienced birders have recorded 125 species present at some time of the year, including migrating sandhill cranes and red crossbills, nesting rose-breasted grosbeaks, scarlet tanagers, and chestnut-sided warblers.

From the trailhead on FR 49, you can hike either the Songbird or Tower Trail. Cross the road and go past the wheelchair-accessible toilets and down a gravel roadway that has been blocked to vehicular traffic. This cove drains into the stream on which the beavers have built a dam, creating a ten-acre pond. Rhododendron and mountain laurel line the pathway to the pond. A clearing is on the right, with forest on the left. Watch for deer, pig, or black bear tracks in the soft ground along this road. Bat boxes have been placed along the trail.

At the pond you may see wood ducks, which nest in cavities in dead trees or the artificial nest boxes that have been placed on poles in the pond. Belted kingfishers use this area along with many other birds and mammals. An observation platform at the side of the pond is an excellent place to sit and watch quietly. The beaver lodge and dam are visible from here. The trail that leads down from the dam and campground intercepts this trail at an information sign. Continuing along the beaver pond, you cross the branch on a footbridge and begin the climb through thick rhododendron for about 100 yards to where the Tower Trail takes off to the right. From here to the fire tower on Grassy Mountain is 1.7 miles.

The Songbird Trail continues through thick rhododendron, laurel, dog-hobble, and other shrubs beneath white pine, hemlock, yellow poplar, buckeye, and other tall forest trees. Pass another opening and expect to see towhees, cardinals, catbirds, brown thrashers, indigo buntings, and other open-habitat species. Benches at strategic places along the trail afford excellent, quiet viewing places. Besides birds and mammals, the pond attracts a wide variety amphibians (turtles, salamanders, frogs, and toads), and insects (dragonflies, damselflies, crane flies, butterflies, and gnats)—all of which can be seen while you're taking advantage of the benches. The trail crosses the upper end of the beaver pond and heads back to the wider, old roadbed. Turn to the right and return to the trailhead.

Miles and Directions

0.0 Start across the road from the parking area.

0.3 The trail on the left is the end of the loop; continue straight.

0.5 Reach the boardwalk to observation platform.

0.6 Come to the connecter trail from campground and directional signs.

0.9 Grassy Mountain Tower Trail continues on the right fork. Take the left fork to continue on the Songbird Trail.

1.4 Close the loop portion of the trail.

1.7 Arrive back at the trailhead and parking area.

Grassy Mountain Tower Trail

The Tower Trail leaves the Songbird Trail, climbs at a moderate grade through a rhododendron thicket, and then opens into a beautiful mixed-hardwood forest with large fern glades of New York, wood, and other ferns. Large clumps of Christmas ferns are scattered about the east- and north-facing slopes. This section of the trail is an exceptional wildflower area. Lady's slippers, showy orchis, rattlesnake plantain, and other orchids are present at different times throughout spring and summer. Solomon's seal, false lily-of-the-valley, bellwort, wood lily, several species of trilliums, mayapple, wild geranium, violets, squawroot, one-flowered cancer root, azaleas, and a host of other flowers bloom in spring. At this elevation, the blooming season is two or three weeks behind lower elevations in the mountains.

The trail reaches the road to the fire tower FR 49 near the crest of Grassy Mountain; walk 0.75 mile on the gravel road to the tower. Here the forest is made up of smaller, somewhat stunted southern red and other oak trees. Blackberries grow abundantly along the road in the open sun along with many other plants, especially daisies, asters, Queen Anne's lace, and other sun-tolerant flowers. At the fire tower you can climb to the first landing for a grand view of the mountains to the northeast in the Cohutta Wilderness, the Ridge and Valley Province to the west, and south to Fort Mountain and Fort Mountain State Park. This is a great place to watch for migrating hawks in the fall and for migrating sandhill cranes on clear days in spring and fall.

At the first switchback down the road, take one of two choices for the return to the trailhead. Either go back down the trail and around the Songbird Trail, or continue down the Forest Service road. The distance is about the same. Birders may wish to take the road for a greater variety of habitats. The blackberries are ripe in early July.

Miles and Directions

0.0 Start at the Overflow Campground trailhead shared with the Songbird Trail. Follow with the Songbird Trail to the forks.

0.8 Leave the Songbird Trail, taking the right fork to the Grassy Mountain Tower Trail.

1.1 Pass a large glade of New York and wood ferns mixed with other species.

1.8 Meet the gravel road to the fire tower.

2.2 Reach Grassy Mountain Tower (3,692 feet elevation). Climb the tower and enjoy the views before retracing your steps.

4.4 Arrive back at the campground trailhead.

Lake Trail

The Lake Trail can be walked from several places in the campground, picnic areas, and boat ramp. It is a level, quiet walk with views of the lake all the way around. The lake is usually crystal clear. Large patches of trout lilies (also known as dogtooth violets) grow under the rhododendron and hemlocks. Ferns are all along the trail. Look for the aromatic heart-leaf and maybe even a pink lady's slipper that has been missed by campers who unthinkingly pick wildflowers. Mountain laurel and rhododendron bloom along the trail from May to July. The 1.0-mile trail is an ideal morning or evening exercise stroll or birding area.

8 DeSoto Falls Trail

There are two falls on the trails that begin at the bridge across Frogtown Creek from the Desoto Falls Campground. The trails are wide and relatively level, with little elevation change. The smaller falls is to the left and DeSoto Falls to the right after the bridge across Frogtown Creek.

Start: At the trailhead across the Frogtown Creek bridge
Distance: Lower Falls, 1.0-mile loop; DeSoto falls, 1.5 miles out and back
Approximate hiking time: Lower Falls, 45 minutes; DeSoto Falls, 1 hour
Difficulty: Easy
Elevation gain/loss: Negligible
Trail surface: Loamy dirt
Season: Year-round hiking; campground open late May to October 30; heaviest water flows in winter and spring

Land status: Chattahoochee National Forest
Nearest town: Cleveland
Fees and permits: No fees or permits required for day use
Maps: USGS Neels Gap; USDA Forest Service map of Chattahoochee National Forest
Trail contacts: USDA Forest Service, Brasstown Ranger District, 1881 Highway 515, Blairsville, GA 30512; (706) 745-6928; www.fs.fed.us/conf

Finding the trailhead: DeSoto Falls Recreation Area is 14.6 miles north of Cleveland on U.S. Highway 129/Highway 11. Park in the day-use parking area for hiking. Reach the trailhead by crossing the Frogtown Creek bridge, following the arrows through the picnic area to the bridge.

From Dahlonega take U.S. Highway 19 to US 129 (12 miles). Turn left and go 4.2 miles to DeSoto Falls Campground and day-use parking. Follow the arrows to the bridge.

The Hike

This trail takes you through a range of forest types—from the thick rhododendron, mountain laurel, and dog-hobble of the streamsides to the more open hardwood forest of oak, hickory, yellow poplar, maple, buckeye, and many other species of large trees. Fine spring flower displays begin as early as March and continue with colorful displays of shrubs and trees like dog-hobble, silverbell, serviceberry, yellow poplar, deciduous magnolias, mountain laurel, rhododendron, and sourwood from April through August. The mountainsides exhibit grand color in mid- to late October. The name DeSoto Falls comes from a legend that a piece of armor found near the falls belonged to Hernando de Soto or one of his men. (**Note:** The Upper Falls Trail is closed and no longer maintained.)

The trail begins at a picturesque footbridge across Frogtown Creek from the campground. After you cross the bridge, a large wooden sign welcomes you to DeSoto Falls Scenic Area. A smaller sign directs you to the left for the Lower Falls in 0.5 mile and to the right to DeSoto Falls in 0.75 mile.

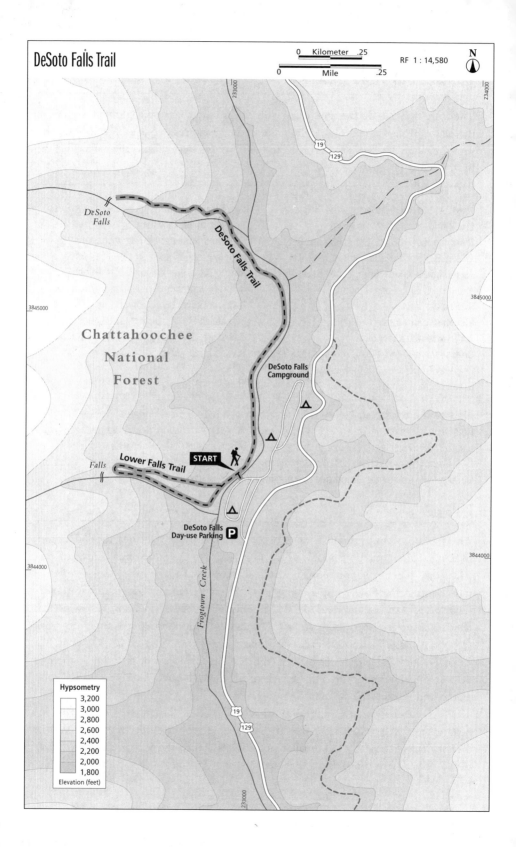

Turning left downstream, you are on the west side of Frogtown Creek. This well-traveled trail leads to **Lower Falls,** a series of cascades dropping about 35 feet on an unnamed tributary to Frogtown Creek. A platform provides a good view of the small but picturesque falls. You walk back down a trail, forming a loop to the creek and back to the trailhead for a 1.0-mile hike.

Returning to the bridge, the trail continues upstream for 0.75-mile to **DeSoto Falls,** also on a tributary to Frogtown Creek. A platform has been constructed for viewing the falls, which cascades down several stages for about 90 feet. The platform provides an excellent point to appreciate this cove-hardwood forest. This picturesque area is abundantly rich in wildflowers during spring. Return to the main trail and the trailhead.

Miles and Directions

To Lower Falls

0.0   Start at the end of the bridge across Frogtown Creek.

0.1   Turn downstream to the falls.

0.4   Reach the observation deck for a view of the falls.

1.0   Arrive back at the bridge to complete the loop.

To DeSoto Falls

0.0   Start at the end of the bridge across Frogtown Creek; turn upstream.

0.7   Cross the stream and turn up another small stream.

0.75 Reach the observation deck at DeSoto Falls. Enjoy the view and then return the way you came.

1.5   Arrive back at the bridge to complete the hike.

More Information

Local Events/Attractions

De Soto's search for gold probably did not take him to Dahlonega Gold Museum or to Smithgall Woods–Dukes Creek Conservation Area, where gold was discovered 10 years before the California gold rush.

Dahlonega Gold Museum Historic Site, #1 Public Square, Dahlonega, GA 30533; (706) 864-2257; www.gastateparks.org/info/dahlonega.

Smithgall Woods–Dukes Creek Conservation Area, 61 Tsalaki Trail, Helen, GA 30545; (706) 878-3087 or (706) 878-3520; www.gastateparks.org/info/smithgall; www.gastateparks.org.

9 Cooper Creek Wildlife Management Area Trails

The trails in this wildlife management area offer nearly 8 miles of easy to moderate hiking. The trails follow old logging trails and new footpaths through a variety of hardwood, mixed pine and hardwood, and white pine and hemlock forests and through a variety of conditions, from old stands of large trees to a tract recovering from fire.

Start: Yellow Mountain and Mill Shoals Creek Trails, at trailheads off Forest Road 236 with steps up the road bank; Eyes on Wildlife Trail, at parking area 0.2 mile upstream on FR 236 across Cooper Creek

Distance: Yellow Mountain Trail, 6.4 miles out and back; Mill Shoals Creek Trail to Forest Road 39, 1.7 miles one-way (featured loop, 4.9 miles); Cooper Creek Trail, 0.4 mile one-way; these three trails and FR 39 interconnect for two loop options; Eyes on Wildlife Trail, 1.7-mile lollipop

Approximate hiking time: Yellow Mountain Trail, 3 hours; Mill Shoals Creek Trail, 1 hour (featured loop, 2.5 hours); Eyes on Wildlife Trail, 1 hour

Difficulty: Easy to moderate; a few short, steep grades

Elevation gain/loss: 800 feet

Trail surface: Clean loamy dirt with leaf litter

Lay of the land: Low mountainous terrain with few steep grades

Season: Year-round; campground open March 23 to October 31; wearing blaze-orange cap or vest recommended during deer and turkey seasons

Land status: Chattahoochee National Forest

Nearest town: Blairsville

Fees and permits: No fees or permits required for day-use; campground $8.00 to $10.00 per site per night in season (mid-April through October)

Maps: USGS Mulky Gap; USDA Forest Service Chattahoochee National Forest map

Trail contacts: For marked trails in the Cooper Creek Scenic Area: Brasstown Ranger District, Chattahoochee National Forest, 1881 Highway 515, Blairsville, GA 30512; (706) 745-6928 For camping in Cooper Creek Recreation Area: Toccoa Ranger District, Chattahoochee National Forest, 6050 Appalachian Highway, Blue Ridge, GA 30513; (706) 632-3031; www.fs.fed.us/conf

Finding the trailhead: From Blairsville travel west on U.S. Highway 515/76 to Old U.S. Highway 76; turn left on Old US 76 and go 2.9 miles to Mulky Gap Road. Turn left and follow the winding Mulky Gap Road 9.9 miles to the Cooper Creek Campground at FR 236; turn left. The trailhead for Mill Shoals Trail is on the left side of the road about 400 yards. The Yellow Mountain trailhead marker is another 150 yards on the left.

From Dahlonega take Highway 60 north 19 miles through Suches to Cooper Creek Road. Look for the sign for Cooper Creek Recreation Area and Cavendar Gap. Turn right and go 0.8 mile to FR 236. You will see the sign for the Cooper Creek Wildlife Management Area (WMA) and the Cooper Creek Recreation Area. Turn left on FR 236 and go 2.3 miles to the bridge across Cooper Creek. The parking area on the right just before the bridge is for the Eyes on Wildlife Trail. Use this parking for Yellow Mountain and Mill Shoals Creek Trails. They are only another 225 yards on the right down FR 236.

Cooper Creek Wildlife Management Area Trails

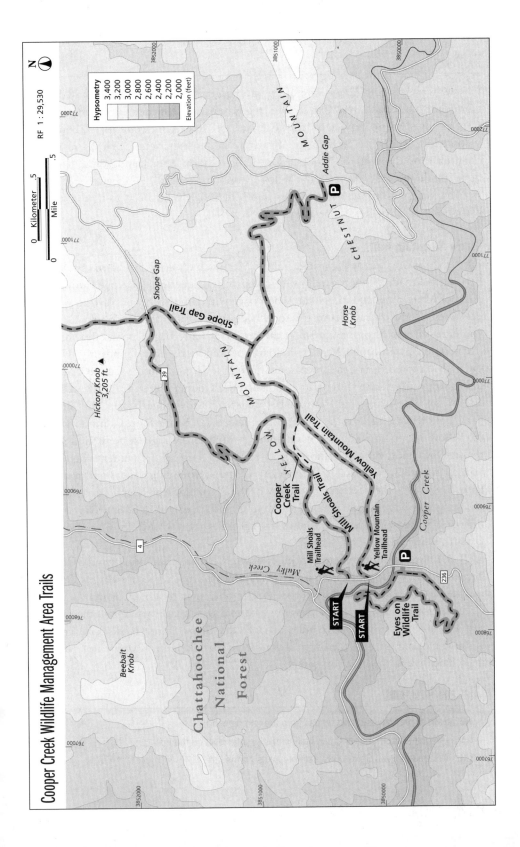

The Hikes

Cooper Creek Scenic Area is one of the more interesting forest areas in the Chattahoochee National Forest. Old timber stands remain untouched except for a few trees removed many years ago. Trout fishing in Cooper Creek and its tributaries, wildflowers, wildlife, and camping add to the hiking experience. The 2,160-foot contour runs through the Cooper Creek Recreation Area campground. From there, the highest elevation on the Yellow Mountain Trail is 2,963 feet.

The trailheads for Yellow Mountain and Mill Shoals Trails are steps up the steep bank from the shoulder of the road.

Yellow Mountain Trail

From the parking area at the bridge, Yellow Mountain trailhead is first on the right. Leaving the road, follow the yellow-blazed path up a gentle ridge slope through a stand of white pines and into a hardwood cove with large yellow poplar and white oak trees. As the trail works to the south side of the ridge above Cooper Creek, you enter an area of mountain laurel thickets with some large flame azalea shrubs that bloom April through May. Trailing arbutus and galax grow abundantly where the path is carved out of the steep south-facing slope going into a flat area. At 1.1 miles, you come to the short spur trail called the Cooper Creek Trail. If you turn left on this blue-blazed trail, you are 0.4 mile from the orange-blazed Mill Shoals Trail. Following it back to the campground makes a 2.2-mile loop. Continuing on the Yellow Mountain Trail, you have a gentle climb to the highest point along the trail, Yellow Mountain (elevation 2,963 feet) at 1.4 miles. In winter when the leaves have fallen, you have a grand view of the surrounding valleys and mountains. This trail is the northern boundary of the Cooper Creek Scenic Area. At 1.6 miles a green-blazed trail takes off to the left. This is the trail to Shope Gap at 0.6 mile and FR 39. This trail continues on 1.8 miles more to Mulky Gap and the Duncan Ridge Trail.

The Yellow Mountain Trail continues down the ridge crest into a stand of large hemlocks and white pines, switching back and forth until it reaches Bryant Creek and dense growths of rhododendron, dog-hobble, and mountain laurel. Bryant Creek is crossed on a log at 2.7 miles. In a couple switchbacks you climb the ridge past a clear-cut area and at 3.2 miles reach Addie Gap at Forest Road 33A. There is ample parking for a shuttle car or if you begin the hike here. If you're not catching a ride, return the way you came.

Miles and Directions

0.0   Start at the trailhead sign across from the campground.

1.1   The blue-blazed Cooper Creek Trail connector intersects on the left.

1.6   The green-blazed Shope Gap Trail intersects on the left.

2.7 Cross Bryant Creek on a foot log.

3.2 Reach the end of the trail at Addie Gap and pick up your shuttle or retrace your path to the trailhead.

6.4 Arrive back at the trailhead.

Mill Shoals Creek Loop

From the Cooper Creek Recreation Area, the Mill Shoals Creek Trail begins across the gravel FR 236. A wooden sign marks the trailhead. On the orange-blazed trail you begin a steady climb through white pines and hardwoods, with small patches of trailing arbutus and galax at the path's edge. Old American chestnut logs and new sprouts from old stumps are reminders of this great tree that was once dominant on these ridges. The path switches back and forth up a steep ridge with patches of mountain laurel, white pines, chestnut oaks, and several species of ferns. At 0.7 mile the trail forks; a signpost gives directions to the campground and blue-blazed Cooper Creek Trail connector between Mill Shoals Creek and Yellow Mountain Trails. The left fork and orange blazes continue the Mill Shoals Creek Trail. It drops down along a north-facing slope with wood and New York ferns and many spring wildflowers. The trail follows a logging road on a gentle grade. The path is now along an old road. You pass a former clear-cut area where another newer logging road has been made. Staying on the logging road, you walk along the creek before crossing Mill Shoals Creek at Mile 1.5 and up to FR 39 (Duncan Ridge Road) at Mile 1.7. You can return to the trailhead or continue to the right along the road for 1.0 mile to Shope Gap and the green-blazed Shope Gap Trail. Turn right and follow the green blazes for 0.6 mile to Yellow Mountain Trail. Turn right (east) and follow the yellow blazes 1.6 miles back to FR 236 and the campground to complete a loop of 4.9 miles.

Miles and Directions

0.0 Start at the trailhead sign across from the campground, about 150 yards north of the Yellow Mountain trailhead.

0.7 The blue-blazed Cooper Creek Trail connector intersects on the right. (**FYI:** This is the other end from the Yellow Mountain Trail.)

1.5 Cross Mill Shoals Creek.

1.7 Reach Duncan Ridge Road (FR 39). (**Option:** Retrace your steps for a 3.4-mile out-and-back hike.) Turn right up the road to continue for a loop trail.

2.7 Reach Shope Gap and the green-blazed Shope Gap Trail; turn right.

3.3 Connect with the yellow-blazed Yellow Mountain Trail; turn right.

4.9 Close the loop at FR 236 and the campground area.

Eyes on Wildlife Trail

At this writing, the Eyes on Wildlife Trail has not been blazed with colored markers. There are only carsonite stakes with directional arrows at major directional turns in the trail. The trailhead is located across FR 236 from the parking area. You cross a small bridge over Tom Jones Branch. A very attractive granite stone designates the trail history and the trailhead. It is best to begin this walk to the left around the 1.7-mile loop. This hike is not recommended until it is more clearly marked with blazes.

Additional Trails
Part of the Yellow Mountain Trail is in the Cooper Creek Scenic Area, which includes the **Old-Growth Forest Trail.** This trail is not maintained, but it is well worth taking the mile walk to see the magnificent yellow poplars, or tulip trees, with circumferences of as much as 11 to 15 feet. This trail starts at the parking area across Cooper Creek where the Eyes on Wildlife Trail begins.

More Information

Local Events/Attractions
Georgia Mountain Fall Festival, 1311 Music Hall Road, Hiawassee, GA 30546; (706) 896–4191; www.georgia-mountain-fair.com/fallfestival.asp. This festival, commonly referred to as the "Mountain Fair," is a ten-day festival in early October. It features great musical performances, educational demonstrations, mountain crafts, a flower show, and Georgia's Official State Fiddler's Convention.

Dahlonega Gold Museum Historic Site, #1 Public Square, Dahlonega, GA 30533; (706) 864–2257; www.gastateparks.org/info/dahlonega.

10 Arkaquah and Brasstown Bald Trails

At 4,784 feet, Brasstown Bald Mountain is the highest point in Georgia. A steep, paved trail leads from the parking area near the concession building to the summit and massive visitor center. For those who have heart problems or who do not want to hike to the summit, a concessionaire operates a shuttle bus from the parking area to visitor center for a fee. The Arkaquah Trail follows along a high ridge and then drops rapidly to Track Rock Gap. On this trail you are in the Brasstown Wilderness, providing spectacular views in a pristine setting.

Start: At the northwest end of the Brasstown Bald parking area at the ARKAQUAH TRAIL sign
Distance: Paved Brasstown Bald Summit Access Trail, 1.2 miles out and back; Arkaquah Trail, 9.0 miles out and back
Approximate hiking time: Summit Access Trail, about 1 hour; Arkaquah Trail, about 10 hours (leave early to prevent hiking this trail in the dark)
Difficulty: Moderate and strenuous, depending on the direction hiked; from Brasstown Bald parking area to Track Rock Gap, moderate; from Track Rock to the higher Brasstown parking area, strenuous; Summit Trail, strenuous
Elevation gain/loss: For Arkaquah Trail from Track Rock Gap end to Buzzard Roost Ridge, 1,408 feet
Trail surface: Clean loamy earth most of the trail; rocky exposed dirt on western steep grade; paved to summit
Lay of the land: Mountainous

Season: Spring through fall; trails open year-round but not advisable to hike the Arkaquah Trail in heavy snow; visitor center open daily from Memorial Day through October and on weekends, weather permitting, from April 2 to May 29
Land status: Chattahoochee National Forest
Nearest towns: Blairsville (north), Helen (south)
Fees and permits: Parking fee $3.00 per car or minivan; $10.00 per large van
Maps: USGS Jacks Gap, Hiawassee, and Blairsville; Chattahoochee National Forest map
Trail contacts: USDA Forest Service, Brasstown Ranger District, 1881 Highway 515, Blairsville, GA 30512; (706) 745-6928; www.fs.us/conf (click on "Brasstown Bald") Brasstown Bald Visitor Center; (706) 896-2556
Brasstown Heritage Association Bookstore at the parking area; (706) 896-3471

Finding the trailhead: From Blairsville go south on U.S. Highway 19/129 for 8.0 miles to Highway 180. Turn east on Highway 180 and go 7.0 miles to Jacks Gap and the Highway 180 Spur. Turn right (north) and travel 4.5 miles to the parking area. This is a very steep drive, gaining almost 1,500 feet in 3.0 miles.

From Helen go north 14.0 miles on Highway 75 to Highway 180. Turn west (left) and go 6.0 miles to Jacks Gap and the Highway 180 Spur; turn north and continue 4.5 miles to the parking area and the trailheads for both tails.

The Arkaquah trailhead is at the northwest corner of the Brasstown Bald parking area. The west end trailhead is at Track Rock Road and the parking area for the Track Rock Archaeological Area. The trail begins on the opposite side of the road 35 yards down from the parking area. The roads are clear during much of the winter; however, an occasional snow makes the road from Highway 180 to the Brasstown parking area impassable.

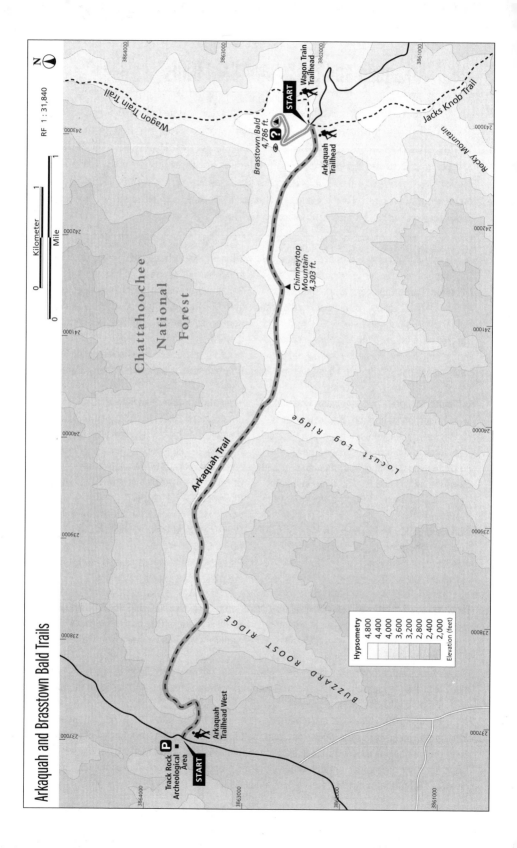

The Hikes

Spring and fall migrations of warblers, tanagers, thrushes, other songbirds, and raptors make the Brasstown Bald area especially popular with birders. Because of the elevation, northern species mingle with southern species to add greatly to the variety of birds. This is just as true for the plants.

Brasstown Bald Trail

The Brasstown Bald Trail to the summit and visitor center is paved. It is steep, climbing almost 500 feet in the 0.6-mile walk. You walk through thick rhododendron and mountain laurel along with stunted hardwoods. During late spring and early summer, this can be a mass of flowering color. In fall the leaf colors are spectacular. The visitor center exhibits tell of "Man and the Mountain" and other features unique to this highest point in Georgia. The visitor center stands above the trees and affords a 360-degree view of the surrounding wilderness and distant villages. On a clear day, four states can be seen from here.

Because of rapidly changing weather conditions of clouds and sunshine at the top of Brasstown Bald Mountain, the view seems to change by the hour as well as with the expected changes that occur with the seasons.

Arkaquah Trail

From the northwest end of Brasstown Bald parking area, the Arkaquah Trail is a moderate 4.5 miles. The trail passes through thick rhododendron and laurel along a southwest-facing slope. Look for pink lady's slippers, bluets, trilliums, and other spring flowers blooming beside the trail in May along with many ferns. As you reach the crest of the ridge, gnarled and stunted yellow birch and dwarfed oak trees are festooned with "old man's beard," a lichen, giving the forest an elfin atmosphere. This is especially true on the many days when clouds shroud the mountain.

For the first 3.8 miles from the parking area, there is relatively little change in elevation. You stay on the ridge crest past Chimney Top Mountain and on along Locust Log Ridge crest at 2.8 miles. The path goes from one gap to the next ridgetop until you reach Buzzard Roost Ridge. From there the trail descends 1,408 feet at a steep grade in 1.7 miles to Track Rock Gap.

Most of the ridge across Chimney Top Mountain to Locust Log Ridge stays above 4,000 feet. This produces a climate that supports plants and animals at their southernmost range and is quite like the southern latitudes of Canada. This is a northern hardwood "cloud forest" of striking old birches and dwarfed red oak and white oak trees festooned with old man's beard. Rhododendron and mountain laurel are some of the few shrubs that can survive here. Wildflower displays are particularly outstanding in the north- and east-facing coves.

Pink lady's slippers bloom along the Arkaquah Trail in spring.

Miles and Directions

0.0 Start at the parking area trailhead.

1.2 Reach the summit of Chimney Top Mountain.

2.3 Pass through Low Gap.

3.3 Reach the crest of Buzzard Roost Ridge. (**Option:** Go west out to Buzzard Roost and return without going down to Track Rock Gap for a round-trip hike of 6.6 miles.)

4.5 Come to the end of trail at Track Rock Gap Road. Unless you've arranged for a shuttle, this is your turnaround point.

9.0 Arrive back at the trailhead.

Option: The stouthearted can hike this trail from the western trailhead at Track Rock Road and the Track Rock Archeological Area. In the first 1.7 miles you climb 1,435 feet and continue to gain elevation on a strenuous hike to the Brasstown Bald parking area. The road distance between the Brasstown Bald and Track Rock trailheads is 23.0 miles. There is no potable water along the trail.

More Information

11 Wagon Train Trail

This is the second trail heading out from the Brasstown Bald parking area. There are no blazes, but the comfortably graded trail is easy to follow. This trail has the greatest change in elevation of all the short trails in the state. You stay at or above the 4,000-foot level for almost a mile and then begin the gentle descent along the old roadbed until you reach the gated road at the national forest and wilderness boundary. From here on you are on a former roadway (Bald Mountain Road) to U.S. Highway 76.

The best hike is from the top down to the gate at the national forest boundary and back up to the top. Primitive camping is permitted in the national forest and wilderness areas; however, be sure to carry water or water purification supplies. Do not make a campfire; instead take a suitable backpack stove for cooking.

Start: Between the gift shop and concession building on the paved path on the north end of the parking area

Distance: From the Brasstown Bald parking area to Young Harris, 6.8 miles one-way shuttle; the last mile before Young Harris, over a steep, rough road on private property.

Approximate hiking time: 4½ hours from Brasstown parking area to Young Harris; 5½ hours from Young Harris to the Brasstown parking area

Difficulty: Moderate or strenuous; hiked from the Brasstown Bald parking area to Young Harris or from Young Harris to the Brasstown Bald parking area in one day, moderate; hiked from the Brasstown Bald parking area to the Chattahoochee Forest boundary line and back to the parking area in one day, strenuous; hiked from Young Harris to the top and back in the same day, strenuous

Elevation gain/loss: A climb of 2,452 feet from Young Harris to Brasstown Bald parking area

Trail surface: Mostly good footing on a wide loamy base

Lay of the land: From the highest mountain in the state, staying above 2,000 feet

Season: Best spring through fall; many pleasant winter days suitable for hiking

Land status: Chattahoochee National Forest

Nearest towns: Blairsville (driving from the top); Young Harris (from lower end or trailhead)

Fees and permits: Brasstown Bald parking area $3.00 per car or minivan; $10.00 per large van

Maps: USGS Hiawassee and Jacks Gap; USDA Forest Service map of Chattahoochee National

Forest; *Trail Guide to the Chattahoochee and Oconee National Forests*
Trail contacts: Brasstown Ranger District, 1881 Highway 515, P.O. Box 9, Blairsville, GA 30512; (706) 745-6928; www.fs.fed.us/conf (click on "Brasstown Bald")

Brasstown Bald Visitor Center; (706) 896-2556
Brasstown Heritage Association Bookstore at the parking area; (706) 896-3471

Finding the trailhead: Brasstown Bald and the parking area are located at the end of the Highway 180 Spur off Highway 180 about 20.0 miles from Hiawassee. From the Brasstown Bald parking area, walk up the paved trail between the gift shop and the concession building. This is the trail to the summit. About 100 yards farther, you come to an unpaved service road with a sign for the Wagon Train Trail.

At the Young Harris College campus, a private road marked by a red gate is the beginning of the road on private property that leads to the national forest boundary. You must get permission from the college to park and begin the hike from this end. There is no other access to the national forest boundary.

The Hike

Beginning at the paved summit trail between the log cabin gift shop and concession building in the parking area, you walk about 100 yards up this trail to an opening in the dense rhododendron. Here is the two-track, grassy road that is the upper end of the Wagon Train Trail. Turn right and follow it 0.3 mile to the gated section of the trail that enters the Brasstown Wilderness. Here the trail loses its two-track character. The path follows under the bald as it winds along the most appropriate contour for a roadbed. You soon pass rock bluffs blasted out to make the road. These cliffs and boulder fields are now covered with rock tripe and other lichens. Sphagnum moss hanging on the rocks, old man's beard on the trees, and club moss flourish in the frequent cloud cover and rain and have healed the blasting scars.

Steep slopes opposite the rock walls afford grand views of the mountains in winter and early spring on clear days. The trail passes along the north-facing slopes through quiet and majestic cove hardwood forests with large yellow poplars, hemlocks, silverbells, yellow birches, basswoods, buckeyes, and maples. On the points and western and southern slopes, the tree canopy becomes oaks, hickories, sourwoods, black gums, and pines, under which may be rhododendron and mountain laurel or one or more kinds of huckleberry.

Along the steep east and west slopes, there are excellent views during winter. This is especially true as you pass to the west and below Chimney Top at 2.5 miles and along Wolf Pen Ridge for the next mile. Even the untrained eye will see how the forest changes as you get lower and lower on the trail. At the higher elevations you will see the more open stands of oaks, yellow birch, and the less common red-berried mountain ash. As you go lower, sweet birch, large yellow poplars, and massive oaks dominate; still farther down, you'll see Virginia and shortleaf pines. From early spring and throughout the warm months you will be able to enjoy a wide variety of wildflower, including four species of trilliums.

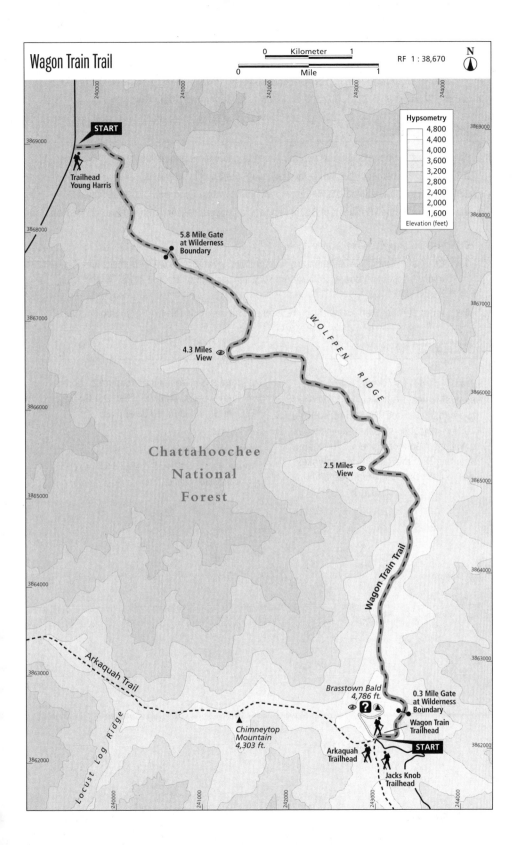

Wagon Train Trail

0 Kilometer 1

0 Mile 1

RF 1 : 38,670

N

Hypsometry

4,800
4,400
4,000
3,600
3,200
2,800
2,400
2,000
1,600

Elevation (feet)

START

Trailhead
Young Harris

5.8 Mile Gate
at Wilderness
Boundary

4.3 Miles
View

W O L F P E N   R I D G E

2.5 Miles
View

Chattahoochee

National

Forest

Wagon Train Trail

Arkaquah Trail

Locust Log Ridge

Brasstown Bald
4,786 ft.

0.3 Mile Gate
at Wilderness
Boundary

Wagon Train
Trailhead

Chimneytop
Mountain
4,303 ft.

Arkaquah
Trailhead

START

Jacks Knob
Trailhead

At Mile 5.8 you reach the gate that marks the forest and wilderness area boundary. If you have arranged for transportation at the Young Harris College or at US 76, you have a mile of rutted, littered road to follow down to the highway.

Miles and Directions

0.0 Start at the paved road between the gift shop and concession building.

0.3 Reach the bar gate that marks the beginning of the wilderness area.

2.5 Come to the west side of Chimney Top Mountain, with a good view into Waterfall Cove.

4.3 Go around the west point of Double Knob and begin to descend on the north of Double Knob Ridge.

5.2 Reach Carrol Gap and Granny Knob.

5.8 Reach the Forest Service boundary line and end of the Brasstown Wilderness Area. This roadway takes you down to private property and the end of the trail at US 76 and Young Harris.

6.8 Arrive at Young Harris. Unless you've arranged for a shuttle, this is your turnaround point.

More Information

Local Events/Attractions

Georgia Mountain Fall Festival, 1311 Music Hall Road, Hiawassee, GA 30546; (706) 896-4191; www.georgia-mountain-fair.com/fall festival.asp. Commonly referred to as the "Mountain Fair," this ten-day festival takes place in early October. It features great musical performances, educational demonstrations, mountain crafts, a flower show, and Georgia's Official State Fiddler's Convention.

Food/Lodging

Brasstown Valley Resort, U.S. Highway 76, Young Harris, GA 30582; (800) 201-3205; www.brasstownvalley.com.

12 Jacks Knob Trail

The blue-blazed Jacks Knob Trail, the third trail out of the Brasstown Bald Parking Area, is a ridgetop trail that at times skirts the crest of several high points before ending at the Appalachian Trail. The trail follows high ridge crests, the county line between Towns and Union Counties, and is most frequently hiked in one of two one-way segments. Brasstown Bald parking area to Highway 180 at Jacks Gap is 1.6 miles and a descent of 1,597 feet. From Jacks Gap to Chattahoochee Gap, 2.2 miles, you climb 570 feet. There are no streams to cross.

Start: South end of the Brasstown Bald parking area at the JACKS KNOB sign and blue blazes

Distance: From Brasstown Bald Scenic Area to Chattahoochee Gap and the Appalachian Trail, 7.8 miles out and back; from Highway 180 to Chattahoochee Gap, 4.4 miles out and back

Approximate hiking time: From the Brasstown Bald parking area to Highway 180, 1 hour; from Highway 180 to Chattahoochee Gap, 1½ hours; the full 7.8-mile out and back, 5½ hours

Difficulty: Moderate to strenuous

Elevation gain/loss: From Jacks Gap to Brookshire Top, 540 feet

Trail surface: Mostly loamy dirt; a few rocky areas

Lay of the land: Mountainous

Season: Year round; many winter days suitable for hiking

Land status: Chattahoochee National Forest

Nearest town: Helen

Fees and permits: Parking at Brasstown Bald Recreation Area $3.00 per car or minivan; $10.00 per large van

Maps: USGS Jacks Gap; Chattahoochee National Forest map

Trail contacts: USDA Forest Service, Brasstown Ranger District, 1881 Highway 515, P.O. Box 9, Blairsville, GA 30512; (706) 745-6928; www.fs.fed.us/conf; www.georgia-atclub.org

Finding the trailhead: One trailhead is at the south end of Brasstown Bald parking area. The other is about the middle of the trail on Highway 180 at Jacks Gap. To get to Jacks Gap from Blairsville, go south on U.S. Highway 19/129 for 8.0 miles to Highway 180. Turn left (east) on Highway 180 and go 7.0 miles to Jacks Gap and the Highway 180 Spur. Turn north and go 4.5 miles to the parking area.

From Helen go north 14.0 miles on Highway 75 to Highway 180. Turn left (west) and go 6.0 miles to Jacks Gap and the Highway 180 Spur; turn north for 4.5 miles to the parking area.

The Hike

All three Brasstown Bald trails are fascinating because of the elevation. Both plant and animal life are noticeably different from other areas in the mountains. Along with a few other high points like Blood, Tray, and Roan Mountains, these ridges support species found at their southernmost geographic range. The trees of the north-facing coves produce an abundant supply of food for wildlife. You are apt to see deer, squirrels, turkeys, ruffed grouse, and a variety of other birds, including ravens, the large crow of the high mountains.

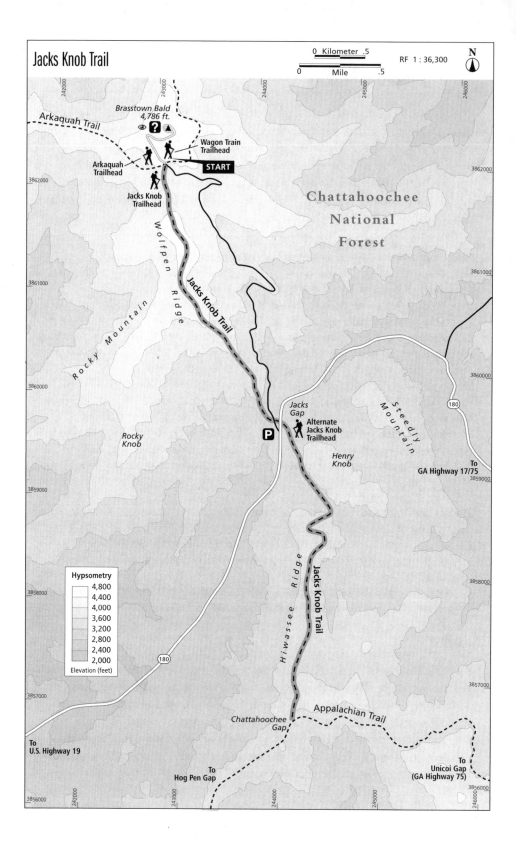

Jacks Knob Trail

0 Kilometer .5
0 Mile .5
RF 1 : 36,300
N

Arkaquah Trail

Brasstown Bald
4,786 ft.

Wagon Train
Trailhead

START

Arkaquah
Trailhead

Jacks Knob
Trailhead

Chattahoochee

National

Forest

Wolfpen Ridge

Rocky Mountain

Jacks Knob Trail

Rocky
Knob

Jacks
Gap

Alternate
Jacks Knob
Trailhead

Steedly Mountain

180

Henry
Knob

To
GA Highway 17/75

Hiwassee Ridge

Jacks Knob Trail

Hypsometry

| 4,800 |
| 4,400 |
| 4,000 |
| 3,600 |
| 3,200 |
| 2,800 |
| 2,400 |
| 2,000 |

Elevation (feet)

180

Appalachian Trail

Chattahoochee
Gap

To
U.S. Highway 19

To
Hog Pen Gap

To
Unicoi Gap
(GA Highway 75)

The blue-blazed trail follows the ridge crest from the highest mountain in Georgia to Chattahoochee Gap where the Chattahoochee River, Georgia's most famous river, has its origin. The trail begins at the south end of the parking area for Brasstown Bald Visitor Center. You enter a rhododendron thicket and continue south on Wolfpen Ridge, climbing steadily to the highest point on the trail (4,561 feet). From here the trail leads down steadily and rather steeply, losing more than 1,500 feet to Jacks Gap and Highway 180. You cross the highway and immediately begin to climb up Hiwassee Ridge. You go around the southwest side of Henry Knob more or less on a contour through a mature hardwood forest with large rock outcrops above the trail. Passing through a stand of white pines, you enter a sweeping north-facing cove of mature hardwoods. Stepping-stones have been placed across the only wet area on this trail.

The trail continues around to the east side of Brookshire Top and drops down into another of several gaps. From here the path is the crest of Hiwassee Ridge and the Towns–Union county line. From the gap south of Eagle Knob just before starting up Jacks Knob, the trail goes around the west side and drops down to Chattahoochee Gap and the Appalachian Trail. Chattahoochee Spring, headwater for the Chattahoochee River, is about 120 yards just below this gap.

From the south end of Jacks Knob Trail at the Appalachian Trail, you can return to Highway 180. Or you can hike east on the Appalachian Trail to the Blue Mountain shelter, 2.25 miles, or to Unicoi Gap (Highway 75), an additional 2.2 miles. If you choose to hike southwest on the Appalachian Trail, you will go past the Low Gap Shelter, 5.0 miles, or an additional 4.2 miles to Hog Pen Gap on the Richard B. Russell Scenic Highway (Highway 348).

This trail offers spectacular views from the high points, and a challenging hike along the higher ridges and into the gaps makes this an interesting one-way trail. Wildflowers from many spring herbaceous plants to the grand display of mountain laurel and rhododendron add to the trail's beauty, and fall leaf colors can be dazzling. Birds of the higher mountains like ravens, hawks, and warblers make this a good birding and wildlife-watching trail.

Note: The Jacks Gap USGS quadrangle shows the trail splitting just north of Jacks Knob, with both prongs ending at the Appalachian Trail at Chattahoochee Gap and near Red Clay Gap. The left fork is not blazed with blue blazes like the right prong of the trail. The trail to the left (southeast) has been used so infrequently it is difficult to follow. Walking the left prong is not advisable unless you have the current Jacks Gap quadrangle and/or a GPS and are experienced in orienteering.

Miles and Directions

0.0 Start at the south end of the Brasstown Bald parking area.

0.3 Reach the Wolfpen Ridge high point (4,561 feet).

1.6 Arrive at Highway 180 and the alternate trailhead at 2,964 feet. Cross the highway and begin the climb to Brookshire Top.

2.2 You have a sweeping view down into a north-facing cove, with many wildlife food–producing trees.

2.6 Reach Brookshire Top, with great views east and west at 3,533 feet.

3.3 Arrive at Eagle Knob; do not be confused by a lateral unmarked trail on the left.

3.7 Jacks Knob crest is on the left.

3.9 Reach the Appalachian Trail, your turnaround point if you're not continuing on the AT.

7.8 Arrive back at the parking area.

13 Lake Winfield Scott Recreation Area Trails

The beautiful Lake Winfield Scott Recreation Area contains three fine trails of easy to moderate hiking, plus several interesting options. The Lake Trail encircles the lake and is an easy loop. Jarrard Gap Trail is a comfortable hike from Lake Winfield Scott to Jarrard Gap on the Appalachian Trail (AT). The Slaughter Creek Trail, with the same trailhead as Jarrard Gap Trail, also leads to the Appalachian Trail. Combining these two trails with the 1.9-mile hike on the AT makes an interesting half-day loop hike of 6.0 miles.

The clear, eighteen–acre lake offers fishing for trout and other species, swimming, camping, and wildflower and bird viewing.

Start: Slaughter Creek and Jarrard Gap Trails, south end of the lake at the information and trailhead signs; Lake Trail, accessed from several points around the lake

Distance: Lake Trail, 0.4-mile loop; Jarrard Gap Trail, 2.4 miles out and back; Slaughter Creek Trail, 5.8 miles out and back; Appalachian Trail between Slaughter Creek and Jarrard Gap, 1.9 miles one-way; Slaughter Gap to Blood Mountain, 1.4 miles up and back

Approximate hiking time: Lake Trail, 30 minutes; Jarrard Gap Trail, 1 hour out-and-back; Slaughter Creek Trail, 3 hours out-and-back; Jarrard, AT, and Slaughter Trail loop, 4½ hours

Difficulty: Lake Loop, easy, following the contour of the lake; Jarrard Gap and Slaughter Creek Trails, easy to moderate; section of the Appalachian Trail from Jarrard Gap to Slaughter Gap, moderate

Elevation gain/loss: Slaughter Creek to the AT, 1,128 feet; Jarrard Gap Trail, 536 feet

Trail surface: Loamy with leaf litter; old roadbeds with dirt and loose rock

Lay of the land: Mountainous

Season: Year-round

Land status: Chattahoochee National Forest

Nearest towns: Blairsville, Dahlonega

Fees and permits: Day-use parking, $3.00 per vehicle per day

Maps: USGS Neels Gap; Chattahoochee National Forest map

Trail contacts: Chattahoochee National Forest, Brasstown Ranger District, 1881 Highway 515, P.O. Box 9, Blairsville, GA 30512; (706) 745-6928; www.fs.fed.us/conf

Finding the trailhead: The entrance to Lake Winfield Scott Recreation Area is 4.5 miles east of Suches on Highway 180 and 7.1 miles west of U.S. Highway 19/129 near Vogel State Park.

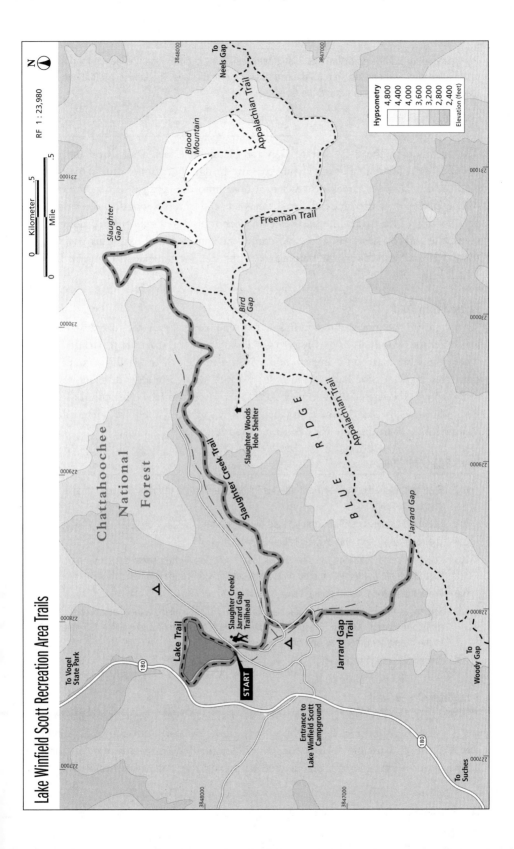

Lake Winfield Scott Recreation Area Trails

RF 1 : 23,980

N

0   Kilometer   .5
0   Mile   .5

Hypsometry

4,800
4,400
4,000
3,600
3,200
2,800
2,400
Elevation (feet)

Chattahoochee
National
Forest

To Vogel
State Park

180

Lake Trail

START

Slaughter Creek/
Jarrard Gap
Trailhead

Entrance to
Lake Winfield Scott
Campground

180

To
Suches

Jarrard Gap Trail

Slaughter Creek Trail

Slaughter Woods
Hole Shelter

B L U E   R I D G E

Appalachian Trail

Jarrard Gap

To
Woody Gap

Bird
Gap

Slaughter
Gap

Freeman Trail

Blood
Mountain

Appalachian Trail

To
Neels Gap

3848000
3847000
3848000
3847000

227000
228000
229000
230000
231000

The trailhead for both Jarrard Gap and Slaughter Creek Trails is on the main entrance road at the information sign and parking area on the southeast side of the lake. The Lake Loop Trail can be reached from several points around the lake.

The Hikes

The common trailhead for Jarrard Gap and Slaughter Creek Trails is on the park entrance road on the right after you cross the bridge. They follow the same wide path beside Slaughter Creek near where it flows into the lake. Just before the footbridge crosses over the creek, the trail turns left and enters a wooded area marked plainly with a blue blaze. The sign refers to both trails. After a short walk along the creek, the path crosses it on a log and comes out onto a gravel road. Turn right on the gravel road and follow the blue blazes to the sign for the Slaughter Creek Trail, which leaves the road to the left.

Jarrard Gap Trail

Turn right on the gravel road and follow the blue blazes. Leave the road at 0.5 mile and enter the woods at a sign indicating the direction and 0.7 mile to Jarrard Gap. There is a blue blaze on a huge boulder in the middle of the trail. You continue through a pleasant cove hardwood forest up Lance Branch in a gentle grade to Jarrard Gap and the Appalachian Trail at 3,290 feet. Here you have the option to turn left and follow the AT 1.9 miles to the end of Slaughter Creek Trail or go down Slaughter Creek to the lake for a 6.0-mile loop hike.

Miles and Directions

0.0 Start at the shared trailhead with the Slaughter Creek Trail, and follow the path to and across the footbridge.

0.2 Leave Slaughter Creek Trail, turning right on the road.

0.4 The road turns right and crosses Lance Branch.

0.5 Leave the road, following the blue blazes into the woods at the JARRARD GAP 0.7 MI. sign. Pass the huge bolder with a blue blaze, and continue up Lance Branch.

0.9 Cross the second of two spring flows.

1.2 You are at the white-blazed Appalachian Trail. If you're not making a loop, this is your turnaround point. (**Option:** Create a loop by turning left on the AT and walking 1.9 miles to the Slaughter Creek Trail and down to the lake.)

2.4 Arrive back at the trailhead.

Slaughter Creek Trail

The Slaughter Creek Trail begins at the same trailhead as the Jarrard Gap Trail and passes through a similar cove hardwood forest, now on the south side of Slaughter Creek. You follow the blue blazes along an old logging road for much of its distance. This is a good example of a regenerated hardwood forest that was heavily logged seventy years ago. After crossing several small streams, you gain 1,050 feet from the lake to Slaughter Gap. This upper section of the Slaughter Creek Trail has been changed recently to avoid the rutted, rocky paths on the old roadway. At the gap (elevation 3,920 feet) trail signs point out directions and miles along the Appalachian Trail. This is the end of the long Duncan Ridge Trail and close to the Coosa Back Country Trail from Vogel State Park.

Option: At Slaughter Gap, you can continue for 0.7 mile on the AT up the relocated rocky and steep switchbacked trail to the crest of Blood Mountain at 4,461 feet with a beautiful 360-degree view. Returning to Slaughter Gap, follow the Appalachian Trail 1.9 miles southeast to Jarrard Gap and return to Lake Winfield Scott for a loop trail with a spur to Blood Mountain of 7.4 miles.

Miles and Directions

0.0 Start on the shared walkway toward Slaughter Creek.

0.2 Reach the creek and cross on a split log; continue on an old road.

0.6 Temporarily leave the roadbed to the right.

0.8 Pick up the old road again and follow it.

2.3 Leave the roadway with a sharp turn to left; walk down to the spring at the beginning of Slaughter Creek.

2.4 At the stream, turn right and walk about 35 yards; begin the climb to the gap.

2.5 At Slaughter Gap, the blue blaze indicates a sharp turn to the right to reach the Appalachian Trail.

2.9 You are at the Appalachian Trail, marked with white blazes. At this point the AT has made an abrupt turn to the south and begins the ascent to Blood Mountain. If you're not making a loop, this is your turnaround point. (Option: Continue 0.7 mile on the AT to the crest of Blood Mountain for the view. Return to Slaughter Gap, follow the AT 1.9 miles southeast to Jarrard Gap, and return to the lake for a 7.4-mile loop.)

5.8 Arrive back at the trailhead.

Lake Loop Trail

The loop is a 0.4-mile walking path around the small but beautiful, clear lake that can be accessed from several points, providing good access to walking and fishing.

14 Sosebee Cove Trail

The hike consists of two easy, connected loops that total about 0.5 mile in the Sosebee Cove Scenic Area. This trail is a must for anyone interested in wildflowers, especially for photography. It is possible to photograph twenty to thirty species of wildflowers in bloom in one day. The trail has been designed to reach as many species of plants as possible in the shortest distance. There are no blaze marks.

Start: At the parking area on Highway 108, 3.0 miles from Vogel State Park
Length: 0.5 mile in two loop trails
Approximate hiking time: 30 minutes—if you don't stop to "smell the roses"
Difficulty: Easy
Elevation gain/loss: Negligible
Trail surface: Loamy and leaf littered; worn to loose stones and dirt in a few places
Lay of the land: Level
Season: Late March to mid-May for the best show of native wildflowers

Land status: Chattahoochee National Forest
Nearest town: Blairsville
Fees and permits: No fees or permits required
Maps: USGS Coosa Bald; Chattahoochee National Forest map
Trail contacts: Chattahoochee National Forest, Brasstown Ranger District, 1881 Highway 515, P.O. Box 9, Blairsville, GA 30512; (706) 745-6928; www.fs.fed.us/conf

Finding the trailhead: From Blairsville, take U.S. Highway 129 south 10.0 miles to Highway 180 near Vogel State Park. Turn right and go 3.0 miles to the Sosebee Cove parking area, with space for three or four vehicles. The trailhead is here.

The Hike

The comparatively flat trail provides access to the 175-acre Sosebee Cove Scenic Area, with its great trees and wildflowers typical of the Southern Appalachian cove hardwood forests. It is a memorial to Arthur Woody, who served as forest ranger from 1911 to 1945. A sign at the beginning of the trail tells of Ranger Woody and the plant life in the cove.

The trail begins from the side of Highway 180 down into this beautiful hardwood forest with two successive loops, the second a little deeper than the first. You are very quickly greeted by one of the largest buckeye trees in the state (15 feet 4 inches in circumference) and by many large yellow poplars. In fact, this is considered to be one of the best second-growth stands of these trees in the nation. As with many other high-elevation Southern Appalachian streams, the small branch flowing through the cove is preferred habitat for salamanders.

Lady's slippers, Solomon's seals, false Solomon's seals, mayapples, hepaticas, several species of trilliums, and many other spring wildflowers grow in great abundance along the deeply shaded trail. There are no steep sections that would prevent anyone with limited walking ability from enjoying the shorter loop.

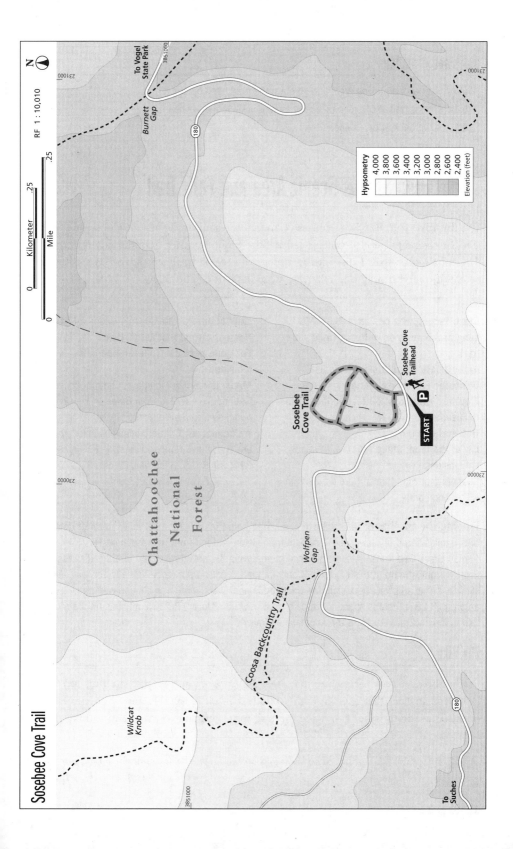

Sosebee Cove Trail

RF 1 : 10,010

N

Hypsometry
- 4,000
- 3,800
- 3,600
- 3,400
- 3,200
- 3,000
- 2,800
- 2,600
- 2,400

Elevation (feet)

Kilometer
0 · .25 · .25

Mile
0 · .25

To Vogel
State Park

Burnett
Gap

180

Chattahoochee
National
Forest

Sosebee
Cove Trail

Sosebee Cove
Trailhead

P

START

Wolfpen
Gap

Coosa Backcountry Trail

Wildcat
Knob

180

To
Suches

231000

230000

3851000

Miles and Directions

0.0   Start at the parking area, and go down the road bank on steps.

0.1   A cross trail at 0.1 mile takes you more quickly to the trailhead.

0.5   Arrive back at the trailhead.

15   High Shoals Scenic Area and Falls Trail

On this hike you visit two impressive and picturesque waterfalls on a downhill trail. The first waterfall, at 1.0 mile, is called Blue Hole. Another 0.3 mile downstream is 100-foot-high Shoals Falls, with an observation deck. In this walk you lose 480 feet in elevation, with only one relatively steep descent or climb.

Start: Parking area on Forest Road 283
Length: 2.6 miles down to both falls and back
Approximate hiking time: 2½ hours
Difficulty: Easy to moderate
Elevation gain/loss: 480 feet on return to trailhead
Trail surface: Dirt
Lay of the land: Steep valleys with narrow streamsides
Season: Year-round; falls more dramatic in winter and spring

Land status: Chattahoochee National Forest
Nearest towns: Hiawassee, Helen
Fees and permits: No fees or permits required
Maps: USGS Tray Mountain; Chattahoochee National Forest Map; *Trail Guide to the Chattahoochee-Oconee National Forests*
Trail contacts: Chattahoochee National Forest, Brasstown Ranger District, 1881 Highway 515, P.O. Box 9, Blairsville, GA 30512; (706) 745-6928; www.fs.fed.us/conf

Finding the trailhead: The trailhead is reached from Highway 75, 11.4 miles north of Helen or 9.5 miles south of Hiawassee. Turn right from Helen and left from Hiawassee on FR 283 (Indian Grave Gap Road). A short distance after leaving the paved road, you ford the Hiawassee River, a small stream at this elevation. Continue for 1.5 miles up a steep grade to the HIGH SHOALS SCENIC AREA AND BLUE HOLE FALLS sign. The trailhead is near the sign at a small, unpaved parking area on FR 283. There is space for three or four vehicles. (**Note:** FR 238 continues up the mountain to Indian Grave Gap and the Appalachian Trail.)

The Hike

High Shoals Creek originates on Tray Mountain, one of the summits on the Appalachian Trail that is more than 4,000 feet in elevation. During winter, freezing weather and high water can make the trail more difficult to reach and to hike.

The lower falls on the High Shoals Scenic Area and Falls ▶
Trail splashes down 100 feet.

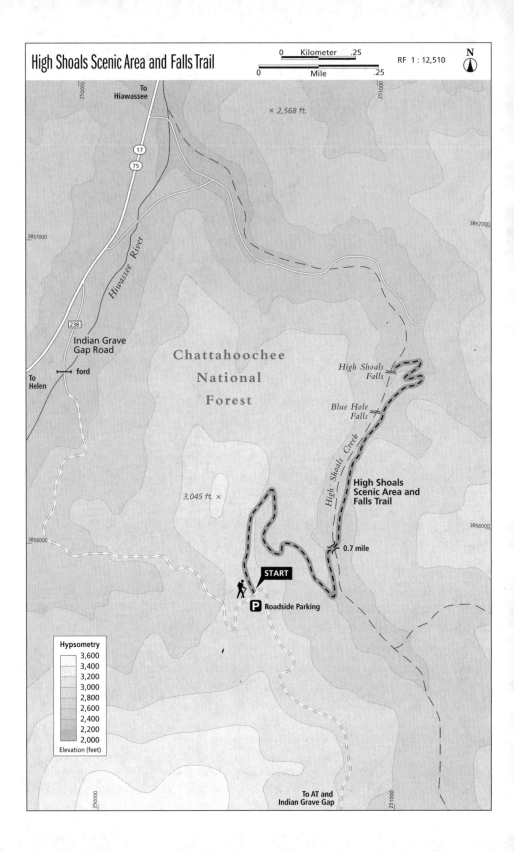

The trail begins with steps going down from the parking area. Blue blazes mark the path throughout its length. The trail descends the steep-sided cove, but two sweeping switchbacks keep the grade moderate for the descent and climb back out. A big oak tree with cavities large enough to have accommodated a hibernating bear stands beside the path before the first switchback. Hardwood trees in the cove give way to large white pines and hemlocks as the trail nears High Shoals Creek. Several spring seeps that cross the path are easily stepped across even during wet weather.

The cascading water of the creek can be heard well before you reach the stream. At the creek the trail abruptly flattens out and follows an old roadbed to the first bridge at 0.7 mile on the trail. It crosses High Shoals Creek in a beautiful, level area in the cove that has been used for many seasons as a primitive campsite. Thick rhododendron covers the stream as you walk downstream. Three footbridges span brooks and spring seeps that cross the path. The cascading creek can be heard but not seen at this point because of the thick rhododendron. The large rock outcrops along the trail indicate the same formations that form the falls. The first turnout in the trail, at 1.0 mile, leads quickly to Blue Hole Falls. This 30-foot waterfall spills into a deep catch pool in front of the wooden platform. A sign warns of the dangers of leaving the trail and climbing on the rocks. The smart hiker will heed these warnings.

Returning to the main trail again, the path leaves the creek temporarily as you ascend and descend quickly through two switchbacks back to the creek at 1.3 miles and to the more dramatic High Shoals Falls and another observation platform. Here the creek falls more than 100 feet, splashing grandly down the steep rock face. Many moisture-tolerant plants, including liverworts, mosses, and wildflowers add to the beauty of the falls. The massive rhododendrons on either side of the stream, large hemlocks, white pines, and hardwood trees complete the enchantment of the site. Backtrack to the trailhead.

Miles and Directions

0.0 Start at FR 238 roadside; walk down from the shoulder on timber steps.

0.6 Reach High Shoals Creek.

0.7 Cross the creek on a footbridge.

1.0 Arrive at the Blue Hole Falls viewing platform.

1.3 Reach the High Shoals Falls viewing platform and the end of the trail.

2.6 Arrive back at the trailhead.

More Information

Local Events/Attractions

Georgia Mountain Fall Festival, 1311 Music Hall Road, Hiawassee, GA 30546; (706) 896-4191; www.georgia-mountain-fair.com/fall festival.asp. Commonly referred to as the "Mountain Fair," this ten-day festival takes place in early October. It features great musical performances, educational demonstrations, mountain crafts, a flower show, and Georgia's Official State Fiddler's Convention.

16 Ellicott Rock Wilderness Trail

On this hike you follow the Chattooga River for 3.4 miles from Burrells Ford Bridge to the North Carolina state line and the Ellicott Rock. You are in sight of the river all the way. All along the way is excellent birding for warblers, thrushes, nuthatches, woodpeckers, and others. The belted kingfisher is frequently seen. Some of the more unusual plants along the way are Dutchman's pipe vine, rough-leaf dogwood, running ground pine, shining club moss, and Clinton's lily. To view Ellicott Rock and the old carvings on it, you must leave the trail at the large hemlock tree with the paint bands and go down the steep riverbank to the water's edge.

Start: Trailhead in South Carolina, 0.1 mile from the Georgia side parking area at Burrells Ford Bridge

Distance: From Burrells Ford Bridge (featured hike), 3.4-miles one-way; from the campground on the South Carolina side, 3.8 miles one-way

Approximate hiking time: 3 hours one-way; 5½ hours out and back

Difficulty: Moderate

Elevation gain/loss: 240 feet

Trail surface: Hard loam; a few rocky areas

Lay of the land: Mountainous streamside

Season: Year-round

Land status: Sumter National Forest, South Carolina

Nearest towns: Clayton, Georgia; Walhalla, South Carolina

Fees and permits: No fees or permits required

Maps: USGS Tamassee; USDA Forest Service map of the Chattooga National Wild and Scenic River

Trail contacts: USDA Forest Service, Tallulah Ranger District, 809 Highway 441 South, Clayton, GA 30525; (706) 782-3320; www.fs.fed.us/conf

USDA Forest Service, Andrew Pickens Ranger District, 112 Andrew Pickens Circle, Mountain Rest, SC 29664; (864) 638-2695; www.fs.fed.us/ (click on "South Carolina Forests" and "Andrew Pickens District")

Finding the trailhead: from Clayton go 23 miles from U.S. Highway 441 and Warwoman Road to Highway 28. Turn right and go 1.7 miles to Forest Road 646 and the BURRELLS FORD sign. Follow this winding gravel road for 7.0 miles to the Chattooga River and Burrells Ford Bridge, the Georgia–South Carolina line. There is a parking area on the Georgia side and the South Carolina side. There are two points near the Burrells Ford Bridge, both on the South Carolina side, from which you can hike this trail. The trailhead closer to the bridge, about 50 yards on the left, is the trailhead for this hike. It is marked with a carsonite post with the hiking icon. The other trailhead is 0.4 mile farther up the road across the parking area for the Sumter National Forest Burrells Ford Campground. This path is similarly marked.

The Hike

Note: The Ellicott Rock section of the trail is included here, even though it is in South Carolina.

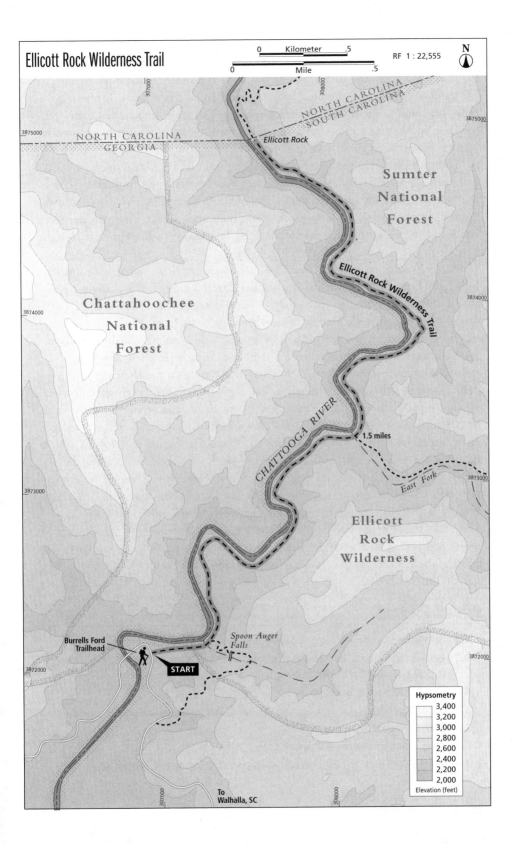

Ellicott Rock Wilderness Trail

0 Kilometer .5
0 Mile .5
RF 1 : 22,555
N

NORTH CAROLINA
SOUTH CAROLINA

Ellicott Rock

NORTH CAROLINA
GEORGIA

Sumter National Forest

3875000

3874000

Ellicott Rock Wilderness Trail

Chattahoochee National Forest

3873000

CHATTOOGA RIVER

1.5 miles

East Fork

Ellicott Rock Wilderness

Burrells Ford
Trailhead

Spoon Auger Falls

START

3872000

To
Walhalla, SC

Hypsometry

3,400
3,200
3,000
2,800
2,600
2,400
2,200
2,000

Elevation (feet)

The trail begins near the Burrells Ford Bridge; the trailhead is about 50 yards up the road on the left side. At first the path is wide and relatively flat through a pleasant stand of hemlock, white pine, yellow poplar, and a few white oak trees. At 0.2 mile you come to the first small stream crossing. This is the branch that forms picturesque Spoon Auger Falls—only about 200 yards up the side trail; several switchbacks help you negotiate the steep slope.

The path now hugs the riverbank, departing from it only where steep rock walls make it impossible to stay close to the water. You frequently go through tunnels of rhododendron, mountain laurel, and dog-hobble. Where the trailside vegetation is more open, the spring wildflowers are more numerous. At 0.6 mile you can see a wide sandy beach on the trail side of the river. This may be a good place to stop for a picnic or just rest and watch the river go by.

At 1.5 miles you reach the East Fork, the creek that flows down from the Walhalla Fish Hatchery. Here you can camp under a great stand of hemlocks, white pines, and yellow poplars. Stop as you cross the East Fork to examine the uniquely constructed footbridge, made entirely of large and small logs. Even the footings are large logs fitted together. Across the bridge begins the 2.5-mile trail to Walhalla Fish Hatchery. From here on, the trail is much less used and changes elevation very little.

At 2.1 miles you cross Bad Creek. There is no bridge across the creek, but most of the time the flow is such that you can rock-hop across it. Ignore the several unmarked paths and stay on the more heavily used path, continuing along the river. At 3.0 miles you cross a small footbridge over an unnamed branch and enter a nice open area above the river. You now reach the Ellicott Rock and the North Carolina state line. Look for a large hemlock wearing a black rectangular blaze with a red bar below. Ellicott Rock is on the streambank below. There, if you look carefully, you may see LAT 35° / A D 1813 / N C + S C engraved in the rock by surveyor Andrew Ellicott in 1813 to establish the boundary between North and South Carolina.

Out in the river are two large boulders. On one is a recent survey control mark set by South Carolina in 1996, labeled CHATTOOGA ROCK, GEODETIC SURVEY. This point in the river is where Georgia, North Carolina, and South Carolina meet. The trail on the South Carolina side is an extension of the Chattooga River Trail.

Miles and Directions

0.0 Start at Burrells Ford Bridge parking area. Cross the bridge to the trailhead, 0.1 mile on left.

0.2 Cross a small branch and come to a trail sign pointing the way to Spoon Auger Falls and to South Carolina Burrells Ford Campground.

0.6 There's a nice sandy beach on the left.

1.5 Reach the bridge across East Fork and the trail to Walhalla Fish Hatchery.

2.1 Rock-hop across Bad Creek.

3.0 Cross a small bridge over an unnamed stream.

3.4 Reach Ellicott Rock and the point where Georgia, South Carolina, and North Carolina meet.

Option: For a longer hike, continue on into the Nantahala National Forest in North Carolina on the Ellicott Rock Trail where it forks. The trail to the right goes to the Forest Road 441 parking area. The one to the left, the Ellicott Rock Trail, crosses Chattooga River and goes to a parking area on Bull Pen Road (North Carolina Highway 1100). This is still within the Ellicott Rock Wilderness Area, parts of which are located in the three states and three national forests.

17 Rabun Beach Recreation Area: Angel Falls Trail

Enjoy a pleasant 1.0-mile walk along Joe Creek, a small cascading stream. The trail ends in a couple of short switchbacks up a steep rhododendron-covered path to Panther and Angel Falls. The trail begins at 1,780 feet and climbs to about 2,500 feet at Angel Falls as you walk along and in sight of cascading Joe Creek. A convenient observation bridge gives you a great view of the falls.

Start: Parking area at the north end of Rabun Beach Campground 2
Distance: 2.0 miles out and back
Approximate hiking time: 1 hour
Difficulty: Easy to moderate
Elevation gain/loss: 720 feet
Trail surface: Loamy dirt; some loose stones at upper end; rock-hopping over narrow stream
Season: Year-round; best waterfall conditions in winter and spring
Land status: Chattahoochee National Forest

Nearest towns: Tallulah Falls, Clayton
Fees and permits: No fees or permits required for trail parking area; parking in other areas in the campground $3.00 per vehicle
Maps: USGS Tiger; Chattahoochee National Forest map
Trail contacts: Chattahoochee National Forest, Tallulah Ranger District, 809 Highway 441, P.O. Box 438, Clayton, GA 30525; (706) 782-3320; www.fs.fed.us/conf/

Finding the trailhead: From U.S. Highway 441, go 3.0 miles north of Tallulah Falls or 9.6 miles south of Clayton; turn west at the RABUN BEACH RECREATION AREA sign on Old 441 Road. Go about 2.5 miles and turn left onto Lake Rabun Road; then go 4.5 miles and turn right into Rabun Beach Campground 2. In the campground turn right and go to the trailhead. The hike to Angel and Panther Falls begins at a gravel parking area for hikers.

The Hike

From the parking area, cross Joe Creek on a footbridge; turn right (upstream) and continue up the left side of the creek. For the first 200 yards you walk in a corridor of dog-hobble, rhododendron, and mountain laurel under the shade of white pines and hemlocks. Farther up the trail you are under a more open canopy of yellow poplars, maples, buckeyes, deciduous magnolias, oaks, and other hardwoods until the path reaches the dense laurel and rhododendron thickets that add enchantment to these pleasant short hikes in the mountains.

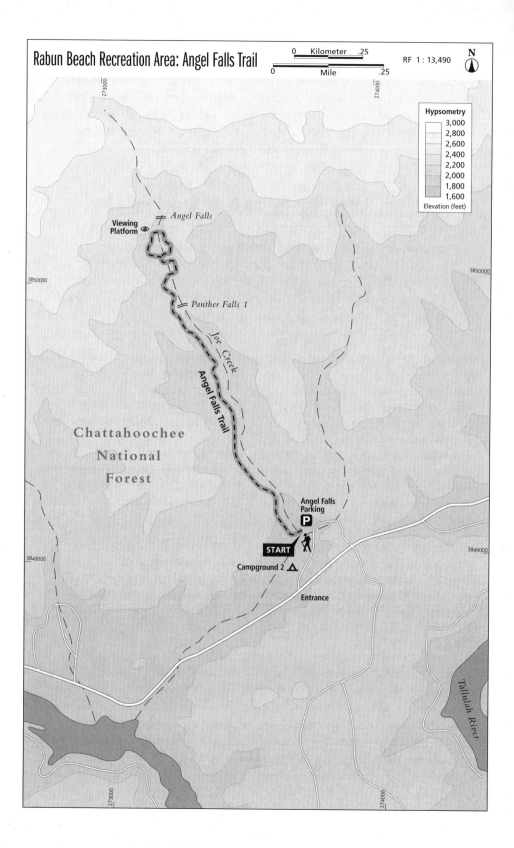

Rabun Beach Recreation Area: Angel Falls Trail

RF 1 : 13,490

N

Hypsometry

3,000
2,800
2,600
2,400
2,200
2,000
1,800
1,600
Elevation (feet)

Angel Falls

Viewing
Platform

Panther Falls 1

Joe Creek

Angel Falls Trail

Chattahoochee

National

Forest

Angel Falls
Parking

P

START

Campground 2

Entrance

Tallulah River

Panther Falls is the first of the two falls on the trail. Joe Creek here drops about 40 feet in a series of steps down a stratified rock formation. During normal flows, the streambed here is exposed rock. It is a quiet place to just sit and watch the water.

A sign points to Angel Falls, another 600 yards upstream. However, the trail to reach the falls is another 0.4 mile. Follow the switchbacks up to an observation platform and bridge with a good view of Angel Falls as it cascades 60 feet over rock formations similar to those of Panther Falls below. The moist rocks alongside and at the foot of the falls support a wide variety of plants specific to this habitat type, including Michaux's (mountain) saxifrage, ragwort, alumroot, ferns, mosses, and liverworts. The trail crosses Joe Creek at the platform and loops back downstream through the great stands of rhododendron to meet the trail back to the trailhead.

Miles and Directions

0.0 Start at the parking area at the north end of Campground 2; cross footbridge and turn right (upstream).

0.6 Panther Falls, the smaller of the two waterfalls on this trail, come into sight.

1.0 Reach the observation bridge below Angel Falls. Cross Joe Creek and head downstream to meet the trail back to the trailhead.

2.0 Arrive back at the parking area.

18 Warwoman Dell Nature Trail and Becky Branch Falls Trail

Walk two short, easy to moderate trails in a beautiful area steeped in history. At the day-use area is the Warwoman Dell Nature Trail with interpretation markers and the Becky Branch Falls Trail. The walk to the falls is a short trail with switchbacks to reduce the steepness. The return is on the same trail.

Start: Warwoman Dell parking area
Distance: Warwoman Dell Nature Trail, 0.4-mile loop; Becky Branch Falls, 0.8 mile out and back
Approximate hiking time: Less than 1 hour for each trail
Difficulty: Warwoman Dell Nature Trail, easy; Becky Branch Falls Trail, moderate
Elevation gain/loss: Becky Branch Falls Trail, 300 feet
Trail surface: Dirt; some pavement
Lay of the land: Mainly flat with a short, steep climb

Season: Year-round; day-use area open mid-March to mid-November
Land status: Chattahoochee National Forest
Nearest town: Clayton
Fees and permits: No fees or permits required
Maps: USGS Rabun Bald; Chattahoochee National Forest map
Trail contacts: Chattahoochee National Forest, Tallulah Ranger District, 809 Highway 441, P.O. Box 438, Clayton, GA 30525; (706) 782-3320; www.fs.fed.us/conf

Finding the trailhead: The Warwoman Dell Day-Use Area is at the park entrance sign, 2.9 miles east of Clayton on Warwoman Road. The trailhead for both trails is in the Warwoman Dell parking area.

The Hikes

Warwoman Dell is better known for its historical significance than for its trails, which are short and easily covered in about an hour of leisurely walking. Other loop trails in the day-use area make excellent optional walks. You can also learn the history of the pre–Civil War Black Mountain Railroad, including the uncompleted tunnel. Picnic shelters, running water, and clean restrooms make this a very pleasant break in a visit to the mountains of northeastern Georgia. The trail system here is joined by a short segment of the Bartram Trail. A metal historic marker on the roadside describes the significance of the trail.

Warwoman Dell Nature Trail

The Nature Trail begins at the west end of the parking area. It was built by a volunteer youth group from the Rabun Gap–Nachoochee School at Dillard. Twenty-five numbered stations identify plants and habitat relationships. The path is easy and

Warwoman Dell Nature Trail and Becky Branch Falls Trail

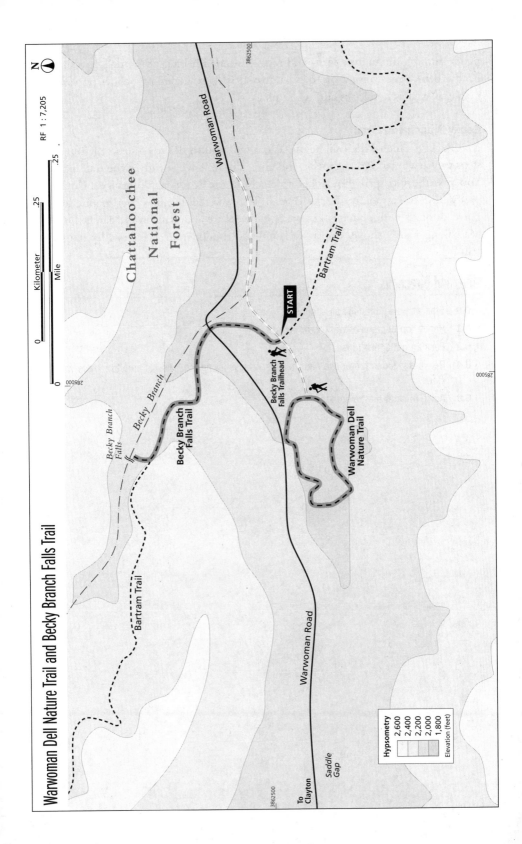

passes through the unique fern- and moss-shrouded habitat of the dell. It is shaded by the dense tree canopy of cove hardwood species, including yellow poplar and maple, as well as hemlocks and white pines.

Becky Branch Falls Trail

The Becky Branch Falls Trail begins at the trailhead in the day-use area. Go up the steps to Warwoman Road, cross it, and enter the well-worn path at the trail marker. You pass the old springhouse before reaching the wooden footbridge below the pretty 20-foot cascade on Becky Branch. The waterfall tumbles over granite ledges down through a rhododendron thicket. Flowers are abundant from March through May, along with a showy display of laurel and rhododendron. Return by the same trail.

Miles and Directions

0.0 Start at Becky Branch Falls trailhead.

0.1 Reach top of steps at Warwoman Road.

0.2 Pass an old springhouse.

0.4 Reach a wooden footbridge and the falls. After enjoying the falls, it's time to retrace your steps.

0.8 Arrive back at the trailhead.

19 Three Forks Trail

Located in the Chattooga National Wild and Scenic River area, this is an easy trail with only a gentle descent to the confluence of three creeks that form West Fork of Chattooga River. The blaze marks are white diamonds; however, there are very few of them. You walk through oak-hickory forest, with occasional rhododendron and mountain laurel thickets.

Start: Parking area at John Teague Gap
Distance: From John Teague Gap to Holcomb Creek, just above Three Forks, 2.4 miles out and back
Approximate hiking time: 1 hour
Difficulty: Easy to moderate, with steep descents and return climbs at the river
Elevation gain/loss: 146 feet
Trail surface: Firm loam
Lay of the land: Mountainous
Season: Year-round

Land status: Chattahoochee National Forest
Nearest town: Clayton
Fees and permits: No fees or permits required
Maps: USGS Satolah; Chattooga National Wild and Scenic River map, available from the USDA Forest Service
Trail contacts: Chattahoochee National Forest, Tallulah Ranger District, 809 Highway 441, P.O. Box 438, Clayton, GA 30525; (706) 782-3320; www.fs.fed.us/conf

Finding the trailhead: From Clayton take Rickman Street to the dead end at Warwoman Road. Turn right and follow Warwoman Road for about 14.0 miles to the bridge across West Fork of Chattooga River. Immediately after the bridge, turn left (north) on the gravel Overflow Creek Road (Forest Road 86). Continue on Overflow Road 4.0 miles to the JOHN TEAGUE GAP trail sign. The trailhead is at the small, unpaved parking area on the right that accommodates three or four vehicles.

The Hike

Three Forks is a great place to explore the many natural history features of the area or to trout fish. The overhanging rock cliffs and river gorge habitat are home to interesting plants and animals. The nests of the secretive Blood Mountain wood rat can be found under the rock shelters along the steep-sided river gorge. Dutchman's pipe vines climb over the alders along the river.

From the parking area and trailhead sign, follow the north face of the ridge and sparsely placed silver-diamond blazes. The trail goes through a pine-oak-hickory forest and an occasional thicket of Catawba or rosebay rhododendron, losing elevation on a gentle slope. The lack of blazes is no problem—the trail is well worn, and there is very little chance of getting off track.

At 0.7 mile a single blue blaze designates the boundary of the Chattooga National Wild and Scenic River area, which encompasses much of the watersheds of the three creeks that form West Fork. At 1.1 miles the trail intercepts an old jeep

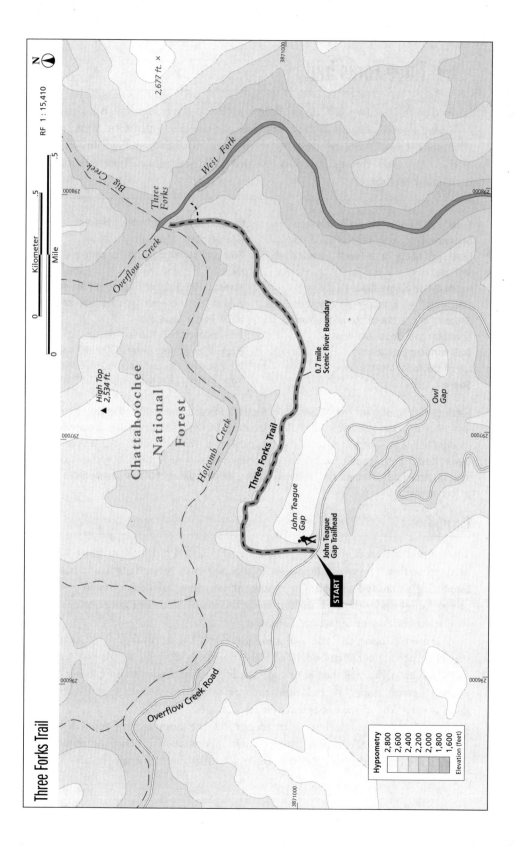

Three Forks Trail

road. Stay to the left, following the old roadbed. Several earthen barriers to stop off-road vehicles have been scraped into the trail and must be sidestepped during wet weather. The trail ends at a wide bedrock area at Holcomb Creek. Here you can see one of nature's greatest works as the full volume of the creek swirls down through a narrow crevice eroded into the rock. If the creek is swollen by recent rains, the sight is awesome.

Miles and Directions

0.0 Start at John Teague Gap trailhead.

0.7 Reach the blue blaze indicating the scenic river boundary.

1.1 Intercept an old jeep road on right; stay to the left, following the old roadbed.

1.2 Reach the Holcomb Creek overlook and your turnaround point.

2.4 Arrive back at the trailhead.

Additional Trails

A short trail branching off the Three Forks Trail where it intercepts the old jeep road is not considered part of the Three Forks Trail. The path leads in a southeasterly direction down to the West Fork below the junction of the three creeks and ends at a steep descent into the river gorge and to a primitive campsite. Here the river cascades in grand fashion from one low waterfall and pool to another. This is truly a wild and beautiful mountain stream. Climb under the laurel and rhododendron upstream for about 0.25 mile to see the three creeks—Holcomb, Overflow, and Big—become the West Fork of the Chattooga River. A fine waterfall is visible just upstream on Big Creek. Return to the steep path and you have about a 100-foot climb back up to more level ground. You can return along a jeep trail back to the trailhead or retrace your path by the Holcomb Creek overlook. Your total distance to the river and back is less than a mile; plan on two and a half hours for the out and back from the trailhead.

20 Anna Ruby Falls and Lion's Eye Nature Trails

Anna Ruby Falls is the most visited waterfall in the north Georgia mountains. A short paved trail with a moderate grade follows picturesque Smith Creek to a beautiful view of the twin Anna Ruby Falls. The Lion's Eye Nature Trail begins at the parking area. It is designed for sight-impaired hikers and is wheelchair accessible. Its entire 100-yard length is within sight and sound of Smith Creek.

See map on pages 100–101

Start: Forest Service visitor center

Distance: Falls Trail, 0.8 mile out and back; Nature Trail, 100-yard loop

Approximate hiking time: Falls Trail, 1½ hours out and back

Difficulty: Moderate

Elevation gain/loss: Falls Trail, 170 feet

Trail surface: Asphalt

Lay of the land: Mountainous

Season: Year-round; possible closures during heavy snowfall

Land status: Chattahoochee National Forest

Nearest towns: Robertstown, Helen

Fees and permits: Forest Service parking area day-use fee, $1.00 per person over age 15; no fee for those on foot or bike

Maps: USGS Tray Mountain; Unicoi State Park Trails map; *Trail Guide to the Chattahoochee National Forest*

Trail contacts: Chattahoochee National Forest, Chattooga Ranger District, 200 Highway 197 North, Clarksville, GA 30523; (706) 754-6221; www.fs.fed.us/conf; www.georgia stateparks.org

Finding the trailhead: Take Highway 75 north from Helen for 1.0 mile. Turn right on Highway 356 for 1.5 miles and then left on Forest Road 242 and the sign for Anna Ruby Falls. Go 3.3 miles to the trailhead at the visitor center and parking area.

The Hikes

Unicoi State Park and Forest Service employees lead guided walks throughout the year to help visitors and hikers recognize and identify the dozens of wildflowers, birds, and other animals and special features along the trail.

Anna Ruby Falls Trail

Spring wildflowers and the beautiful tumbling Smith Creek are the foremost attractions of this trail. During April and May, thirty to forty species of wildflowers are likely to be in bloom at the same time. The large boulders along Smith Creek support some of the largest colonies of rockcap ferns in the state.

A paved 0.4-mile trail from the parking area and visitor center extends along Smith Creek to Anna Ruby Falls. The hike is easy to moderate, with benches along the way providing comfortable resting places for those who need to take it easy. An observation bridge and deck and a second deck at the end of the trail provide great views of the twin falls. The trail can be slippery when wet or with snow, so walking shoes are recommended. This is a good trail to take children hiking. The pavement is safe, and the moderate grade is not too difficult, even with children in strollers. A complete canopy of hardwood trees shades the trail during the warm months.

Miles and Directions

0.0 Start at the trail to the left of the visitor center.

0.2 Reach the bridge over Smith Creek with trailside bench.

0.4 Arrive at the bridge observation deck.

0.45 Enjoy the view from the falls observation deck before retracing your steps.

0.8 Arrive back at the visitor center.

Lion's Eye Nature Trail

The Lion's Eye Nature Trail, designed for the visually impaired, begins at the northeast corner of the parking area and goes along the creek. This short loop with Braille interpretive signs and guide rails describes the sounds, smells, and texture of the forest. The paved trail is easily traveled by wheelchair.

21 Smith Creek Trail

This 4.6-mile one-way hike is a good practice trail for longer hikes. Starting at the visitor center, you walk along a paved walkway to Anna Ruby Falls. From the falls, you then follow the north side of Hickorynut Ridge for about halfway, cross to the southeast side, and then descend to the Unicoi State Park Road trailhead. The observation bridge at Anna Ruby Falls is 2,211 feet. The trail goes up to 2,645 feet on Hickorynut Ridge and back to 1,760 feet at the campground.

Start: Anna Ruby Falls Visitor Center
Distance: From visitor center to Little Brook Campground, 4.6 miles one-way/shuttle
Approximate hiking time: From visitor center to the campground, 3½ hours; from the campground to the falls and back, about 6 hours
Difficulty: Moderate one-way, strenuous as a round-trip hike
Elevation gain/loss: Total climb 983 feet; total descent 1,429 feet
Trail surface: Paved, dirt, and firm loam; loose stones in short segments; branch crossing
Lay of the land: Mountainous
Season: Year-round; late fall to early spring for good views of surrounding mountains
Land status: Chattahoochee National Forest

Nearest towns: Robertstown, Helen
Fees and permits: Parking at Anna Ruby Falls Visitor Center, $1.00 per person over age 15 (no fee for those on foot or bike); parking at Unicoi State Park campground road trailhead, $3.00 per vehicle per day
Maps: USGS Tray Mountain and Helen; Chattahoochee National Forest map; Unicoi State Park map
Trail contacts: Chattahoochee National Forest, Chattooga Ranger District, 200 Highway 197 North, Clarkesville, GA 30523; (706) 754-6221; www.fs.fed.us/conf
Unicoi State Park, 943 Anna Ruby Falls Road, Helen, GA 30545; (706) 878-3983; www.gastateparks.org

Anna Ruby Falls and Lion's Eye Nature Trails; Smith Creek Trail

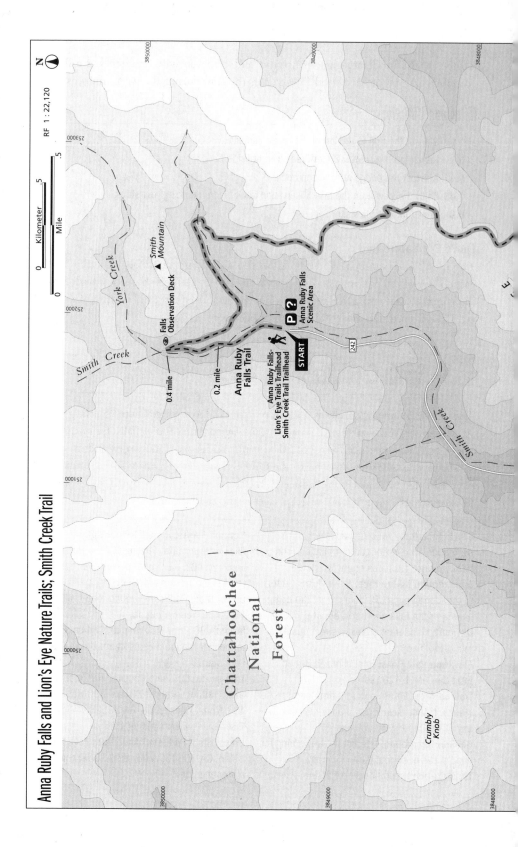

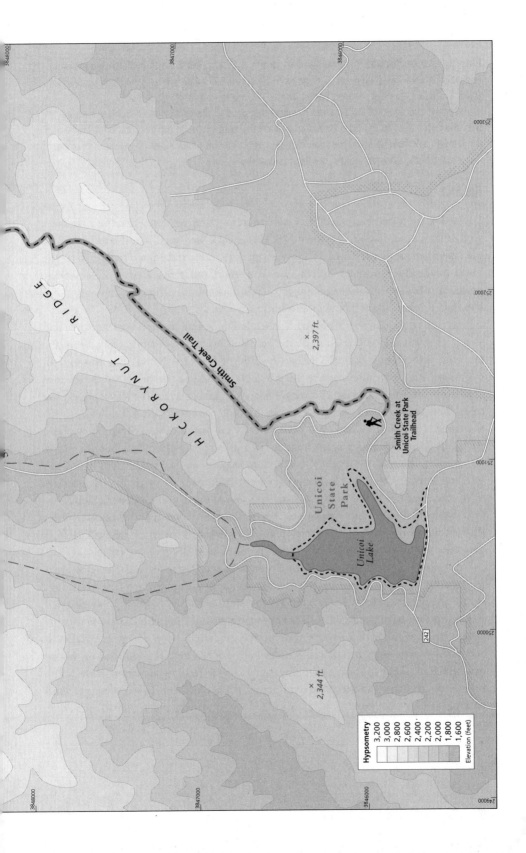

HICKORYNUT RIDGE

Smith Creek Trail

× 2,397 ft.

Smith Creek at
Unicoi State Park
Trailhead

Unicoi State Park

Unicoi Lake

242

× 2,344 ft.

Hypsometry

3,200
3,000
2,800
2,600
2,400
2,200
2,000
1,800
1,600

Elevation (feet)

Finding the trailhead: The starting point for this hike is at the Anna Ruby Falls Visitor Center and parking area. Take Highway 75 north from Helen for 1.0 mile. Turn right on Highway 356 and travel 1.5 miles, then turn left on Forest Road 242, the road to Anna Ruby Falls.

For the Unicoi State Park trailhead, follow the signs to the campground. Turn left and go past the cabin area to the gravel parking area on the right opposite the Information A-frame and the Little Brook Campground. The trailhead sign at the parking area reads: SMITH CREEK TRAIL, ANNA RUBY FALLS 5 MILES, ESTIMATED WALKING TIME ONE WAY 3 HOURS.

The Hike

Located in the Chattahoochee National Forest and Unicoi State Park, this hike takes you along the west side of Hickory Nut Ridge on a well-used blue-blazed trail. The road distance from the Anna Ruby Falls parking area, the upper trailhead, to the lower trailhead is 4.6 miles. Unicoi State Park and Conference Center offers weekly programs on a wide variety of subjects, including mountain music, arts and crafts, conducted hikes, and wildflower and birding walks.

An easy to moderate walk along a paved 0.4-mile trail from the parking area and visitor center brings you to Anna Ruby Falls and bridge observation deck. From the falls, the path climbs gradually along the side of Hickory Nut Ridge through an open hardwood cove and beside a small branch with dense patches of rhododendron and mountain laurel. During the winter and early spring when the leaves are off the trees, there are excellent views of the surrounding mountains. At 1.9 miles, high on the ridge across Smith Creek, you have a clear view to the west of Steep Creek Falls. At about 2.0 miles, you pass through an area of very large boulders. Several spring brooks cross the trail, all of which can be stepped over easily. Timber steps have been installed in places to help you negotiate short, steep banks. American chestnut logs from trees that fell in the mid-1930s are still visible on dry southwestern slopes.

The path dips in and out of the coves between ridge spurs. Rhododendron thickets along the steep side of the ridge add pleasant variety to the walk, which generally follows a contour as you travel the northwest slope of the ridge.

You come to the crest of Hickory Nut Ridge at 2.2 miles and pass close to a jeep road at 2.5 miles, visible to the east and south. On this crest, the forest is mostly shortleaf pines that have been damaged by southern pine beetles. Trees that fell across the path have been sawed to permit easier passage. Switchbacks on the steepest segments of the path keep the grade only moderately steep. You walk parallel to and then cross a pretty brook at 3.8 miles before it reaches the jeep road on Hickory Nut Ridge. Staying just above the paved service road to the campgrounds, the hike ends (or starts) at the park road across from the Little Brook Campground entrance and a few yards from a parking turnout, kiosk, and trailhead sign with miles and directions.

Miles and Directions

0.0 Start at Anna Ruby Falls Visitor Center on the paved trail along Smith Creek.

0.4 Arrive at Anna Ruby Falls bridge observation deck.

1.9 Come to a view of small waterfall on Steep Creek on the opposite mountain.

2.0 Pass through an area of large boulders.

2.2 Reach the crest of Hickory Nut Ridge.

2.5 A jeep road is visible on the left.

3.8 Cross a branch near the end of the trail.

4.6 Reach the end of trail at the campground parking area. (**Option:** Begin at the campground and hike up to Anna Ruby Falls and return for a strenuous 8.4-mile round-trip day hike.

22 Andrews Cove Recreation Area Trail

This easy to moderate hike traverses an old logging road for much of its length. This is an excellent example of a cove hardwood forest, with large yellow poplars, maples, oaks, and streamside rhododendron and mountain laurel thickets. The attractive trout stream, Andrews Creek, is visible during the lower half of hike. The blue-blazed trail ends at Indian Grave Gap (3,120 feet elevation) on the Appalachian Trail (AT).

Start: Campground near Campsite 6

Distance: 4.0 miles out and back

Approximate hiking time: 2½ hours

Difficulty: Easy to moderate

Elevation gain/loss: From campground to Indian Gap, 520 feet

Trail surface: Dirt with occasional large weathered rocks and stony sections.

Lay of the land: Mountainous, on the slopes of 4,430-foot Tray Mountain

Season: Year-round hiking; campground open from early April to the end of October

Land status: Chattahoochee National Forest

Nearest town: Helen

Fees and permits: Parking $3.00 per vehicle per day

Maps: USGS Tray Mountain; Chattahoochee National Forest map

Trail contacts: USDA Forest Service, Chatta-hoochee National Forest, Chattooga Ranger District, 200 Highway 197 North, Clarkesville, GA 30523; (706) 754-6221; www.fs.fed.us/conf; www.georgia-atclub.org

Finding the trailhead: The campground entrance is 5.5 miles north of Helen on Highway 17/75. The trail begins just beyond Campsite 6 and is designated by a wooden sign with ANDREWS COVE TRAIL—APPALACHIAN TRAIL 2 MILES.

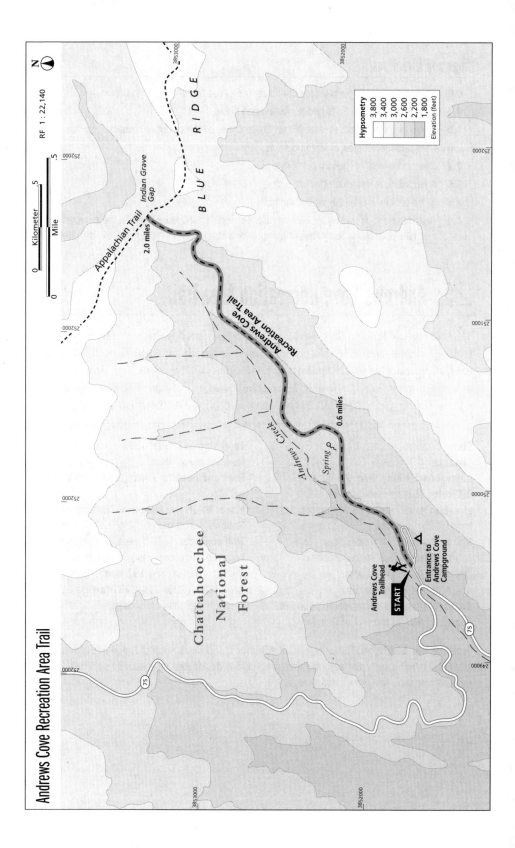

Andrews Cove Recreation Area Trail

RF 1 : 22,140

Elevation (feet)

Hypsometry
3,800
3,400
3,000
2,600
2,200
1,800

N

Appalachian Trail

Indian Grave Gap

BLUE RIDGE

2.0 miles

Andrews Cove Recreation Area Trail

Chattahoochee National Forest

Andrews Creek

Spring

0.6 miles

Andrews Cove Trailhead

START

Entrance to Andrews Cove Campground

75

75

The Hike

The Andrews Cove Recreation Area is situated in a picturesque cove hardwood forest. The trail leads to Indian Grave Gap and the Appalachian Trail. Along the trail you'll find evidence of former living in the cove by mountain homesteaders and gold mining during the late 1800s. The recreation area has excellent campsites, a comfort station, and drinking water from a hand pump. The large trees and rhododendron provide seclusion even though the area is within earshot of the heavily traveled mountain highway.

Marked with a blue blaze, the trail climbs easily but steadily in the beautiful hardwood cove with maples, oaks, yellow poplars, buckeyes, white pines, hemlocks, and an undergrowth of dogwoods and other flowering shrubs. Andrews Creek is a beautiful, tumbling trout stream on the left side of the trail as you go to the Indian Grave Gap. The path leads around a spring that emerges from beneath a massive boulder as it flows to the creek. Rock piles indicate former homesites. Rock fields along the side of Tray Mountain to the right or southeast side of the trail are resplendent with wildflowers and provide habitat for several species of less common small mammals, especially shrews and voles.

The trail becomes progressively steeper toward the end of the cove, and the path begins the ascent to the gap. The cove hardwood forest gives way to a drier, better drained forest of chestnut, black, and southern red oaks. The trail ends at Forest Road 238 and the Appalachian Trail. From here, the Appalachian Trail can be hiked in either direction. To the right (northeast) is Tray Mountain, which reaches to 4,000 feet. The trail to the left (southwest) leads to Unicoi Gap and Highway 17/75.

Miles and Directions

0.0 Start at the trailhead sign near Campsite 6.

0.6 Go around a running spring on the right, flowing from beneath a huge bolder.

1.1 To the right up the steep slope is a typical boulder field of the Blue Ridge highlands.

1.5 Begin climbing the switchbacks as the grade gets steeper.

2.0 Reach the trail's end at Indian Grave Gap and the Appalachian Trail. It's downhill all the way back to the trailhead.

4.0 Arrive back at the trailhead.

23 Dukes Creek Trail

From a trailhead elevation of 2,120 feet, this trail takes you down a steep-sided gorge to a tumbling mountain creek. You walk down a well-planned path with very little steep grade. As you descend 340 feet, the vegetation changes from the well-drained, drier ridgetop of pine and oak through dense rhododendron and mountain laurel to the stream edge with large yellow poplar and buckeye trees. An understory of silverbells, dogwoods, and rhododendron and mountain laurel add their masses of color from early spring into early summer. Smithgall Woods–Dukes Creek Conservation Area, 2.0 miles back down the Scenic Highway, offers regularly scheduled programs, lectures, and hikes.

Start: Paved section of Dukes Creek Falls parking area
Distance: 2.0 miles out and back
Approximate hiking time: 1½ hours
Difficulty: Easy to moderate; first segment of the trail to the observation deck is wheelchair accessible
Elevation gain/loss: 340 feet
Trail surface: Beginning paved section, followed by short expanse of fine gravel; lower trail, mostly firm loam
Lay of the land: Steep-sided gorge
Season: Year-round; best in spring and fall; waterfall most impressive during spring flows;

possible closings of Richard Russell Scenic Highway during heavy snow
Land status: Chattahoochee National Forest
Nearest town: Helen
Fees and permits: No fees or permits required
Maps: USGS Cowrock; Chattahoochee National Forest map
Trail contacts: USDA Forest Service, Chattahoochee National Forest, Chattooga Ranger District, 200 Highway 197 North, Clarkesville, GA 30523; (706) 754-6221; www.fs.fed.us/conf; www.gastateparks.org/info/smithgall

Finding the trailhead: From Helen go north 1.5 miles on Highway 17/75. Turn left on Highway 75 Alternate and go 2.3 miles to Richard Russell Scenic Highway (Highway 348). Turn right and go 2.0 miles; the Dukes Creek Falls parking area is on the right. The trail begins at the south end of the paved parking area.

The Hike

Dukes Creek Trail descends in several hairpin turns down into Dukes Creek gorge, ending at the creek across from Dukes Creek Falls. Dukes Creek Falls is actually on Davis Creek and falls about 300 feet in a very scenic spray. The beginning of the trail is completely wheelchair accessible to the viewing deck. The remainder of the trail is an easy walk into the gorge. A restroom, benches, and picnic tables are available at the parking area.

Where the gorge slope is especially steep, a beautifully engineered boardwalk has been installed. The paved walkway at the beginning of the trail has turnouts

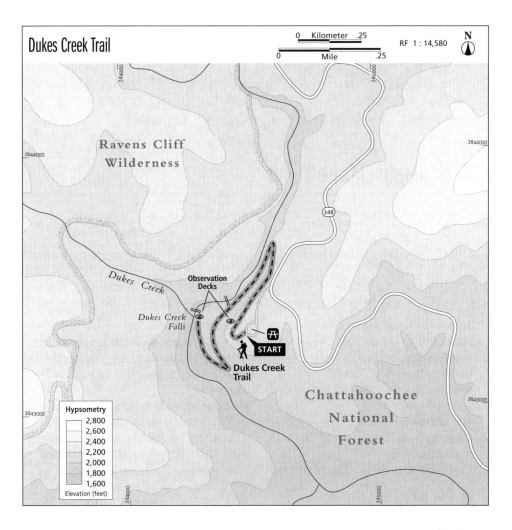

0 Kilometer .25

0 Mile .25

RF 1 : 14,580

N

Ravens Cliff
Wilderness

Dukes Creek

Observation
Decks

Dukes Creek
Falls

Dukes Creek
Trail

START

Chattahoochee

National

Forest

Hypsometry
2,800
2,600
2,400
2,200
2,000
1,800
1,600
Elevation (feet)

permitting wheelchairs to pass without touching. A wide platform overlook affords a clear view of the falls and the gorge. The platform is equipped with benches. This is the limit for wheelchair accessibility.

After the paved stretch, the trail surface is fine gravel or natural loamy soil. It is usable in most weather conditions, although rain, ice, or snow might make the footing slippery. The pathway is relatively flat, and at no point except the creek's edge is the grade more than a gentle slope. The trail passes through dense rhododendron thickets growing on the very steep gorge slope. About halfway down, the forest changes to the typical cove hardwood trees. On some of the drier sites, oaks, hickory, and Virginia pine dominate. As with many trails in the mountains, spring migrating warblers can be heard as they pass through on their northern flight.

Once at the bottom, you can reach the actual water's edge only with some difficulty. Dukes Creek is a series of beautiful cascades, rapids, and pools. Because of the thick cover of rhododendron, mountain laurel, dog-hobble, and other woody vegetation, it is very difficult to walk along the stream's edge either upstream or down. But this is a fine trout stream, and fishermen who want to expend the energy can be rewarded with some fine catches of rainbow and brown trout.

24 Raven Cliff Falls Trail

This trail in the Raven Cliffs Wilderness Area follows the noisily cascading Dodd Creek. It begins at the parking area where Bear Den Creek crosses the highway to join Dodd Creek. The trail follows a relatively gentle grade to Raven Cliff, through which the creek flows to form two waterfalls. Blue blazes mark the trail throughout its course, making it easy to follow. This is a fine trail for family hiking.

Start: Trailhead sign in the parking area
Distance: 4.8 miles out and back
Approximate hiking time: 3 hours
Difficulty: Moderate
Elevation gain/loss: 856 feet climbing; 321 feet descending
Trail surface: Dirt with firm loam
Lay of the land: Mountain stream valley
Season: Year-round
Land status: Chattahoochee National Forest

Nearest town: Helen
Fees and permits: No fees or permits required
Maps: USGS Cowrock; USDA Forest Service map for Chattahoochee National Forest in Georgia
Trail contact: USDA Forest Service, Chattahoochee National Forest, Chattooga Ranger District, 200 Highway 197 North, Clarkesville, GA 30523; (706) 754-6221; www.fs.fed.us/conf; www.gastateparks.org/info/smithgall

Finding the trailhead: Take Highway 75 north out of Helen for 1.5 miles to Highway 75 Alternate. Travel 2.3 miles to the Richard B. Russell Scenic Highway (Highway 348). Turn right; after passing the DUKES CREEK RECREATION AREA sign, continue another 1.3 miles to the parking area on the left side, where Bear Den Creek flows under the road. The trailhead is at the closed road just below the parking area.

The Hike

You begin the hike at the closed road and continue on the former roadbed for about 150 yards as it passes old primitive campsites. This area is heavily used by trout fishermen. Leaving the white pine and hemlock flat area, where Bear Den and Dodd Creeks join to become Dukes Creek, you begin to see the blue blazes as the path leads upstream along cascading Dodd Creek in a northwesterly direction to the cliffs. Campsites along this early part of the trail demonstrate this area's heavy use. The trail alternately brushes up against the stream and climbs 30 to 50 feet above the water level when the steep-sided valley makes it necessary.

Raven Cliff Falls Trail

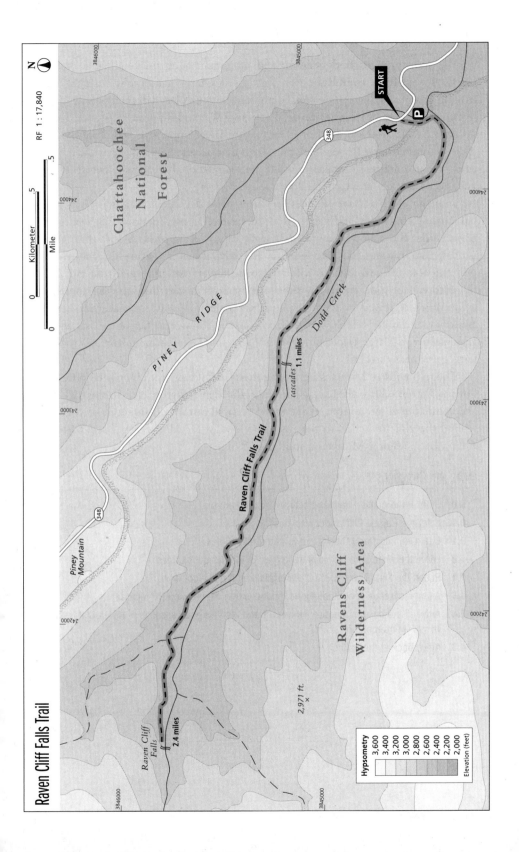

RF 1 : 17,840

N

Chattahoochee
National
Forest

START

P

348

Dodd Creek

cascades
1.1 miles

PINEY RIDGE

Raven Cliff Falls Trail

348

Piney
Mountain

Raven Cliff
Falls
2.4 miles

2,971 ft.
x

Ravens Cliff
Wilderness Area

Kilometer
Mile
.5   0   .5

Hypsometry	
	3,600
	3,400
	3,200
	3,000
	2,800
	2,600
	2,400
	2,200
	2,000
Elevation (feet)	

You pass through rhododendron and mountain laurel thickets that form passageways with thick overhead cover. Spring seeps and small brooks cross the trail, making wet places that can be crossed on conveniently placed stepping-stones. During rainy weather, portions of the trail are quite wet and slippery.

At 1.1 miles you see the first of several small yet impressive waterfalls and cascades before reaching Raven Cliff Falls. Trees that occasionally fall across the trail are easily stepped across or walked around. The largest of the cataracts before Raven Cliff is at 1.3 miles and tumbles down about 30 feet.

Large hemlock and white pines, yellow poplars, deciduous magnolias, hickories, oaks, maples, buckeyes, and many other trees thrive along the moist valley sides and floor. Under this canopy, a resplendent array of flowering plants bloom throughout early spring, summer, and into late fall. Hepatica, dwarf iris, trout lily, Jack-in-the-pulpit, Solomon's seal, various trilliums, foam flower, parasitic squawroot and one-flowered cancer root, and many other spring flowers start the show beginning in early March; followed by wild geranium, saxifrages, asters, white snakeroot, mountain mint, and other wildflowers to finish out the show. Bunches of Christmas fern and spleenworts; large glades of New York fern; and beech, maidenhair, and rockcap ferns grow near the cliffs.

The trail ends at 2.5 miles below the massive cliff face from which Dodd Creek flows as Raven Cliff Falls. The stream flows through a narrow cleft in the rock wall and comes out at the bottom in a series of falls and cascades. A side trail leads up and around the cliff for access to the top and views of Dodd Creek valley, 3,620-foot Adams Bald, Wildcat Mountain, and Piney Ridge.

Miles and Directions

0.0 Start at the marked trailhead near the parking area.

0.06 Enter the Ravens Cliff Wilderness Area.

0.1 Bear Den and Dodd Creeks join to form Dukes Creek.

0.3 Leave the white pine-hemlock tree cover for the deciduous trees.

1.1 Reach the first of several small waterfalls, about a 10-foot drop.

1.3 A larger cascade seen through the rhododendron has about a 30-foot fall.

2.4 Arrive at the base of massive Raven Cliff and the falls and cascades of Raven Cliff Falls. This is your turnaround point.

4.8 Arrive back at the trailhead.

25 Lake Russell Recreation Area: Sourwood Trail

This is an easy walk to a small waterfall and beaver ponds. The loop takes you through a variety of forest habitats, from clear-cuts and new pine plantations to maturing hardwood coves with large yellow poplars, oaks, hickories, and pines, as well as open areas and small streams. This is an ideal trail for introducing children to a wide variety of plants and animals.

Start: Bridge across the stream flowing into Nancy Town Lake
Distance: 2.7-mile loop
Approximate hiking time: 2 hours
Difficulty: Easy
Elevation gain/loss: Negligible
Trail surface: Dirt and unpaved roadway
Lay of the land: Rolling foothills
Season: Year-round hiking; campground open late April to end of November

Land status: Chattahoochee National Forest
Nearest town: Mount Airy
Fees and permits: No fees or permits required
Maps: USGS Ayersville; page-size maps available from the Chattooga District Ranger office in Clarksville
Trail contacts: Chattahoochee National Forest, Chattooga Ranger District, 200 Highway 197 North, Clarksville, GA 30523; (706) 754-6221; www.fs.fed.us/conf

Finding the trailhead: From Cornelia take U.S. Highway 123 for 2.0 miles to Mount Airy. Turn right (south) on Lake Russell Road (Forest Road 59) at the LAKE RUSSELL RECREATION AREA sign; go 2.0 miles and turn left at the group camp entrance. A sign designates trail-use parking. The trailhead is on Red Root Road at the bridge at the head of Nancy Town Lake.

The Hike

Start at the bridge across a small branch flowing into Nancy Town Lake. A trail sign marked SOURWOOD TRAIL, A 2.7-MILE LOOP TRAIL, NANCY TOWN FALLS 1.5 MILES is beside the road. Blue blazes mark the trail that follows an old roadbed for about 200 yards along a steep hillside with a noticeable stand of Christmas ferns and mountain laurel. After crossing the branch on a footbridge, the path leads up a gentle slope through loblolly pines planted in an old clear-cut area. You now enter a more mature forest until the trail crosses Nancy Town Road at the highest point on this hike. Here you enter a hardwood forest, very open and composed of white, chestnut, black, and southern red oaks, along with scattered hickories and other nut-producing trees. Look for places in the leaves where turkeys have been scratching in search of acorns and other food. Deer tracks will almost always be present in the exposed clay soil of the path.

After the trail crosses two branches on footbridges and traverses low ridges, the grasses in the shallow beaver pond on Nancy Town Creek make a large opening in the woods. The path comes down to the small stream at the head of the pond. At this point you have the option of taking the trail spur upstream to Nancy Town Falls.

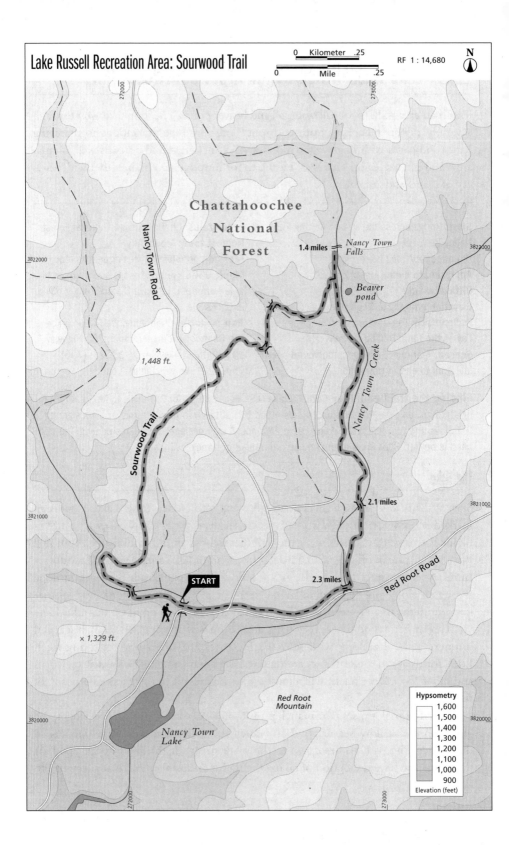

Lake Russell Recreation Area: Sourwood Trail

0 Kilometer .25

0 Mile .25

RF 1 : 14,680

N

Chattahoochee
National
Forest

Nancy Town Road

× 1,448 ft.

Sourwood Trail

Nancy Town Creek

1.4 miles — Nancy Town Falls

Beaver pond

2.1 miles

START

2.3 miles

Red Root Road

× 1,329 ft.

Red Root Mountain

Nancy Town Lake

Hypsometry

	1,600
	1,500
	1,400
	1,300
	1,200
	1,100
	1,000
	900

Elevation (feet)

The main trail continues downstream along the edge of the beaver pond. In late November look for the blue soapwort gentian blooming at the water's edge. Grape ferns, Christmas ferns, and brown-stemmed spleenwort grow along the trail where it passes the side of the beaver pond.

A short distance up the small rocky stream, at 1.4 mile, you see pretty Nancy Town Falls cascading over a rock ledge about 20 feet high. This small but delightful falls is well worth the diversion. Returning to the loop, the pathway follows close to the creek, crosses a metal footbridge, and goes down the left bank through laurel and rhododendron. The creek cascades over rock ledges just before you reach Red Root Road at 2.3 miles. Turn right, cross Nancy Town Creek again, and walk along the road back to the trailhead. There is only one Y in the road; stay to the left to return to the trailhead bridge and close the loop.

Miles and Directions

0.0 Start at the trailhead at the bridge and parking area.

0.1 Cross a stream on a bridge.

0.2 Make a sharp turn and follow blue blazes up the ridge.

0.8 Cross Nancy Town Road.

1.1 Cross a bridge over a small stream, followed shortly by another bridge.

1.4 Intersect the spur trail to Nancy Town Falls. (**Option:** Make the short trek to view the falls before returning to the loop.)

2.1 Cross Nancy Town Creek on a metal bridge.

2.3 Come to Red Root Road; turn right and recross the same creek.

2.7 Cross the bridge on Red Root Road and close the loop.

26 Panther Creek Trail

This blue-blazed trail makes an excellent one-way day hike with arrangements for transportation at the end. Or you can hike to the falls in 3.6 miles and return to the day-use area for 7.2-mile day hike. You follow a beautiful tumbling, cascading stream through a steep-sided valley with rocky cliffs to the dramatic and impressive Panther Creek Falls. The trail leads down to the pool for a grand view of the falling water and the large pool catching it. The trail continues through some especially grand hardwood stands. The USDA Forest Service has designated parts of this area as a Protected Botanical Area. The parking area at this end of the trail is quite remote and not secure for overnight parking.

Start: Panther Creek Day Use Area
Distance: Panther Creek Trail, 7.2 miles out and back; one-way shuttle to Davidson Creek, 5.8 miles
Approximate hiking time: Panther Creek Trail, 4 hours; one way to Davidson Creek, 6 hours
Difficulty: Easy to moderate; short, more difficult places negotiating rock ledges
Elevation gain/loss: 740 feet
Trail surface: Dirt, bare rock surface, and firm loam
Lay of the land: Streamside path, forested rolling foothills

Best season: Year-round
Land status: Chattahoochee National Forest
Nearest town: Clarkesville
Fees and permits: No fees or permits required
Maps: USGS Tallulah Falls and Tugaloo Lake; USDA Forest Service map of the Chattahoochee National Forest
Trail contacts: Chattahoochee National Forest, Chattooga Ranger District, 200 Highway 197 North, Clarkesville, GA 30523; (706) 754-6221; www.fs.fed.us/conf

Finding the trailhead: Take U.S. Highway 23/441 for 9.0 miles north from Clarksville or 3.0 miles south from Tallulah Falls to the Panther Creek Recreation Area. The trailhead is across Old U.S. Highway 441 from the recreation area. The eastern end of the trail can be reached by taking Highway 184 from Taccoa for 9.0 miles to Yonah Park at Yonah Dam. Across the bridge, turn left on an unpaved road and go 2.0 miles to Panther Creek. You are a few yards above the mouth of Davidson Creek on the opposite side. Fording Panther Creek in a standard passenger car or two-wheel-drive pickup is not recommended. The trailhead is on the other side; just wade across.

The Hike

Note: Because Panther Creek and most of its tributaries flow out of farm or residential land, the water along the trail is not safe for drinking. If you plan to camp along this trail, be prepared to treat the water for drinking and cooking.

A view of Panther Creek Falls at mile 3.6 on the Panther Creek Trail. ▶

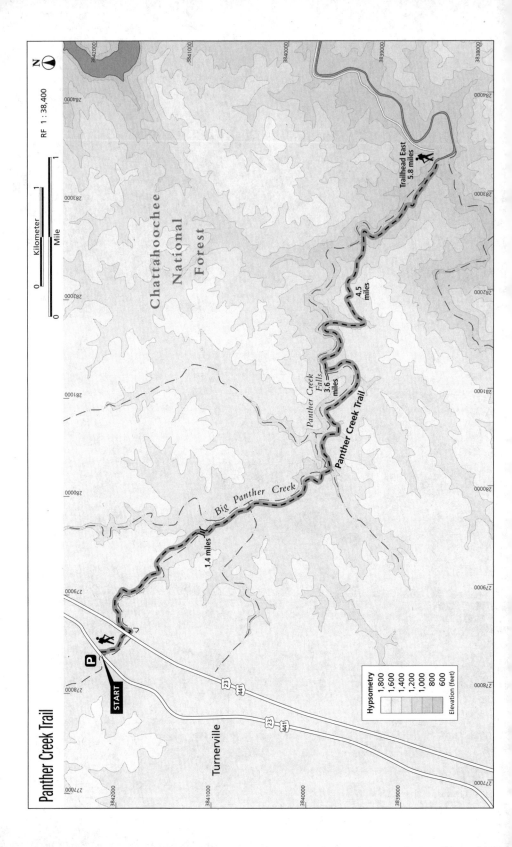

Panther Creek Trail

RF 1 : 38,400

Kilometer

Mile

N

Chattahoochee National Forest

Turnerville

START

P

Big Panther Creek

1.4 miles

Panther Creek Falls
3.6 miles

Panther Creek Trail

4.5 miles

Trailhead East
5.8 miles

Hypsometry
1,800
1,600
1,400
1,200
1,000
800
600
Elevation (feet)

23
441

23
441

The trail begins on the opposite side of Old US 441 at the Panther Creek Day Use Area and paved parking area. Look for a trailhead sign. Blue blazes mark the trail to Davidson Creek. The trail then goes under the new US 23/441 bridge that crosses Panther Creek at 0.27 mile. You soon enter a mixed forest of oaks, hickories, yellow poplars, and pines. Trailing arbutus grows abundantly along the first half mile. One patch is close to the trailhead, and large patches of the earth-hugging, sweet-smelling plant occur regularly along the south- and west-facing sections of the trail. Mountain laurel thickets border the pathway and bloom en masse in May, followed in June and July by the great white rhododendron (rosebay) growing along the stream.

The trail then goes down the northeast (left) side of Panther Creek. Cascading water can be seen or heard throughout much of the hike, sometimes forming small waterfalls. Two rock overhangs only a few feet apart are encountered at 0.9 miles. If you do not pay attention to the two blazes on a white oak at the second cliff overhang, it is easy to pass by the sharp left turn through the rocks for several yards to gain access to the earth path above the thick laurel and rhododendron. (**FYI:** If you miss this turn and find yourself on a slightly worn path *without* blue blazes, don't feel bad—others have done it before you. This faux-path follows close to the creek and you must climb through the thick laurel and rhododendron more than 200 yards. It eventually comes out again on the blazed trail.)

Following the relatively easy-grade blazed section of the trail, you return to the creek at a stand of hemlock and white pine at a level area with a primitive campsite and fire ring. At 1.4 miles cross Panther Creek on a footbridge to a peaceful level area going down the right (west) bank. Little Panther Creek enters the main stream from the east at 1.5 miles. This level area is rich in wildflowers, ferns, ground pine, and other plants thriving in the rich alluvial soil. Several small tributaries are crossed either on low footbridges or stepping-stones.

At 2.2 miles the creek makes an abrupt turn to the east. On the opposite side is the mouth of Horse Creek. You now enter an area of more steep-sided rock cliffs, where two steel-wire guard fences have been installed to prevent mishaps. The Forest Service recommends that hikers with heavy packs use extra caution walking under the rocky overhangs. Panther Creek picks up speed here and dashes over several beautiful cascades. This is Mill Shoals, a former mill site, not Panther Creek Falls. The main show is still 0.3 of a mile along the trail. Panther Creek Falls is three separate cascades, each with its own pool. The trail leads out onto a large rock overlook for the upper and middle section of the falls. At 3.6 miles a side path to the lower cascade takes you below the falls and to the edge of the large catch pool. This is one of the more visible and showy of the north Georgia waterfalls.

From the falls, the trail remains on the south and east side of the creek as it cascades in a tight gorge for about 0.5 mile. The trail now leaves sight of the creek and gains elevation through more open deciduous woods to reach the flat top of a pine ridge, the highest point on this hike. Keep a sharp eye for the blue blazes; there are sharp turns. The trail drops down to the left from the ridge as you return to a forest of large oaks and yellow poplars to the creek again at 5.0 miles. Follow it another 0.8 mile to the eastern trailhead and the mouth of Davidson Creek at 5.8 miles.

Sections of both sides of the Panther Creek below the falls have been designated by the Forest Service as a Protected Botanical Area because of the richness and diversity of plant life. This area lies in the Brevard Fault Zone, characterized by a narrow band of limestone that supports vegetation not commonly found in northeast Georgia. Regionally rare gay-wings bloom along the Panther Creek Gorge.

Miles and Directions

0.0 Start at the day-use area across Old US 441. Walk down toward the dual highway bridge.

0.9 Look for the double blaze on a white oak tree. (**FYI:** If you don't see the blaze, you missed a sharp left turn.)

1.4 Coming back to creek side, cross Panther Creek on a footbridge.

1.5 Look across Panther Creek at a wide, flat area. This is Little Panther Creek.

2.2 Begin to come to the steeper valley sides as Horse Creek enters Panther Creek on the opposite side.

2.8 The rock ledges now become the valley side as you hold onto cable for support on the narrow ledge. (**FYI:** Be careful of large backpacks bumping the rock overhangs, causing you to lose balance.)

3.2 Do not be misled by the beautiful cascading water here; this is not Panther Creek Falls.

3.5 Reach Panther Creek Falls on the left; continue a little farther for a better look.

3.6 This side trail takes you to a spectacular view of the wide, plunging waterfall into an equally pretty catch pool below. (**Option:** Return to the trail to go back upstream and the day-use area for a 7.2-mile out-and-back hike.) Turn left and continue another 1.2 miles.

4.1 Leave the creek and start to climb up the ridge.

4.5 Enter more open woods as you reach the high point on the trail at 1,300 feet.

5.0 Come back to the stream again in a much flatter area.

5.8 Reach the east-end trailhead at Davidson Creek. Hopefully you have a vehicle on the other side of Panther Creek at the road's end from Tugaloo River at Yonah Lake Spillway.

State Park and Wildlife Management Area Trails

27 Fort Mountain State Park Trails

Fort Mountain State Park trails offer an assortment of cultural, natural, and human history subjects. The park lies on the southwestern edge of the Southern Appalachian range and melds into the Ridge and Valley province, giving it a wide variety of habitat types and geological diversity, including old gold mines and active talc mines. There are 14 miles of hiking trails of varying length and difficulty—from a short walk along the ancient stone wall from which the mountain got its name to a backpacking trail with campsites (free permit required)—and additional miles of bike and horse trails. The seven hiking trails are well marked, interesting, and easy to follow. All access trails are marked with a red blaze.

Start: Interconnected trails with several starting points; specific trailheads noted in trail discussions

Distance: Old Fort Loop and Stone Wall Trails, 1.6-mile loop; Cool Springs Overlook Trail, 2.0 miles out and back; Big Rock Nature Trail, 0.7-mile loop; Lake Loop Trail, 1.1-mile loop; Gahuti Backcountry Trail, 7.2-mile loop; Gold Mine Creek Trail, 2.3-mile loop

Approximate hiking time: Short trails 1 to 1½ hours; Gahuti Trail, all-day hike or overnight camping trip

Difficulty: Easy to moderate; some strenuous stretches on the Gahuti Trail

Trail surface: Mostly dirt; some paved or unpaved roads

Lay of the land: Mountainous

Season: Year-round, limited only during infrequent heavy snowfall; spring and fall for wildflower, foliage color, and bird migrations

Land status: Georgia State Parks Division

Nearest town: Chatsworth

Fees and permits: Park Pass $3.00 per vehicle per day; free permit required for camping on Gahuti Trail

Maps: USGS Crandall; page-size map showing all trails, lengths, and blaze colors available at park office

Trail contacts: Fort Mountain State Park, 181 Fort Mountain Park Road, Chatsworth, GA 30705; (706) 695–2621; www.gastate parks.org

Finding the trailhead: The park is located 7.0 miles east of Chatsworth on Highway 52 in Murray County. The trailhead for the Old Fort Loop Trail is at the Old Fort parking area on the north end of the park. The trailhead for the Gahuti Backcountry Trail is at the Cool Springs Overlook parking area. This trail also can be accessed at other points in the park. Trailheads for the Big Rock Nature Trail and Gold Mine Creek Trail are located on the Lake Trail.

The Hikes

Several long bike and horse trails add miles to the marked hiking trails. If you choose to hike these trails, remember that cyclists and equestrians have the right-of-way. Dogs are not welcome on the horse trails, even on leashes. The Pinhoti Trail links into a section of the Fort Mountain trails.

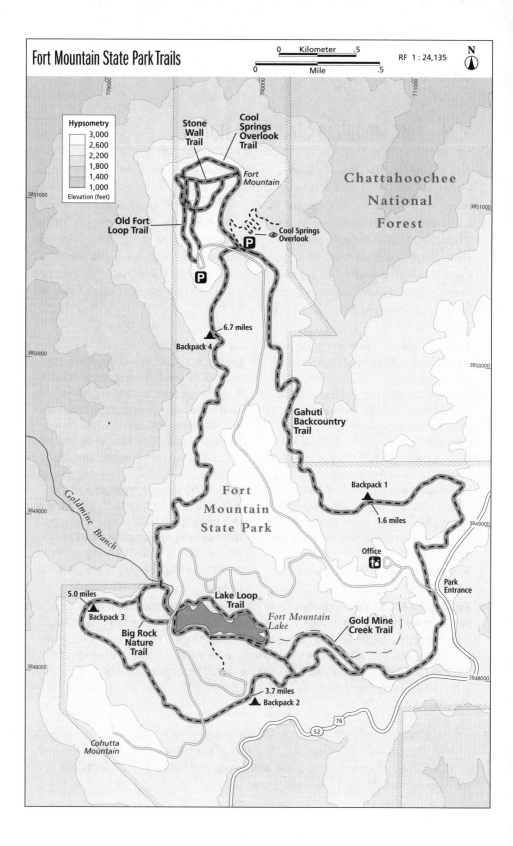

Fort Mountain State Park Trails

0   Kilometer   .5

0   Mile   .5

RF 1 : 24,135

N

Hypsometry

	3,000
	2,600
	2,200
	1,800
	1,400
	1,000

Elevation (feet)

Stone Wall Trail

Cool Springs Overlook Trail

Fort Mountain

Chattahoochee

National

Forest

Old Fort Loop Trail

P

P

Cool Springs Overlook

6.7 miles

▲ Backpack 4

Gahuti Backcountry Trail

Backpack 1

▲

1.6 miles

Office

Park Entrance

Fort Mountain State Park

Goldmine Branch

5.0 miles

▲ Backpack 3

Big Rock Nature Trail

Lake Loop Trail

Fort Mountain Lake

Gold Mine Creek Trail

3.7 miles

▲ Backpack 2

76

52

Cohutta Mountain

Old Fort Loop and Stone Wall Trails

The most popular trail in the park leads to the ancient stone wall. Many generations of explorers, archaeologists, geologists, historians, and sightseers have wondered about the identity of the unknown builders and the purpose of the stone wall. From the brink of the cliff on the east side of the mountain, the wall extends 855 feet to another precipice on the west side. Its highest part measures about 7 feet, but generally it rises to a height of 2 or 3 feet. There are twenty-nine pits scattered fairly regularly along the wall, with the wings of a gateway at one point. Speculation regarding the builders and their purpose includes references to sun worship and last-ditch defense by prehistoric white peoples, bloody warfare between rival Indian tribes, defense fortification by Spanish conquistadors hunting gold, and honeymoon havens for Cherokee Indian newlyweds. Nobody knows which of the many legends and theories is true or false. The true answer still lies buried somewhere in antiquity and may never be unearthed.

At the beginning of the trail, a large metal plaque placed in 1968 by the Georgia Department of State Parks tells of the mystery and legends of the stone wall and the mountain. The trail to the north leads to the mysterious prehistoric wall of rocks from which Fort Mountain takes its name. From the sign, the yellow-blazed trail leads to the stone wall and two more plaques that tell of additional mysteries regarding arrangement of the stones.

Beyond the wall about 200 yards, the trail reaches the stone tower built in the 1930s by the Civilian Conservation Corps on the summit of Fort Mountain. The trail along the stone wall is marked by a blue blaze. A red-blazed access trail extends a short distance to the west from the Old Fort Loop Trail to an overlook deck. It provides an excellent view to the west and the town of Chatsworth. The Cool Springs Overlook Trail is only a short distance from the parking area to the observation deck. A bike trail also comes through this parking area and descends 1.3 miles in a series of switchbacks.

The trees on the Fort Mountain summit show the weathering of wind, rain, ice, and snow and are much older than they look. During spring migration of warblers and other small birds, this area offers a unique opportunity to see, not just hear, many species at close range.

Big Rock Nature Trail

The trail begins at the sign along the park road a few yards south of the dam on Gold Mine Creek. This 0.7-mile path is marked by a yellow blaze and is the jewel of the park. After going under a power line, the trail leads through a stand of small Virginia pines and then into a more dominantly deciduous hardwood forest of oaks, maples, sourwoods, black gums, and yellow poplars. The undergrowth is thick with sweet shrub and spicebush along with mountain laurel as the trail dips into a wet area. Dropping sharply to the bluff line, it intercepts the Gahuti Backcountry Trail, turns to the right, and follows the rocky bluff line. The view from here is spectacular.

Catawba rhododendron is in bloom during May and June along with mountain laurel and many species of spring wildflowers. Rockcap fern is abundant on the large rocks near the wooden steps and short boardwalk that lead to an overlook and down to the falls of Gold Mine Creek.

The orange-blazed Gahuti continues along the bluff line, while the Big Rock Nature Trail turns upstream beside the picturesque cascades as the creek pours over the rock ledges. Above the tumbling water, the creek and trail become flatter until the base of the dam is reached. Then the trail ascends steeply to the road.

Lake Loop Trail

The Lake Loop Trail is an easy, flat path around the lake marked in blue blazes for a distance of 1.1 miles. It can be accessed at several places from the dam around to the swimming area and campgrounds on the north side. On the north side there are several wet areas where you might see such wildlife as frogs, salamanders, and other aquatic and semiaquatic animals. Patches of large cinnamon ferns grow in these wet glades along with aquatic plants like lizard-tail, arrowhead, and smartweed. The trail passes cabins, picnic areas, swimming area, fishing dock, and campgrounds. Boardwalks cross some of the wet areas. On the east end and south side of the lake, mountain laurel and rhododendron form a canopy over the trail. This is an excellent birding trail with both water birds and forest species present. A day-use parking area with picnic shelters is on the south end of the dam.

Gold Mine Creek Trail

Gold Mine Creek Trail takes off from the Lake Loop Trail on the southeast end of the lake as a red-blazed access to the white-blazed loop trail. Turning left following the white blaze, you walk along an old roadbed up a gentle slope and then turn down the watershed of Gold Mine Creek. Walking beside the small creek for 0.6 mile, you turn up a gentle cove to the intersection with the Gahuti Backcountry Trail. You turn right and hike with the Gahuti Trail about a mile until the white-blazed trail turns right and the orange-blazed Gahuti Trail continues. Follow the white blazes for about 0.3 mile to the access trail. Turn left and follow the red blazes back to the lake.

Gahuti Backcountry Trail

This 7.2-mile loop of the Gahuti Backcountry Trail travels around the crest of Fort Mountain. The trail is marked by an orange blaze and can be hiked in either direction. A grand view of the Cohutta Mountains and Wilderness Area greets you at the very beginning. During late fall, winter, and early spring, the colors and vistas are exceptional. For the most part, the trail is easy to moderate; however, there are some short steep climbs and descents as the trail leads through the ravines and around the ridge crests. These can be slippery when wet or when covered with snow. Four campsites are strategically located along the trail for backpackers. Free permits must be obtained from the park office for use of these campsites. No permit is necessary for day use of the trail.

Miles and Directions

0.0 Start at the trailhead at the Cool Springs Overlook parking area.

0.8 Enjoy a great view to the west.

1.6 Reach Backpack Site 1.

2.6 Cross road at park entrance.

3.3 The Gold Mine Creek Trail is on the right; look for yellow blazes.

3.6 The Gold Mine Connecter Trail is on the right; leave yellow blazes.

3.7 Pass trail to Backpack Site 2.

5.0 Reach Backpack Site 3, with a great view to the north and west.

5.2 Join the green-blazed Big Rock Nature Trail; this is another view area.

5.3 Leave green-blazed Big Rock Nature Trail, and cross over Gold Mine Branch.

6.7 Backpack Site 4 is on the left.

7.1 Cross the paved park road.

7.2 Arrive back at the trailhead and parking area.

28 Amicalola Falls State Park Trails

Amicalola is a Cherokee word meaning "tumbling waters," and Amicalola Falls, formed as Little Amicalola Creek plunges 729 feet in several cascades, is the highest waterfall east of the Mississippi River. The state park has nine hiking trails totaling 6.0 miles and two staircases with 602 steps. You can choose from a variety of easy to short, strenuous climbs. Most are directly associated with Amicalola Falls or are designed to reach a better view of the falls. All trails are well marked and carefully maintained.

Start: Amicalola Falls Visitor Center
Distance: Base of the Falls Trail, 0.6 mile out and back; Spring Trail, 0.4-mile one-way; West Ridge Falls Access, 0.3 mile one-way; Mountain Laurel Loop, 1.0 mile; Creek Trail, 0.6 mile one-way; AT Approach Trail, one-way from visitor center to Appalachian Trail at Springer Mountain, 7.4 miles
Approximate hiking time: 30 minutes to 1 hour for most trails; AT Approach Trail to Springer Mountain, 5 hours
Difficulty: Easy to strenuous
Elevation gain/loss: AT Approach Trail, 1,963 feet

Season: Year-round
Nearest towns: Dahlonega, Ellijay
Fees and permits: Park Pass $3.00 per day per vehicle
Maps: USGS Amicalola and Nimblewill; detailed trail map available at visitor center; USDA Forest Service map of Chattahoochee National Forest and Georgia section of Appalachian Trail
Trail contacts: Amicalola Falls State Park and Lodge, 240 Amicalola Falls Park Road, Dawsonville, GA 30534; (706) 265-4703; www.gastateparks.org; www.georgia-atclub.org lodge: (706) 265-8888; www.Hike-Inn.com

Finding the trailhead: Amicalola Falls State Park Visitor Center is 20.0 miles east of Ellijay and 14.0 miles west of Dahlonega on Highway 52. Trailheads for all trails below the falls are at or across the road from the visitor center.

The Hikes

Campground and cabin accommodations are available in the park. The Amicalola Lodge offers buffet-style meals with a great view of mountains and excellent hotel accommodations. Park personnel and special guests lead special outdoor programs throughout the year. This area can be exceptionally beautiful during fall leaf color and in winter with snow. The road to the lodge from the visitor center is steep and may be closed during snow or icy conditions.

Base of the Falls Trail

The Base of the Falls Trail, an easy to moderate one-way paved trail, begins at the reflection pool. A longer extension starts across the road and Little Amicalola Creek bridge from the visitor center. In either case, you follow the creek to the lower observation deck. Little Amicalola Creek is shaded by a fine stand of yellow poplars.

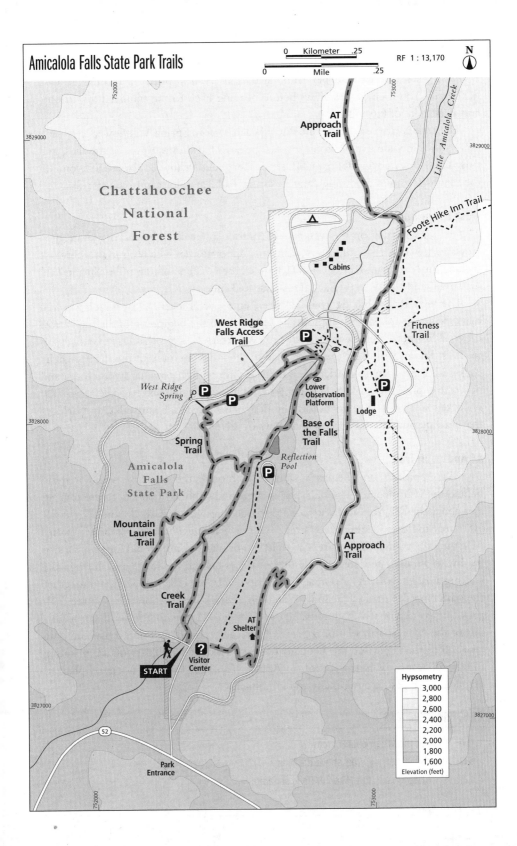

Amicalola Falls State Park Trails

Kilometer

0 .25

Mile

0 .25

RF 1 : 13,170

N

Chattahoochee
National
Forest

Little Amicalola Creek

AT
Approach
Trail

Foote Hike Inn Trail

Cabins

West Ridge
Falls Access
Trail

Fitness
Trail

West Ridge
Spring

Lower
Observation
Platform

Spring
Trail

Base of
the Falls
Trail

Lodge

Amicalola
Falls
State Park

Reflection
Pool

Mountain
Laurel
Trail

AT
Approach
Trail

Creek
Trail

AT
Shelter

START

Visitor
Center

52

Park
Entrance

Hypsometry

	3,000
	2,800
	2,600
	2,400
	2,200
	2,000
	1,800
	1,600

Elevation (feet)

Spring flowers abound along this trail from March through May. The trail ends with a 177-step staircase to a steeper climb at the observation platform nearest the base of the falls. You'll enjoy the views before heading back to the trailhead for an out-and-back hike of 0.6 mile.

The trail is markedly different during each season. Spring wildflowers put on a great show, including bloodroot, several species of trilliums, Virginia cowslips, and trout lilies. Dogwood, redbud, maple, serviceberry, and yellow poplar are just some of the shrubs and trees blooming early in spring. Fall leaf color can be spectacular.

West Ridge Trails

The network of trails on the west side of Amicalola Creek, all easy to moderate, provide a variety of forest conditions and scenic opportunities. The trails in this network include the Mountain Laurel Loop (1.0 mile), the Creek Trail (0.6 mile), Spring Trail (0.4 mile) and the West Ridge Falls Access (0.3 mile).

The West Ridge Spring Trail is broken into several loops, all of which are well marked and identified with appropriate blazes. From the beginning of the trail, across the road from the visitor center, there are NATURE TRAIL signs that lead eventually to the West Ridge Spring on the paved road to the lodge. Because of the many switchbacks, this trail is easy to moderate and travels through lush cove hardwood forest and open, dry, pine and oak ridge exposures. This trail complex has been carefully reworked so that it leads to beautifully designed stairways, boardwalks, and bridges that provide outstanding acccess and views of the falls.

AT Approach Trail

The AT Approach Trail begins as you walk through the attractive stone archway behind the visitor center. The blue-blazed trail climbs about 1,000 feet to the parking area above the falls. You start with a gentle grade through a hardwood forest for about 100 yards and then begin a steep grade with several switchbacks for another quarter mile through a laurel thicket. At 0.25 mile you break out onto an old logging/service road with a moderately steep grade until it passes behind the lodge and through the parking area. Here the AT Approach joins the Len Foote Hike Inn Trail, and together the trails cross the road to the lodge. You then go back into the forest where the trails part. The AT Approach Trail continues to Springer Mountain, the southern terminus of the Appalachian National Scenic Trail. The Leonard E. Foote Hike Inn Trail takes off to the right (see the Leonard E. Foote Hike Inn Trail). If you are planning to hike all or any extended part of the Appalachian Trail, this park is a good place to practice and break in equipment and clothing.

Miles and Directions

0.0 Start at the visitor center archway.

1.2 Reach the parking area above the falls.

1.5 The AT Approach and Hike Inn Trails separate.

4.1 Arrive at Frosty Mountain crest and lookout tower.

4.7 Meet with trail on right to the Foote Hike Inn Trail.

5.3 Arrive at Nimblewill Gap.

6.6 Arrive at Black Mountain.

7.4 Arrive at Springer Mountain, the southern end of the AT.

Note: It is anticipated that the southern end of the Appalachian Trail will be moved to Amicalola State Park. It seems that most "through-hikers" for the AT use the Amicalola State Park approach. Springer Mountain, the current official southern terminus of the AT, is not a secure place to leave a vehicle.

More Information

Local Events/Attractions

Dahlonega Gold Museum Historic Site, #1 Public Square, Dahlonega, GA 30533; (706) 864-2257; www.gastateparks.org/info/dahlonega.

29 Leonard E. Foote Hike Inn Trail

Yellow rectangular blazes mark the way for this 4.9-mile trail to the Leonard E. Foote Hike Inn. The inn, a welcome sight after your hike, offers the opportunity to spend a night in the wilderness without the need for sleeping bag, tent, or other camping gear. If you're staying overnight at the inn, you must check in at the Unicoi State Park Visitor Center and receive your permit by 2:00 P.M. the day of your reservation to ensure that you complete the hike to the inn before dark.

Start: Top of the falls parking area

Distance: 9.8 miles out and back from the designated parking area

Approximate hiking time: 6 to 8 hours

Difficulty: Moderate with several short, steep grades

Elevation gain/loss: 707 feet

Trail surface: Firm loam; a few rocky segments

Lay of the land: Mountainous without being strenuous

Season: Year-round

Land status: Chattahoochee National Forest; Hike Inn managed by Georgia State Parks Division

Nearest towns: Ellijay, Dahlonega

Fees and permits: Parking at designated Hike Inn guests parking area, $3.00 per vehicle for the duration of the trip; advanced reservations required for the inn

Maps: USGS Nimblewill and Amicalola; trail map available at the park visitor center when checking in; Hike Inn brochure with excellent map of the trail, available by mail when making reservations

Trail contacts: Amicalola Falls State Park, 240 Amicalola Falls State Park Road, Dawsonville, GA 30534; (706) 265-4703; www.gastateparks.org; www.georgia-atclub.org; for overnight reservations and costs at the Leonard E. Foote Hike Inn: (800) 581-8032; www.Hike-Inn.com

Leonard E. Foote Hike Inn Trail

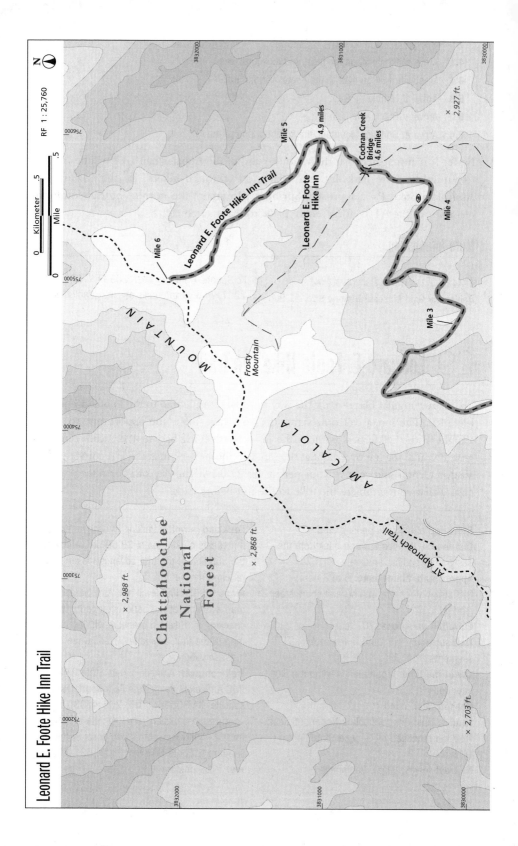

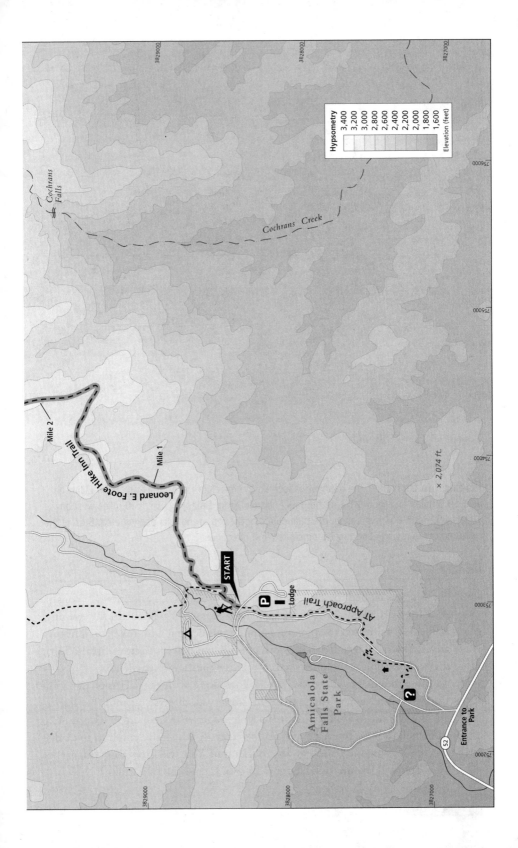

Leonard E. Foote Hike Inn.

Finding the trailhead: The trailhead is located at Amicalola Falls State Park. From Ellijay go east 19.0 miles on Highway 52 to the park entrance. From Dalhonega go 15.0 miles west on Highway 52 to the park entrance. The trailhead is at the top of the falls parking area. Stop at the visitor center to register and receive brochures and directions.

The Hike

The Hike Inn was named for Leonard E. Foote (1918–1989), a consummate conservationist who spent his life in research and management of wildlife. In the evening, guests at the inn are treated to entertaining programs dealing with the natural history of the area, including illustrated discussions of birds and flowers. Visitors can also learn about the conservation techniques used to manage the facility efficiently.

From the parking area above the falls, follow along with the AT Approach Trail across the paved road where the path at the stone wall directs you into the woods. Stay with the Approach Trail to about 0.3 mile, where the Leonard E. Foote Hike Inn Trail branches off to the right and up the ridge. It is a steady climb to the ridge crest on a well-maintained and easy-to-follow trail. You will cross four ridges, but the highest one will require only about a 500-foot climb in 1.25 miles.

The forest floor has been relatively clear to this point, but now you encounter a thick growth of low vegetation in summer consisting of grasses, herbaceous plants, and many young sassafras trees. At 0.9 mile you reach the crest of this first ridge and a log bench with a view of surrounding mountains. Changes in vegetation will continue throughout the hike as you go from west- to east-facing and south- to north-facing ridge exposures.

In spring look for the abundance of blooming wildflowers, including trailing arbutus, sessile and Vasey's trilliums, jack-in-the-pulpits, and pink lady's slippers. Among the trees and shrubs are silverbells, dogwoods, redbuds, buckeyes, yellow poplars, and mountain laurel. Along the trail are glades of New York ferns as well as marginal wood, lady, Christmas, and bracken ferns, and spleenworts.

You might be surprised at the number of seedling and sprouting American chestnuts along the trail. Unfortunately they will soon succumb to the chestnut blight that killed the parent trees.

Mammals in the area include black bears, white-tailed deer, foxes, squirrels, chipmunks, raccoons, and opossums along with smaller deer mice, shrews, and moles. Most are only seen as tracks in the soft ground or as signs of feeding. This is an excellent birding trail in spring and fall for migrating warblers, grosbeaks, orioles, and others. Besides the migrant birds there are many resident species like warblers, towhees, wrens, hawks, owls and, at higher elevations, ravens.

At 3.3 miles you pass a rock cairn left by workers during the original building of the trail. Stop for a moment at 3.9 miles to take in the views from the rock ledge. You are looking down the Cochrans Creek Valley toward Cochrans Falls. You cross several small brooks and moist areas until you come to Cochrans Creek at 4.6 miles, crossed on a footbridge. At this rhododendron- and mountain laurel–lined stream in a quiet cove hardwood forest, you are not far from the end of the trail and the unique experience of the Leonard E. Foote Hike Inn at 4.9 miles.

You have gained 500 feet in elevation, and even in the warm months of summer it is several degrees cooler on the ridge. You are ready for a refreshing drink at this remarkably designed, energy efficient inn.

After your stay at the inn, you can backtrack along the same trail to return to the park. Or you can make a long loop by heading north to Nimblewill Gap, connecting with the AT Approach Trail, and following it back to Amicalola Falls and the parking area. You can also turn north (right) and go 3.4 miles to Springer Mountain, currently the southern terminus of the Appalachian Trail.

Miles and Directions

0.0 Start at the designated parking area at top of the falls. The yellow-blazed Hike Inn and blue-blazed AT Approach Trails share same pathway for 0.3 mile.

0.3 The Hike Inn Trail leaves the AT Approach Trail to the right and begins a gentle climb.

0.9 Reach a bench rest with views and a section of trail with many sassafras trees.

3.3 A rock cairn on the left was constructed during the original trail work.

3.9 Come to a view down Cochrans Creek Valley toward Cochrans Falls.

4.6 Cross Cochrans Creek on a footbridge.

4.9 Arrive at the Leonard E. Foote Hike Inn. Enjoy your stay and/or your walk back to the parking area. (**Option:** Make a 10.4-mile loop by going north 1.0 mile to Nimblewill Gap. Turn left [south] at the gap and follow the AT Approach Trail 4.5 miles to the parking area and trailhead.)

9.8 Arrive back at the parking area.

30 Vogel State Park Trails

One of the oldest state parks in Georgia, Vogel is also one of the most scenic. Wolf Creek runs through the park and is impounded to make beautiful little Lake Trahlyta. The park's four trails total more than 20 miles and cover a wide variety of conditions, including elevation changes, difficulty, and forest habitats.

Start: Coosa Backcountry and Bear Hair Trails, about 100 yards from the office/visitor center toward the camping areas; Byron Reece Nature Trail, about 250 yards along the start of the Coosa Trail; Trahlyta Lake Trail, from several points around the lake

Distance: Coosa Backcountry Trail, 12.7-mile loop, plus an additional 2.0-mile round-trip to Coosa Bald; Bear Hair Trail, 4.2-mile lollipop, including spur to the overlook; Trahlyta Lake Trail 1.0-mile loop; Nature Trail, 0.5-mile loop

Approximate hiking time: Coosa Backcountry Trail, 2 days if camping or a long, strenuous day hike; Bear Hair Trail, 4 hours; Trahlyta Lake and Nature Trails 1 hour each

Difficulty: Trahlyta Lake and Nature Trails, easy; Bear Hair and Coosa Backcountry trails, moderate to strenuous

Elevation gain/loss: Bear Hair Trail, 1,000 feet; Nature Loop Trail, 170 feet

Trail surface: With few exceptions, dirt and old logging roads

Lay of the land: Mountainous

Season: Year-round; short periods of severe weather possible in winter

Land status: Georgia State Parks Division and Chattahoochee National Forest

Nearest town: Blairsville

Fees and permits: Parking $3.00 per day per vehicle; free permit required for camping on Coosa Backcountry Trail, available at park office

Maps: USGS Coosa Bald and Neels Gap; page-size map of park is available from the visitor center

Trail contacts: Vogel State Park, 7485 Vogel State Park Road, Blairsville, GA 30512; (706) 745-2628; www.gastateparks.org; www.georgia-atclub.org
USDA Forest Service, Brasstown Ranger District, 181 Highway 515, P.O. Box 9, Blairsville, GA 30512; (706) 745-6928; www.fs.fed.us/conf

Finding the trailhead: Vogel State Park is 11.0 miles south of Blairsville. A single trailhead serving the Coosa Backcountry, Bear Hair, and Nature Trails is located about 100 yards from the office/visitor center toward the camping areas. The Trahlyta Lake Trail can be accessed from several points around the lake.

The Hikes

Wildflowers begin blooming in Vogel State Park in late February and March, and some species are in bloom until late November. Songbird migrations begin in late March. Warblers, thrushes, tanagers, grosbeaks, and finches head north through the mountains as late as May. Many will end their northward trip in the Georgia mountains and begin nesting here. Fall leaf color by mid-October can be spectacular due to the many tree species.

Trahlyta Lake Loop Trail

Trahlyta Lake Loop Trail is a comfortable walk around the lakeshore. Canada geese and other waterbirds, mammals, and amphibians add to the enjoyment of this short but scenic trail.

Byron Reece Nature Loop Trail

The Byron Reece Nature Trail is a short hike with interpretive signs along the path describing the interesting natural features of the forest. The loop trail begins off the access trail for the park's two longer hikes.

Bear Hair Trail

The Bear Hair loop is a steady climb along tumbling Burnett Branch. One crossing is on a footbridge. Other crossings require rock hopping and are easy except after a hard rain. You climb through a cove hardwood forest until you get to the level of the laurel and Catawba rhododendron. Here a slightly steeper path tunnels through the thick shrubs that bloom in late May and June. The path comes to a gap where you will intersect a spur trail on the left. Marked with a green blaze, the spur leads to the top of the ridge and an overlook platform. From the vista clearing at the end of the spur trail, you look right down on Lake Trahlyta in the park. At the ridgetop you are at 3,280 feet and have climbed 1,000 feet.

Backtracking to the loop trail, you soon follow near an old roadbed along a contour. This is a particularly peaceful and easy-to-walk part of the trail through a fine hardwood forest with yellow poplars, hemlocks, white pines, oaks, hickories, Fraser magnolias, buckeyes, and smaller dogwoods, sourwoods, high-bush blueberries. There are some exceptionally large grapevines growing up the taller trees. Dwarf crested iris, wood lily, showy orchis, pink and yellow lady's slippers, trilliums, bloodroot, and mayapples are just a few of the wildflowers that bloom in spring along the path.

The trail crosses Wolf Creek and drops quickly through Catawba rhododendron and mountain laurel thickets. It passes a boulder field as you look down on the stream. The junction with the yellow-blazed Coosa Backcountry Trail is next. Signs here mark the way to the park and to the Bear Hair, Coosa Backcountry, and Appalachian Trails. You cross Wolf Creek again on foot logs; the path with both

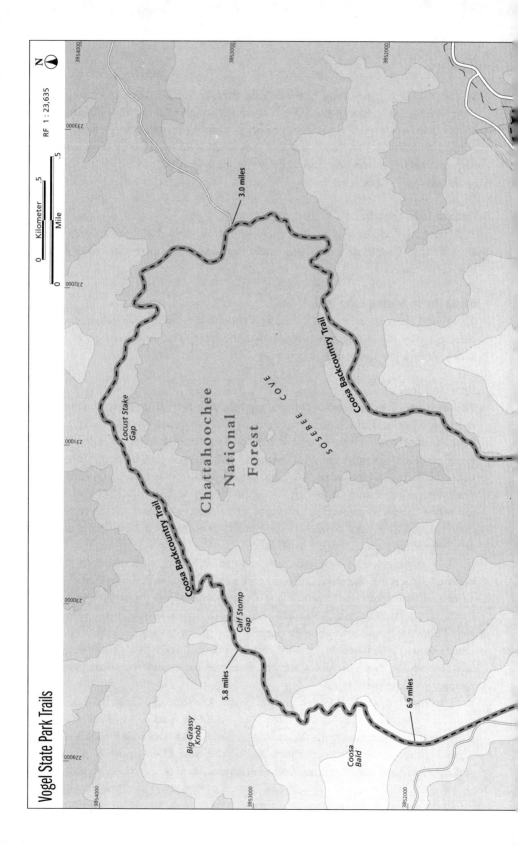

Vogel State Park Trails

RF 1 : 23,635

N

Kilometer

Mile

3.0 miles

Locust Stake
Gap

Coosa Backcountry Trail

Chattahoochee
National
Forest

SOSEBEE COVE

Coosa Backcountry Trail

Coosa Backcountry Trail

Calf Stomp
Gap

5.8 miles

Big Grassy
Knob

Coosa
Bald

6.9 miles

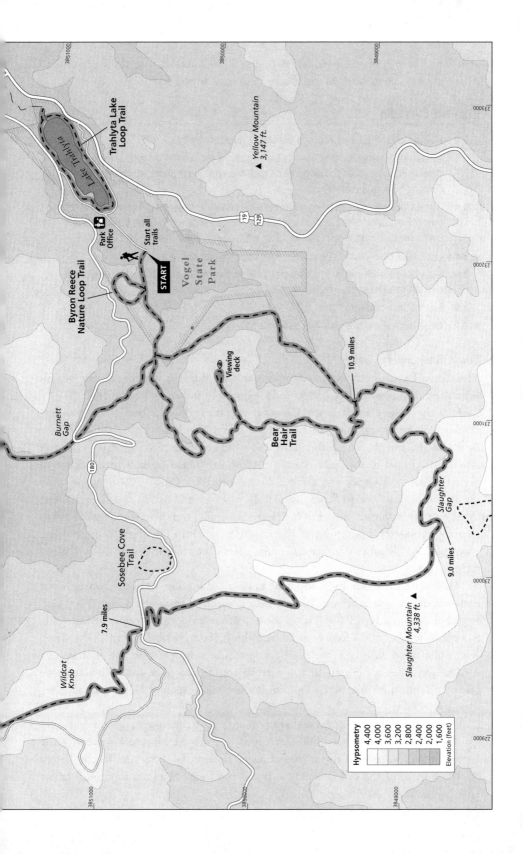

Trahlyta Lake
Loop Trail

Yellow Mountain
▲ 3,147 ft.

Park
Office

Start all
trails

START

Vogel
State
Park

Byron Reece
Nature Loop Trail

Viewing
deck

10.9 miles

Bear
Hair
Trail

Burnett
Gap

180

Slaughter
Gap

Sosebee Cove
Trail

9.0 miles

7.9 miles

Slaughter Mountain
▲ 4,338 ft.

Wildcat
Knob

Hypsometry
4,400
4,000
3,600
3,200
2,800
2,400
2,000
1,600
Elevation (feet)

yellow and orange blazes levels out through tall trees and back to the access trail to closed the loop. A turn to the right takes you back to the trailhead.

Miles and Directions

0.0 Start at the shared trailhead with the Coosa Backcountry Trail.

0.4 The two trails separate. Bear Hair Trail goes straight ahead; stay straight and follow the loop counterclockwise. Follow Burnett Creek and cross on a bridge, climbing to another crossing back to the other side.

1.4 A green-blazed spur trail takes off to the left. Follow the spur trail 0.1 mile to a platform overlook at 3,280 feet elevation and a beautiful view looking down on Trahlyta Lake. Backtrack to the Bear Hair loop and turn left.

2.4 Cross Wolf Creek; turn left and head east down several switchbacks.

2.6 Meet Coosa Backcountry Trail's yellow blazes and continue down to a more level area; turn left to head north.

3.6 End the loop and turn right.

4.2 Arrive back at the trailhead and parking area.

Coosa Backcountry Trail

The Coosa Backcountry Trail is strenuous and more than a day hike. A free permit from the park visitor center is required for camping overnight on this trail.

Like the Bear Hair Trail, the Coosa Backcountry loop is best hiked counterclockwise. It branches off to the right at the end of the access trail where it and the Bear Hair Trail begin. The path climbs up to Burnett Gap across Highway 180 and down an old road to the right of Forest Road 107. This road is followed down to West Fork of Wolf Creek and across it on a footbridge. Cross FR 107 and begin a steady climb up to Locust Stake Gap. This gap is used frequently as a campsite. The forest up to this point is similar to the Bear Hair Trail. From here you begin to experience the ridgetop hiking so plentiful in the mountains. The forest is more open, with oaks and hickories dominant. Virginia pines occur on the dry south- and west-facing slopes.

The trail climbs one high, rounded knob after another, only to drop between each one down to another gap. You reach Calf Stomp Gap, which is near 3,200 feet, as you cross Forest Road 108. This is about halfway around the loop. The next mile is a climb to the 4,000-foot contour and the junction with Duncan Ridge Trail, which is marked with blue blazes. The ridgetop here is open and flat, another area used frequently as a campsite. If you turn sharply to the right and follow the blue blaze for about 0.25 mile along Duncan Ridge Trail, you come to Coosa Bald (elevation 4,280 feet).

Off the trail to the southwest there is a large rock outcrop. In winter and early spring before the leaves have fully developed, you have an impressive view of the Cooper River Valley and the surrounding mountains. Backtracking to the Coosa Backcountry Trail, the yellow and blue blazes run together all the way to Slaughter

Gap, where Duncan Ridge Trail ends and Coosa Backcountry Trail drops down to Wolf Creek.

From Coosa Bald, the trail passes through Wildcat Gap and up Wildcat Knob. The elevation of the trail here is about 3,800 feet. The path now drops steeply to Wolfpen Gap and crosses Highway 180 again at Mile 7.9 (elevation 3,320 feet). One of the steepest climbs on the trail now winds up to the next knob at 4,145 feet, drops only slightly into a high gap over 4,000 feet, and then levels out as you go around the east side of Slaughter Mountain. The trail is on an old logging road and is very pleasant, with excellent conditions for spring and early-summer wildflowers. If you are hiking in April, this is also a good place to stop and watch for spring migrating birds. Ravens frequent this high ridge. A gentle slope down to Slaughter Gap connects you with the Appalachian Trail. Just before you get to the gap, the Coosa Backcountry Trail turns to the left (east) and descends rapidly for about a mile before it joins Bear Hair Trail and continues back to the park trailhead.

An interesting side trip from the Coosa Backcountry Trail is from Slaughter Gap to Blood Mountain on the Appalachian Trail. From Slaughter Gap it is only a 1.0-mile one-way hike up the Appalachian Trail to the top of Blood Mountain, the highest point in Georgia on this famous trail. At the mountaintop there is a stone trail shelter and grand views of the surrounding valleys and mountains. The hike up to Blood Mountain is a series of switchbacks along a well-worn path through Catawba rhododendron and mountain laurel thickets and gnarled oaks. The elevation at Blood Mountain is 4,461 feet, a climb of 580 feet from the gap.

Miles and Directions

0.0 Start at the shared trailhead for both Bear Hair and Coosa Backcountry Trails, 0.2 mile from the park office on the road to the campground.

0.4 The two trails separate. Bear Hair goes straight ahead. Turn right to follow the Coosa Backcountry Trail. (**FYI:** The trail to the left is the return path for both trails.)

1.0 After a steady climb, cross Highway 180 at Burnett Gap and follow an old road to the right of FR 107.

3.0 Cross Wolf Creek on a footbridge and quickly cross FR 107; begin a steady ascent in a westerly direction.

4.5 Reach the first of the ridge crests, Locust Stake Gap. This is a popular campsite.

5.8 Reach Calf Stomp Gap at about halfway around the loop; there's another campsite here. Begin walking in a more southerly direction.

6.9 At this relatively level area, meet the Duncan Ridge Trail (see Honorable Mentions). A sharp turn to the right takes you 0.25 mile on the blue-blazed trail to Coosa Bald at 4,271 feet. Return to the Coosa Backcountry Trail as Duncan Ridge and Coosa Backcountry run together, with both yellow and blue blazes.

7.9 Cross Highway 180 again, this time at Wolfpen Gap, and begin the steepest climb on the loop.

8.9 At the crest of an unnamed knoll, you are 4,145 feet above sea level.

9.0 Reach Slaughter Gap. Signs point the way to the Appalachian Trail and Blood Mountain. Make a sharp turn left (east) and head down to the Bear Hair Trail. (**Side trip:** Hike 2.0 miles out and back on the AT from Slaughter Gap to Blood Mountain, the highest point on the trail in Georgia at 4,461 feet.)

10.9 Meet the Bear Hair Trail with its orange blazes. Very quickly come to and cross Wolf Creek on foot logs. Continue down to a comparatively flat area, and turn north with the yellow and orange blazes.

12.3 Close the loop and turn right.

12.7 Return to the trailhead and parking area.

31 Unicoi State Park Trails

Unicoi State Park, conveniently located as a gateway into the higher mountains of the Southern Appalachians, is one of the most popular parks in Georgia. Three well-marked trails in the park provide hikers with diverse habitat and degree of difficulty. The featured Unicoi Lake Trail is an almost level walk around beautiful Unicoi Lake. Park personnel lead scheduled interpretive walks along the Lake and Bottoms Loop Trails, especially during spring flower and fall foliage seasons.

Start: Intersection of Highway 356 and the road to the Unicoi Lodge

Distance: Unicoi Lake Trail, 2.5-mile lollipop; Bottoms Loop Trail, 1.7-mile loop; Unicoi to Helen Trail, 4.8 miles out and back

Approximate hiking time: Unicoi Lake and Bottoms Loop Trails, 2 hours each; Unicoi to Helen Trail, 3 hours

Difficulty: Easy to moderate

Trail surface: Mostly dirt; a few short segments on paved and unpaved roads

Lay of the land: Rolling foothills very close to the higher mountains

Season: Year-round

Land status: Georgia State Parks Division

Nearest town: Helen

Fees and permits: Park Pass $3.00 per vehicle per day

Maps: USGS Helen and Tray Mountain; page-size Unicoi State Park trail maps available at the lodge

Trail contacts: Unicoi State Park, 943 Anna Ruby Falls Road, Helen, GA 30545; (706) 878-2201; www.gastateparks.org; www.georgia-atclub.org

Finding the trailhead: From Helen, travel north 1.0 mile on Highway 17/75 to Robertstown. Turn right on Highway 356 and go 1.0 mile to the UNICOI STATE PARK sign. A common trailhead for all hiking trails is at the junction of Highway 356 and the entrance to the Unicoi Lodge and Conference Center. These trails can also be accessed from the conference center parking area. The Unicoi to Helen Trail can also be hiked from Helen; that trailhead is on White Strasse, about 100 yards below the water tower.

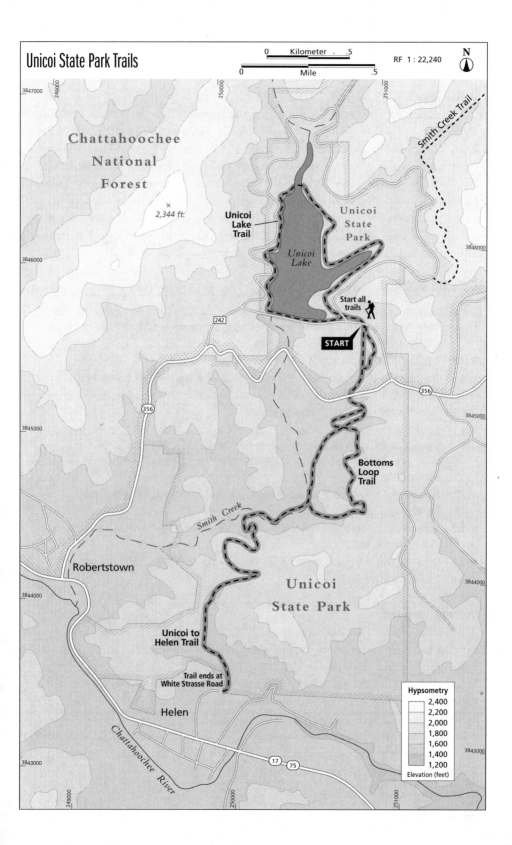

Unicoi State Park Trails

0 Kilometer .5
0 Mile .5

RF 1 : 22,240

N

Chattahoochee
National
Forest

× 2,344 ft.

Smith Creek Trail

Unicoi Lake Trail

Unicoi
State
Park

Unicoi
Lake

Start all trails

START

242

356

356

Bottoms
Loop
Trail

Smith Creek

Robertstown

Unicoi
State Park

Unicoi to
Helen Trail

Trail ends at
White Strasse Road

Helen

Chattahoochee River

17 75

Hypsometry

Elevation (feet)
2,400
2,200
2,000
1,800
1,600
1,400
1,200

The Hikes

Unicoi Lake Trail

The Unicoi Lake Trail is the easiest and most accessible trail in the park. The yellow-blazed path can be picked up at several locations. From the trailhead, it crosses the highway and continues around the lake, passing the cabins on the east side of the lake. After passing the Trading Post, the trail returns to the lakeshore. A floating footbridge crosses Smith Creek where it enters the lake. You can continue the hike up Smith Creek to a picnic area, where you cross the creek on a bridge. Here the trail turns back downstream to the floating bridge. Along the west side of the lake, the trail passes the day-use beach area and goes along the lake to the information center A-frame. You return to the lodge area by walking along the road crossing the dam.

Miles and Directions

0.0 Start at the common trailhead at the junction of Highway 356 and the road to the lodge. Cross the highway and turn left. Cross the road to the cabins and campground and head into the woods, following the yellow blazes.

0.2 Behind the cabins you begin to see the lake through the trees.

0.5 Cross the first stream behind the Trading Post. Continue into the open hillside field along the lakeshore.

0.75 Leave the open area and go into the woods.

1.1 Reach the floating footbridge across the Smith Creek arm of the lake. Cross the floating bridge; turn left and walk along the lakeshore. (**Option:** Continue up Smith Creek to a picnic area. Cross the creek on a bridge, then follow the trail back downstream to the floating bridge.)

1.2 Pass the day-use area with dock and swimming area; continue to follow the yellow blazes along the shore.

1.7 Arrive at the parking area, information A-frame, and Highway 356. Turn left and cross the dam along the road.

2.0 Close the loop at the road to the cabins. Continue across Highway 356 to the trailhead.

2.5 Arrive back at the trailhead.

Bottoms Loop Trail

The yellow-blazed Bottoms Loop Trail is an easy 1.7-mile hike that takes you through a variety of habitat types, including hardwood forests, dry pine stands, old homesites, wetland areas, streamside, and meadow. The trailhead is the same as for Unicoi Lake Trail. Park staff conducts scheduled guided walks, especially for spring flowers, on this well-marked and interesting trail. This is an excellent hike for a morning or late-afternoon hike. The terrain and habitat types are quite different from the older growth hardwood forest areas. Smith Creek is a much slower stream here and yet is still a good trout stream. The open fields offer a better opportunity to see deer and other mammals and birds.

Unicoi to Helen Trail

The Unicoi to Helen Trail, marked with green blazes, takes you to the resort town of Helen in 2.4 miles. You begin at the junction of Highway 356 and the road to the lodge, same as with the park's other trails. The path coincides with Bottoms Loop Trail for 0.7 mile, leaving it at the Smith Creek bridges. From here you follow Smith Creek 0.2 mile and cross the creek. You now begin to climb with switchbacks up one low ridge. At the ridge you traverse a contour on a pleasant wooded pathway for about 1.0 mile to the White Strasse trailhead at 2.4 miles. Up to the right you see a large water tower as you break out onto the road high on a ridge. To go into the town of Helen, follow White Strasse 0.2 mile down the road to Highway 17/75. Turn left to visit the main area of gift shops before your return hike.

32 Smithgall Woods and Dukes Creek Conservation Area Trails

The 5,604 acres of mountain woodlands here were acquired in 1994 as a gift to the state from conservationist Charles A. Smithgall. The Dukes Creek Conservation Area was dedicated to the purpose of protecting existing landscape, maintaining wildlife diversity, providing environmental education, and permitting low-impact recreational activities. The five marked trails here—all relatively short—are designed to interpret the natural and cultural history of the area. The featured Laurel Ridge Trail takes you from a moist streamside area to the drier ridge habitat and back. In addition to the hiking trails, more than 12 miles of paved and unpaved roads are available for walking and bike riding.

Start: Tsalaki Trail, the paved single-lane road through the park that begins at the entrance and visitor center
Distance: Laurel Ridge Trail, 1.5-mile loop
Approximate hiking time: 1 hour
Difficulty: Easy to moderate
Elevation gain/loss: 375 feet
Trail surface: Dirt; bark chip in a few places
Lay of the land: Rolling foothills next to the mountains
Season: Year-round
Land status: Georgia State Parks Division

Nearest towns: Helen, Cleveland
Fees and permits: Parking $3.00 per day per vehicle
Maps: USGS Cowrock and Helen; page-size map of conservation area with trails, available from the visitor center
Trail contacts: Smithgall Woods–Dukes Creek Conservation Area, 61 Tsalaki Trail, Helen, GA 30545; (706) 878-3087 or (706) 878-3520; www.gastateparks.org/info/smithgall; www.gastateparks.org

Finding the trailhead: From Helen go north 1.0 mile on Highway 75 to Robertstown. Turn left on Highway 75A and go 2.5 miles to the entrance for Dukes Creek Conservation Area on the left.

Smithgall Woods and Dukes Creek Conservation Area Trails

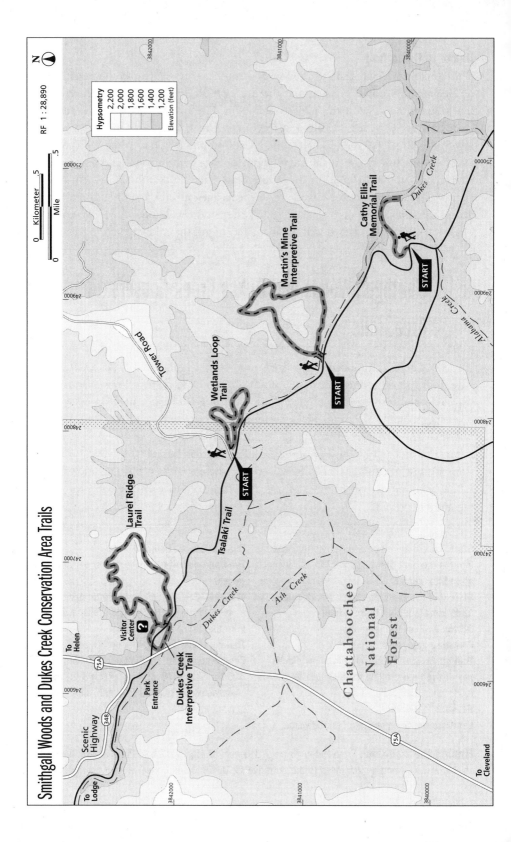

From Cleveland go north on U.S. Highway 129 for 3.0 miles to Highway 75A. Turn right and go 5.7 miles to the entrance on the right. The visitor center is on the left, and the Laurel Ridge Trail trailhead is at the visitor center parking area.

The Hike

Dukes Creek was the center of gold discovery in 1828, more than ten years before the California gold rush. Dukes Creek is also a fine trout stream managed for catch-and-release. Trout fishing using artificial lures with barbless hooks is permitted on Wednesday, Saturday, and Sunday. Although the 12 miles of narrow paved and unpaved roads are not described here, visitors are invited to walk or mountain bike the roads. Permits for hiking, biking, and fishing are available at the visitor center.

The visitor center is well worth the time spent here. You can pick up a map of the conservation area and get information about the trails in addition to permits for hiking, biking, and fishing. You can also take advantage of educational programs designed by the Smithgall Woods Conservation Education Team—a unique educational opportunity for students of all ages.

The 1.5-mile Laurel Ridge Trail is the most fascinating trail in the conservation area because of its variety of habitats. There are twenty-five marked places on the way, interpreted by a leaflet that discusses features at each waypoint. The trail begins at the end of the paved walkway, about 50 yards from the visitor center. A large information sign helps orient you to what you may see.

A well-marked bark-chip pathway leads to the first stop at the footbridge over a small brook that is habitat for trout. Along the streambank is yellowroot, one of the favorite medicinal plants of mountain people. From here the path enters a quiet forest of tall yellow poplars, hemlocks, white pines, maples, sourwoods, and dense thickets of rhododendron and dog-hobble. In summer, New York ferns form a green deep-pile carpet on the moist forest floor. In spring, trilliums, jack-in-the-pulpits, white baneberries (also called doll's eyes), Solomon's seals, and a host of other flowering plants bloom here and along the trail.

The path goes up the ridge and into a tunnel of rhododendron and mountain laurel, then into another cove and across another footbridge. White pines, maples, hemlocks, yellow poplars, and white oaks shade the ridge slope here. Under the canopy, the trail is lined with bear-huckleberry and other low shrubs. Ferns and mosses among the leaf-litter cover the porous soil.

Another footbridge crosses a permanent brook. At the end of the bridge is a tree trunk supporting a patch of resurrection fern. From here to the top of the ridge, the trail passes from the moist coves to the higher, drier forests. It does not take much elevation to do this, only a better-drained soil. Oaks, hickories, sourwoods, Virginia pines, thickets of mountain laurel, low-bush blueberries, and daisy-like flowering plants dominate. The nuts, acorns, and berries, called soft mast, are staple foods for deer, squirrels, opossums, black bears, chipmunks, and many birds. Another interesting plant beside the path is switch cane, which more frequently grows along river and creek banks. It is a close relative of the giant, or river, cane also found along creeks.

This ridge area is a great place to watch for fall migrations of hawks and vultures. In spring there will be an increase in the number of small birds in the trees as they migrate through.

For about 0.25 mile the trail goes along the crest of the ridge, rich with blueberry bushes and other thick vegetation. The bare trees of winter allow great views of the surrounding mountains. In summer the shade from the trees is welcome. A large opening in the trees affords a view of Yonah Mountain to the southeast. Very soon the trail descends a steep slope back into the cove. On the way down, the vegetation changes rapidly until you reach the mountain laurel and rhododendron tunnels and back to the New York fern glades as you close the loop.

Miles and Directions

0.0 Start at the visitor center trailhead. Walk down the pathway about 50 yards to the information sign and cross the footbridge.

0.2 Cross the first small bridge after walking through a corridor of mountain laurel and rhododendron.

0.7 Reach the top of the ridge with a view toward Helen.

1.0 Start the descent, first through open forest and then thick mountain laurel.

1.2 You're back to the trailhead level.

1.25 Turn right and walk through the fern glade to close the loop.

1.5 Arrive back at the trailhead.

Additional Trails

Four additional short trails in the conservation area are well worth walking.

Dukes Creek Interpretive Trail (0.3-mile loop; 30 minutes) is a short, flat walk beside a typical mountain trout stream. The trailhead is located at the Visitor Center on the paved Tsalaki Trail.

The **Wetlands Loop Trail** (0.6-mile loop; 30 minutes) is a good example of what happens in this mountain area when water is impounded by either beavers or humans. The trailhead is on Tsalaki Trail, 1.1 miles from the visitor center.

The **Martin's Mine Interpretive Trail** (1.5-mile loop; 1 hour) walks you through the history of early gold mining. Special guided tours are available by advanced registration (check Web site for dates). The trailhead is on Tsalaki Trail at the bridge across Dukes Creek, 2.2 miles from the visitor center

The **Cathy Ellis Memorial Trail** (1.0 mile out and back; 1 hour) is a pleasant walk to a small but beautiful cascading waterfall on Alabama Branch—where "gold mining began with the discovery of a gold nugget in 1828 by a salve of Major Franck Logano." The trailhead is on Tsalaki Trail, 3.0 miles from the visitor center on the left.

More Information

Food/Lodging

Tucked away in a forested wilderness setting, the Lodge at Smithgall Woods offers upscale rustic accommodations with gourmet cuisine.

For information and reservations call (800) 864-7275 or visit www.gastateparks.org/info/smithgall.

33 Moccasin Creek Wildlife Trail and Hemlock Falls Trail

The two trails on Moccasin Creek are accessed by the same road and are so close together they can be hiked as one or separately. The Wildlife Trail is a 1.2-mile loop. Hemlock Falls Trail goes through a typical hardwood forest, with Moccasin Creek in sight most of the way, to a waterfall. The road to the Hemlock Falls trailhead bisects the Wildlife Trail. At the first crossing you are only about 0.5 mile from this trailhead, making it easy to combine the two trails for a combined hike of about 3.0 miles.

Start: Wildlife Trail, at the fenced picnic area as you turn onto Andersonville Road; Hemlock Falls Trail, 0.5 mile farther at the boulder marked with the trail name

Distance: Wildlife Trail, 1.2-mile loop; Hemlock Falls Trail, 2.2 miles out and back; hiked together, total hiking distance about 3.5 miles up and back to the falls

Approximate hiking time: Wildlife Trail, 1½ hours; Falls Trail, 2 hours; both trails combined, 4 hours

Difficulty: Easy

Elevation gain/loss: Wildlife Trail, 158 feet; Falls Trail, 374 feet

Trail surface: Dirt; some gravel road

Lay of the land: Mountain streamside

Season: Year-round: best spring and fall

Land status: Georgia Department of Wildlife Resources and Chattahoochee National Forest

Nearest town: Clayton

Fees and permits: No fees or permits required

Maps: USGS Lake Burton; page-size map of the Wildlife Trail, available at the Lake Burton Fish Hatchery Office

Trail contacts: USDA Forest Service, Tallulah Ranger District, Highway 41, P.O. Box 438, Clayton, GA 30525; (706) 782-3320; www.fs.fed.us/conf

Moccasin Creek State Park, Route 1, Box 1634, Clarksville, GA 30523; (706) 947-3194; www.gastateparks.org

Lake Burton Fish Hatchery, Route 1, Box 1638, Clarksville, GA 30523; (706) 947-3112; www.gofishgeorgia.com; www.georgiawildlife.com

Finding the trailhead: From Clayton go west 11.5 miles on U.S. Highway 76 to Highway 197. Turn left and go 3.8 miles to the MOCCASIN CREEK STATE PARK sign; turn right on Andersonville Road. The trailhead for the Wildlife Trail is directly across Highway 197 from the Lake Burton State Fish Hatchery and Moccasin Creek State Park on Andersonville Road at the fenced parking area on the right. The trailhead for the Hemlock Falls Trail is at the end of the same road. Continue 0.5 mile past the parking area for the Wildlife Trail to the backcountry camping area. The name of the trail has been carved into a large boulder that serves as a barrier to vehicles.

Moccasin Creek Wildlife Trail and Hemlock Falls Trail

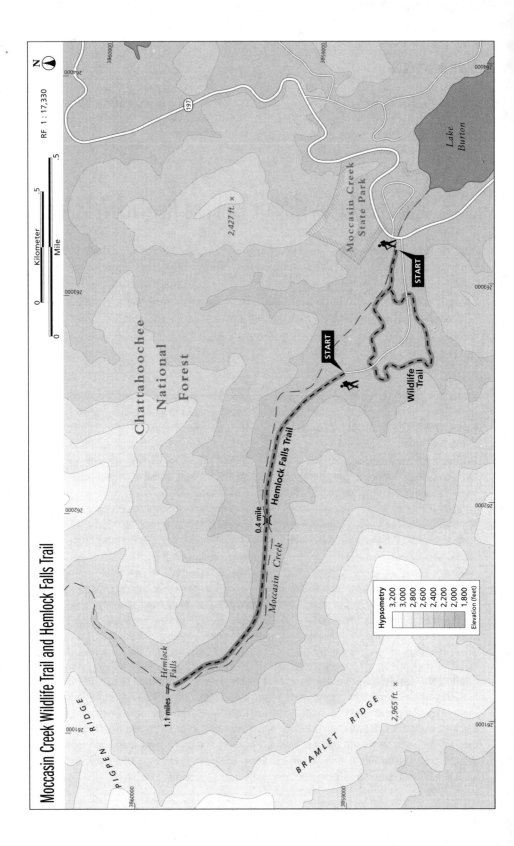

Lake Burton, Moccasin Creek State Park, and Lake Burton Fish Hatchery are a few yards away. Aside from RV and tent camping at Moccasin Creek State Park, there is trout fishing in a section of the creek reserved for children under age twelve and senior citizens. At the hatchery there is a pond just for children's fishing. Boating, sightseeing, and quality fishing are at Lake Burton.

Wildlife Trail

The Wildlife Trail is a team effort by the Georgia Department of Natural Resources personnel from the Lake Burton Fish Hatchery, Lake Burton Wildlife Management Area, and Moccasin Creek State Park. The trail is designed to show some of the wildlife management principles and structures that are beneficial to both game and nongame animals. Along the path are interpretive signs describing fish and wildlife management practices or some of the devices used to monitor habitat and populations.

The well-marked trail begins at the small fenced park with picnic tables. The trail is on the bank of Moccasin Creek at the water-control dam that supplies water for the fish hatchery. An information board describes the trail and its purpose. Stakes with a metal disc, an orange stripe around the top, and an arrow direct you around the loop. As you walk the trail, you cross the small streams and branches on sturdy footbridges.

Interpretive signs and markers provide information and are placed strategically along the trail. The first of these is a bat box on a yellow poplar. The next interpretive sign describes a wildlife food plot. Another talks about the watershed, and so on as you walk. This is an exceptionally good trail for children to see and learn more about plants and wildlife and how they relate. The last sign describes some of the techniques used to improve the trout-holding capacity of streams. You are now near the end of the trail, which completes the loop back to the picnic and parking area.

Option: To combine the Wildlife and Falls Trails, start with the Wildlife Trail. When you hit the road that leads to the Falls Trail, turn right and follow the road 590 feet to the trailhead. Hike the Falls Trail out and back and when you return to the intersection of the road and the Wildlife Trail, turn right and complete the loop to the trailhead.

Hemlock Falls Trail

Hemlock Falls Trail is an easy walk along Moccasin Creek, a beautiful, tumbling trout stream, to a waterfall. The trail begins at the end of the access road. You pass the parking area for the Wildlife Trail and the check station for the Lake Burton Wildlife Management Area. At the end of the road is a backcountry campsite and parking area. The large boulder in the road engraved with the trail name is the trailhead. The trail is blazed with small metal diamonds attached to trees along the way.

For the first 200 or 300 yards, the trail follows an old roadbed that at one time was also a railroad bed for hauling saw logs out of the forest. Along the streamside and well up the bank along the trail, rosebay rhododendron is the most obvious cover. Dog-hobble, mountain laurel, bear-huckleberry, dogwood, and many other shrubs contribute to the dense trailside vegetation. In spring, before the leaves are on the trees, trilliums, jack-in-the-pulpits, anemones, and many other flowers are in bloom. Dogwoods, silverbells, yellow poplars, buckeyes, and other trees bloom along with shrubs like dog-hobble and sweet shrub. The predominant ferns are the New York and Christmas ferns. White pine, hemlock, yellow poplar, oak, maple decidu-ous magnolia, birch, and beech are the predominant forest trees.

At 0.3 mile, look across the creek for a small waterfall on a tributary branch of Moccasin Creek. It may not be flowing during very dry weather. Just a few yards far-ther you will see a large rock overhang on the left side of the trail. Should you get caught in one of the frequent spring or summer thundershowers, think rain shelter.

A wooden footbridge crosses Moccasin Creek at 0.4 mile. After this the trail con-tinues up the right side of the stream. The valley is narrower, the ridges are higher, the stream is more turbulent, and you are in shade even at midday. The path is nar-rower right up to the falls. You have just gained about 520 feet in elevation. Hem-lock Falls is not very high, only about 30 feet, but it is an attractive, wide flow as it plunges into a large pool—a favorite with trout fishermen. The large broken boul-ders outside the pool make rustic benches. This is one of those delightful areas in the mountains where a quiet rest is welcome and rewarding. The trail ends at the falls, so retrace your steps to the trailhead.

Note: The unmarked trail above the falls follows Moccasin Creek and South Fork Moccasin Creek, which flows down from the highland ridge that includes Tray Mountain. You eventually reach Addis Gap and the Appalachian Trail.

Miles and Directions

0.0 Start at the large boulder in the road engraved with the trail name.

0.3 Look for a small but picturesque waterfall on the opposite side of Moccasin Creek.

0.4 Cross a footbridge over Moccasin Creek.

1.1 Arrive at Hemlock Falls, trail's end and your turnaround point.

2.2 Arrive back at the trailhead.

34 Black Rock Mountain State Park Trails

At 3,640 feet, Black Rock Mountain State Park is the highest state park in Georgia. The park's trails offer a variety of mountain environments and unusual plant diversity. Ada-Hi Falls Trail is a series of steps down to an observation deck providing a good view of the falls. The yellow-blazed Tennessee Rock Trail loops through a north-facing mountain slope that supports a wide variety of wildflowers and breaks out on top of Black Rock Mountain (elevation 3,280 feet), following the Eastern Continental Divide. The orange-blazed James E. Edmonds Backcountry Trail shares a trailhead and similar habitat with the Tennessee Rock Trail but descends lower into the valley before climbing to a grand view at the Lookout Mountain bluff.

Start: Ada-Hi Falls, at the campground concession and trading post; Tennessee Rock and Backcountry Trails, at the day-use area near the springhouse on Black Rock Road
Distance: Ada-Hi Falls Trail, 0.4 mile out and back; Tennessee Rock Trail, 2.2-mile loop; James E. Edmonds Backcountry Trail, 6.3-mile lollipop
Approximate hiking time: Ada-Hi Falls Trail, 1 hour; Tennessee Rock Trail, 1½ hours; James E. Edmonds Backcountry Trail, 3 hours
Difficulty: Ada-Hi Falls Trail, strenuous; Tennessee Rock Trail, moderate; James E. Edmonds Backcountry Trail, moderate to strenuous
Elevation gain/loss: Ada-Hi Falls, 220 feet

Trail surface: Dirt and firm loam; Ada-Hi Falls, wooden stairway
Lay of the land: Mountainous
Season: Spring to early summer for wildflowers; fall for spectacular fall foliage; road closed to top of mountain during winter snow and ice
Land status: Georgia State Parks Division
Nearest towns: Mountain City, Clayton
Fees and permits: Park Pass $3.00 per vehicle per day
Maps: USGS Dillard; detailed page-size map available from visitor center
Trail contacts: Black Rock Mountain State Park, Mountain City, GA 30562; (706) 746-2141; www.gastateparks.org; www.georgia-atclub.org

Finding the trailhead: From Clayton go north 3.0 miles on U.S. Highway 441 to Mountain City. Turn left (west) at the BLACK ROCK MOUNTAIN PARK sign and go 2.5 miles into park. The Ada-Hi Falls trailhead is at the concession and trading post area near the campground. The trailhead for the Tennessee Rock and James E. Edmonds Backcountry Trails is at the graveled day-use parking and picnic area on the main access road near the large free-flowing spring and springhouse.

The Hikes

Located in the northeast corner of Georgia, the park's 1,502 acres lie along the ridgeline of the Eastern Continental Divide, 2,700 feet above the valley at Clayton. Many scenic overlooks offer views of the surrounding southern Appalachian Mountains. The park offers a variety of activities for visitors, including wildflower programs, nature walks, and overnight backpacking trips.

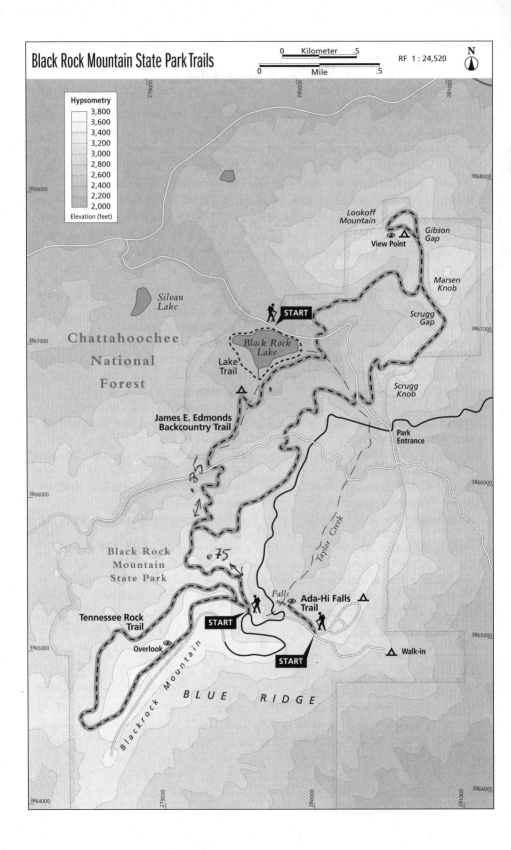

Black Rock Mountain State Park Trails

Kilometer | .5
Mile | .5

RF 1 : 24,520

N

Hypsometry

3,800
3,600
3,400
3,200
3,000
2,800
2,600
2,400
2,200
2,000
Elevation (feet)

Silvan Lake

Chattahoochee

National

Forest

Lookoff Mountain

View Point

Gibson Gap

Marsen Knob

Scrugg Gap

START

Black Rock Lake

Lake Trail

Scrugg Knob

James E. Edmonds Backcountry Trail

Park Entrance

85

Taylor Creek

75

Black Rock Mountain State Park

Falls

Ada-Hi Falls Trail

Tennessee Rock Trail

START

Overlook

START

△ Walk-in

Blackrock Mountain

B L U E   R I D G E

Ada-Hi Falls Trail

This strenuous trail takes you down from the concession and trading post area. It is only 0.2 mile one-way, but in that short walk the trail drops 220 feet. As hikers say "It's 0.2 mile down and 5.2 miles back up." But it is a beautiful hike with nice views in winter when the leaves have fallen. A series of steps made from stone, log, and wood lead down to a small but enchanting waterfall in a dense rhododendron thicket. Rock ledges and overhangs add variety to the setting. The path ends at a level observation platform, affording fine views of the stream cascading and sliding down about 80 feet of sheer granite.

Tennessee Rock Trail

The yellow-blazed Tennessee Rock Trail starts at a moderate climb up log steps. It then follows the contour wherever possible through a hardwood forest of oaks, hickories, yellow poplars, sourwoods, dogwoods, and black gums. Turning into the north-facing slope, the cooler, moister habitat is marked by moss-covered logs and ferns, including marginal, Christmas, New York, and wood ferns. Spring wildflowers include hepatica, bloodroot, halberd-leaved and Canada violets, and showy orchid. Mountain laurel blooms later in spring, with rhododendron in June. This trail is designed as a self-guided nature trail. A leaflet, available at the park office, explains conditions and species at some of the twenty-five stations along the way. The trail leads through several beautiful coves below boulder fields, some with springs.

The path joins an old roadbed for a short distance. The walking becomes much easier as it enters a white pine stand and climbs to the ridge crest, where a sign indicates that the trail turns sharply to the left. You now walk to the top of Black Rock Mountain. Here the elevation is 3,640 feet, and during late fall and winter, when the trees are bare, neighboring mountain ranges are visible. The old skeletal remains of American chestnut trees are still easy to recognize along the way. Some are much larger than any of the living oaks and hickories that have replaced them. Hiking now on the south face of the mountain, the view is straight down to the town of Clayton, about 2,000 feet below. This crest of the ridge is the Eastern Continental Divide. Water on the south side goes into the Atlantic Ocean by way of the Savannah River. The north drainage flows into the Tennessee and Mississippi River systems and into the Gulf of Mexico.

One of the most magnificent views in the north Georgia mountains is from the granite outcrop reached by a set of wooden steps. On a clear day, the Great Smoky Mountains in North Carolina can be seen on the far horizon. Walking through a tunnel of rhododendron, the trail comes very close to one of the roads that lead to a cottage area. You continue with the yellow blazes back down the mountain to the trailhead, completing a 2.2-mile loop.

Miles and Directions

0.0 Start at the common trailhead with the Backcountry Trail at 3,280 feet elevation.

0.1 Turn right at the fork and begin the loop.

0.3 You are in the north-facing cove with many species of flowering plants, especially those that bloom in spring.

0.6 Turn right and begin a climb to an old roadbed.

0.7 At the road turn left at the ridge crest—a major drainage divide.

1.5 After crossing the divide, follow the blazes and climb the steps to the observation deck. This the high point on the trail (elevation 3,640 feet).

2.1 Close the loop.

2.2 Arrive back at the trailhead.

James E. Edmonds Backcountry Trail

This backcountry trail shares a trailhead with Tennessee Rock Trail but is marked with orange blazes. Instead of beginning a climb up the mountain, this trail begins a 0.5-mile gradual descent that is moderately steep in some places until it reaches a fork in the path. The right fork takes you in a counterclockwise direction around a loop that comes back to the fork and then backtracks uphill to the trailhead.

As the trail breaks out of the evergreen rhododendrons into the hardwood coves, you can look down on Black Rock Lake through the trees. Great patches of galax grow all along the trail. (Galax sometimes emits an odor resembling the scent of skunk.) Other spring wildflowers are abundant all along the trail. You cross a tributary of Greasy Creek in another of the frequent rhododendron thickets that are beautiful when in bloom.

Following along an old roadbed, the path comes out in a gap and soon crosses the road from Mountain City to Germany Valley. Crossing the road into another rhododendron tunnel, the trail alternates from open hardwoods to streamside rhododendron as it follows Taylor Creek. The trail crosses the creek on a footbridge and bends back, climbing to a gravel road to Black Rock Lake. Across the road the path begins the long, steady 600-foot climb up to Scruggs Knob and along the watershed divide through Scruggs Gap. It then goes along an old roadbed under the crest of Marsen Knob into Gibson Gap. Here the trail turns back down the mountain toward Black Rock Lake or goes up the steeper climb to Lookoff Mountain. The spur trail to Lookoff Mountain is a loop that goes to the granite outcrop that gives the mountain its name. The view from here is spectacular. A cable fence with stone-masonry pillars protects the edge of the sheer drop. The north-by-northwest view looks down more than 1,000 feet to the headwater valley of the Little Tennessee River and the attractive farms on its floodplain.

Returning to Gibson Gap, you've completed half of 6.3-mile hike. The return trail drops quickly to the head of Black Rock Lake. Cross Taylor Creek on a footbridge at a lower point than before, and follow along the south side of the lake to

Greasy Creek. Greasy Creek is a small, very pretty mountain stream that literally slides down the mountain over the exposed granite that is covered in places with algae. The algae gives the stream a slick appearance, hence the name. In most places, the creek slides through a thick cover of rhododendron. You cross the creek on another footbridge before the trail returns to the end of the loop section and climbs about 700 feet back to the trailhead.

Miles and Directions

0.0 Start at the common trailhead with Tennessee Rock Trail.

0.6 Meet the fork in the trail that starts the loop. Go right.

0.8 Cross a small tributary of Greasy Creek.

1.4 Cross Hell Cat Creek Road.

1.7 You can look down on Black Rock Lake through the trees.

1.9 Cross Taylor Creek and Taylor Chapel Road.

2.3 Pass on the north side of Scrugg Knob and continue on a ridge to Scrugg Gap.

2.8 On the west side of Marsen Knob, come to the spur path leading to Lookoff Mountain.

3.0 Begin the loop to the granite outcrop edge of the mountain.

3.2 Reach the "lookoff" at about 3,100 feet elevation. (**FYI:** The stone pillars were placed here years ago to keep people from getting too close to the edge.)

3.6 Complete the lookoff loop and backtrack to the main trail. Turn right, heading down to Black Rock Lake.

4.3 Cross Taylor Chapel Road again

4.4 Cross Taylor Creek on a footbridge.

4.8 Cross Greasy Creek on a footbridge.

5.2 Cross the small headwater stream of Greasy Creek and begin to regain all the elevation lost from the trailhead.

5.7 Meet the trail to close the loop; continue to climb.

6.3 Arrive back at the trailhead.

Additional Trails

The easy **Black Rock Lake Loop Trail** (0.8-mile loop; 1 hour) is a pleasant, level walk with good opportunities to see wildlife, especially native and migratory waterbirds.

More Information

Food/Lodging

Dillard House, 1158 Franklin Street, Dillard, GA 30537; (800) 541-0671 or (706) 746-5348; www.dillardhouse.com/dining.html. An old family-style restaurant with mountain atmosphere and fine lodging accommodations.

35 Tallulah Gorge State Park Trails

Opened in 1992, Tallulah Gorge State Park is one of the newest state parks in Georgia, the result of a lease agreement between the Georgia Power Company and the Department of Natural Resources. The word *Tallulah* has its origin in the Cherokee language but cannot be translated. There are more than 20 miles of trails in the park, including hiking and biking trails. A free permit, available at the interpretive center, is required for trails going down into the gorge. The featured Stoneplace Trail is completely out of the gorge as it winds along the ridges and old logging roads of the upland. Near the end of the trail you come to the jeep road down to Tugaloo Lake at a canoe and small boat launching access. The High Bluff side loop bypasses about 0.6 mile of the Stoneplace Trail.

Start: Jane Hurt Yarn Interpretive Center parking area

Distance: Stoneplace Trail, 9.2 miles out and back; 10.4 miles out and back with High Bluff side trail

Approximate hiking time: Stoneplace Trail with High Bluff side trail, 5 hours

Difficulty: Stoneplace Trail, moderate to strenuous

Elevation gain/loss: 1,592 feet descending; 750 feet climbing

Trail surface: Varied, including shredded auto tire composition, asphalt paved, and dirt

Lay of the land: River gorge and upland

Season: Year-round

Land status: Georgia State Parks Division

Nearest towns: Clayton, Clarkesville

Fees and permits: Park Pass $3.00 per day per vehicle; special permits required for certain of the more dangerous or strenuous trails and for use of Adirondack shelter

Maps: USGS Tallulah Falls and Tugaloo Lake; page-size maps of trails, available at the Jane Hurt Yarn Interpretive Center

Trail contacts: Tallulah Gorge State Park, P.O. Box 248, Tallulah Falls, GA 30573; (706) 754-7970; www.gastateparks.org/

Finding the trailhead: From Clarkesville go 9.0 miles on Highway 365 to U.S. Highway 441/23. Go 17.0 miles to TALLULAH GORGE STATE PARK sign and turn right on Jane Hurt Yarn Drive. From Clayton go south 21.0 miles on US 441 to the TALLULAH GORGE STATE PARK sign. Turn left on Jane Hurt Yarn Drive and go 0.8 mile to the Jane Hurt Yarn Interpretive Center. All park trails can be accessed from the interpretive center and its parking areas. The South Rim trails can also be accessed from a private parking area off US 441/23.

The Hike

The Tallulah Gorge area has a long history as a scenic area and summer resort, beginning in the mid-1880s. The park's Jane Hurt Yarn Interpretive Center exhibits the rich history of the Victorian town of Tallulah Falls along with the rugged terrain and fragile ecosystem of the area. On July 18, 1970, aerialist Karl Wallenda crossed the gorge on a high wire.

Tallulah Gorge. ▶

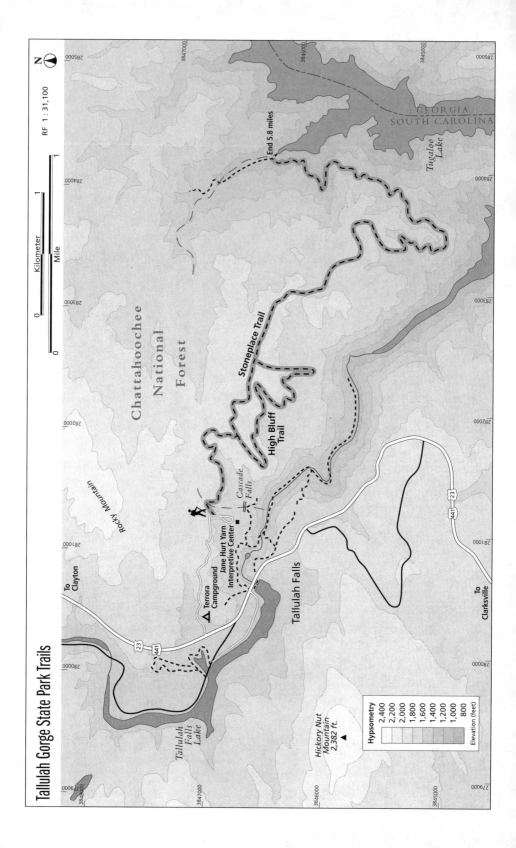

Tallulah Gorge State Park Trails

The yellow-blazed Stoneplace Trail reaches Tugaloo Lake in 4.6 miles. (If you follow the High Bluff side trail to the lake, the one-way hike is 5.8 miles.) Tugaloo Lake is on the Chattooga River, tributary to the Tallulah River, which flows through the gorge.

The trailhead is at the end of the parking area from the interpretive center. Instead of passing along the gorge, the trail uses old logging roads that traverse the ridges and valleys of the area to the north and east of the gorge. The Stoneplace Trail varies from 1,700 feet at its highest point to 900 feet at the level of Tugaloo Lake. (The rim trails are at about 1,600 feet.) Stoneplace Trail is designated for hiking and biking, which should pose little problem—the logging roads are wide enough for hikers and bikers to pass without incident. The 1.7-mile High Bluff Trail is designated hiking only.

At first you go through a cove with yellow poplars, pines, sourwoods, and oaks. Grapevines, high-bush huckleberries, and an abundance of seedling sourwood trees make a green wall beside the trail. In spring there will be many flowering plants in bloom, especially in the coves where the hillside is steep above and below the trail. The surface of the trail is sandy clay. Impressions of animal tracks are easy to see. After the cove area, you are in a more open area as you reach the top of a ridge. Other roads join the trail road; just follow the yellow blazes.

At 0.8 mile you intersect the beginning of the blue-blazed High Bluff Trail. Turn right to follow this more scenic path (the loop returns to the Stoneplace Trail in 1.7 miles). You go through a shaded, moist cove with rhododendron, galax, and spring flowers along with white oak, yellow poplar, dogwood, black gum, and maple trees. You hike under a high power line. The trail follows around a more exposed, western slope where bracken ferns grow, with a view of the opposite side of the gorge. In summer this view is partially blocked by tree leaves; it is more scenic in winter. The trail goes in and out of the dry ridge site to the moister cove areas with rhododendron, yellow poplar, hemlock, and white pine. The low vegetation includes galax, partridgeberry, and ferns, and the usual spring wildflowers. You come back to the yellow-blazed trail; turn left to hike back 1.3 miles to the interpretive center, or turn right to continue to Tugaloo Lake.

At 4.9 miles you come to an Adirondack shelter on the right several yards below the trail. Overnight camping permits for this shelter are available at the interpretive center.

The last mile of the trail is through a more moist forest with steep slopes. When you reach the gravel road, you know you are at the lake—even though you cannot see it in summer. Turn right, go down the road, and cross a small stream. Four-wheel-drive vehicles can get to this point by another road, which is used to launch canoes or small boats in Tugaloo Lake. This lake is on the Chattooga River, which forms the state line between Georgia and South Carolina. As it comes out of the gorge, the Tallulah River joins the Chattooga River. Georgia Power Company's Tugaloo Dam impounds both rivers at this confluence.

Miles and Directions

0.0 Start at the interpretive center parking area trailhead, and follow the yellow blazes.

0.8 Turn right onto the blue-blazed High Bluff Trail.

1.0 Reach the first of the wintertime viewpoints that afford a great view of the gorge area. Follow the trail around to the left.

2.2 After following close to the 1,600-foot contour, come to the second point with a good view of the gorge area. Turn left and continue uphill.

2.5 Rejoin the Stoneplace Trail. Turn right to continue to Tugaloo Lake. (**Bailout:** Turn left to return to the interpretive center in 1.3 miles.)

3.8 Pass under the high power line.

4.8 Return to the power line, indicating that you have changed directions 180 degrees.

4.9 Just below the trail is an Adirondack shelter. (**FYI:** A free permit, available at the interpretive center, is required to camp at this shelter.)

5.7 Cross a small stream and come to the gravel road leading down to the lake.

5.8 Arrive at Stoneplace, with a small craft launching site. This is a good place to picnic or rest before your return hike to the interpretive center. It is 4.6 miles back without retracing the High Bluff Trail.

10.4 Arrive back at the trailhead.

Additional Trails

The North and South Rim Trails provide the best views and understanding of the gorge and local and natural history. A free permit, available at the interpretive center, is required for these trails. Several species of plants and animals are found in the gorge and nowhere else in the area, including the endangered persistent trillium and the rare green salamander. The rim trails are easy. Stairway trails into the gorge and crossing on the bridge, a 600-foot wooden stairway down to the bottom of the gorge, and the Wallenda Cable Trail are strenuous and not recommended for visitors with health problems.

The **North Rim Trail** (1.4 miles out and back; 1 hour) and **South Rim Trail** (1.2 miles out and back; 1 hour) follow the gorge escarpment. These time frames allow for time spent at the ten strategically placed overlooks along the rim. Hiked together by crossing the suspension bridge, the rim trails are about 5.0 miles out and back.

The **Hurricane Falls Bridge** connector trail and the **South Gorge Access Trail** (about 1 hour each) comprise a series of wonderfully crafted stairs to the bottom of the gorge connected by a 600-foot suspension bridge 80 feet above the river.

The **Wallenda Cable Trail** (2.0 miles out and back from Overlook 10; 1 hour) reaches the bottom of the gorge downstream. A permit is required to use this trail.

36 Victoria Bryant State Park Trails

Four interconnected trails totaling 10.6 miles give you many hiking options of varying lengths and habitats. The Perimeter Trail goes around the park boundary through a variety of wildlife habitats, including an observation platform over a wildlife food plot. The Victoria's Path Nature Trail, with interpretive signs and an overlook, takes you along both sides of Rice Creek. The newer Broad River Trail takes you outside the main park area to two watercourses and an observation platform on a beaver pond.

Start: Victoria's Path Nature Trail, at the parking area on Rice Creek; Perimeter and Broad River Trails, at the fishpond near the park entrance
Distance: Victoria's Path Nature Trail, 0.5 mile loop; Perimeter Trail, 2.7-mile loop; Inner Loop Trail, 2.5-mile loop; Broad River Trail, 3.5-mile loop
Approximate hiking time: Victoria's Path Nature Trail, 30 minutes; Perimeter Trail, 1½ hours; Inner Loop Trail, 1 hour; Broad River Trail, 3½ hours
Difficulty: Victoria Path Nature Trail, easy; Perimeter Trail, easy to moderate; Inner Loop Trail, moderate; Broad River Trail, moderate

Elevation gain/loss: Perimeter Trail, 210 feet climbing, 156 feet descending; Broad River Trail, 351 feet climbing, 430 feet descending
Trail surface: Dirt; some paved roadway
Lay of the land: Rolling foothills of the upper Piedmont
Season: Year-round
Land status: Georgia State Parks Division
Nearest town: Royston
Fees and permits: Park Pass $3.00 per day per vehicle
Maps: USGS Carnesville; page-size map, available at the park office
Trail contacts: Victoria Bryant State Park, 1105 Bryant Park Road, Royston, GA 30662; (706) 245-6270; www.gastateparks.org

Finding the trailhead: From exit 166 off Interstate 85, go right (south) 1.5 miles on Highway 145 to Carnesville. Continue 8.1 miles to U.S. Highway 29. Turn left and go about 100 yards; turn left on Highway 327 and go 0.7 mile to the park entrance on the left. The trailhead for the Victoria's Path Nature Trail is the parking area on Rice Creek just below the office and concession building. The trailhead for the Perimeter Trail is at the fishpond only a few yards from the park entrance. The Broad River Trail is accessed at Mile 1.0 on the Perimeter Trail.

The Hikes

The entire Victoria Bryant State Park system is interconnected, providing a wide variety of hiking options. All trails except Victoria's Path Nature Tail are for both hiking and biking. The park has an eighteen-hole Highland Walk golf course, a swimming pool, tent and trailer camping, and a wheelchair-accessible fishing pond.

Victoria's Path Nature Trail

The Nature Trail is an attractive loop walk beginning at the parking area on Rice Creek. This trail, constructed by Scout Troop 70 as an Eagle Scout project in 1984,

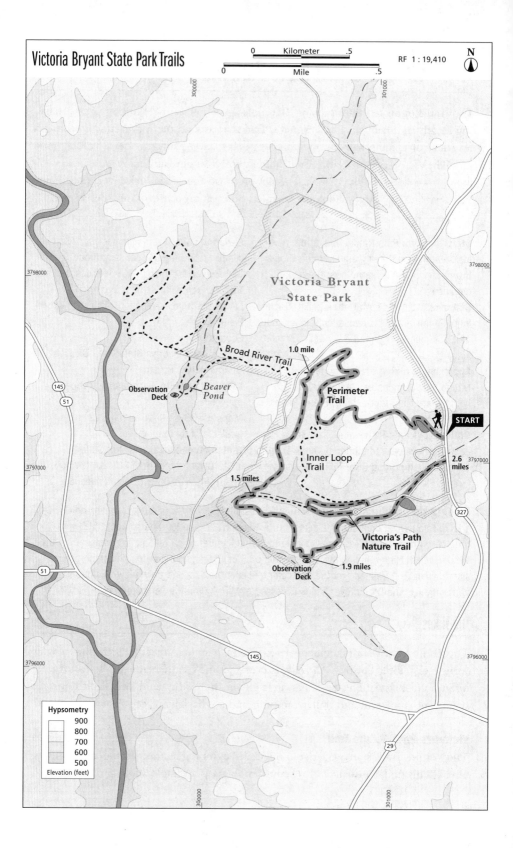

goes downstream through the mountain laurel and dog-hobble that are thick on both sides of the stream. Sixteen numbered stations, described in a pamphlet available from the park office, explain the points of interest along the trail. An overlook platform affords a nice view of the creek and dense laurel thicket. This side of the creek is a north-facing slope where galax, Christmas ferns, Robin's plantain, and a number of other shade-tolerant plants grow. The forest is mostly hardwoods, with dogwoods growing beneath the larger trees. You get a good look into the creek from the footbridge that takes the trail up the other side of the creek. Switch cane growing along the river here gives the trail a tropical atmosphere. This walk is especially interesting during early spring when wildflowers are in bloom. Mountain laurel blooms from late April into May along with the dog-hobble. You cross rock outcrops with the help of wooden railings, then continue through the laurel to the roadway, up to another bridge, and on to the parking area.

This walk provides a good look at the difference between the plant life on the north-facing slope on the downstream side and the south-facing slope on the opposite side. More ferns, mosses, and shade-tolerant plants live on the north-facing side. The south-facing side is drier and has more open forest floor.

Perimeter Trail

The Perimeter Trail begins at the fishpond on the entrance road. It is paved and barrier free for about 100 yards, offering wheelchair access to an observation deck that overlooks the two-acre pond. This is an excellent place for viewing wildlife or fishing. Canada geese nest on a small island near the deck. At the end of the pavement, the wide path climbs the side of the small valley.

Fiberglass posts with arrows point the way of the trail. The forest here is a second-growth stand of typical Piedmont hardwoods—oaks and hickories—with dogwoods, redbuds, and other smaller trees growing underneath. The flowering trees put on a great show in spring. The Inner Loop Trail takes off to the left at 0.5 mile. Stands of switch cane grow in the bottom of the sharp valleys with intermittent streams. At 1.0 mile the Broad River Trail takes off to the right. Erosion gullies, now healed, indicate past farming in the area. You pass an impressive stand of American holly and mountain laurel interspersed with switch cane. This evergreen area merges with the vegetation of Rice Creek, which you cross on a sturdy footbridge at 1.5 miles. In early spring look for silverbell trees blooming here. The trail follows downstream to the corner of the park property line. This is a fine birding area, along with most of the trail, which passes through a wide variety of habitats. Many spring wildflowers grow along the trail.

A barbed-wire fence marks the boundary between the park and private land. *Do not trespass onto the private property.*

The path winds uphill to an open wildlife planting with an elevated observation platform on the crest of the hill at 1.9 miles. This is a great place to sit quietly and watch for birds and mammals, especially in early morning or at twilight. Deer and turkeys use the clearing along with other wildlife; watch for their tracks in the soft ground along the trail.

From the observation platform, you go through a moist depression with an especially large patch of ground pine (or club moss), a fern relative. The barbed-wire property line is again evident near the trail before the path reaches the dam for the campers' fishpond, another good wildlife-watching area.

From the pond back to the trailhead, the way is marked with footprints painted on the pavement. Use the platform stepway down to the level of Rice Creek; cross the creek on a footbridge, and follow the footprints to the end of the trail.

Miles and Directions

0.0 Start at the fishpond on the park entrance road.

0.5 Inner Loop Trail takes off to the left.

1.0 Broad River Trail begins on the right.

1.8 Barbed-wire fence marks the park boundary

1.5 Cross Rice Creek on a footbridge.

1.9 Come to a wildlife observation platform with wildlife planting.

2.4 Reach the campground fishing pond.

2.6 Cross Rice Creek on a footbridge.

2.7 Arrive back at the fishpond and trailhead.

Additional Trails

The **Broad River Trail** is an excellent longer hike. You visit two different streams: the larger Broad River and a small stream with an observation overlook at a beaver pond—an excellent place to view a wide variety of wildlife associated with the wetland area.

More Information

Ty Cobb Museum, 461 Cook Street, Royston, GA 30662-3903; (706) 245–1825; www.tycobbmuseum.org.

Elberton Granite Museum, 1 Granite Place, Elberton, GA 30635; (706) 283-2551; www.ega online.com/home/association/museum.shtml.

37 Lake Russell Wildlife Management Area: Broad River Trail

This trail follows beautiful, cascading Dicks Creek and Broad River. The unpaved roads in the wildlife management area are nice, quiet places to walk and offer good opportunities to see more wildlife. This trail can be hiked in either direction, but it is easier to hike down from Dicks Creek than up from the parking area at Broad River Bridge, the southern trail end. By road it is 2.9 miles between the trailheads.

Start: Northern (upstream) trailhead, 120 yards from Dicks Creek Bridge on the right at a sign with history of the trail
Distance: 4.2 miles one-way; 7.1-mile loop with a return on Forest Road 87
Approximate hiking time: 3½ hours one-way or 5 hours as a loop
Difficulty: Easy to moderate
Elevation gain/loss: 172 feet
Trail surface: Compacted loamy dirt
Lay of the land: Rolling foothills beside fast-moving stream

Season: Year-round; blaze-orange cap and/or jacket advised during managed deer hunts
Land status: Chattahoochee National Forest
Maps: USGS Ayersville; Chattahoochee National Forest map
Trail contacts: USDA Forest Service, Chattooga Ranger District, 200 Highway 197 North, Clarkesville, GA 30523; (706) 754-6221; www.fs.fed.us/conf Georgia Wildlife Resources Division, Game Management, 2150 Dawsonville Highway, Gainesville, GA 30501; (770) 535-5700; for hunting seasons: www.gohuntgeorgia.com

Finding the trailhead: From Cornelia go east 11.0 miles on U.S. Highway 123 to the Ayersville Road at the large Milliken Plant sign. Go 1.0 mile on the Ayersville Road to unpaved FR 87 (marked as Guard Camp Road on the management area map). A small sign here points to the CHECKING STATION for the management area. On FR 87 go about 2.9 miles to Dicks Creek, passing the checking station building on the way. The trailhead is about 100 yards beyond Dicks Creek bridge on the right (west) side of the road.

The Hike

Note: At the end of this hike, you will be at the footbridge across Kimbell Creek and the intersection of FR 87 and Forest Road 92 and the vehicle bridge across Broad River. Road names here can be confusing. The Ayersville USGS quadrangle does not list the Forest Service roads. FR 87 is Sellers Road, and the wildlife management area map refers to it as Guard Camp Road.

From the parking area at Dicks Creek, you walk 120 yards to begin the hike at the large sign with a short history of the trail. Although the sign says the trail is 3.8 miles long, it is actually 4.2 miles. This difference is relatively unimportant, since the trail is not strenuous and there are no side trails or old roadbeds to confuse you.

Raccoons are plentiful throughout the state.

After following the blue-blazed path through a weedy area with blackberry briars, you enter the woods. Here you should see a wide variety of spring wildflowers before the leaves are on the trees. You are now in the typical streambank vegetation of mountain laurel and dog-hobble thickets. Closer to Dicks Creek, you can hear the cascading water more than see it.

At 0.6 mile you pass a flat area with white pines, hemlocks, and yellow poplars that would be a nice lunch stop or campsite. The trail leads under several picturesque rock overhangs.

At 1.0 mile you reach the confluence with Broad River. At this point, Dicks Creek seems to be larger than Broad River. The path comes right down to the bank of the river and goes through a flat alluvial area for a short distance. Dog-hobble, or fetterbush, grows along the bank.

Turning south you follow Broad River as the path goes in and out of several coves following contours away from the river. You cross small wet areas and streams on small bridges or foot logs, the first one at 1.7 miles.

Near the end of the trail, 3.6 miles, the path comes right to the edge of the river and passes under a low rock ledge, making it necessary to rock-hop and step on the sandy stream edge until you can climb back up the bank and away from the water.

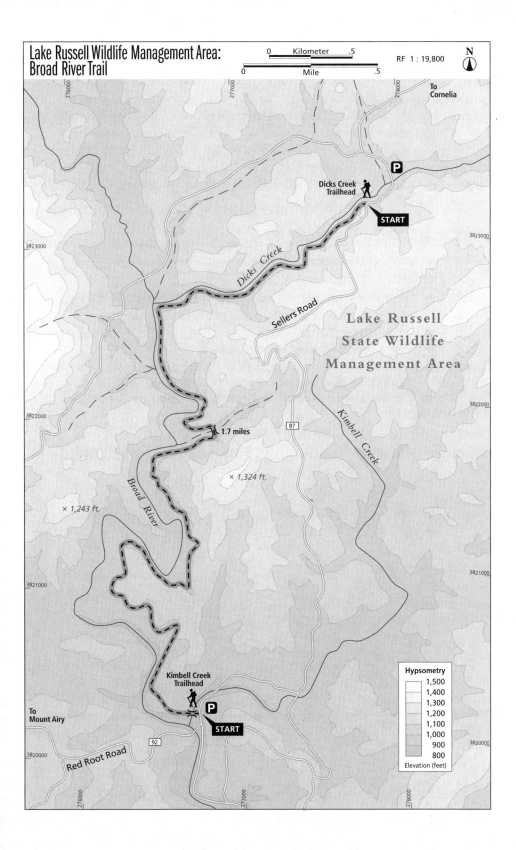

Lake Russell Wildlife Management Area: Broad River Trail

0   Kilometer   .5

0   Mile   .5

RF 1 : 19,800

N

To
Cornelia

P

Dicks Creek
Trailhead

START

276000

277000

278000

3823000

3823000

Dicks Creek

Sellers Road

**Lake Russell
State Wildlife
Management Area**

3822000

3822000

Kimbell Creek

1.7 miles

87

× 1,324 ft.

Broad River

× 1,243 ft.

3821000

3821000

3821000

Kimbell Creek
Trailhead

P

To
Mount Airy

START

92

3820000

3820000

Red Root Road

276000

277000

278000

Hypsometry	
	1,500
	1,400
	1,300
	1,200
	1,100
	1,000
	900
	800
	Elevation (feet)

If the river is up a few feet at this point, you'll have to climb through the mountain laurel thicket above the rock ledge. At 3.8 miles you hike through a flat area growing thick with blackberry canes and other tall annual plants. An unusual number of American holly trees also grow here. The trail ends at 4.2 miles where Kimbell Creek enters Broad River, a few yards above the vehicle bridge across the river.

You cross Kimbell Creek on a bridge to a parking area where FR 87 and FR 92 join. To complete a 7.1-mile loop back to the parking area at Dicks Creek, walk 2.9 miles north on FR 87. (**Option:** Park at the Broad River Bridge and walk the road up to Dicks Creek and the trail back.)

Miles and Directions

0.0   Start at the Dicks Creek trailhead, about 100 yards past the FR 87 bridge.

1.0   Dicks Creek joins Broad River at a flat area.

1.7   Cross the first small branch on a low footbridge. You cross other wet area on foot logs.

3.6   The trail goes under a rock ledge, making it necessary to walk on the sand at the stream's edge.

3.8   Walk through tall blackberry canes and other tall weeds.

4.2   Cross Kimbell Creek on a footbridge and to FR 87 with roadside parking. Walk north 2.9 miles on FR 87 to the Dicks Creek parking area for a 7.1-mile loop. (**Option:** Start at the Broad River Parking area, walk north 2.9 miles on FR 87 to Dicks Creek, and hike the trail back.)

7.1   Arrive back at the Dicks Creek trailhead.

Honorable Mentions

C Holcomb Creek Trail

This year-round trail is a pleasant 3.0 miles of easy to moderate hiking to waterfalls. The path goes through a beautiful cove hardwood forest. Large yellow poplars, buckeyes, and other hardwoods form a dense canopy over smaller silverbells and dogwoods. Holcomb Creek falls in a succession of drops for about 120 feet. Standing at the bottom where a bridge crosses the creek, it is hard to see the entire cascade. An observation deck at Ammons Creek Falls affords a good view of the falls as the creek plummets under the deck through narrow rock crevices. The best waterfall conditions are in winter and spring.

The trail starts at the junction of Overflow Road and Hales Ridge Road (Forest Road 7). The HOLCOMB CREEK FALLS sign marks the trailhead. The trail goes through a steep cove lined with rhododendron, mountain laurel, hemlock, white pine, and a wide assortment of hardwoods. Switchbacks keep the grade at a moderate rate of descent. In places, the trail is completely covered over by white rosebay rhododendron, which blooms from late May through the summer after the mountain laurel blooms. These two large shrubs add much color and pleasant shade to the walk during the warm months. The noise of the water can be heard well before the cascade is in sight. The trail ends at Hales Ridge Road where it crosses Holcomb Creek. An easy 0.6-mile walk on the road back to the starting point completes the loop.

For more information: Chattahoochee National Forest, Tallulah Ranger District, 809 Highway 441 South, Clayton, GA 30525; (706) 782–3320; www.fs.fed.us/conf.

DeLorme: Georgia Atlas and Gazetteer: Page 16 A4

D Aska Area Trails

A group of four trails in the Aska area total 17.8 miles of hiking and mountain biking paths. You will be able to hike along the clear waters of Lake Blue Ridge, climb to mountains reaching to 3,000 feet with great views, pass through rich hardwood coves with trout streams, and tunnel through thickets of mountain laurel and rhododendron. Three trails—Flat Creek Loop, Green Mountain Trail, and Stanley Gap Trail—can be started at Deep Gap on Aska Road, 4.7 miles south of Blue Ridge. Stanley Gap Trail can also be accessed at Stanley Gap, 7.6 miles farther south on Aska Road. The Long Branch Loop trailhead is 1.6 miles south of Deep Gap.

All trails are interconnected so that you can have 17.8 miles of hiking or cycling with only a few miles of backtracking. Bulletin boards at the Deep Gap and at Long Branch Loop trailheads show a map of the trail system. Parking at these trailheads is free. The trails are open year-round, with spring and fall best for wildflowers and spectacular leaf colors, respectively.

For more information: Chattahoochee National Forest, Toccoa Ranger District, 6050 Appalachian Highway, Blue Ridge, GA 30513; (706) 632–3031; www.fs .fed.us/conf.

DeLorme: Georgia Atlas and Gazetteer: Page 14 C4

E Duncan Ridge National Recreation Trail

This 35-mile-long trail is a challenging hike covering a wide variety of trail conditions from easy to strenuous. At its eastern end it connects with the Benton MacKaye and Appalachian Trails (AT) at Long Creek. The trail quickly leaves the AT, continuing with the Benton MacKaye Trail across the Toccoa River and soon heads east on ridgetops to the Coosa Backcountry Trail. These two trails travel together to Slaughter Gap and connect with the AT at the end of the Duncan Ridge Trail. From here you can go back west to Springer Mountain on the AT and close a 60-mile backpacking loop.

There are good wilderness campsites all along the trail, except for long stretches with very little water. In addition to the scenic features along this trail, you cross the 260-foot suspension bridge over the Toccoa River, one of the longest swinging bridges just for foot travel in the eastern United States.

For more information: Chattahoochee National Forest, Toccoa Ranger District, 6050 Appalachian Highway, Blue Ridge, GA 30531; (706) 632–3031; www.fs .fed.us/conf; www.georgia-atclub.org; www.bmta.org.

DeLorme: Georgia Atlas and Gazetteer: Page 14 D6

F Lake Russell Recreation Area: Ladyslipper Trail

This 6.2-mile hiking and equestrian loop offers glimpses of different forest management practices and offers good wildlife viewing opportunities. Blue blazes mark the way throughout the trail. The trail is of moderate difficulty, with a few short, steep grades and some wet, muddy areas along the trail where horse travel has caused standing water at spring seeps crossing the trail. This is a year-round hiking area; however, the recreation area is open only from Memorial Day to Labor Day. The trails, boat ramps, and lakes are open year-round. Because the area is located on the edge of the Piedmont and Blue Ridge provinces, species from both physiographic areas are present, adding variety to the hike. This is especially true for the many wildflowers and flowering shrubs and trees you will see during spring and summer. Look for pink lady's slipper orchids growing along the path where there is a mixture of mature pines and hardwoods.

The hike begins at the parking area at Nancy Town Lake dam on a blue-blazed trail. Open fields have been planted to grasses and other wildlife food plants. These areas are developed by the Georgia Wildlife Resources Division specifically to add variety to the habitat types for wildlife. Deer and turkeys are the most obvious species, and their tracks are evident. Such areas also support many nongame species. Songbirds, rabbits, squirrels, wood and field mice, hawks, owls, and a great variety of other species have benefited from the openings in the forest.

For more information: USDA Forest Service, Chattooga Ranger District, 200 Highway 197 North, P.O. Box 1960, Clarkesville, GA 30523; (706) 754–6221; www.fs.fed.us/conf.

DeLorme: Georgia Atlas and Gazetteer: Page 16 G3

G Brasstown Valley and Mountain Park

Brasstown Valley Resort, in the mountains of north Georgia, is about 1.0 mile north of Young Harris on U.S. Highway 76/Highway 2. Located in 503-acre Mountain Park, the resort lies under the highest point in the state, Brasstown Bald, and was designed to blend into the mountain environment. There are four interconnected loop trails with a combined distance of about 8.0 miles. These loops may be walked in several ways to accommodate the distance and difficulty one chooses. Collectively they are moderate to strenuous difficult. The longest, the 5.5-mile Brasstown Trek Loop, leads to Rocky Knob and back to the parking area. All trails can be accessed at the upper parking area for the resort.

April to late October is best for the full range of wildflower blooming times and fall leaf color. Summer temperatures are pleasant, and many winter days are suitable for hiking. A small map for these trails is available at the registration desk at Brasstown Valley Resort and from the Mountain Park office.

For more information: Mountain Park, P.O. Box 115, Young Harris, GA 30582; (706) 379–2040; www.gadnr.org.

DeLorme: Georgia Atlas and Gazetteer: Page 15 B8

H Tugaloo State Park

On a peninsula tucked away on Lake Hartwell's 55,590 acres, 393-acre Tugaloo State Park has delightful hiking trails. Another of Georgia's well-kept secrets, the park is surrounded by water on all but about 110 yards through which the park road passes. Located on the northern edge of the Piedmont Plateau, the area supports an interesting range of plants and animals found in both the mountains and plateau. The four interconnected trails total 4.2 miles. Crow Tree and Muscadine Nature Trails take you through woods of oak, walnut, mulberry, and cherry trees along with many low shrubs. The north and south sections of the loop trails combine for 3.2 miles of wooded, gently rolling topography. Lake Hartwell is noted for its fine fishing for largemouth and striped bass.

For more information: Tugaloo State Park, 1763 Tugaloo Sate Park Road, Lavonia, GA 30553; (706) 356–4362; www.gastateparks.org.

DeLorme: Georgia Atlas and Gazetteer: Page 17 H6

| Benton MacKaye Trail

This grand, long trail begins at Springer Mountain with the Appalachian Trail and extends in a sweeping S-shape to the north and west. The trail lies mostly in the Chattahoochee National Forest. Although the trail crosses major roads in the mountains when necessary, it has many remote stretches and provides true wilderness hiking. The hike follows rhododendron- and laurel-lined trout streams and crosses one of the longest hiker's suspension bridges in the country. Mountains and ridges with scenic views, mature and regenerating forests, and paved and unpaved mountain roads are all part of the trail, with a variety of optional side trips of shorter loops along the route.

This new trail will provide a challenge for any serious hiker. The section through Georgia has been completed to the Tennessee line in the Cohutta Wilderness at Double Springs Gap, and work is in progress on the Tennessee section. The Benton MacKaye Trail Association reports 78.6 miles as the total trail length in Georgia. Hopefully the Tennessee and North Carolina portions will be completed soon. Then a grand loop hike from Springer Mountain to Great Smoky Mountains National Park on the Benton MacKaye Trail and back on the Appalachian Trail will be possible, passing through some of the finest wilderness areas in the East.

For more information: The Benton MacKaye Trail Association, P.O. Box 53271, Atlanta, GA 30355-1271; www.bmta.org. Chattahoochee National Forest, 1755 Cleveland Highway, Gainesville, GA 30501; www.fs.fed.us/conf.

DeLorme: Georgia Atlas and Gazetteer: Page 14 F5

⌡ Cohutta Wilderness Area

Steep, rugged, and heavily forested, the Cohutta Mountains are true wilderness today. But only sixty-five years ago, this area on the Tennessee-Georgia border was intensively logged. Some of the old railroad beds used to haul the timber are still evident. There also were attempts at mining here, but these scars have healed and are not noticeable. Year-round hiking is possible.

At 37,000 acres, this is the third largest mountain wilderness in the East. One-lane dirt Forest Service roads define much of the boundary. These roads are pleasant to walk along and can be incorporated with the fourteen named trails into loop trails to get back to a parking area and trailhead. More than 75 miles of backcountry trails lead to grand forests, scenic beauty, fishing, hunting, and exploring. More than forty species of rare and uncommon plants and a variety of game animals abound in the wilderness, and the many cold-water streams support fine trout populations. Birding, wildflower photography, fishing, and hunting for small and big game provide something for everyone.

For more information: Chattahoochee National Forest, Armuchee-Cohutta Ranger District, 3941 Highway 76, Chatsworth, GA, 30705; (706) 695–6736. A large-scale map of the Cohutta Wilderness Area is available for sale from the Forest Service; www.fs.fed.us/conf.

DeLorme: Georgia Atlas and Gazetteer: Page 13 B10

Central Georgia:
Piedmont and Fall Line Area

Covered bridge at Watkins Mill Bridge State Park (Hike 43).

38 Oconee River Recreation Area Trails

Remains of old buildings, Indian mounds, the relatively unchanged river, and three short trails make this a fine day trip and hiking destination. Scull Shoals Trail follows along the bank of the Oconee River and at times can be muddy or temporarily underwater. Boarding House Trail, a short walk to the historic ruins, is well above water level. Indian Mound Trail takes you away from the river and through a bottomland hardwood forest. The area supports an excellent bird population, with both river and upland forest habitat. The Oconee River floodplain is rich in wildflowers and tree species.

Start: Scull Shoals Trail, Scull Shoals Day Use Area; Boarding House Trail, Scull Shoals Historic Area; Indian Mound Trail, at the end of Forest Road 1231A parking area with trailhead carsonite stake
Distance: Scull Shoals Trail, 2.2 miles out and back; Boarding House Trail, 0.4 mile out and back; Indian Mound Trail, 2.0 miles out and back
Approximate hiking time: 2 hours out and back for each trail
Difficulty: Easy
Elevation gain/loss: Negligible
Trail surface: Sandy loam (and clay for Scull Shoals Trail)

Lay of the land: Flat river floodplain
Season: Year-round
Land status: Oconee National Forest
Nearest town: Greensboro
Fees and permits: No fees or permits required for day use; camping $5.00 per site per night
Maps: USGS Barnett Shoals, Maxeys, and Greshamville; Oconee National Forest map; *Trail Guide to the Chattahoochee and Oconee National Forests*
Trail contacts: USDA Forest Service, Oconee Ranger District, 1199 Madison Road, Eatonton, GA 31024; (706) 485–7110; www.fed .us/conf

Finding the trailhead: From Greensboro, go north 12.0 miles on Highway 15. The Oconee River Recreation Area is on the right at Oconee River Bridge. The trailhead for the Scull Shoals Trail is at the boat-launching ramp in the recreation area.

For the Boarding House Trail, go 1.1 miles south of the bridge on Highway 15 to Macedonia Road (paved). Turn left on Macedonia Road; go 2.5 miles and turn left on Forest Road 1234, an unpaved road (labeled Scull Shoals Road in *DeLorme Georgia Atlas & Gazetteer* and on USGS quad maps). Follow the signs 1.8 miles to Forest Road 1231. Bear left and go 0.9 mile to Scull Shoals Historic Area. The trailhead is at the parking area near the information sign. This is also the northern terminus for the Scull Shoals Trail.

For the Indian Mound Trail follow FR 1234 from Macedonia Road for 2.0 miles to FR 1231 and go 0.5 mile to FR 1231A. Turn right on FR 1231A and go 0.5 mile to the end of the road and parking area. The trailhead is at the end of the parking area at the brown carsonite post with the hiker icon and marked Trail 102.

Ruins of a building at Scull Shoals Village, Oconee River Recreation Area.

The Hikes

The Scull Shoals area of the Oconee River is steeped in history, going back to the late 1700s and, even further, to prehistoric American Indian mounds. The origin of the name Scull Shoals has been lost in antiquity. It may be from Indian skulls washed up after floods or from a family named Scull. The name was first recorded in 1788 by Elijah Clarke as "Schel-sholes." Located in the town of Scull Shoals were Georgia's first paper mill, one of the first cotton gins, and an early textile factory.

Scull Shoals Trail

Scull Shoals Trail follows the river upstream, crossing several small tributaries with steep banks. Water oak, hackberry, sweet gum, red maple, and yellow poplar are some of the most obvious trees along the trail. Mountain laurel on the moist north-facing banks blooms in late April, and many other spring wildflowers add color and interest to this easy walk that ends at the historic site of Scull Shoals Village.

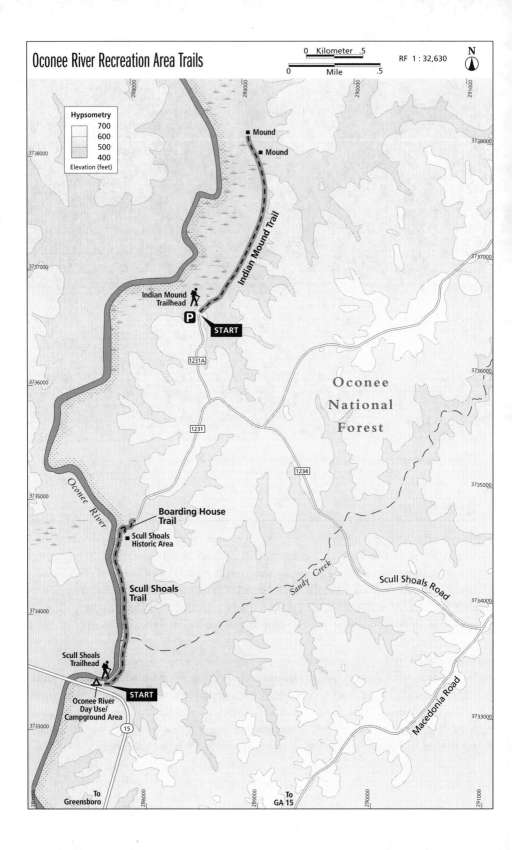

Miles and Directions

0.0 Start at the boat launch area and go upstream.

0.3 Cross a small stream on a bridge.

0.4 (**FYI:** From the bridge to this point and all along the riverbank, look for beaver cuttings on trees and saplings.)

1.1 Reach the Scull Shoals Historic Area. After exploring the site, retrace your steps.

2.2 Arrive back at the trailhead.

Boarding House Trail

This trail is a short walk through flat pine woods to the ruins of the boardinghouse. Interpretive signs explain some of the history and identify the building remains. An excellent brochure, available from the Oconee District Ranger's office, provides a good historical account of Scull Shoals Village and the industry that took place here from the late 1700s to the early 1900s. William Bartram, for whom the Bartram Trail is named, may have been one of the first white visitors at this site, in 1773. The settlement began in 1784; Indians ceded the area to white settlers about 1790.

Indian Mound Trail

The trail begins at the parking area at the end of FR 1231A. The marker post bears TRAIL 102, and the white blazed path enters a wooded area with a clearing on the left. This trail passes through a fine example of Piedmont floodplain forest. Instead of following close to the river, the trail follows along the base of the low ridges on the east side of the Oconee River. Very large water oaks and loblolly pines are along the trail, as well as red maples, sweet gums, white and red oaks, hackberries, and yellow poplars. A patch of ground pine grows by the path, and flame azalea and other wildflowers bloom here in spring.

The first of the two Indian mounds is 0.6 mile on the trail. A large plaque on a loblolly pine warns visitors not to take artifacts of any kind from the site. These regulations are designed to protect archaeological sites on public lands. The mound rises 25 feet above the floodplain and is completely covered with trees, indicating that the mound has not been disturbed for many years. Light-blue blazes and rings on selected trees mark the mound site. The second mound is about 0.25 mile farther along the white-blazed trail. Here the trail passes through a splendid floodplain forest of very large trees. Some of the large loblolly pines have been killed by southern pine beetles and have become homes for cavity-nesting birds using holes made by several species of woodpeckers, including the pileated woodpecker.

39 Twin Bridges Trail

Wind through low, gently rolling low ridges and valleys in a mixed hardwood-pine forest on the Little River arm of Lake Sinclair. Lake Sinclair, a Georgia Power Company reservoir, is in sight most of the hike. A number of large trees along the trail have cavities that are used by small mammals, birds, and other animals. Because of the variety of small openings in the forest and the adjacent lake, this trail is an exceptionally productive birding area.

Start: Camp Loop B
Distance: 3.6 miles out and back
Approximate hiking time: 2 hours
Difficulty: Easy
Trail surface: Soft loam with tree leaves
Lay of the land: Gently rolling hills
Season: Year-round; campground closed from December to March 30
Land status: Chattahoochee-Oconee National Forests

Nearest towns: Milledgeville, Monticello
Fees and permits: Parking $3.00 per day per vehicle; other charges for camping
Maps: USGS Resseaus Crossroads; Oconee National Forest map
Trail contacts: USDA Forest Service, Oconee Ranger District, 1199 Madison Road, Eatonton, GA 31024; (706) 485-7110; www.fs .fed.us/conf

Finding the trailhead: From Monticello go east on Highway 212 where Highway 16 splits off. Continue east 17.0 miles on Highway 212 to Twin Bridges Road. Turn left and follow the signs 1.6 miles to the Lake Sinclair Recreation Area entrance, then go 0.25 mile to the Camp Loop B parking area. The trailhead is off the road from the parking area at a marker with trail number 119. From Milledgeville go north 11.2 miles on 212 to Twin Bridges Road; turn right and follow directions above.

The Hike

The white-blazed Twin Bridges Trail is marked number 119. This is a fine morning or afternoon hike for campers or day-use visitors. Small streams, lakeshore, wildflowers, and wildlife add special interest. You walk down a gentle slope from Camp Loop B to a small creek. Turn up the creek (to the right) to the first of two footbridges at 0.2 mile. A large patch of trout lilies, sometimes called dogtooth violets, bloom in March. Beaver cuttings on many of the larger trees can be seen along the streambank. After crossing the bridge, you go through a small canebrake thicket, then through a stand of young pines and into a more mature hardwood forest. Several paths leading off to the left show where fishermen reach the lake for bank fishing. Lake Sinclair is a good fishing lake for largemouth bass and crappie. The tree cover extends right to the edge of the water, making a nice shady place to fish from the bank.

Twin Bridges Trail

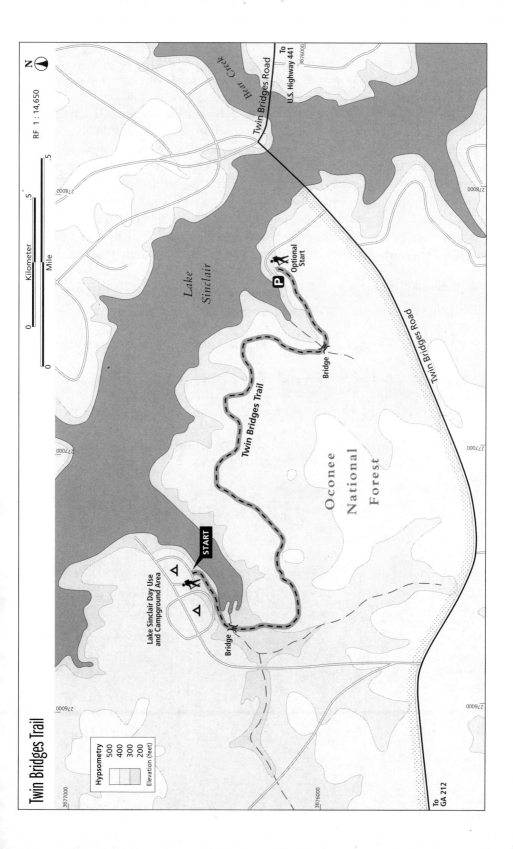

Hypsometry

Elevation (feet)
500
400
300
200

RF 1 : 14,650

N

Kilometer
0   .5

Mile
0   .5

Lake Sinclair

To Bear Creek

Twin Bridges Road

To U.S. Highway 441

Optional Start

P

Bridge

Twin Bridges Trail

Oconee National Forest

Twin Bridges Road

START

Lake Sinclair Day Use and Campground Area

Bridge

To GA 212

At 1.4 mile you cross a short footbridge over a gully that's a remnant of earlier farming. The old gullies have healed with mosses, ferns, trees, and soil-retention plants. Wildflowers are well represented throughout the trail, including the Piedmont azalea, with pink flowers on 4- or 5-foot-high bushes blooming in spring, and the crane-fly orchid, whose slender stalks of tiny greenish-yellow flowers bloom in mid-summer. At the bridge is a mature yellow poplar with a large cavity at the base filled with dirt and decayed wood in which a heartleaf, or wild ginger, plant has become established. This small, sweet-smelling plant may last in one place like this for fifteen to twenty years. The trail ends at 1.8 miles at a Forest Service primitive campground-parking area. Here you are 0.3 mile from the bridge over the Little River arm of the lake. Across that bridge 0.1 mile is another bridge over Bear Creek. You can use this end as a trailhead by driving 2.4 miles on Twin Bridges Road from Highway 212.

Miles and Directions

0.0 Start from Camp Loop B on the white-blazed trail. Walk down a gentle slope to a small creek.

0.2 Cross the first of two footbridges. Look for beaver cuttings on sweet gum and other smaller trees.

0.5 Pass through a switch cane thicket. These canebrakes provide important wildlife cover and food.

1.4 Cross another small footbridge over one of the erosion gullies, now healed and well vegetated.

1.8 Reach the primitive camping and parking area. This is your turnaround point. You are 0.3 mile from the first of the Twin Bridges.

40 Red Top Mountain State Park Trails

Beautiful views of Allatoona Lake; abundant deer, squirrels, wild turkeys, and other wildlife; birding; wildflowers; and forest make this a fascinating day-hike area.

The paved Lakeside Trail, total distance 0.75 mile, is designed for physically challenged visitors. Crossway paths break the trail into smaller loops. The featured Homestead Trail in the gently rolling hills is the most varied and interesting trail in the park. The Sweet Gum Nature Trail branches off the Homestead Trail for another 1.2 miles and even more variety. The Iron Hill Trail, for the more ambitious hiker or biker, is close to the campground. A connector trail in the middle of the loop provides a shorter option.

Start: Paved Lakeside and White Tail Trails, at the lodge; all other trails, at the visitor center
Distance: Lakeside Trail, 0.75 mile of connected loops; White Tail Trail, 0.8 mile out and back; Sweet Gum Nature Trail, 1.2-mile loop; Visitor Center Loop Trail, 0.5-mile loop; Campground Trail, 1.0 mile out and back; Homestead Trail, 4.9-mile lollipop
Approximate hiking time: Homestead Trail, 2½ hours; other trails, approximately 30 minutes each
Difficulty: Easy to moderate
Trail surface: Dirt; some paved road sections
Lay of the land: Rolling hills

Season: Year-round; spring and fall for the best animal, wildflower, and foliage opportunities
Land status: Georgia State Parks Division
Nearest town: Cartersville
Fees and permits: Park Pass $3.00 per day per vehicle
Maps: USGS Allatoona Dam; page-size map of the trails, available at the park office
Trail contacts: Red Top Mountain State Park and Lodge, 781 Red Top Mountain Road SE, Cartersville, GA 30120; www.gastateparks.org; park office: (770) 975-0055; lodge: (800) 864-7275

Finding the trailhead: From Atlanta go north on Interstate 75 to exit 285. Go east on Red Top Mountain Road 1.5 miles; the trailhead for all trails is at the visitor center except the paved Lakeside and White Tail Trails, which start at the lodge.

The Hike

The trailhead for the Homestead Trail is at the visitor center building. This 4.9-mile yellow-blazed trail is the most varied and interesting of all the trails in the park. It leads you through a wide variety of habitats. Mile-marker posts have been placed along the path, a handy reference for the beginning hiker. At 0.9 mile you cross the paved road to the lodge. The trail divides just beyond the road. The loop starts here and goes around to the right (counterclockwise). The path drops down to one of

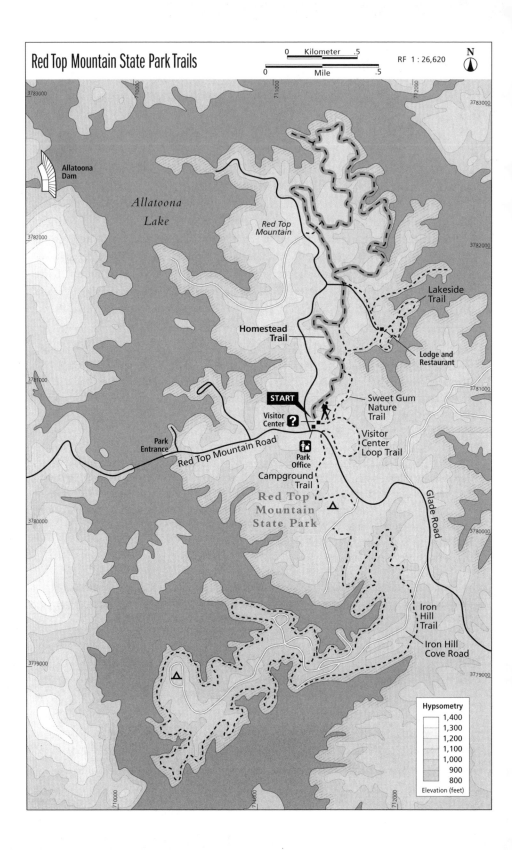

the arms of Lake Allatoona, where you come to a higher ridge providing scenic views of the lake. At 2.6 miles, a blue-blazed trail leads down to a point overlooking the lake. From this spot you can see Allatoona Dam to the west. This is a nice place to be just before sunset. Return to the yellow-blazed trail and pass near one of the old homesites that were occupied when iron ore and clay were mined from Red Top Mountain. Small clearings in the forest have been planted with grasses for wildlife, especially deer and turkeys.

You can expect to see deer on any of the trails here; the wild turkeys are much more wary and difficult to spot. You're sure to see squirrels and many species of birds.

The path loops back again to the paved road and back to the visitor center, or you can walk down the trail to the lodge and return to the visitor center via the red-blazed Lodge Trail.

Miles and Directions

0.0   Start at the visitor center.

0.3   Join the orange-blazed Sweet Gum Nature Trail until it angles off to the right in about 20 yards.

0.8   Rejoin Sweet Gum Trail.

0.9   Cross the paved road that leads to the lodge. The Sweet Gum Trail turns off to the right toward the lodge; continue straight ahead on the yellow-blazed Homestead Trail.

1.0   The trail divides; take the right fork to follow the loop counterclockwise. For the next 1.9 miles, the trail continues in and out of several coves of Lake Allatoona with good views of the lake, especially in winter and early spring.

2.6   A short trail takes off to the right (**Option:** Take this 400-foot trail out and back for a good view of the lake and Allatoona Dam.)

2.9   One of several old home site ruins on Red Top Mountain is visible here.

3.2   Intersect a blue-blazed shortcut trail. (**Option:** Follow the shortcut to a left turn onto the Park Marina Road. You can either take the road all the way to the visitor center or detour onto Cottage Road to reach the cottage area.)

3.5   The trail makes a U-turn, providing another good view of Allatoona Lake and Dam.

3.7   Meet the shortcut trail again.

3.9   Close the loop and head back to the visitor center.

4.9   Arrive back at the visitor center.

Additional Trails

The following trails are great options for short walks in the woods.

The **Lakeside Trail** is completely barrier free and wheelchair accessible. It is a good trail for anyone interested in wildlife. Bird feeders and bird and mammal nest boxes are placed at appropriate places along the trail. White-tailed deer come right to the trail. They are well conditioned to people and easily seen if you remain quiet. Many birds, including hummingbirds and a variety of songbirds, are attracted to the area. Lake Allatoona is visible throughout most of the walk.

Two cross paths make it possible to return to the trailhead without making the entire loop or backtracking. A small field, mixed hardwood-pine forest and lake edge give the walk an interesting mixture of habitat types.

The red-blazed **Visitor Center Loop Trail** begins at either the visitor center or the lodge parking lot. The undulating path, a 0.5-mile loop, takes you through stands of almost pure loblolly pine and into a forest of large hardwood trees and beside and across a small stream. Hiked from the lodge, a blue-blazed trail turns off to the right, picks up the yellow-blazed trail, and continues for a short distance to the road leading back to the lodge. Two footbridge crossings add charm to the forest walk. The Sweet Gum Nature Trail is a loop off this trail.

The **Sweet Gum Nature Trail,** marked with orange blazes, makes a loop through a dry ridge of white, chestnut, and red oaks, with dogwoods, huckleberries, and other shrubs growing underneath. This is a good place to look for spring wildflowers. The trail overlooks a small, quiet valley. Two observation decks allow you to sit and watch for wildlife. In 0.5 mile you are back to the red-blazed trail and can continue back to the visitor center.

The very interesting 0.5-mile **Campground Trail** leads from the campground to the visitor center. It passes an opening in the woods where deer are likely to be seen, crosses three bridges, and passes the stone ruins of an old homestead. The trailhead is located in the campground near comfort station No. 2.

More Information

Food/Lodging

Red Top Mountain State Park and Lodge, 50 Lodge Road, Cartersville, GA 30121; (800) 864-7275; www.gastateparks.org (click on Red Top Mountain State Park).

Organizations

Friends of Red Top Mountain State Park; www.gastateparks.org (click on "Red Top Mountain" then on "Friends of Red Top Mt. St. Park").

41 Richard B. Russell State Park Trails

Richard B. Russell State Park is on a peninsula formed by the embayment of Vans and Coldwater Creeks on Richard B. Russell Lake. The featured Blackwell Bridge Trail takes you away from the main park activity area to a pleasant walk along the lake to the historic Blackwell Bridge. Five other interconnected trails totaling 4.3 miles allow you to walk rather than drive to almost anywhere else in the park, with the opportunity to see plant and animal life along the way.

Start: Parking area trailhead for the Blackwell Bridge Trail
Distance: Blackwell Bridge Trail, 1.3-mile loop
Approximate hiking time: Blackwell Bridge Trail, 1 hour
Difficulty: Easy
Trail surface: Dirt; short paved road section
Lay of the land: Gently rolling hills
Season: Year-round
Land status: Georgia State Parks Division

Nearest town: Elberton
Fees and permits: Park Pass $3.00 per day per vehicle
Maps: USGS Lowndesville; trail map, available from the park office
Trail contacts: Richard B. Russell State Park, 2650 Russell State Park Road, Elberton, GA 30635; (706) 213-2045; www.gastate parks.org

Finding the trailhead: From Elberton go north 3.0 miles on Highway 77 to Highway 368. Turn right and go 7.7 miles, then turn right on Russell State Park Road to the park entrance. The office and information center is on the left. Continue 4.0 miles to the beach parking area. The Blackwell Bridge trailhead is at the corner of the parking area.

The Hike

The 1.3-mile Blackwell Bridge Trail is the primary hiking trail in the park. It is under a hardwood forest for most of the way, so even in the heat of summer the hike is mostly shaded. The principal trees are several species of oaks, maples, sycamores, sweet gums, black gums, yellow poplars, and dogwoods; shrub vegetation includes high-bush huckleberries, blueberries, and hawthorns. Spring wildflowers begin to show under the leafless trees in late February and continue until May. Bloodroots, trilliums, dwarf irises, and many others grow in the moist coves. Other common plants seen are Christmas ferns, spleenworts, and patches of the almost white pincushion moss and reindeer-moss lichen, which occurs from the arctic to north Florida.

This second-growth forest has become good habitat for white-tailed deer, gray and fox squirrels, opossums, raccoons, and other small mammals. It is also a fine birding area in spring and fall migrations, with many species of songbirds, hawks, owls, and crows. Near the lake coves you may see such waterbirds as egrets, herons, ducks, and geese.

Richard B. Russell State Park Trails

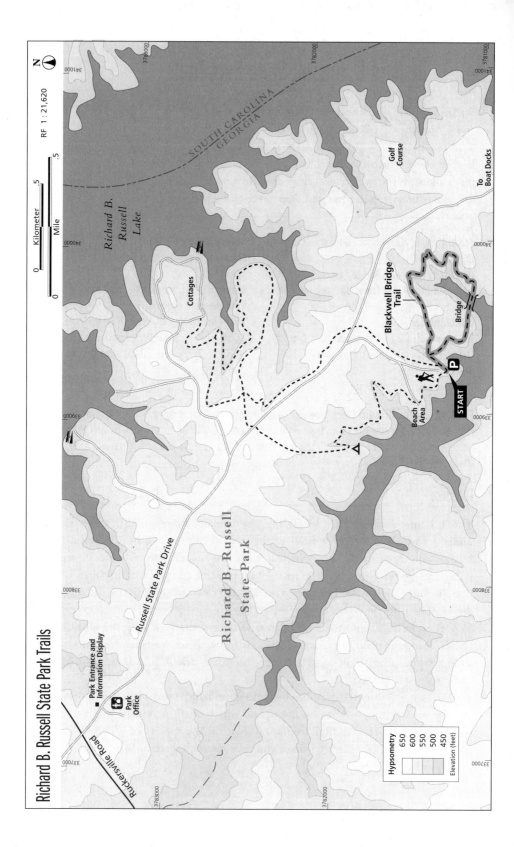

The Blackwell Bridge Trail begins with a paved path down to a footbridge and an information sign with map. The remainder of the trail is unpaved. The pathway follows around the coves and points of the lake so that the lake is visible for much of the way. (It is much more visible in winter with the leaves off the trees.) At 0.4 mile you come to the historic steel bridge. This is the last remaining steel bridge in Elbert County. It was constructed in 1917, and a historical marker describes the structure. Take your time here and enjoy the history and view of the lake. The trail continues on up and around a low ridge where, at 0.7 mile, you begin to see the exposed granite outcrops. This very attractive and durable stone has been used in famous buildings throughout the world.

Prior to impoundment of Russell Lake, several American Indian sites were excavated. The Ruckers Bottom site yielded artifacts such as Clovis points, indicating that American Indians used the area as much as 10,000 years ago. The pathway loops back to the starting point and the paved path to the parking area.

Miles and Directions

0.0 Start at parking area at direction sign.

0.05 Walk down the shredded tire-paved path to the information sign; turn right to go around the loop counterclockwise.

0.15 Walk down into a small cove with a good lake view for the next 0.3 mile.

0.4 Reach the steel bridge for which the trail was named.

0.7 After a short climb, begin to hike on a contour from one cove to the next.

0.9 Look for the large granite boulders for which Elbert County is world famous.

1.0 This is the high point on the trail; walk through the pleasant deciduous forest.

1.2 Close the loop and return to the paved walkway.

1.3 Arrive back at the parking area.

Additional Trails

Five interconnected trails throughout the park provide 4.3 miles of additional hiking: **Beach/Cottage Trail,** 1.6 miles; **Cottage Loop,** 1.3-mile loop; **Beach Connector Trail,** 0.3 mile; **Campground–Cottage Connector,** 0.5 mile; **Campground—Picnic Area Connector,** 0.6 mile

More Information

Local Events/Attractions

The **Georgia Guidestones** are located 8.7 miles north of Elberton on Highway 77. A sort of "American Stonehenge," each of the five 19-foot-high, one-piece granite pillars is inscribed with different modern and ancient languages.

42 Hard Labor Creek State Park Trails

Two interconnecting trails pass through farmland abandoned in the mid-1930s, now in mature pine-hardwood forest. Bridges across small, eroded ravines offer a different view of the forest floor and vegetation and provide a nice place for quietly watching birds and other wildlife. Some bridges have rest benches. Both loops can be walked so that the only repetition is the short access trail between the loops. These interlocking trails provide a pleasant ninety-minute hike through mixed pine and hardwood forest and along beaver pond and marsh. Horse and bike trails provide 23 miles of additional trails for hiking.

Start: All trails, about 100 yards in front of the office/trading post
Distance: Brantley Nature Trail, 1.0-mile loop; Beaver Pond Trail, 1.1-mile loop; trails combined, 2.2-mile loop
Approximate hiking time: Individual trails, 1 hour each trail; combined loops, 90 minutes
Difficulty: Easy
Trail surface: Dirt with leaf litter
Lay of the land: Gently rolling hills

Season: Year-round.
Land status: Georgia State Parks Division
Nearest town: Rutledge
Fees and permits: Parking $3.00 per vehicle per day
Maps: USGS Rutledge North; trail maps available at the office/trading post
Trail contacts: Hard Labor Creek State Park, P.O. Box 247, Rutledge, GA 30663; (706) 557-3001; www.gastateparks.org

Finding the trailhead: From Atlanta take Interstate 20 east to exit 185. Go north on Newborn Road 2.0 miles to Rutledge and continue 2.6 miles on Fairplay Road to Knox Chapel Road. Turn left and go 0.4 mile to Campground Road. Turn right; the office/trading post is 0.1 mile on the right. The trailhead for Brantley Nature Trail is about 100 yards in front of the office on the road to the campground. The trail begins on the left. A short trail connects the loops of Brantley Nature and Beaver Pond Trails.

The Hikes

Both loop trails, hiked together or separately, are interesting and delightful any time of the year. Wildlife you're likely to encounter includes deer, turkeys, squirrels, waterfowl, beavers, and aquatic and other animals attracted by the two lakes and the beaver pond.

The **Brantley Nature Trail** winds through rolling ridges and terraces still visible from early farming practices and a mixed pine-hardwood forest with most of the trees less than sixty years old. Loblolly pine, several oak species including very large white oaks, hickories, dogwood, sourwood, yellow poplar, and beech make up most of the forest species. Undergrowth plants include redbud, gooseberry, muscadine, Christmas ferns, and a great assortment of wildflowers in spring. The rare Piedmont barren strawberry grows along this trail as well as elsewhere in the park. This low plant spreads by subsurface stems like the cultivated strawberry. The five-petaled white flowers bloom from April to June.

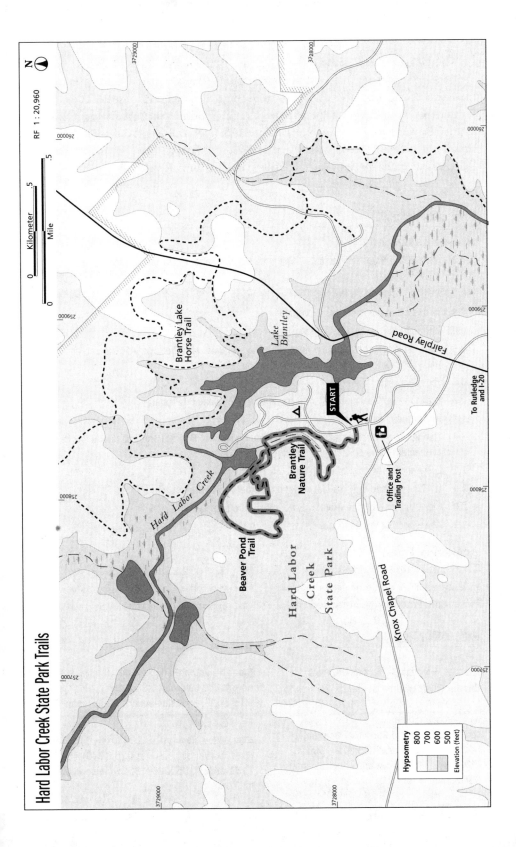

Hard Labor Creek State Park Trails

The **Beaver Pond Trail** is much like the Brantley Nature Trail, except that it includes areas of older trees and the beaver pond. One very large yellow poplar on the inside of the loop about 20 yards from the trail is well over 5 feet in diameter. Standing water in the beaver pond killed a number of trees that have become excellent habitat for cavity-nesting birds, including the colorful wood duck. The pond is almost completely covered with vegetation and is a favorite place for quiet birding. Pileated and other species of woodpeckers, wading birds, flycatchers, and other forest birds are easily observed.

Miles and Directions

Combined Loop Trails

0.0 Start at the Brantley Nature Trail trailhead and sign, about 100 yards in front of the office/trading post.

0.2 Take the right fork at the beginning of the loop.

0.4 Turn left and cross the small branch.

0.45 Turn right to join the Beaver Pond Trail.

0.5 Pass the beaver pond on the right. (**FYI:** The standing dead trees provide habitat for many different cavity-nesting birds and mammals.)

0.6 The marsh is on the right.

0.7 Leave the wetland area and start to climb a well-forested hillside.

1.2 Reach the crest of the hill.

1.6 Through four switchbacks in the trail, close the loop on Beaver Pond Trail and follow the connector up the small branch on the Brantley Nature Trail.

1.7 Leave the moist cove to climb up a low ridge.

1.9 You have gained only 80 feet elevation as you turn to the left.

2.0 Close the loop on the Brantley Nature Trail; turn sharply right.

2.2 Arrive back at the trailhead.

Additional Trails

There are 23 miles of equestrian and biking trails east of the lakes, which can be hiked in a number of different configurations. Horses and riders have the right-of-way on these trails. For safety reasons, dogs are not permitted on the horse trails even on a leash.

More Information

Local Events/Attractions

Charlie Elliott Wildlife Center, 543 Elliott Trail, Mansfield, GA 30055; (770) 784-3059; www.georgiawildlife.com.

The State Botanical Garden of Georgia, 2450 South Milledge AvenueAthens, GA 30605; (706) 542-1244; www.uga.edu/botgarden/Contact.html.

Stone Mountain Park, located 16 miles east of downtown Atlanta on U.S. Highway 78; (770) 498-5600; www.stonemountainpark.com.

Food/Lodging

Blue Willow Restaurant, 294 North Cherokee Road, Social Circle, GA 30025; (770) 464-2131 or (800) 552-8813; www.bluewillow inn.com.

43 Watson Mill Bridge State Park Trails

Watson Mill Bridge State Park is named for the 229-foot covered bridge, constructed in 1880, located at its original site across the South Fork Broad River, colloquially known as just South Fork River. The area is characteristic of the Piedmont Plateau physiographic province. This park has a compact series of short trails that touch the history of early river life and waterpower. The story is amply told with information boards and pamphlets. The trails provide a good cross section of the numerous habitat types.

Start: The small concession building for trails on the south side of the river and covered bridge; parking area 0.1 mile north of the bridge for hiking trails on the north side of the river
Distance: Trails on the south side of the river: Nature and Powerhouse Trails combined, 2.0 miles out and back; on the north side: Beaver Creek Loop, 1.5-mile loop; Ridge Loop, 0.75-mile loop; Hiking/biking Loop Trail, 2.0-mile loop
Approximate hiking time: South-side trails, 2 hours; Beaver Creek Loop, 1 hour; Ridge Loop, 30 minutes
Difficulty: Easy for all trails

Elevation gain/loss: Negligible
Trail surface: Loamy dirt; walkways, bridges, and steps
Lay of the land: Low rolling hills
Season: Year-round
Land status: Georgia State Parks Division
Nearest towns: Comer, Elberton, and Athens
Fees and permits: Park Pass $3.00 per day per vehicle
Maps: USGS Carlton; small map of the park with the hiking and biking trails, available at the park office
Trail contacts: Watson Mill Bridge State Park, 650 Watson Mill Road, Comer, GA 30629; (706) 783-5349; www.gastateparks.org

Finding the trailhead: From Athens go 13.0 miles east on Highway 72 to Comer. At Comer go south 3.1 miles on Highway 22 to Watson Mill Road. Turn left; the park entrance is 3.0 miles on the right. From Elberton go west 13.4 miles on Highway 72 to New Town Church Road. Turn left (south); cross railroad track and turn left on Old Fork Cemetery Road. Go 0.3 mile to Watson Mill Road and then 0.7 mile to the park entrance. The covered bridge is 0.4 mile farther south.

The trailhead for the trails downstream of the covered bridge and along the river is at the small concession building on the south side of the river. The Beaver Creek and Ridge Loop Trails can be hiked from either parking area on the north side of the covered bridge. The second parking area, a gravel loop off the main road 0.1 mile north, is the preferred trailhead for both trails.

The Hikes

The waterpower from the river at this scenic shoal was once used to drive a gristmill for corn and wheat, a cotton gin, a wool factory, and a woodworking shop. In 1905 the hydroelectric powerhouse, raceway canal, and dam were added. The only remains of this era are the canal that was hewn from the granite wall on one side

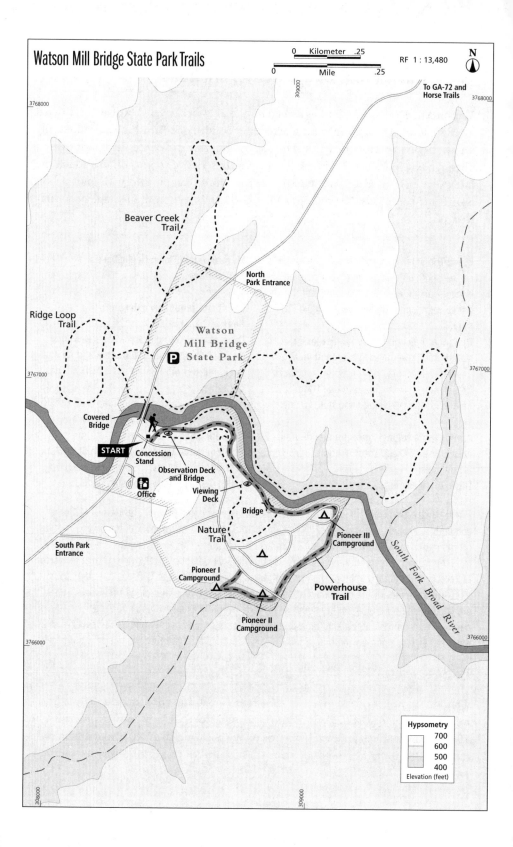

and the powerhouse ruins and a levee on the other side. One of the trails follows along the top of this levee.

A total of 3.5 miles of the park's trails are dedicated to hiking; an additional 4.75 miles are hiking/biking trails. Hikers are welcome to use the 12.0 miles of horse trails. The hiking trails on the river are all easy, with bridges and steps.

South-side Trails

From the concession building below the dam, the path leading to a footbridge over the canal is the access to the interconnected system of trails on the south side of the river. Here a large observation platform provides a view of the covered bridge and dam, with water flowing over the grand shoals below the bridge.

The **Nature Trail** can be hiked down the canal levee to the powerhouse ruins. As you walk down the levee, notice the exposed granite wall on the other side. During the warm months you may see frogs and toads as they hop into the canal waterway. At the end of the levee at the powerhouse, you can go down a few steps to the section of the trail that follows up the river with excellent views of the river tumbling over boulders and down the wide, steep shoals. Numerous ferns and flowers thrive in the moist riverside habitat. Chain ferns, spleenworts, and Christmas ferns grow along with many spring flowers. Dog-hobble and mountain laurel are among the shrubs growing in the moist shade. At times the river may overflow parts of this trail. Large riverine trees—beeches, ironwoods, yellow poplars, sycamores, water oaks, and others—provide shade during the warm months. An exceptionally large loblolly pine is right beside the trail. Before the leaves are on the trees, the early spring wildflowers begin to show. Look for tracks of deer, raccoons, squirrels, beavers, otters, and other animals in the soft, sandy soil along the path. This path leads back to the steps up to the overlook platform.

At the powerhouse ruins you can cross the canal on the footbridge and return on the other side of the canal to the observation platform, or you can continue on the Powerhouse Trail downriver for 0.6 mile and up Big Clouds Creek for another 0.4 mile. This is a one-way trail, or you may return by way of the Nature Trail.

The well-used **Powerhouse Trail** is easy to follow. There are no blaze marks, only direction signs at each intersection. As you go down the river, you come to a large observation platform that provides an easy view of the river. If you have time to sit here for a while, you may see a wood duck, other waterbirds, beavers, turtles, and many kinds of birds among the trees. Trees along the trail include beech, ash, hickory, yellow poplar, sycamore, and water oak—all providing food and nesting sites for the animals. Along the way is a variety of flowering plants. Heartleaf and elephant's-foot are visible most of the year. Trilliums, Solomon's seals, false Solomon's seals, trout lilies, hepaticas, windflowers, and many others will be blooming here in spring.

You cross a footbridge over a well-healed erosion gully that affords a nice view of an attractive cove of hardwood trees. Right after you cross the bridge, the Nature

Trail turns off to the right. Here you can walk back to the covered bridge area or continue on to Pioneer Campground III, only about a hundred yards farther.

A rather large and pretty creek, Big Clouds Creek, enters the river at the campground. The trail continues for 0.5 mile up this creek past Pioneer Campsite II and ends at Pioneer Camp I. The path passes under a piece of history in the form of an old, abandoned steel bridge. Only a few steel bridges of this type are left. The bridge is now covered with vines of muscadine, honeysuckle, and trumpet creeper and provides roosting and nesting places for birds. Big Clouds Creek flows through a typical bottomland hardwood forest, a productive habitat for plants and animals. Thick patches of switch cane grow along the path. In places the creek changes character and tumbles over granite boulders, creating nice places to wade. In the quiet water above and below are good places to fish for small bass, sunfish, and catfish. There are many animal tracks left by deer, squirrels, beavers, and wild turkeys in the soft sandy-clay path. From here you can backtrack on the Powerhouse Trail or take the short spur trail to the service road for 0.2 mile to the Nature Trail and back to the concession stand.

Miles and Directions

0.0   Start at the concession stand.

0.1   Reach the observation deck and bridge.

0.15 The Nature Trail turns to the left going down steps, following the Powerhouse Trail.

0.2   Pass the other end of the Nature Trail.

0.25 Go up to the powerhouse ruins and observation area, then continue downstream.

0.4   Reach the viewing deck. Take the time to sit, look, and listen.

0.45 Cross the bridge and shortly meet the Nature Trail on the right.

0.6   Cross the road to Pioneer Campsite III and go around the campsite to Big Clouds Creek, where the trail continues upstream.

0.8   Pass under the old steel bridge, and come in view of Pioneer II.

1.0   Reach the end of this trail at Pioneer I. Backtrack to Pioneer III and the concession stand trailhead. (**Option:** Take a 300-foot spur trail to the Park Service road and go another 0.1 mile to the Nature Trail on the right. You can follow this trail back to the powerhouse ruins and the concession stand, a shorter route.)

2.0   Arrive back at the trailhead.

North-side Trails

The **Beaver Creek Loop** and **Ridge Loop Trails** on the north side of the covered bridge are hiked from the sign marked PARKING, PICNICKING AND HIKING TRAILS. The trails begin near the entrance end of the parking area. These biking and hiking trails are excellent, as is the 2.0-mile **Hiking/Biking Loop Trail** on the opposite side of Watson Mill Road. These are excellent wildflower and birding areas. If you walk quietly, you can expect to see or hear deer, squirrels, and wild turkeys.

44 High Falls State Park Trails

Three trails varying in length and difficulty provide access to the falls as well as historical and natural areas of the park. The featured Non-Game Nature Trail changes 140 feet in elevation walking through the ridges; the Falls Nature and Historic Ruins Trails take you from the High Falls Road bridge level to Towaliga River level below the falls, a 120-foot change in elevation. Streamside overlooks provide excellent views of the river and falls.

Start: For trails on the west side of High Falls Road Bridge, from the roadside at the bridge; for trails on the east side of the bridge, at the sign across the road from the campground entrance

Distance: Non-Game Nature Trail, 2.3-mile lollipop; Falls Nature Trail, 1.1-mile loop; Historic Ruins Trail, 0.5 mile out and back

Approximate hiking time: Non-Game Nature Trail, 1½ hours; Falls Nature Trail, 1 hour; Historic Ruins Trail, 1 hour

Difficulty: Easy to moderate for all three trails

Elevation gain/loss: 140 feet

Trail surface: Loam with leaf litter; occasional rocky areas

Lay of the land: Rolling hills; some steep streamside cliffs

Season: Year-round

Nearest town: Forsyth

Fees and permits: Parking $3.00 per vehicle per day

Maps: USGS High Falls; detailed maps of the park and trails, available from the park office

Trail contacts: High Falls State Park, 76 High Falls Park Drive, Jackson, GA 30233; (912) 994-3053; www.gastateparks.org

Finding the trailhead: From Forsyth go 10.0 miles north on Interstate 75 to exit 198, High Falls Road/High Falls State Park. Turn right on High Falls Road and go 1.5 miles to the park entrance. From Atlanta go south 50 miles on I-75 to exit 198. The park is located 1.5 miles east on High Falls Road. Trailheads for the Historic Ruins and Nature Trails are at opposite ends of the High Falls Road bridge. The trailhead for the Non-Game Nature Trail is on the west side of the bridge at a parking area 0.2 mile from the High Falls Road on Towaliga River Drive to Camping Area 2.

The Hike

This is an area of remarkable natural beauty and historic significance, with something of interest throughout the year, including spring wildflowers, fishing, fall colors, and bird migrations. Waterfalls that drop almost 100 feet in multiple cascades over granite outcrops give the area and the state park its name. Pay close attention to the warning not to climb on the rock surfaces around the falls. Fatal accidents have occurred.

The rockwork for the gristmill that operated intermittently here from the mid-1800s until 1960 is still in place. The mill was burned during the Civil War and rebuilt in 1866. The park office has excellent historical information on the many businesses that once flourished on the power supplied by the falling water.

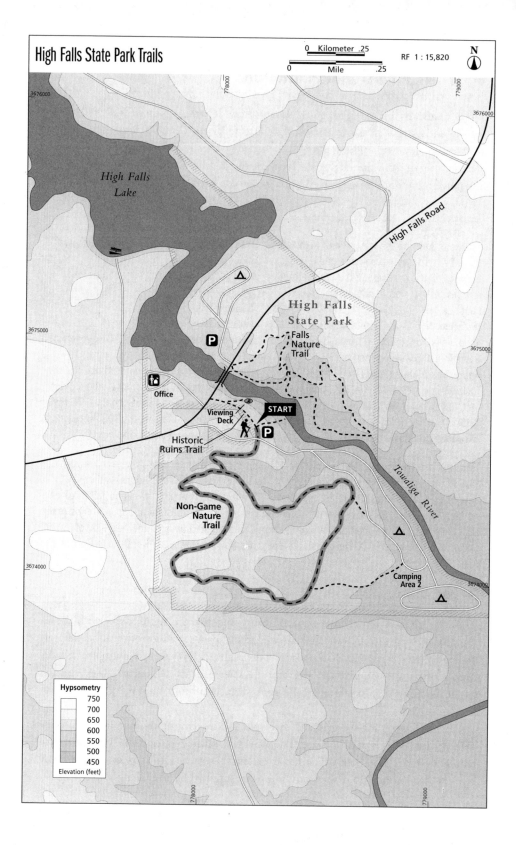

The 2.3-mile **Non-Game Nature Trail** can be accessed from several points along the loop. You can start at the High Falls Road with the Historic Ruins Trail or from two other points from Camping Area 2. You might see deer, turkeys, squirrels, foxes, skunks, and many songbirds.

For this hike, start at a parking area 0.2 mile on the left side of Towaliga River Drive, which turns off High Falls Road about 100 yards west of the park entrance. From the parking area, cross the road and follow the yellow-blazed trail down to a small stream. Cross the stream on a small wooden bridge and go up to the junction with the loop trail at 0.3 mile. Go to the right and climb up through a hardwood forest to a more level area. At Mile 0.75 you pass a small break in the more mature forest and start a descent to one of the several gullies resplendent with Christmas ferns that children hiking the trail have dubbed "Fern Gully" for the movie of the same name. All along the trail, footbridges cross the small brooks and erosion gullies, making that part of the trail easy to negotiate. At Mile 1.2 you come to an access trail from Camping Area 2. At 1.5 miles you reach another access trail to a different point in Camping Area 2. You pass along a steep hillside at 1.8 miles and close the loop at 2.0 miles. Follow the path to the right 0.3 mile back to the parking area.

Miles and Directions

0.0 Start at the parking area. Cross the road to the path with a short stone border. (**FYI:** The park staff residence visible to the left.)

0.2 Reach a small footbridge after coming down a slope with a switchback.

0.3 Meet the loop portion of the trail. Turn right and go around counterclockwise.

0.5 Come around a low ridge, following a contour.

0.7 Enter a stand of young trees, regeneration from a cleared area.

0.8 Start down into a steep cove, with an intermittent stream on the right.

1.2 Meet the first connector trail on the right from the campground.

1.5 Intersect the second connector, from another location in the campground.

1.8 Hike along a steep hillside to the right.

2.0 Close the loop and turn right.

2.3 Return to the parking area and trailhead.

Additional Trails

The **Historic Ruins Trail,** on the south side of the river near the park office, and the **Falls Nature Trail** are popular and are well worth the hike, although unmarked "shortcuts" make staying on the blazed trail quite difficult. This is a beautiful area to walk in if you are not concerned with staying on a specific trail.

From early spring through the summer and fall you will be able to enjoy numerous flowering plants along these trails. At a number of points, you will have excellent views of the river and the falls. With the lake and river nearby, this is an excellent birding hike.

45 Mistletoe State Park Trails

An interconnected group of easy to moderate trails offer campers and hikers 11.4 miles of pathways with only about a 130-foot change in elevation. You pass through a variety of wooded and open areas. You cross two small streams without bridges and go through frequent changes in habitats adding to the variety and interest of the hikes. The combined Cliatt Creek and Nature Trails and the Hiking/Biking Backcountry Trail are the featured trails. A kiosk across the road from the park office has a map of the trails and other useful information about the area.

Start: Kiosk across the road from the park office

Distance: Cliatt Creek and Nature Trails combined, 2.3-mile loop; Canyon Trail, 0.3-mile loop; Hiking/Biking Backcountry Trail, 5.6-mile lollipop; Return connector trail for Backcountry Trail, 0.9 mile one-way

Approximate hiking time: Combined Cliatt and Nature Trails, 1 hour; Hiking/Biking Backcountry Trail, 3 hours

Difficulty: Cliatt and Nature Trails, easy; Hiking/Biking Backcountry Trail, moderate

Elevation gain/loss: 130 feet

Trail surface: Clay loam; short sections of paved road

Lay of the land: Low hills

Season: Year-round

Land status: Georgia State Parks Division

Nearest town: Thomson

Fees and permits: Park Pass $3.00 per vehicle per day

Maps: USGS Leah and Woodlawn; park map with trails, available at the park office

Trail contacts: Mistletoe State Park, 3723 Mistletoe Road, Appling, GA 30802; (706) 541-0321; www.gastateparks.org

Finding the trailhead: From exit 175 off Interstate 20, go north 7.8 miles on Highway 150 to Winfield. Take Winfield Road north 1.9 miles to Mistletoe Road and then go 1.0 mile to the park entrance. Turn left and go about 250 yards to the information kiosk across the road from the park office. The trailhead for the Cliatt Trail is here. From it you have access to all other trails in the park.

The Hikes

The park takes its name from Mistletoe Junction, a local area that derived its name from the large, extensive growth of mistletoe in the oak trees. Young men and women used to meet here during the holiday season and pick the mistletoe. The forests in the park are the result of forest regeneration after farms were abandoned in the mid-1930s and consist of old and young growth pine and hardwoods. The area is excellent for birding. Deer, turkeys, squirrels, chipmunks, foxes, raccoons, and opossums may be seen if you walk quietly. Park staff and resource people schedule events all year covering a wide range of subjects. Visit www.gastateparks.org and click on "Summer News Letter" for a list of events.

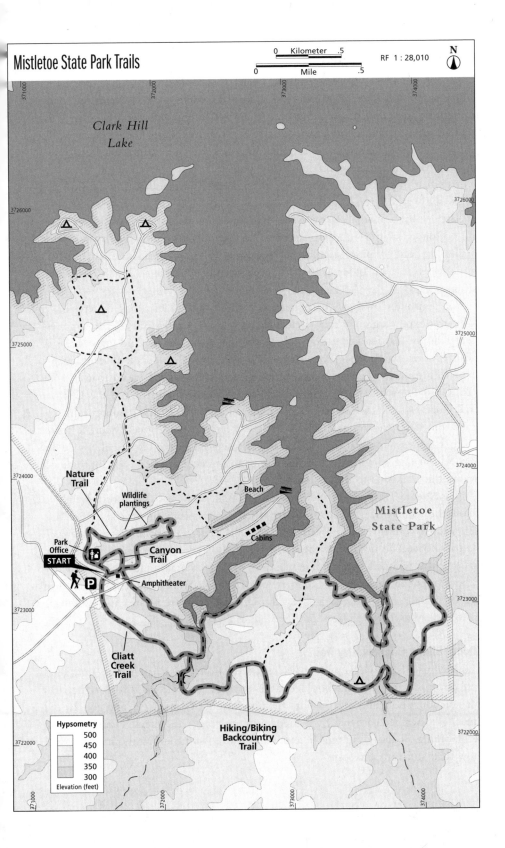

Mistletoe State Park Trails

0 Kilometer .5
0 Mile .5

RF 1 : 28,010

N

Clark Hill Lake

3726000

3725000

3724000

Nature Trail

Wildlife plantings

Beach

Mistletoe State Park

Park Office

START

P

Canyon Trail

Cabins

Amphitheater

3723000

Cliatt Creek Trail

Hiking/Biking Backcountry Trail

3722000

Hypsometry

500
450
400
350
300

Elevation (feet)

Cliatt Creek and Nature Trails

From trailhead kiosk, the white-blazed **Cliatt Creek Trail** can be hiked in either direction. For this hike, walk southeast toward the park entrance, across the roads, and into a young mixed hardwood-pine forest with a few older trees like the white oak that most frequently marks the site of a former farmhouse. These trees were the best shade trees and not as subject to lightning strikes as pines and taller, faster growing hardwoods like sweet gum and yellow poplar.

You go through terraces constructed on former farmland to stop erosion and spread the water better to the crops. Much of this land was in crops as recent as the late 1930s. The small farms were abandoned because the land was worn out and no longer supported a farm family. The fallow fields rapidly gave way to tree species like loblolly pine, sassafras, and persimmon. From these more recent clearings, you go into an older hardwood forest of beech, maple, yellow poplar, oaks, and hickories.

You continue down to Cliatt Creek at 0.7 mile and go left along the creek as it flows over exposed granite rocks before it empties into Clarks Hill Lake. A large resident flock of Canada geese from Clarks Hill Lake use the bay and grassy areas of the park. Leaving the lakeshore, the trail winds through older hardwoods where many spring flowers grow. Returning uphill you come to the paved road at Mile 1.25. Cross the road and in a few yards reach the amphitheater and the **Canyon Trail**. Turn right along a deep erosion gully. The clay soils of the Piedmont quickly erode into deep narrow gullies. This one is so large it has a small waterfall beside which an observation platform has been constructed. The age of the gully since the land was farmed is evident from the size of the trees growing in it. Continue on around this trail back to the trailhead.

The **Nature Trail** part of the Cliatt Creek Trail starts here as you turn right and follow the white blazes. There are lettered stations pointing out special natural history features you pass. A pamphlet with each of the letters described is available from the park office. You may enjoy the trail more if you pick one up before you go. On this trail you will pass two wildlife plantings of various grains and grasses attractive to birds, deer, rabbits, squirrels and many other animals. You continue downhill to an arm of a small cove of the lake. Cross through this more moist area and walk back up to the red and white blazes and the trailhead.

Hiking/Biking Backcountry Trail

The Hiking/Biking Backcountry Trail takes off from the Cliatt Creek Trail, 0.65 mile down the trail at a large boulder at the junction of an old roadbed. A sign marks this junction. The trail drops down to the floodplain of Cliatt Creek and goes by the stream as described earlier for 0.2 mile and then crosses the creek. Dogwoods will be blooming all along the trail here in early April. Later the Piedmont azaleas will show their soft-pink blossoms.

At 1.4 mile a connector trail turns to the left. This trail along a power line right-of-way gives you the option of crossing over to the Hiking/Biking Trail and returning to the Cliatt Creek Trail and the trailhead kiosk for a 3.4-mile loop.

Continue on the blue-blazed trail. All along the trail there are large boulders, part of the erosion-resistant gneiss and granite formations that extend from Augusta diagonally across the state to Columbus. Crossing over a low ridge, you come to another creek valley. At 2.1 miles you are at the backcountry camping area.

At 2.3 miles you come to Bohler Creek. It is much the same as Cliatt Creek, with many wildflowers and large trees in the floodplain. The very large sweet gums, yellow poplars, water and willow oaks, and river birches form a delightful cove. Once more you leave the moist, shaded creeks and cross a low ridge, following old roadbeds. Grasses grow in the trail, and the small, naturally regenerated fifteen-year-old loblolly pines form thickets beside the wide path. You descend down to the head of an embayment of Clarks Hill Lake at 3.2 miles.

You cross several old erosion gullies. These have healed, with little or no erosion today. At one point the path leads right down one of these gullies, which ends in a pleasant open hardwood cove with large loblolly pines, beeches, yellow poplars, and an impressive rock outcrop. This is particularly beautiful in spring when the trout lilies, hepaticas, trilliums, and other spring wildflowers are in bloom. Azaleas, dogwoods, dwarf pawpaws, and other shrubs bloom later in spring.

At 3.4 miles you are now on the bank of Bohler Creek. At 3.7 miles you will cross this small creek at a natural dam formed by a single large boulder that extends from bank to bank and forms a small pool above and a pretty little waterfall. There is no bridge at this crossing, and it may be necessary to get your shoes wet to cross over. After following along the creek downstream for a short distance, the trail again leaves the creek for the drier hillside. At 3.9 miles you begin to see more of the great boulders that have weathered into many shapes and sizes. Some elongated boulders have split lengthwise. One has a colony of resurrection ferns growing on top.

The trail now passes around the highest knoll on the way and again comes back to Cliatt Creek. After crossing the creek, you are back to the Cliatt Creek Trail at 4.9 miles. Follow the signs to the right and head back to the common trailhead.

Miles and Directions

0.0   Start at the kiosk trailhead for Cliatt Creek. Walk 0.65 mile to Backcountry Trail marker at the old road and large stone; turn right.

0.7   Start upstream on Cliatt Creek.

0.9   Cross bridge over Cliatt Creek

1.4   Intersect the connector trail on the left that follows a power line. (**Option:** Take the connector to return to the Cliatt Creek Trail and the trailhead kiosk for a 2.7-mile loop.)

2.1   Pass a backcountry campsite.

2.3 You are at Bohler Creek in a different watershed.

2.8 Climb to top of knoll through a stand of young pines, and begin back down toward the lake.

3.4 Pass Clarks Hill Lake on the right where Bohler Creek enters. (**FYI:** This embayment may be dry in winter months.)

3.7 Reach the rock dam on Bohler Creek; there is no bridge at this crossing.

4.3 Cross the connector trail again.

4.8 Walk along a steep ridge on left with the lake on your right.

4.9 Cross Cliatt Creek and rejoin the yellow-blazed Cliatt Creek Trail. Follow the signs to the right to return to the trailhead.

5.6 Arrive back at the kiosk trailhead.

Additional Trails

The park's other trails and three connector trails are excellent hiking options close to the campgrounds and the park office: **Camping–Beach Trail,** 1.7-mile one-way (45 minutes); **Camping Loop Trail,** 0.9-mile loop; **Office Connector Trail,** 0.5 mile one-way.

46 Piedmont National Wildlife Refuge Trails

Three well-marked loop trails take you through a wide range of habitats. The featured Red-cockaded Woodpecker Trail goes through typical pine-hardwood forest to an active nesting site of this small, endangered bird. Benches have been placed so that you can sit quietly to watch for the birds at their nest cavities in live pine trees. The Pine-Creek Trail forms one loop from the visitor center. Allison Lake Trail takes you along the lake to an observation deck and a photo blind. These trails are definitely worth your time and effort.

Start: Red-cockaded Woodpecker Trail, the information kiosk at the end of County Road 262; Pine-Creek and Allison Lake Trails, the visitor center parking lot
Distance: Red-cockaded Woodpecker Trail, 2.9-mile lollipop; Pine-Creek Trail, 1.3-mile loop; Allison Lake Trail, 1.0-mile loop
Approximate hiking time: Red-cockaded Woodpecker Trail, 1½ hours without waiting at nest cavity site; Pine-Creek and Allison Lake Trails, 1½ hours combined
Difficulty: Easy
Elevation gain/loss: Negligible

Trail surface: Clay loam; bridges over streams and permanently wet spots
Lay of the land: Gently rolling hills
Season: Year-round
Land status: U.S. Fish and Wildlife Service
Nearest towns: Forsyth, Monticello
Fees and permits: No fees or permits required
Maps: USGS Dames Ferry and Hillsboro; trail maps, available at the visitor center; Oconee National Forest map
Trail contacts: Refuge Manager, Piedmont National Wildlife Refuge, 718 Juliette Road, Round Oak, GA 31038; (478) 986-5441; www.piedmont.fws.gov

Finding the trailhead: From Macon go north on Interstate 75 to exit 186 in Forsyth and travel east on Juliette Road. Go 9.4 miles to a bridge across the Ocmulgee River. Continue on Round Oak Juliette Road 8.2 miles to the REFUGE VISITOR CENTER/OFFICE sign; turn left onto CR 262. The visitor center/office and parking area are 0.5 mile on the right. Trailheads for Pine-Creek and Allison Lake Trails are located here. Continue to the end of the road for the Red-cockaded Woodpecker Trail.

From Monticello take Highway 11 south 14.3 miles to the refuge sign and Round Oak Juliette Road; turn right (west). There is a fire tower at this intersection. Go 3.1 miles to the REFUGE VISITOR CENTER/OFFICE sign; turn right and follow the directions above.

The Hike

Piedmont National Wildlife Refuge was established in 1939 to manage the wildlife potential of the exhausted farmland. Natural history and some human history are

Piedmont National Wildlife Refuge Trails

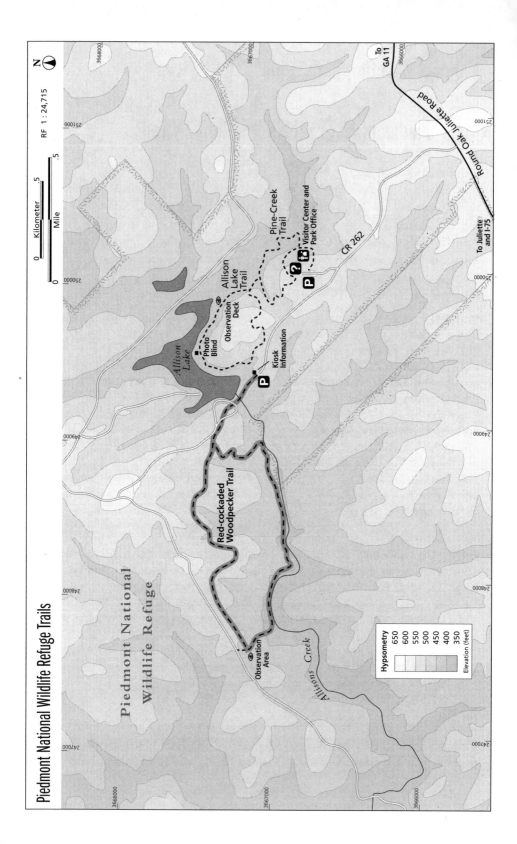

interpreted in the Allison Lake Nature Trail guide. In addition to the hikes described here, there are several more miles of unmarked trails and a wildlife drive on the refuge.

The information kiosk has basic information about the red-cockaded wood-pecker and other wildlife and their needs. Another sign cautions about ticks, which can transmit diseases, including Lyme disease. For your protection, use the following precautions when walking refuge trails: Wear protective clothing, tuck pants into footwear, use a strong insect repellent, and check for ticks both during and after the hike.

The Red-cockaded Woodpecker Trail begins at the parking area and information kiosk at the end of CR 262. The trail follows an unpaved service road across the Allison Lake dam. Nest boxes for wood ducks are placed about the lake and are easily seen from the trail. This area was one of the pioneer places for experimental wood duck nest boxes to improve the population of this most beautiful of our native ducks. Across the dam the trail continues on the service road for another few yards before it turns into a pine forest on a wide path. Fiberglass posts with hiker symbols mark the path throughout the loop.

As the trail enters wetter sites, oak, yellow poplar, sweet gum, and other hardwood trees replace the pines. The undergrowth of dogwood and occasional redbud trees blooms profusely in early spring. Wildlife along the trail includes deer, fox and gray squirrels, turkeys, and a number of songbirds. At 0.4 mile the path divides. The right prong leads to the red-cockaded woodpecker colony; the left prong is the return path to complete the loop.

Erosion gullies indicate the extent to which this area was farmed during the early 1930s before it became a national wildlife refuge. At slightly more than a mile, you reach the mature loblolly pines, the focal point of the trail. A white ring is painted about 8 feet up the towering pines on selected trees. These designate the nest trees of the endangered red-cockaded woodpecker, which excavates its nest cavity in old, live pine tree that have a fungus disease called red-heart. The small woodpeckers chip away at the bark around the nest cavity, causing the resin to flow down around the tree. The cavities are 15 to 20 feet and higher above the ground. A bench has been provided for watching the trees for a glimpse of these rare birds. Quiet observation often results in seeing the 8.5-inch-long woodpecker, described as zebra-backed with a black cap and a white cheek. They live in family colonies and use the same nest cavity for several years. Pay close attention to the carsonite trail markers and the white blazes; do not get confused and walk toward the white-banded nest cavity trees.

The trail leads away from the nesting colony down to Allison Creek and returns to the junction and back to the trailhead. Along the creek there is evidence of beaver cuttings and slides on the creekbank. Wildflowers, ferns, and other plants that prefer moist soils are abundant along the floodplain. The beautiful Piedmont azalea grows here, blooming in April and May.

Miles and Directions

0.0 Start at the information kiosk at end of CR 262. Follow the unpaved road across the Allison Lake dam.

0.3 Leave the refuge road to follow the loop trail, marked by the fiberglass post with hiker symbols.

0.4 The trail forks; take right fork.

0.5 Cross the first footbridge.

0.8 Cross the second footbridge.

1.4 Arrive at the benches near the red-cockaded woodpecker nest site. (**FYI:** White bands placed 8 feet high designate trees with a nest cavity. Sit quietly and watch for the small, rare birds to return to their nests.) Follow the trail marker posts, continuing around the loop.

1.6 Reach Allison Creek; turn left (east) and walk along the creek.

2.4 Turn left, leaving the creek.

2.7 Close the loop and turn right to return to the trailhead.

2.9 Arrive back at the parking area and the information kiosk.

Additional Trails

The following trails can be combined for a ninety-minute ramble.

The **Pine-Creek Trail** is interesting because of the variety of habitat through which it passes. The 1.3-mile loop begins at the refuge visitor center parking area as a concrete-paved wheelchair-accessible section 500 feet long. A backyard wildlife habitat demonstration area with a small pool and plantings attracts birds, butterflies, and other animals. The path drops down the slope to the creek. The forest changes from a mostly pine overstory to deciduous hardwoods. A bench at the spring invites you to stop and take in the quietness of this pleasant microhabitat.

The Pine-Creek Trail connects at an observation deck to the **Allison Lake Trail.** This 1.0-mile loop takes you through loblolly pine and bottomland hardwood forests beside attractive Allison Lake. A completely covered photo blind provides an excellent observation point and should be approached quietly.

Honorable Mentions

K Charlie Elliott Wildlife Center

The 6,400-acre Charlie Elliott Wildlife Center encompasses the Marben Public Fishing Area, the Clybel Wildlife Management Area, and the Charlie Elliott Visitor Center. This is a must-visit area for hiking, birding, fishing, and family outings. Located 3.0 miles south of Mansfield or 14.0 miles north of Monticello on Highway 11, the center is a museum of the history of modern conservation in Georgia, demonstrated in the life of conservationist, wildlife administrator, and outdoors writer Charlie Elliott. Children will find much to do at the visitor center, including interactive displays and window viewing of birds and other animals with binoculars provided by the center.

Five short loop trails, totaling 7.4 miles, are easy to moderate as they pass through a diverse wildlife management area. The visitor center is the ideal starting point for most of the hikes. The trails encompass a wide variety of habitats from dense woodlands, open fields, and lakeshores to granite outcrops with unique fauna and flora. There are twenty man-made lakes in the area, with the trails touching two. Fishing is permitted, and one lake is reserved for children ages twelve to sixteen years old.

For more information: Georgia Department of Natural Resources, Wildlife Resources Division, Charlie Elliott Wildlife Center, 543 Elliott Trail, Mansfield, GA 30055; (770) 784–3059; www.gohuntgeaogia.com.

DeLorme: Georgia Atlas and Gazetteer: Page 27 FG9

L Rum Creek Wildlife Management Area Nature Trail

This trail is located in the Number 4 unit of the Rum Creek Wildlife Management Area. It was developed with funds from the T.E.R.N. (The Environmental Resources Network) organization. The trailhead is adjacent to the Wildlife Resources Division, Nongame-Endangered Wildlife office. The 1.2-mile loop has eighteen points of interest, interpreted with well-designed information plaques. The trail passes through predominately second-growth hardwoods and pines—hickory, oak, sweet gum, black gum, wild cherry, loblolly pine—with an understory including dogwood, small red buckeyes, beauty berry, muscadine, and the ever-present poison ivy.

Walking the trail you border a wetland area and cross a small creek by bridge. The trail is in direct conjunction with the Wildlife Resources Division, Nongame-Endangered Wildlife Office. Near the trailhead, a butterfly and hummingbird flower garden is maintained along with an array of bird feeders. The area is used frequently by both adults and school groups and offers an exceptional opportunity for children. The funds for maintaining the Nature Trail and demonstrations are provided by T.E.R.N.

For more information: Nongame-Endangered Wildlife Office, 116 Rum Creek Drive, Forsyth, GA 31029; (478) 994–1438; www.georgiawildlife.com. T.E.R.N. Inc., 116 Rum Creek Drive, Forsyth, GA 31029; (478) 994–1438; www.TERNfor wildlife.org.

DeLorme: Georgia Atlas and Gazetteer: Page 34 D4

M Ocmulgee River Trail

This trail is 3.0 miles of easy walking through the bottomland hardwoods and pines of the Ocmulgee River. The trail is listed and managed by the USDA Forest Service for both hiking and horseback riding. Explore the riverbank of the historically important Ocmulgee River. Spring wildflowers, birding, wildlife watching, camping, fishing, and small and big game hunting in season are all available.

What this trail lacks in grand scenery, it makes up in interesting wildlife and wildflower habitat. Deer, raccoons, fox and gray squirrels, and other mammals are evident from the many tracks left in the soft sandy and silty loam of the riverbank. Wild turkeys, wood ducks, hooded mergansers, woodcocks, quail, and other game birds may be seen or heard. An amazing variety of songbirds use the area as residents and during the spring and fall migrations. Beavers, minks, muskrats, and even an occasional otter may be seen along the river's edge, with turtles sunning on the exposed logs in the river. The hillsides above the floodplain are excellent areas for spring wildflowers. Trout lilies (also called dogtooth violets) bloom on the floodplain in late February and early March.

Two interconnected Kinnard Creek and Wise Creek Trails are accessible from the Ocmulgee River Trail. The Kinnard Creek Trail is designated for horseback riding, although hikers are welcome to use the trail. Wise Creek is for both hikers and equestrians.

For more information: Chattahoochee-Oconee National Forests, Oconee Ranger District, 1199 Madison Road, Eatonton, GA 31024; (706) 485–3180; www.fs.fed.us/conf.

DeLorme: Georgia Atlas and Gazetteer: Page 34 B3

N Bobby Brown State Park

Bobby Brown State Park is located on a forested peninsula formed by the Savannah and Broad Rivers at the headwaters of Clarks Hill Reservoir. The tip of the peninsula is the site of the colonial town of Petersburg, the third largest town in the state in 1790. The park is named for Robert T. Brown, USN, who lost his life during World War II. The 2.2-mile-long trail is ideal for family hiking. It is relatively easy, with only two short, steep sections. Part of the trail follows the path William Bartram trod in 1791 while he was exploring the region for useful plants to be sent back to England for commercial purposes (see the Bartram National Heritage Trail).

Well-made footbridges cross all low and wet areas, and the trail follows contours as it crosses the low ridges. Clark Hill Lake can be seen through the trees for most of the way. An observation platform at the end of the peninsula provides full view of the lake, surrounding you on three sides. From here you may see bald eagles, ospreys, ducks, geese, herons, and other birds associated with Clarks Hill Reservoir. An information board tells about the colonial town of Petersburg and the Petersburg boat used to take people, cotton, and produce to Augusta during the last years of the 1790s and early 1800 (see the Augusta Canal National Heritage Area Trail). More trails are planned.

For more information: Bobby Brown State Park, 2509 Bobby Brown State Park Road, Elberton, GA 30635-5727; (706) 213–2046; www.gastateparks.org.

DeLorme: Georgia Atlas and Gazetteer: Page 31 B9

○ Ocmulgee National Monument

Six miles of easy trails interconnect to provide access to the significant areas within the monument. The well-marked Human Cultural Trails make it easy for you to visit all the key features in the lives of the earliest Americans. From these trails you can walk the Wildflower Trail to the McDougal Mound or the Opelofa Trail around the wetland area to the Loop Trail around a wooded knoll of hardwoods and pines and the River Trail that, at this writing, is being reclaimed from two disastrous floods.

Located on the eastern edge of Macon on U.S. Highway 80 East, this national monument is convenient to local residents, especially students who frequently take field trips to the area. Evidence of 12,000 years of human habitation is wonderfully interpreted on the ground and in the fine visitor center, which houses a major archaeological museum. Between 900 and 1,100 A.D. the people known as Mississippians, skillful at farming, built the mounds so evident at this site. The park was established as a memorial to the antiquity of man in this southeast corner of the United States. The trails connect all archaeological and natural history features. Since the mounds are located on the floodplain of the Ocmulgee River, the only significant elevation changes are in various mounds, such as the 45-foot-high Temple Mound. This is a fine place to watch for birds and deer along with squirrels and other small mammals.

For more information: Ocmulgee National Monument, 1207 Emory Highway, Macon, GA 31217-4399; (478) 752–8257; www.nps.gov/ocmu.

DeLorme: Georgia Atlas and Gazetteer: Page 34 G6

47 Sweetwater Creek State Conservation Park Trails

Sweetwater Creek is a beautiful, fast-flowing stream that wends its way through a granite-boulder streambed in a well-protected wooded valley. Six miles of trails pass the ruins of a Civil War–era textile mill and follow along a stream that meanders through mature hardwood forests. The short Factory Ruins Trail leads to the ruins along the river. The featured trail combines the Ruins and Falls Trail with the Jacks Hill Trail for a 3.7-mile loop past the old factory ruins and down Sweetwater Creek to a waterfall overlook before returning to the trailhead. All trails are hiking only. Park Ranger Don Scarbrough Jr. has recorded more than 120 wildflowers in bloom along the trails in the park from early February to mid-June. The old area of Lithia Springs, a few miles to the north, was a favorite area of early Native Americans because of the salt (lithium) springs.

Start: Parking area near the visitor center
Distance: Four loop trails, totaling about 7.8 miles; Ruins and Falls Trail with Jacks Hill Trail, 3.7-mile loop
Approximate hiking time: 4 hours for all trails; Factory Ruins–Jacks Hill loop, 2 hours; shorter loops, about 1 hour each
Difficulty: Mostly easy to moderate; a few strenuous sections
Elevation gain/loss: 220 feet
Trail surface: Clay loam; some paved and short rocky and gravel sections
Lay of the land: Rolling low hills

Season: Year-round; spring for more than one hundred species of wildflowers and fall for spectacular foliage
Land status: Georgia State Parks Division
Nearest town: Lithia Springs
Fees and permits: $3.00 per vehicle per day
Maps: USGS Austell, Campbellton, Mableton, and Ben Hill; trail map, available from the park office
Trail contacts: Sweetwater Creek State Park, P.O. Box 816, Lithia Springs, GA 30057; (770) 732-5871; www.gastateparks.org

Finding the trailhead: From Atlanta take Interstate 20 West to exit 44 at Thornton Road. Turn left and go 0.25 mile to Blairs Bridge Road. Turn right and go 2.1 miles to Mt. Vernon Road. Turn left and go 1.15 miles to the park entrance on the left. Go 0.7 mile on Factory Shoals Road to the visitor center and parking area. The parking area is the trailhead for all trails.

Alternate route from Atlanta: Take I-20 west to exit 41, Lee Road. Turn left (south) on Lee Road and continue south 1.0 mile to Cedar Terrace and turn left. Cedar Terrace dead-ends into Mt. Vernon Road; turn right and go 0.3 mile to the main park entrance, Factory Shoals Road. Turn left for the visitor center and parking area for the trails.

Sweetwater Creek rapids as seen from the observation deck.

The Hike

Sweetwater Creek State Conservation Park has a wilderness feel, offering many species of wildflowers and wildlife, a beautiful forest, and cascading Sweetwater Creek—all only minutes from downtown Atlanta. During the Civil War, cloth was manufactured at the New Manchester Manufacturing Company for Confederate troops. This proved the factory's undoing. General Sherman ordered the factory and other buildings to be burned on July 9, 1864. The mostly women and children working at the mill were told to pack for a long trip, loaded into wagons, and eventually placed in a prison camp in Louisville, Kentucky.

The remnants of the brick mill, millrace, and other historical points of interest are seen from this trail, along with a wide variety of plants that include native azaleas and mountain laurels.

A tree-covered gravel walkway leaves the parking area under a canopy of a dozen species of trees. The trails are well marked and are interpreted in a leaflet, available at the park office. The wide, well-used path leads to Sweetwater Creek and downstream to the factory ruins.

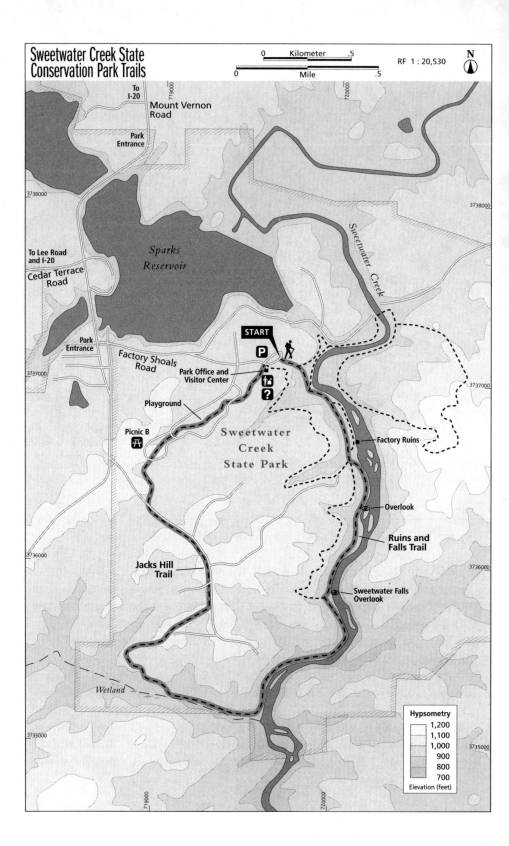

Sweetwater Creek State Conservation Park Trails

0 Kilometer .5
0 Mile .5

RF 1 : 20,530

N

To I-20

Mount Vernon Road

Park Entrance

Sweetwater Creek

3738000
3738000

Sparks Reservoir

To Lee Road and I-20

Cedar Terrace Road

Park Entrance

Factory Shoals Road

START

P

Park Office and Visitor Center

Playground

Picnic B

Sweetwater Creek State Park

3737000
3737000

Factory Ruins

Overlook

Ruins and Falls Trail

Jacks Hill Trail

3736000
3736000

Sweetwater Falls Overlook

Wetland

Hypsometry

1,200
1,100
1,000
900
800
700

Elevation (feet)

3735000
3735000

The beauty of the creek and valley is just as fascinating as the trail's historical features. Numbered markers correspond to the interpretive leaflet. Return to the parking area on the same trail, continue downstream to the Blue-Blazed Trail, or continue around the white-blazed loop trail.

Beautiful views of the Georgia Piedmont are visible downstream from the factory ruins at the falls. The granite cliffs along the bank and cascades are spectacular. A well-designed set of steps and a platform enable a grand view of the creek and falls.

The rock cliffs support many interesting plants, such as rockcap fern, liverworts, and mosses. If you are returning via the Blue-Blazed Trail, you leave the creek and follow a gentle contour through several pleasant coves with fern glades and tributary branches rich in wildflowers growing on the forest floor. This trail is 1.7 miles back to the parking area and trailhead.

Continuing downstream from the falls, the white-blazed Jacks Hill Trail follows the creek for another 0.6 mile before turning to the right up a brook flowing over gravel and granite. This setting is within thirty minutes of downtown Atlanta. With a cascading stream, steep hillsides, trees, and flowering plants, the area is very reminiscent of the mountains. Large chain ferns, cinnamon ferns, Christmas ferns, and other moist-soil plants are abundant along the brook. You follow the brook for 0.7 mile and then climb steadily up the side of the ridge until it opens out on an unpaved road overlooking a long, narrow lake frequented by beavers, turtles, wood ducks, herons, and other waterbirds and mammals. From this point the trail follows the unpaved road through a forested area and into open fields. The fields with young trees like persimmon, sumac, loblolly pine, and oaks add an interesting diversion from the more mature forest. Several service roads are crossed or branch off the trail. It is necessary to keep the white blaze in sight. After going through pine stands and some hardwoods, the trail goes through a campground and back to the parking area and trailhead.

Miles and Directions

0.0 Start at end of the parking area.

0.1 Pass the Army Bridge–Sweetwater Creek Trail, or Yellow Trail, on left.

0.15 Pass the Bridge–Ruins Creek Connector on the left.

0.3 Factory Ruins Spur Trail begins on the left.

0.5 The Factory Ruins Spur returns to the main trail. (**FYI:** At this point you are at the factory ruins on the left, and only 150 feet from the return of the Blue-Blazed Trail, and 1.0 mile from the trailhead.) Continue on the Factory Ruins and Falls Trail.

1.0 Reach the end of the Ruins and Falls Trail, start of the white-blazed Jacks Hill Trail, and Sweetwater Fall Overlook—a grand place to stop and enjoy the view.

1.1 Enjoy a grand view of the rapids.

1.6 Make a 90-degree right turn, leaving Sweetwater Creek to go up a small branch; begin the upland portion of the Jacks Hill Trail.

1.9 Make a right turn and then a quick left turn around the base of an old dam.

2.1 You are going around the "Jack Hill Environmental Education Area."

2.2 Make a right turn, going almost due east.

2.5 Begin walking on Jacks Hill Road as you turn left back north.

3.0 Leave Jacks Hill Road, turning right. (**FYI:** You are at 1,000 feet elevation after leaving Sweetwater Creek at 780 feet.)

3.2 Go through or around Picnic Area B and the playground area.

3.7 Arrive back at the parking area, closing the loop at the common trailhead.

Additional Trails

Although the **Army Bridge–Eastside Trail,** or **Yellow Trail,** is not associated with the historical significance of Sweetwater Creek, it's well worth your time. Starting at the common trailhead, this 2.2-mile loop crosses the bridge over Sweetwater Creek on the way to a steep ridge that affords excellent views of the area.

More Information

Local Events/Attractions

Georgia Aquarium, 225 Baker Street, Atlanta, GA 30313; (404) 581-4000; www.georgia aquarium.org.

Six Flags over Georgia Theme Park, located on Interstate 20, at exit 46; (770) 948-9290; www.sixflags.com/parks/overgeorgia/index .asp.

48 Panola Mountain State Conservation Park Trails

Four trails totaling 6.5 miles offer easy interpretive walks through this unique park. Panola Mountain rises to 940 feet, only 260 feet above South River, which flows along its northern edge. There is very little change in elevation along the two self-guided trails described here. The Rock Outcrop and Micro-watershed interpretive trails provide information on the area's geology, fauna, flora, and history. A trail to the top of the mountain is available only as a scheduled hike guided by park personnel.

Start: Visitor center and office
Distance: Rock Outcrop Trail, 0.75-mile loop; Micro-watershed Trail, 1.25-mile loop; Fitness Trail, 1.0-mile loop; limited-use Panola Mountain Trail, 3.5-mile double-loop lollipop
Approximate hiking time: Rock Outcrop and Micro-watershed Trails, 1 hour; Panola Mountain Trail, 3 hours
Difficulty: Easy
Elevation gain/loss: Negligible
Trail surface: Dirt and gravel
Lay of the land: Massive granite outcrop with low rolling hills

Season: Year-round; most colorful in spring and fall
Land status: Georgia State Parks Division
Nearest towns: Lithonia, Stockbridge
Fees and permits: Parking $3.00 per vehicle per day; annual parking passes available at the park
Maps: USGS Redan and Stockbridge; page-size map of the park and trails, available at the park office and interpretive center
Trail contacts: Panola Mountain State Park, 2600 Highway 155 SW, Stockbridge, GA 30281; (770) 389-7801; www.gastate parks.org

Finding the trailhead: From exit 68 off Interstate 20, take Wesley Chapel Road south 0.3 mile to Snapfinger Road. Go 1.8 miles to Highway 155, and then 5.0 miles on Highway 155 to the Panola State Park entrance on the left. All trails share the same trailhead at the interpretive center.

The Hikes

Of the several granite domes in the vicinity, Panola Mountain is the only one left undisturbed. Unique granite outcrops and the endemic plants and animals are associated with this peculiar habitat. Wildlife including deer, squirrels, rabbits, raccoons, opossums, skunks, and chipmunks may be seen along with lizards and other reptiles. Butterflies abound during the summer months, feeding on the wide variety of flowering plants.

The park will eventually tie in with the much more extensive network of paved trails that lead to Davidson-Arabia Mountain Nature Preserve, the town of Lithonia, and the Stonecrest Mall. There will be more than 13 miles of 10-foot wide, paved trails constructed in conjunction with The Path Foundation, Dekalb and Rockdale Counties, and the Georgia State Parks and Historic Sites Division (DNR).

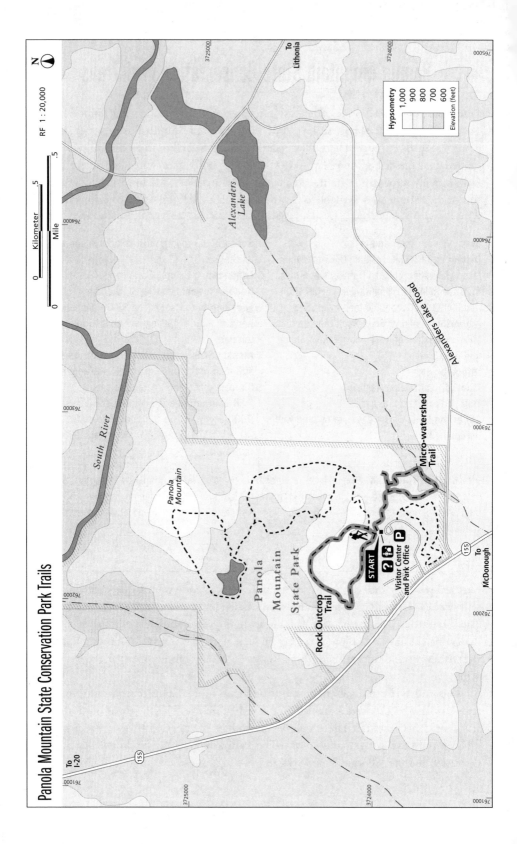

Panola Mountain State Conservation Park Trails

The Micro-watershed and Rock Outcrop Trails are ideal for family walks. The interpretive center has excellent displays of local geology, plants, and wildlife; park personnel offer frequent nature walks for children and adults. The 1,126-acre park borders a rapidly growing residential area and provides excellent educational outdoor activities for its neighbors.

Micro-watershed Trail

The Micro-watershed Trail leads off to the right behind the interpretive center and passes through a mixed pine-hardwood forest with undergrowth of sweet gum, sassafras, maple, and yellow poplar saplings along with dogwood trees and honeysuckle and muscadine vines. Strawberry bush is common with its strikingly colorful fruits in fall. Ferns are abundant and include bracken, Christmas, wood, and cinnamon ferns and brownstem spleenwort. The first interpretive sign explains, with illustrations, the workings of a watershed. Other signs along the trail point out special features such as the deeply eroded gullies and past farming activities. A platform affords a good perspective of the deepness of the eroded ravines. Dropping into a small creek bottom, the forest is almost completely hardwoods with large sweet gums, yellow poplars, beeches, several species of oaks, and an occasional large loblolly pine. The stream is crossed on a short bridge. Large patches of New York ferns grow in the moist alluvial soil along the creek. The loop returns to the trailhead through a much younger growth of pines and deciduous trees, regenerating from past controlled fires. This practice is explained on an interpretive sign.

Rock Outcrop Trail

The short but very attractive Rock Outcrop Trail makes a loop through a boulder-strewn woods with interesting vistas of large exposures of granite and many colorful plants. During late summer and fall, masses of yellow flowers, locally known as Confederate daisies and found only on and around these granite domes, add spectacular color to the otherwise gray rock outcrops. Interpretive stations along the trail provide educational insight to a naturally fascinating trail. The loop is less than a mile, but the rock formations and plant and animal life give it a special charm.

Additional Trails

A number of exercise devices are located along the 1.0-mile **Fitness Trail.**

The 3.5-mile **Panola Mountain Trail** is designed to provide a closer look at the undisturbed one hundred–acre granite dome atop the mountain. To protect the natural condition of the very fragile plant communities, the trail is available only as a scheduled guided hike. The staff leaders interpret the special features throughout the hike.

More Information

Local Events/Attractions
Fernbank Museum of Natural History, 767 Clifton Road, NE, Atlanta, GA 30307; (404) 929-6400.
Stone Mountain Park, Exit 8 off of Highway 78, Atlanta, GA; (770) 498-5690 or (800) 401-2407; www.stonemountainpark.com.

Zoo Atlanta, 800 Cherokee Avenue SE, Atlanta, GA 30315; (404) 624-WILD; www.zooatlanta.org.
Georgia Aquarium, 225 Baker Street, Atlanta, GA 30313; (404) 581-4000; www.georgia aquarium.org.

49 Davidson–Arabia Mountain Nature Preserve Trails with Arabia Mountain Trail

Davidson–Arabia Mountain Nature Preserve encompasses another of the prominent rock outcrops called a monadnock—an isolated hill standing above the surrounding area. These rock outcrops support a unique environment with a wide variety of microhabitats that support a number of endemic plant and animal species. There are four trails in the preserve plus the long Arabia Mountain Trail, which passes through the preserve. These trails have been designed to expose you to as many of the different habitats as possible. The featured hike combines the Forest and South Lake Trails to create a 1.9-mile loop that begins and ends at the Nature Center.

Start: Nature Center for Forest, South Lake, and Fern Trails; south parking area for the Bradley Mountain Peak Trail and the unmarked mountain loop trail; several road crossing throughout the preserve for the paved Arabia Mountain Trail

Distance: Forest Trail, 1.8 miles out and back; South Lake Trail, 2.0 miles out and back; Fern Trail, 0.4 mile out and back; Bradley Peak Trail, 1.2 miles out and back; unmarked mountain loop trail, 2.4 miles in addition to Bradley Peak Trail; Arabia Mountain Trail, 13.4 miles total, including spurs

Approximate hiking time: Forest Trail with South Lake Trail, 1 hour; Bradley Peak Trail, 1 hour (with the unmarked mountain loop trail, 1½ hours) Arabia Mountain Trail, Lithonia to Nature Center, 1½ hours; Nature Center to Evans Mill Road, 2½ hours

Difficulty: Bradley Peak Trail, moderate; Forest Trail, easy; South Lake Trail, easy with moderate sections of uneven granite surface; Fern Trail, easy; Arabia Mountain Trail, easy to moderate

Elevation gain/loss: Bradley Mountain Peak Trail, 165 feet; other trails negligible

Trail surface: Dirt and sandy loam; natural, uneven granite and exposed quarry stone surface in Nature Preserve; Arabia Mountain Trail, 10-foot-wide concrete pavement

Lay of the land: Gently rolling hills, granite dome

Season: Year-round

Land status: Dekalb County Parks, Path Foundation, Georgia Department of Natural Resources, Panola Mountain State Conservation Park, City of Lithonia

Nearest towns: Lithonia, Conyers

Fees and permits: No fees or permits required
Maps: USGS Conyers and Redan; map of Davidson-Arabia Mountain Nature Preserve, available at Nature Center
Trail contacts: Davidson-Arabia Mountain Nature Preserve, 3787 Klondike Road, Lithonia, GA 30038; (770) 484-0603; www.arabiaalliance.org

Arabia Mountain Heritage Area Alliance; www.arabiaalliance.org
Path Foundation, P.O. Box 14327, Atlanta, GA 30324; (404) 875-7284; www.path foundation.org; path@pathfoundation.org
Panola Mountain State Conservation Park; (770) 389-7801; www.gastateparks.org

Finding the trailhead: From Interstate 20 take exit 74 (Evans Mill Road and Lithonia). Turn right and go 0.1 mile through the next traffic light on Woodrow. Continue 0.8 mile to Klondike Road; turn right and go 1.2 miles to the DAVIDSON–ARABIA MOUNTAIN NATURE PRESERVE sign. Turn right into parking area at the kiosk and Nature Center. The south parking area for the Bradley Peak Trail is 1.0 mile farther south on Klondike Road.

The Hikes

Arabia Mountain is said to be 100 million years older than its three local granite-dome cousins. Arabia is noted for the swirling rock pattern characteristic of "Lithonia gneiss," formed when the mountain's original granite metamorphosed into gneiss. The history of human settlement in this region is intimately connected to its geological resources, starting more than 7,000 years ago with the quarrying and trading of soapstone. Included in the park is the former rock quarry donated by the Davidson family, who operated it until 1972.

Arabia Mountain is home to two federally protected species (black-spore quill-wort and little amphianthus) as well as several other rare plants and plants that are unique to the granite-outcrop environment, such as the brilliant red diamorpha or Small's stonecrop and Georgia oak. Other plants you can expect to fine here include sunnybells, sparkleberry, and fringe tree. Mosses and lichens are well adapted to the harsh rock outcrop. Lichens are very fragile, especially when dry, and very susceptible to foot-traffic damage. A plant endemic to these mountains that will not escape your notice is the yellow daisylike flower affectionately called the "Confederate daisy" *(Viguiera porteri)* that blooms in masses in late summer.

Bradley Peak Trail

The Bradley Peak Trail starts at the south parking area. It is a 0.6-mile trail up Arabia Mountain (954 feet) to its highest point, which affords a 360-degree view of the lower Piedmont forestland. After you leave the parking area and walk along the log-fenced area, you are on the beginning gentle slope of the granite dome. Loblolly pines grow in isolated spots where roots can get started. The path is easy to follow, with only a slight incline at first.

At 0.3 mile you break away for the pines and low shrubs to begin the steeper climb with only the uneven granite and quarry stone. Here you will not see a trodden path, since there are few marks from foot travel. Cairns, carefully stacked cut granite stones with mortar, 2 to 3 feet high are now the only trail blazes. As soon as you get to one cairn, you will be able to see the next. Watch for an occasional lichen grasshopper (locally called the "lichenhopper") that might fly up in front of you only to plop down a few yards away. If you take your eyes off the spot where it landed, you probably won't be able to find it again, so splendidly is it camouflaged to match the color and pattern of the lichen patches.

Continuing on up, the way gets steeper until at 0.6 mile you reach the crest of this dome, highest of the two prominent, rounded areas called Bradley Mountain Peak. On the way you will see a number of rounded depressions that hold water following rains. The larger pockets hold water long enough for several plants species to become established. At the top you have a 360-degree view across the landscape and down on the pine-hardwood forests. You quickly realize that this is the only prominent hill in the area. Morning and evening you can see some truly spectacular sunrises and sunsets. A 1.7-mile unmarked trail extends to the north, losing about 80 feet in elevation before crossing an old road to a former quarry site. The path bends around the north side of the other, lower dome; turns to the east, following around to the south along the eastern side of the mountain; and ends by intercepting the Bradley Peak Trail and following it back to the parking area.

Forest Trail

The Forest Trail begins at the Nature Center and goes through a pleasant pine-hardwood forest to a picnic shelter at Arabia Lake. You will go to right of and parallel to the wide, paved Arabia Mountain Trail and then cross it at 0.2 mile to continue on toward the lake. The most impressive forest feature here is the thickness of the undergrowth and the large loblolly pines. You continue northwest on a soft pine needle and leaf loamy trail in an area that could be anywhere in north Georgia's remote forests, and yet you are only a mile from a busy, bustling residential community. At 0.4 mile you go through an area of large, old gnarled pines that show the scars of past fires that were common fifty years ago. Openings in the undergrowth give you views of small areas of exposed granite lined with trees and supporting patches of moss and lichens along with bunches of flowering plants. The topography over the areas around the larger granite domes is relatively flat; however, there is stream erosion that creates small valleys. You come to one of these now at 0.6 mile and go down a few feet to a pretty little stream flowing under and sometime over a huge boulder. The small catch pool below the boulder harbors salamanders, frogs and toads, tadpoles, and myriad aquatic insects.

At 0.7 mile you come to an old road to the lake from private property. A gate on the right is the property line. Follow the road to the left; as you might expect, you now must cross the small stream that has puddled in ruts in the road. The road forks; take the left fork to continue on the east side of the lake, or go right to go around the lake. A fine alternate route crosses the larger Stephenson Creek on a bridge.

Davidson–Arabia Mountain Nature Preserve Trails with Arabia Mountain Trail

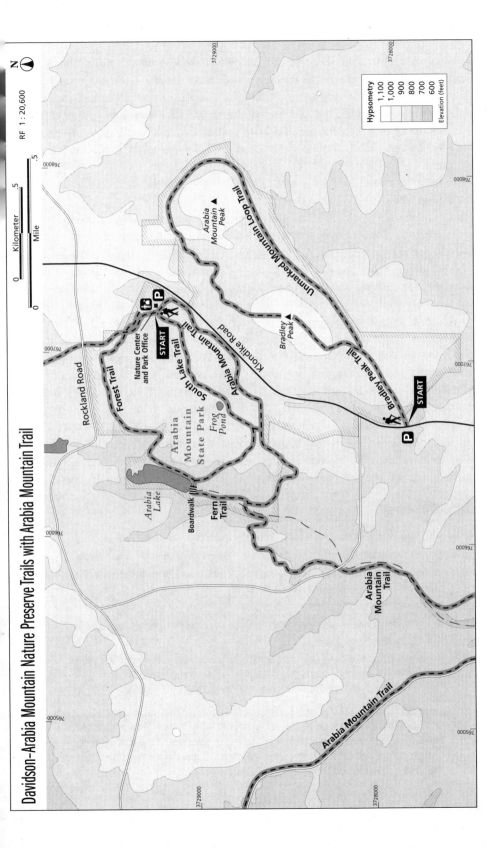

You continue straight ahead to the lake, which is now on the right. This is a pleasant, scenic area. You may see resident wood ducks, great blue herons, or any of the local or migrant waterbirds. At 0.8 mile you come to the large exposed-granite rock area that takes you right to the edge of the water. This is a small but pretty, clear lake impounded years ago. Beavers, muskrats, amphibians, and other aquatic creatures find ideal habitat here. Continue south along the lakeshore to the picnic shelter at 0.9 mile.

South Lake Trail

You can begin the South Lake Trail at the Nature Center or use it as a continuation of the Forest Trail from the picnic shelter. Leaving the picnic shelter from the Forest Trail, you are on open granite. Here are unique lichens and mosses, with patches of plants such as yellow daisies or an occasional pine that has managed a root-hold. You walk over quarried sections and on the natural granite. Without the stone cairns that serve as trail markers, it would be quite difficult to follow the designated path.

You walk across uneven areas in places, over nice flat smooth areas, and over scattered large stones of cut granite. You will see, as on the trail up to Bradley Peak, the round pockets that hold water. At 0.3 mile you come to the remains of the old quarry office and weigh station and the paved Arabia Mountain Trail. To continue on the South Lake Trail, turn north and continue following the cairns. At 0.4 mile you have on the left a larger, deeper pool with permanent water. This is the Frog Pond. An information plaque explains the significance of this small pond. At 0.8 mile you are at the historic quarry building remains and very shortly enter the pine and hardwood forested area. Leaving the cairns as markers, the trail is a well-defined path that takes you along an old roadbed back to the Nature Center area at 1.0 mile.

Miles and Directions

The following hike combines the Forest and South Lake Trails to create a 1.9-mile loop.

0.0 Start at the Nature Center on the paved Arabia Mountain Trail that leads to Lithonia.

0.1 At the short post with arrow leave the paved trail for the soft loamy trail. Side trails to small, treeless granite areas are along the path.

0.4 Start down a slightly steeper way.

0.7 A short spur path on the left goes a few yards to a pretty little stream falling over and flowing under a huge boulder.

0.75 Come to a gated grass and dirt roadway that goes to private property turn left and cross the stream you saw just a moment ago. (**Option:** Go around the lake by crossing Stephenson Creek on a bridge.) This area is used extensively by beavers.

0.8 You can walk to the lake edge on a large sloping granite area.

0.9 Continuing along the east side of the lake, come to the picnic shelter with benches and tables. From here the South Lake Trail begins for the hike back to the Nature Center. Leave the picnic shelter and follow the stone cairns. (**Option:** Turn right to take the Fern Trail down to Stephenson Creek below the dam.)

1.2 Pass the remains of the old quarry office and weigh station. Turn back to the left toward the exposed granite.

1.3 On the left is one of the few permanent pockets of water on the rock. (**FYI:** Frogs and toads use this little pond regularly.) An information plaque describes the Frog Pond.

1.7 The historic quarry remains are on the right. Leave the open granite for the forested area.

1.9 Arrive back at the Nature Center.

Fern Trail

The Fern Trail leaves the south end of the lake and the picnic shelter. It follows Stephenson Creek down through a pleasant, moist habitat with many flowering plants, ferns, and lichens. The trail ends at the long boardwalk of Arabia Mountain Trail.

Arabia Mountain Trail

The multiuse Arabia Mountain Trail, a combined effort of state, county, and private organizations, is an 11.0-mile paved hiking/biking trail from Lithonia to Panola Mountain State Conservation Park. Lying in part on the old railroad right-of-way between Lithonia and the former quarries—one of which is now the Davidson–Arabia Mountain Nature Preserve—the trail is extensively used by the community as an exercise and recreation path. The 10-foot-wide concrete-paved path with boardwalks and arched granite bridges has large signs at frequent intervals with elevation, miles from Lithonia, and other pertinent trail information. The trail passes close to some private homes but for the most part is quite secluded from public eye except where it crosses or passes parallel to a roadway. You walk through forests and pastures, beside streams, and through the nature preserve. Three spur trails lead to the Murphy Candler Elementary School and the planned environmental high school (0.4 mile), to Evans Mill Road on Flat Rock spur (1.4 miles), and to the attractive Mall at Stonecrest (0.6 mile) with restaurants, hotels, and many shops. **Note:** At this writing, a 3.6-mile section of trail from the Flat Rock Spur to the South River Bridge has not been completed. It is not shown on the map.

More Information

Local Events/Attractions

Fernbank Museum of Natural History, 767 Clifton Road, NE, Atlanta, GA 30307; (404) 929-6400.

Stone Mountain Park, Exit 8 off of Highway 78, Atlanta, GA; (770) 498-5690 or (800) 401-2407; www.stonemountainpark.com.

Zoo Atlanta, 800 Cherokee Avenue SE, Atlanta, GA 30315; (404) 624-WILD; www.zooatlanta.org.

Georgia Aquarium, 225 Baker Street, Atlanta, GA 30313; (404) 581-4000; www.georgia aquarium.org.

Chattahoochee River National Recreation Area

The Chattahoochee River begins as a spring in Chattahoochee Gap at the Appalachian Trail, high in the north Georgia mountains near the end of Jacks Knob Trail. It collects water from hundreds of tributaries along its meandering course before it reaches Atlanta as the largest and most important river and water source for the metropolitan Atlanta area. The Chattahoochee River National Recreation Area was established in 1978 to preserve the river corridor and provide recreation under management of the National Park Service. Fourteen tracts of land have been developed for recreation on the 48 miles of river flowing through the north and west regions of metro-Atlanta. Four of the tracts with hiking trails are discussed here. Most of the other units have similar hiking trails.

A detailed map of the Chattahoochee River from Buford Dam down to Atlanta is available from the National Park Service. It shows access roads to the fourteen units of land administered by the Park Service (www.nps.gov/chat).

The flow of the Chattahoochee River is controlled for hydroelectric power generation at Buford Dam. Depending on releases from the dam, the river may be very full or quite low with many rocks exposed in the shoals. The water discharged from Buford Dam is cold—50 to 60 degrees—year-round. The State Wildlife Resources Division manages the river for a very popular rainbow and brown trout fishery. Visit www.wildliferesources, www.chattahoochee.org, or www.riverthroughatlanta.com for more information.

50 East Palisades Trail

About 4.5 miles of winding forest footpaths along the steep bluffs overlooking the east side of the river provide access to some high bluff along the river. Only short sections of the East Palisades Trail are steep and strenuous for hiking. An observation platform and bluff areas afford scenic views of the river and surroundings. The elevation change from the river to the highest point in the unit is about 200 feet.

Start: Indian Trail Road parking area
Distance: 2.4-mile loop
Approximate hiking time: 3 to 4 hours
Difficulty: Mostly moderate; short strenuous stretches on bluff areas
Elevation gain/loss: 200 feet
Trail surface: Dirt and loam; sandy loam along the river's edge
Lay of the land: Steep river bluff with narrow flood zone
Season: Year-round; many winter days suitable for hiking

Land status: Chattahoochee River National Recreation Area
Nearest town: Roswell
Fees and permits: Parking $3.00 per vehicle per day
Maps: USGS Sandy Springs; page-size map, available from the National Park Service office and from www.nps.gov/chat
Trail contacts: National Park Service, Chattahoochee River National Recreation Area, 1978 Island Ford Parkway, Atlanta, GA 30350; (770) 399-8070; www.nps.gov/chat

Finding the trailhead: Exit Interstate 285 at Northside Drive (exit 22). Follow this residential road south to Indian Trail. Turn right and go 0.5 mile to the parking area and to the trailhead. Another trailhead is off Harris Trail, which turns off Northside Drive 0.5 mile beyond Indian Trail. Go 0.8 mile to Whitewater Creek Road and then go 0.1 mile to the Park Service road. Follow the park road 0.3 mile to the parking area and trailhead. This hike begins at the Indian Trail Road trailhead.

The Hike

The East Palisades Unit comprises 393 acres of hardwood forest with rock outcrops, ravines, and a narrow river floodplain. An overlook provides a view of the river shoals. River boatmen in the eighteenth and nineteenth centuries called these rapids Devil's Race Course Shoals. They called the granite palisades the Devil's Stairsteps.

Beginning at the Indian Trail Road parking area, the trail follows an old roadbed for a few yards before dropping down in a series of switchbacks to Whitewater Creek and the river. A bridge crosses Whitewater Creek at the lower trailhead. At the river the path is only a few feet from the bank. This is a good place to look for tracks of muskrats, beavers, raccoons, minks, and other mammals using the river's edge. The exposed rocks when the river is down or the white water when the river is up makes it easy to see why it once was called Devil's Race Course Shoals. Large patches of shrubs and switch cane grow in the wet areas along the bank. You cross a footbridge, and the path begins the climb up along the palisades. One of the largest rock shel-

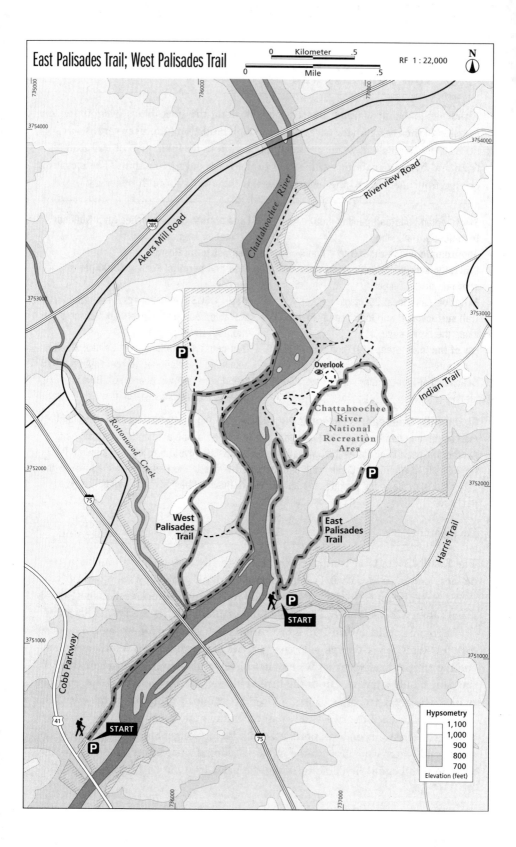

East Palisades Trail; West Palisades Trail

RF 1 : 22,000

N

Kilometer

Mile

Chattahoochee River

Akers Mill Road

Riverview Road

Overlook

Chattahoochee
River
National
Recreation
Area

Indian Trail

Cottonwood Creek

West
Palisades
Trail

East
Palisades
Trail

Harris Trail

P

START

P

START

Cobb Parkway

Hypsometry

	1,100
	1,000
	900
	800
	700

Elevation (feet)

ters along the river is to the right. This is the steepest way to the overlook. To the left is a much shorter climb over rock outcrops.

Indians lived along the river for many years, their villages flourishing. But they disappeared with little trace.

From the overlook you get a grand view of the river and appreciate the height of the bluffs. Retracing your steps from the overlook, you can return to the trailhead or turn left and go back down to the river through a beautiful mature hardwood forest of large yellow poplars, white oaks, chestnut oaks, and an occasional deciduous magnolia with exceptionally large leaves. This is an especially good area for spring wildflowers. At the river you can hike upstream along the bank to the end of the Park Service boundary. Private property is close on all sides. Careful hikers will respect the privacy of those who have adjoining property.

Backtrack up the moderate grade to return to the trailhead. The trail comes out on the road about 200 yards from the parking area.

Miles and Directions

0.0 Start from parking area at end of Indian Trail Road.

0.5 After coming down about 180 feet elevation, White Water Creek is on the left.

0.6 Cross footbridge over White Water Creek and begin walking up the Chattahoochee River's east bank. Dense thickets of privet and switch cane grow along this moist, narrow floodplain.

0.7 Cross the next footbridge over a wet area and continue upstream, with picturesque rapids formed by the river.

1.2 The loop trail turns sharply back to the right as you begin an ascent to the overlook. (**Side trip:** Continue about 200 yards along the river to walk under the cliffs and view rock overhangs that form a large sheltered area. This is a one-way trail.)

1.3 Start the climb through several switchbacks.

1.5 The trail on the left leads to a point with an excellent view of the river and surroundings. (**FYI:** This 0.4-mile spur bypass returns to the loop trail farther up.)

1.7 Intersect the scenic spur trail on the left to the overlook deck. Turn left to visit the overlook.

1.8 Arrive at the overlook.

1.9 Return to the loop trail. (**FYI:** You'll be hiking through an exceptionally beautiful cover area with large trees and many kinds of wildflowers that bloom from early spring through summer and into fall.)

2.4 Turn right onto Indian Trail Road and walk back to the parking area to close the loop.

More Information

Local Events/Attractions

Chattahoochee Nature Center, 9135 Willeo Road, Roswell, GA 30075; (707) 992-2055.

Georgia Aquarium, 225 Baker Street, Atlanta, GA 30313; (404) 581-4000; www.georgia aquarium.org.

51 West Palisades Trail

The West Palisades Unit comprises 302 acres along 1.5 miles of shoals in the Chattahoochee River. The trail follows the riverbank and into the rocky palisades. A variety of habitats with open fields, dense woods, tumbling streams, and rocky cliffs make this area especially interesting. This is a trail for all seasons. Spring wildflowers begin blooming in early March. Migrating warblers and other songbirds pass through in April and May, and leaves change colors in October. Trout fishing in this section of the river is year-round.

See map on page 224
Start: End of the public use parking area off Cobb Parkway.
Distance: 3.6-mile lollipop
Approximate hiking time: 2 to 3 hours
Difficulty: Mostly easy to moderate; one short section of difficult rock formations
Elevation gain/loss: From the river to the highest point, about 100 feet
Trail surface: Sandy loam; stretches of uneven rock outcrops
Lay of the land: Steep riverside cliffs and rolling hills

Season: Year-round
Land status: Chattahoochee River National Recreation Area
Nearest town: Roswell
Fees and permits: $3.00 per day per vehicle
Maps: USGS Fayetteville; page-size map, available from the ranger station, the park office at Island Ford, or www.nps.gov/chat
Trail contacts: National Park Service, Chattahoochee River National Recreation Area, 1978 Island Ford Parkway, Atlanta, GA 30350; (770) 399-8070; www.nps.gov/chat

Finding the trailhead: There is no direct access from the interstate highways. Access to the trailhead is from Cobb Parkway (U.S. Highway 41) at the Chattahoochee River Bridge at Paces Mill Road. The trailhead is at the upstream end of the parking complex in the Paces Mill Day Use Area with restrooms, boat launching ramp, and picnic tables. A second access point and parking area is off Akers Mill Road to Akers Drive and Akers Ridge Road, which ends at the park property line and parking area.

The Hike

This trail system is at the junction of Interstates 285 and 75. The I-75 bridge over the Chattahoochee River crosses over the trail. In sight of Atlanta's skyscraper skyline, you have an almost backwoods-type hiking experience. Cliff-edge views of the Chattahoochee River and stream-edge trails make this a very popular morning or afternoon hike for local residents as well as those who drive miles just for the experience, which includes wildflowers, birding, fishing for trout, nature photography, and the Akers Mill ruins.

The West Palisades Unit has much less mature forest than the East Palisades Unit. The trail begins on the west side of the river across from the toe of Long Island. The first 0.5 mile is a wide trail with fine gravel. This section is wheelchair accessible.

Go under the large I–75 bridge to a high bank overlooking the river. A footbridge crosses Rottenwood Creek and the narrower path continues upriver under typical riverbank trees, including sycamore, sweet gum, water oak, river birch, ironwood, and box elders. The ridge to the left of the trail supports many wildflowers, including azalea, mountain laurel, dogwoods, trout lilies, trilliums, Solomon's seal, phlox, and violets. Privet shrubs have invaded the riverbank in places, forming dense thickets. Large yellow poplars, loblolly pines, and an occasional deciduous magnolia are in the coves leading away from the river. In October the hickories, maples, sassafras, dogwoods, sumacs, red oaks, and other hardwood trees and shrubs put on a beautiful show of color.

Short spur trails used by fishermen lead to the riverbank. Look for the great blue heron feeding in the river and for mammal tracks in the moist sandy-clay areas. Belted kingfishers, wood ducks, Canada geese, and other waterbirds can be seen regularly along this portion of the trail. Signs of beaver activity are common.

At 0.8 mile, a loop trail leads off to the left. Most of the trail junctions have a map mounted on a post showing where you are. Continue up the riverbank to the steep, rocky area with mountain laurel, rhododendron, and several species of ferns. Climb through the rocky bluff and the trail reaches the ridge with chestnut oaks, white oaks, and hickories. It is easy to imagine yourself in the more remote mountains instead of metropolitan Atlanta. The sound of traffic gives way to the sounds of the river and forest. The next section of trail is difficult because of the rock outcrops. But the river is especially scenic here.

The path drops back down to the river and splits into two paths to the floodplain area with a restroom on the left side. A wide, sandy beach appears a few more yards ahead at the river's edge. The trail ends at the property line.

Backtracking to the restroom area, you follow the trail up a steep slope to the ridgetop and to the old road from the Akers Ridge Road trailhead. Stay to the left to return through a pleasant series of low ridges and coves with lots of spring flowers. This trail leads back to the bridge at Rottenwood Creek.

The trail up Rottenwood Creek is a tedious 1.0-mile one-way hike. It is not recommended unless you are especially interested in the old mill ruins or trout fishing. The creek is a rocky-bottomed, cascading stream that looks more like a mountain trout stream than a warm Piedmont watercourse. It is lined with mountain laurels and rhododendrons, oaks, sweet gums, hickories, yellow poplars, and loblolly pines. The old rockworks of the mill dam and the brickwork ruins of the old Akers Mill are at the end of the trail.

Miles and Directions

0.0 Start at the parking area for the large public-use area off Cobb Parkway. A sign at the end of the wide fine-gravel path directs you upstream toward the I-75 bridge that spans Chattahoochee River.

0.6 Pass under the I-75 bridge and over the footbridge across Rottenwood Creek.

1.0 After walking close to the river, turn away from river in a wide cove area.

1.1 Come to a 0.2-mile connector trail on the left. (**Bailout:** For a short loop, follow the connector uphill to the loop trail and return to the trailhead.)

1.5 The trail forks. Take the right fork and continue upstream close to the river. (**FYI:** The left fork is the end of a short loop back to the trailhead.)

1.6 Cross a small footbridge.

1.7 Pass a short cross trail on the left. You will come back to this.

1.8 Make a sharp turn to the left to return back downstream. (**Side trip:** Take a 0.1-mile one-way trail along the cliffs and return.)

1.9 Arrive back at the short cross trail.

2.0 Continue uphill to complete the loop. (**FYI:** The trail on the left backtracks along the river trail to the trailhead.)

2.1 Reach the junction of the trail that leads 0.2 mile to the Akers Ridge Drive parking area and trailhead. (**FYI:** This loop trail also can be started at this point.) Turn left and continue along the ridgetops and coves through the woods full of wildflowers, wildlife, and large trees.

3.0 Close the loop at the bridge over Rottenwood Creek.

3.6 Arrive back at the parking area trailhead, public-use area, and restrooms.

More Information

Local Events/Attractions

Chattahoochee Nature Center, 9135 Willeo Road, Roswell, GA 30075; (707) 992-2055. **Georgia Aquarium,** 225 Baker Street, Atlanta, GA 30313; (404) 581-4000; www.georgia aquarium.org.

River Through Atlanta Chattahoochee River Guide Service, 710 Riverside Road, Roswell, GA 30075; (770) 650-8630; www.river throughatlanta.com.

52 Johnson Ferry North Trail

The Johnson Ferry unit comprises 108 acres entirely on the floodplain of the Chattahoochee River. A three-loop trail takes you around a unique and extensive wetland area with five footbridges. For half the distance you are in almost constant view of the river. The return is along a very straight walkway with both open, brushy cover and larger trees.

Start: The trailhead sign very close to Johnson Ferry Road

Distance: 2.0-mile loop

Approximate hiking time: 1½ hours

Difficulty: Easy

Elevation gain/loss: Negligible

Trail surface: Sandy loam; short gravel section

Lay of the land: Flat river floodplain

Season: Year-round

Land status: Chattahoochee River National Recreation Area

Nearest town: Sandy Springs

Fees and permits: Parking $3.00 per day per vehicle

Maps: USGS Sandy Springs; page-size map, available from the Park Service office at Island Ford or from www.nps.gov/chat

Trail contacts: National Park Service, Chattahoochee River National Recreation Area, 1978 Island Ford Parkway, Atlanta, GA 30350; (770) 399-8070; www.nps.gov/chat

Finding the trailhead: From Interstate 285 take exit 25 (Roswell Road) and go north on Roswell Road 0.9 mile to Johnson Ferry Road. Turn left and go 2.25 miles across the Chattahoochee River Bridge. Immediately across the bridge, turn right at the sign for the Chattahoochee Outdoor Center. The trailhead is at the parking area very close to Johnson Ferry Road.

The Hike

This trail is on the west side of the river upstream from Johnson Ferry Road. This is an exceptionally good birding area with aquatic, open, brushy and forested habitats. Ducks, herons, beavers, muskrats, raccoons, opossums, otters, turtles, frogs, and toads are some of the wildlife associated with the wet area and river; the forested area attracts many songbirds.

The Chattahoochee Outdoor Center is not open at this writing, but the boat-launching site is available for use. Johnson Ferry South Trail is an optional trail to a pleasant picnic area on the south side of Johnson Ferry Road.

This trail is an easy but interesting path that goes around a natural wetland area. From the parking area, walk 0.25 mile across an open field. During spring and summer, you may see killdeers in the gravel and grassy areas. After you pass the buildings of the Chattahoochee Outdoor Center, you cross a short footbridge and enter the wooded walk up the river. Spur trails made by fishermen lead off the trail at irregular intervals. During periods when the water in the river is very clear or low, it is possible to see a V-shaped dark area crossing the channel. This is the remains of

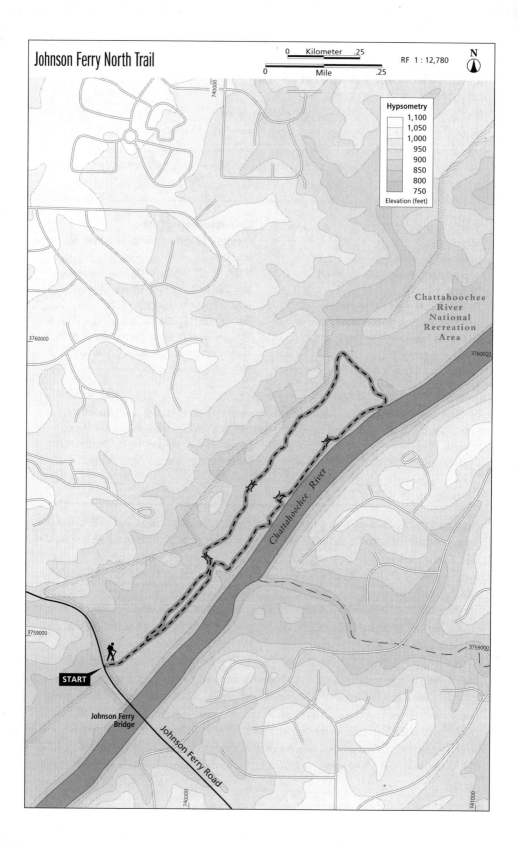

a fish trap used by early settlers. It is believed that white settlers learned to build and use fish traps from the Indians.

Privet shrubs and switch cane grow in dense thickets along the trail close to the river. The privet is an escaped horticultural plant. The cane is native and in the past extended in great patches along many of the rivers of the Southeast. The large cane-brakes of the past were used extensively by both wildlife and humans.

You can now turn toward the ridgeline and hike back downstream on the oppo-site side of a wet, and sometimes flooded, area. This open brushy area is the pipeline right-of-way. It adds a very important wildlife habitat type called an edge, where the wooded area and open areas meet. It is particularly important for such birds as car-dinals, yellow-breasted chats, brown thrashers, catbirds, and mockingbirds. Many other forms of wildlife thrive along this edge, using both the woods and open area as needed.

Wood duck nest boxes were placed on posts in the natural, shallow pond. In late fall and winter, wood ducks frequently gather here in small flocks. The ridge side of the trail is rich in wildflowers and ferns. There is an endless parade of blooming flowers from early spring to early winter.

The loop is completed back at the bridge; backtrack across the field to the park-ing area.

Miles and Directions

This trail is very level and easy to follow. The Chattahoochee River is on your right for the 0.8-mile walk north. The return on the opposite side of the floodplain has the forested habitat on the right. This is a trail to walk slowly and absorb the wildlife and flora of the riverside.

53 Island Ford Trail

The Island Ford Trail is a pleasant hike in a mature hardwood forest. The main trail is blue blazed and takes you through all the habitat types with flat, easy walks and moderate climbs in the hilly upland. From the river to the crest of the low ridges is about 50 feet. It is almost all shaded during the warm months and an open forest canopy in winter. The several paths here are interconnected, and you may start hiking from four different points around the main trail from the paved road. The closeness to the river and the riverine habitat adds to the variety.

Start: The trailhead nearest the entrance to the Island Ford Unit, located 130 yards on the left at a picnic and parking area

Distance: 3.0 miles of trails in several loops

Approximate hiking time: 2½ hours

Difficulty: Easy to moderate

Elevation gain/loss: From the river to the ridge crest, 50 feet

Trail surface: Mostly clay-loam in mixed pine-hardwood forest

Lay of the land: River bank and low rolling hills

Season: Year-round

Land status: Chattahoochee River National Recreation Area

Nearest town: Roswell

Fees and permits: Parking $3.00 per vehicle per day

Maps: USGS Sandy Springs; page-size map, available from the Park Service office or from www.nps.gov./chat

Trail contacts: National Park Service, Chattahoochee River National Recreation Area, 1978 Island Ford Parkway, Atlanta, GA 30350; (770) 399-8070; www.nps.gov./chat

Finding the trailhead: From Interstate 285 take exit 27 and follow Highway 400 north 5.0 miles to exit 6 (North Ridge Road). Turn right and go back across Highway 400. Turn right at the traffic light to Roberts Road. Go 1.2 miles to the National Park Service entrance sign; turn right on Island Ford Parkway. The first trailhead is 130 yards on the left at the parking area. For this hike, continue 0.7 mile to the parking and picnic area on the left and the pond on the right. The NPS Chattahoochee River National Recreation Area office is another 0.4 mile.

The Hike

This 297-acre tract has been retained in as natural a condition as possible, first by the original private owners and by the National Park Service for more than seventy-five years. The mature hardwood forest at this site is a fine example of what the Piedmont area of Georgia might have looked like before it was cleared and developed. This is a great place, especially in the highly residential area of Metropolitan Atlanta, to find a variety of spring and summer wildflowers, trees, and wildlife.

This well-designed system of trails enables you to see a wide variety of habit types in a relatively small area. All the trails are clearly marked and easy to follow.

Using the trailhead nearest the entrance, you leave the parking area from the end of the clearing. Enter the wooded area as the trail drops down toward the river

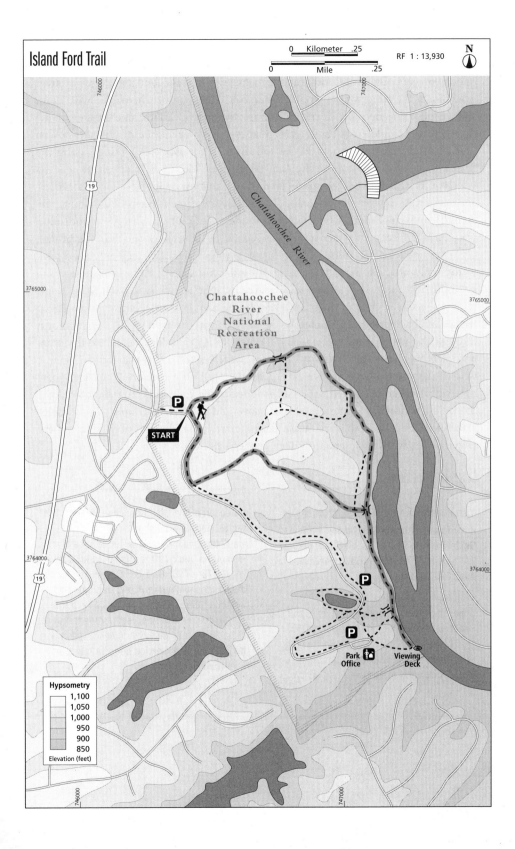

Island Ford Trail

Chattahoochee River

Chattahoochee
River
National
Recreation
Area

START

Park
Office

Viewing
Deck

Hypsometry

| 1,100 |
| 1,050 |
| 1,000 |
| 950 |
| 900 |
| 850 |

Elevation (feet)

through a moist cove with a small stream. A luxurious growth of plants, including spleenworts and Christmas and other ferns, line the trail. Redbud and dogwood trees grow under the larger yellow poplar, white oak, American beech, maple, sweet gum, and loblolly pine trees that form the canopy overhead. A footbridge crosses the little creek at 0.2 mile. At 0.4 mile you are at the river, where one of the early-return green-blazed trails leads back up the hill through the woods. Continue along the river for splendid views of the shoals as the river divides to form an island.

River birch, ironwood, sycamore, red maple, and a number of other water tolerant trees grow right to the riverbank. Mosses, liverworts, and ferns help stabilize the bank. Belted kingfishers, wood ducks, a resident flock of Canada geese, and other waterbirds are frequently seen along this section of the trail. At the next footbridge, 0.7 mile, a yellow-blazed loop trail returns up the moderately steep ridge and back to the trailhead. Following the river at 1.0 mile, you cross the third footbridge and go about 100 yards to an observation area and canoe launch site at the river's edge, with an excellent view of the river both upstream and down. Retrace your steps to the second bridge. Here, 1.5 miles into your walk, you can turn to the left and return through alternating stands of pine and hardwoods up a moderate climb to the other end of the green-blazed trail at 1.8 miles, which takes off to the right. This trail would take you back to the river in 0.3 mile. Continue 0.2 mile to the paved road; turn right and go 0.2 mile to the parking area at the trailhead. You have completed 2.4 miles. Another 0.6 mile of alternate cross and short trails connect to the blue-blazed trail from the other trailheads near the river, the Hewlett play field, and the viewing area with an observation deck at the river's edge.

More Information

Local Events/Attractions

River Through Atlanta Chattahoochee River Guide Service, 710 Riverside Road, Roswell, GA 30075; (770) 650-8630; www.river throughatlanta.com.

Organizations

Upper Chattahoochee Riverkeepers, 615F Oak Street, Suite 1000, Gainesville, GA 30501; (770) 531-1064; www.chattahoochee.org. An independent environmental organization whose mission is to advocate and secure protection of the Chattahoochee River, its tributaries, and its watershed.

The Chattahoochee Cold Water Tailrace Fishery Foundation, Inc., 710 Riverside Road, Roswell, GA 30075; (770) 650-8630; www .chattahoocheefoodwebs.org. Dedicated to protecting the coldwater trout fishery in the Chattahoochee River and supporting the work of the Georgia Wildlife Resources Division and the National Park Service effort to manage these waters.

Honorable Mentions

P Kennesaw Mountain National Battlefield Park

Kennesaw Mountain rises abruptly 1,000 feet above the surrounding Piedmont Plateau to the southeast and the Ridge and Valley area to the northwest. The national park was established to protect, memorialize, and interpret the Civil War Battle of Kennesaw Mountain that occurred in June 1864. This beautiful wooded, rocky ridge offers much more than just Civil War history. The trails lead through hardwood forests, some of which have been relatively undisturbed for nearly one hundred years. The views from the top of Kennesaw and Little Kennesaw Mountains are grand, looking southeast to the Atlanta skyline and over the Piedmont Plateau and north to the mountains and ridges. Several loop trails, from 16.0 to 2.0 miles long, lead through beautiful wooded country with expansive views. The trail across Kennesaw Mountain to Burnt Hickory Road is moderate to strenuous. Other trails' segments are easy to moderate.

Civil War history, military research, grand views, mature hardwood forest, rich variety of plant life, and diverse wildlife populations are available to hikers very near the metropolitan population of Atlanta. The lowest elevation is near the headquarters area at 850 feet; the highest is the top of Kennesaw Mountain at 1,808 feet. All trails can be started at the park headquarters parking area.

The park entrance is 3.0 miles west of Marietta on Highway 120. The park is open year-round for hiking. Trail maps detailing battle history and trail distances are available from the park visitor center. Georgia native Hugh Morton used the steep climbs up Kennesaw and Little Kennesaw Mountains as a training ground, carrying a heavy pack to get into shape for his successful Mount Everest ascent.

For more information: Kennesaw Mountain National Battlefield Park, 905 Kennesaw Mountain Drive, Kennesaw, GA 30152; (770) 427–4686; www.nps.gov/kemo.

DeLorme: Georgia Atlas and Gazetteer: Page 19 G10

Q Chattahoochee River National Recreation Area: Cochran Shoals

The Cochran Shoals Unit comprises 968 acres, the largest and most popular park along the Chattahoochee River National Recreation Area. There are fields, woodlands, wetlands, and river habitats. Ten miles of interconnected trails offer a variety of natural and historic attractions. Most of the trail system is on jogging, fitness, and bike trails. The wheelchair-accessible fitness trail is a 2.5-mile loop that follows close to the river. This is a good birding and wildlife-watching trail. Two other trails, about 1.5 miles each, lead away from the heavily used areas into forested hiking paths. Ruins of the old Marietta Paper Mill add historic interest to the area. The Cochran Shoals area is located close to major office and residential areas of Atlanta, and hundreds of hikers, bikers, joggers, and others use it daily.

This area is just north of the Interstate 285 bridge across the Chattahoochee River. A page-size map is available from the Park Service office. Degree of difficulty varies from easy to moderate. All trails can be reached on foot from three parking areas on the west side of the river. The unit is accessible year-round.

For more information: National Park Service, Chattahoochee River National Recreation Area, 1978 Island Ford Parkway, Atlanta, GA 30350; (678) 538–1200; www.nps.gov/chat.

DeLorme: Georgia Atlas and Gazetteer: Page 20 H2

Augusta City Area

54 Augusta Canal National Heritage Area Trail

The Hiking/Biking Trail, or towpath, is the main hiking trail from the headgates to Augusta's water pumping station. You walk on what was originally the path used by draft animals to pull cargo boats upstream to the locks. It is a hard, level, sand/clay surface. The first 3.5 miles to the Pump Station is in an almost pristine natural setting that's ideal for a half-day hike down to the Pump Station and back with plenty of things to see. This hike covers part of a much longer, historically significant multiuse trail along the old canal and on city streets.

Start: Headgates of the lock and dam
Distance: Hiking trail to water pump station, 7.0 miles out and back
Approximate hiking time: 3 to 4 hours
Difficulty: Easy
Elevation gain/loss: Negligible
Trail surface: Hard, sand/clay
Lay of the land: Flat
Season: Year-round
Land status: Augusta Canal National Heritage Area, managed by the Augusta Canal Authority for the City of Augusta

Nearest town: Augusta
Fees and permits: No fees or permits required
Maps: USGS Martinez, Augusta West, and Augusta East; map with canal and Augusta Canal history, available from Augusta Canal Authority
Trail contacts: Augusta Canal Authority, 801 Broad Street, Room 107, Augusta, GA 30901; (706) 722-1071; www.augustacanal.com

Finding the trailhead: From Interstate 20 turn north on Washington Road. Immediately turn right on Claussen Road and go 0.25 mile to Stevens Creek Road. Turn left (north) and go 2.8 miles to Evens South Lock Road (also called Evens to Lock Road). Turn right (east) and go 1.0 mile to Savannah Rapids Park and Pavilion of Columbia County (August City Lock and Dam). The Hiking/Biking trailhead is at the headgates of the lock and dam and is reached by walking from Savannah Rapids Park parking area across to the historic lockworks.

The Hike

History, scenery, birding, and wildlife watching are a few of the fascinating things waiting for you as you hike this rustic, rural, and urban trail. One of the largest loblolly pine trees you will ever see stands beside the trail. Wildlife includes bald eagles, wood storks, deer, wild turkeys, beavers, muskrats, and even an occasional alligator.

There are several other walking trails in the Augusta area in addition to the Hiking/Biking Trail: the Historic Trail, Downtown Riverwalk Trail, Lake Olmstead Trail, and the new Bartram Trail. Canoers and kayakers have a number of access points to the canal and the river; boat tours are conducted periodically.

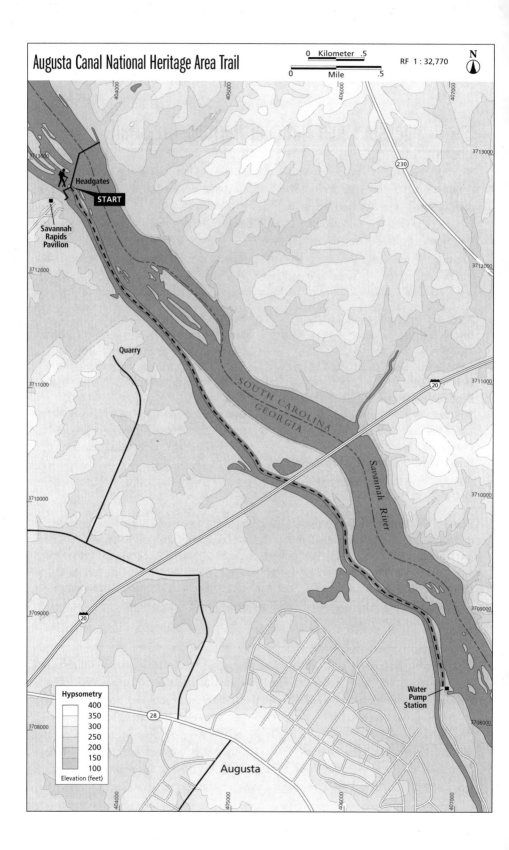

Augusta Canal National Heritage Area Trail

RF 1 : 32,770

N

0   Kilometer   .5

0   Mile   .5

Headgates

START

Savannah
Rapids
Pavilion

Quarry

SOUTH CAROLINA
GEORGIA

Savannah River

Water
Pump
Station

Hypsometry
400
350
300
250
200
150
100
Elevation (feet)

Augusta

This unique trail is upriver from the city of Augusta on the towpath between the historical Augusta Canal and the Savannah River. You walk the actual towpath on which the mules traveled to haul cargo barges up the canal. It follows along beautiful river scenery and many kinds of wildlife and plants associated with the river habitat, ending at the Augusta Water Pump Station. The canal banks were free of trees then to give free passage for the ropes used to pull the barges.

Today the 3.5-mile walk down to the water pumping station has many features both natural and man-made. Across the canal you can look into the mouth of Reed Creek as it tumbles into the canal, looking very much like a mountain trout stream. The forested wetland between the canal and the river is home and resting area for many forms of wildlife. Deer, turkeys, river otters, raccoons, beavers, and squirrels live in this fertile zone. Waterbirds including gulls, herons, egrets, cormorants, ducks, and even ospreys and bald eagles can be seen along and over the river. A fish ladder was installed with the diversion dam in 1852 to allow striped bass, white bass, and American shad to continue their spawning migration upriver. A one-hundred-year-old rock quarry operates on the opposite side of the canal. I–20 crosses over the trail at Mile 1.25, before you reach the pumping station that supplies the domestic water for Augusta. This is the end of the Hiking/Biking Trail. Return to the headgate area.

To walk the rest of the canal, go through the fenced parking area and you can walk the additional 4.5 miles to the downstream end at the Eighth Street Riverwalk in downtown Augusta. The Bike Trail continues on the Augusta Levee Road for another 1.3 miles to Goodrich Street. At this writing a detailed map is being prepared by The Augusta Canal Authority.

The Augusta Canal Authority is to be commended for developing this fine trail, which is open to both walkers and cyclists. Bicycles must yield to pedestrians. Canoers and kayakers use the canal extensively. Motor vehicles are not permitted on the towpath between the pumping station and the dam at the upstream trailhead. No gas-powered motor craft are permitted in the canal.

Miles and Directions

0.0   Start at the headgates for the lock and dam.

0.3   The mouth and falls of Reed Creek enter the canal on the right.

0.7   On the right, pass the quartzite granite quarry. (**FYI:** Active since the initial canal construction, the quarry is operated today by Martin-Marietta. This is also the county line between Columbia and Richmond Counties. The islands visible in the river were occupied by various Native American peoples in the past.)

1.2   The canal turns away from the river to expose a wider floodplain.

2.1   Walk under the I-20 bridge over the Savannah River.

2.8   You are now back closer to the riverbank on the left. Warren Lake, fed by Rock Creek, enters the canal on the right.

3.2   Islands are again visible, as are the picturesque rapids.

3.5 Reach the Augusta Water Pump Station and the end of the Hiking Trail. This is your turn-around point.

7.0 Arrive back at the headgates.

More Information

Organizations

Augusta Canal National Heritage Area, 1450 Greene Street, Suite 400, Augusta, GA 30901; (706) 823-0440; www.augustacanal.com. The Canal Authority was established to promote public interest in the historic and unique nature of the canal by encouraging educational and recreational activities associated with this waterway.

Southwest Georgia: Coastal Plain

Freshwater bay and boardwalk in George T. Bagby State Park (Hike 58).

State Park Trails

55 Sprewell Bluff State Park Trails

The Sprewell Bluff trails are a series of interconnected paths with one main trail along the Flint River. The trails are marked with carsonite posts and are not blazed. The Main River Trail starts at the lower parking area on the Flint River. The other trails connect to this trail from the upper parking area on the ridge. This interconnection makes it possible to hike any of several loops through 3.0 miles of marked and maintained trails.

Start: The public-use area parking lot at the river

Distance: Main River Trail, 3.0 miles out and back; 2.5-mile loop as described

Approximate hiking time: 2 hours for the Main River Trail and a loop back

Difficulty: Easy to moderate

Elevation gain/loss: From the river to the upper parking area, about 210 feet

Trail surface: Dirt and clay

Lay of the land: High ridges and river bluffs

Season: Year-round

Land status: Georgia State Parks Division

Nearest town: Thomaston

Fees and permits: Park Pass $3.00 per vehicle per day

Maps: USGS Roland and Sunset Village

Trail contacts: Sprewell Bluff State Park, 740 Sprewell Bluff Road, Thomaston, GA 30286; (706) 646–6026; www.gastateparks.org

Finding the trailhead: From Thomaston go west on Highway 74 (West Main Street) for 1.6 miles. Continue 4.0 miles on Highway 74 to Old Alabama Road. Turn left (south) and go 3.9 miles to Sprewell Bluff Road, a continuation of Old Alabama Road. Go 2.2 miles to the park entrance and 0.1 mile to the parking area on the right. This is the upper parking area on Pine Woods Ridge and access to all trails. Continue 0.25 mile to the lower parking area, the trailhead for all trails along the river, and the day-use area.

The Hike

Sprewell Bluff State Park is one of Georgia's newest state parks, the property acquired in 1995. Located at the eastern end of the Pine Mountain Formation, the southernmost granite ridge formation in the state, the park comprises 1,372 acres of forested ridges, bluffs, and narrow river floodplain. The Flint River twists and turns its way through the valleys between the sharp ridges, forming an area of scenic beauty. Park animals include white-tailed deer, squirrels, raccoons, skunks, and wild turkeys. The Flint River corridor with its surrounding ridges is an excellent birding area. The day-use area is a long, sandy, pebble-and-rock beach on the inside of a wide bend in the river. It is equipped with restrooms, picnic tables, a playground, and other facilities.

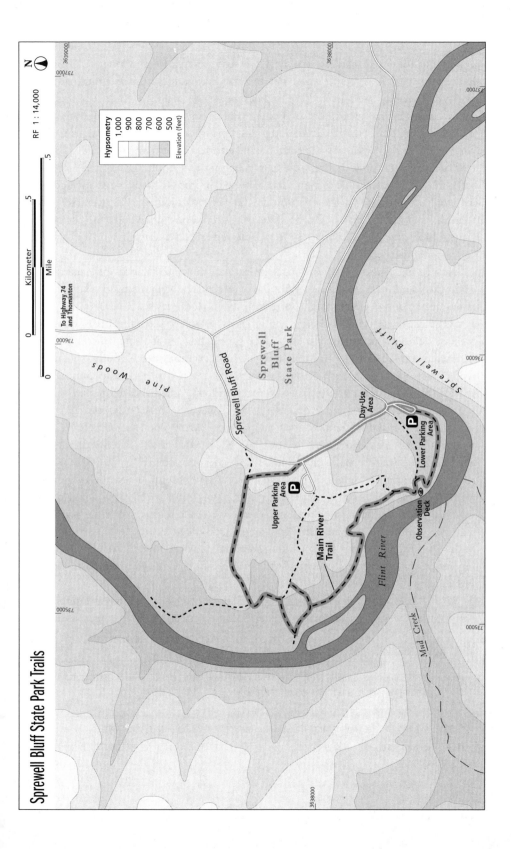

Start at the lower parking area near the day-use area for the longest and most interesting loop. A carsonite stake bearing the hiking stickman and international marks that prohibit vehicles and hunting designates the trailhead. The rest of this and other trails here are clearly brushed and maintained. At the start, the forest cover includes sweet gums, maples, oaks, and pines. Spring flowers will be along the right bank of the trail. Very shortly the path goes by an area that was once subject to severe erosion when the soils were exposed after logging and other agricultural use. The scars are still faintly visible but no longer eroded, protected by the vegetative cover. The trail continues above the river so that you can look down on the river. Here the trees are chestnut oaks, black oaks, hickories, sourwoods, dogwoods, and shortleaf pines. Under the trees throughout the trail are red buckeyes, dwarf pawpaws, azaleas, and sparkleberry bushes.

At 0.3 mile you reach the well-made overlook platform that affords excellent views of the river and surrounding ridges from a rocky bluff. Leaving the overlook, the path continues up and over the bluff as you drop down to the river again. Here the trees are water oaks, sycamores, hickories, and other more water-tolerant plants. Mayapples, trilliums, bloodroots, anemones, and other spring flowers are abundant in season. Mountain laurel, blooming in April and May, grows on the rock bluffs. Linden, ironwood, river birch, and very large hickories grow in the narrow, fertile floodplain.

The trail continues up the river around overflow ponds with temporary standing water. In late winter and spring, the wet season, these areas are important to the tree-nesting wood ducks and hooded mergansers. During flood stage, the river may be out of its banks and temporarily cover the trail. At this point, 0.8 mile, the first of the branching trails turns to the right, as does the next one in 75 yards. Here you turn to the right and in about 100 yards meet a trail coming down the ridge. The final branching trail, turning to the right at 1.1 miles, also leads to the upper parking area. Continue upstream along the river for 0.4 mile to the end of the one-way segment and the end of the River Trail. You have walked 1.5 miles. Return on any of the trails leading to the upper parking area, hike down the road to the lower parking area, or take the connecting trail to the observation deck and to the lower parking area for a loop of 2.8 miles.

Using the well-marked side trails, you have the options of several interesting loops. At this writing, additional trails are planned to continue downriver.

Miles and Directions

0.0 Start at the lower parking area. A flat carsonite stake marked with a hiker and symbols excluding vehicles and hunting shows the way.

0.3 Leave the river edge and come to the observation deck.

0.35 Intersect the first trail coming down from the upper parking area on the right.

0.5 This bluff area affords you another view of the Flint River, its islands, and the high land around.

0.6 Return to the river on an outside bend with a steep bank. (**FYI:** The level floodplain stretching ahead has overflow pools that attract waterfowl, especially wood ducks.)

0.8 The upper parking area loop trail joins the River Trail from the right.

0.9 The second spur trail from the upper parking area enters on the right.

1.0 Leave the river floodplain to continue with the upper parking area loop trail.

1.1 The trail on the right is the return part of the loop trail to the upper parking area. Continue on the last part of the River Trail.

1.5 Reach the end of the River Trail. This long section of the Flint River floodplain continues for another 0.8 mile to the next bluff without a trail. Backtrack to the first trail on the left.

1.8 At this trail, you have the choice of going uphill to the parking area and the Sprewell Bluff Road for diversity or backtracking along the River Trail to the lower parking area and day-use area. Go uphill.

2.2 Arrive at the park entrance road and parking area. Walk down the road to the river and trailhead.

2.5 Close the loop at the lower parking area trailhead.

56 Providence Canyon State Park Trails

Most of the park's 1,003 acres have been reforested and are no longer eroding. These rolling hills are covered with a wide variety of plants from large loblolly and longleaf pines to mature deciduous trees and showy rhododendrons and azaleas. Two loop trails totaling 8.7 miles offer a remarkable hiking experience. The 7.0-mile Backpacking Trail has six designated campsites. A permit is required for camping. Two pioneer campsites are available for Boy Scout use. The Canyon Loop Trail gives you a close-up visit to the exposed 100-foot or more canyon walls.

Start: Office/interpretive center
Distance: Canyon Loop Trail, 3.0-mile loop; Backpacking Trail, 5.2 miles one-way; Backpacking Trail plus 1.8 miles of the Canyon Loop, 7.0-mile loop
Approximate hiking time: Canyon Loop Trails, 1 to 2 hours; Backpacking Trail, without camping, 3½ hours
Difficulty: Easy to moderate; a few very short, steep grades
Elevation gain/loss: 130 feet from rim to the canyon floor
Trail surface: Clay loam; sand and sandy clay

Lay of the land: Rolling hills around steep-walled canyon
Season: Year-round
Nearest town: Lumpkin
Fees and permits: Park Pass $3.00 per vehicle per day
Maps: USGS Lumpkin; page-size maps, available at the interpretive center; www.gastateparks.org for map and photos
Trail contacts: Providence Canyon State Park, Route 1, Box 158, Lumpkin, GA 31815; (229) 838-6202; www.gastateparks.org

Finding the trailhead: Take U.S. Highway 27 to Lumpkin from the north or south. From Lumpkin go west 7.3 miles on Highway 39C to the park entrance. The canyons, parking, and picnic areas are only a few yards from the highway. The trailhead for both the Canyon Loop and Backpacking Trails is at the office/interpretive center.

The Hikes

Canyon Loop Trail

The 3.0-mile loop begins at the Interpretive Center near the overlook. Park personnel provide maps, directions, and instructions for both trails in the park. This white-blazed trail is on a moderate grade, with switchbacks and widely spaced steps between log railings down to the canyon floor. You go from a very dry, well-drained ridge to the moist and shaded canyon floor. The trees on the dry slopes include white, southern red, and blackjack oaks; shortleaf and loblolly pines; and hickories. Dogwoods, blueberries, hawthorns, and numerous wildflowers grow beneath the taller trees.

The canyon bottom is a flat alluvial bed of sandy clay eroded from the canyon walls. The canyons are numbered. There are nine you can walk into on this trail, and a map provided by the park office identifies these canyons, numbered from west to east. Walking up the canyon floor, which is actually the streambed, gives you a better perspective of the massiveness of the erosion that has taken place. When wet, the sandy streambed appears slightly muddy, but the sand makes it surprisingly hard; you can walk without sinking. Rhododendron and the rare plumleaf azalea grow in the canyons along with thick stands of alders and many other shrubs and trees.

After the optional walk into the canyon fingers, you cross a boardwalk and begin the climb up the hill to the surrounding level on the other side. The trail then follows around the canyon rim to the left just outside a protective railing. A number of overlooks at strategic places around the rim provide excellent photographic opportunities and views of the colorful canyon walls as you return to the trailhead and interpretive center.

The complex geological history of the canyons is skillfully interpreted at the interpretive center. Each of the colors along the canyon wall represents a different age and composition. Iron ore, manganese, kaolin, mica, and sandy clays are just a few of the substances contributing to the many colors you see.

Backpacking Trail

About 40 miles south of Columbus, Providence Canyon State Park is frequently called "Georgia's Little Grand Canyon." The soils are very soft and easily eroded. The rolling topography and the geological formation, coupled with clearing the land in the early 1800s for lumber and farming, caused sever erosion gullies. By 1850 the gullies were 3 to 5 feet deep. Once the water cut through the erosion-resistant surface layers, the softer sandy soils of the Providence Formation eroded rapidly. This has resulted in canyons 150 feet deep with exposed sides that are exceptionally colorful.

Colorful canyon walls are seen from Canyon Loop Trail.

Birding along this trail is limited to forest and small open-field habitats. All of Georgia's woodpeckers can be seen here, as well as many warblers, thrushes, several owls, and turkeys. Mammals include the white-tailed deer, red and gray foxes, gray and fox squirrels, raccoons, and armadillos, which have extended their range throughout the Coastal Plain. The diggings seen along the trail are most frequently that of the armadillo searching for insects and other food in the forest leaf litter and sandy soil.

The Backpacking Trail goes into the canyon with the Canyon Loop Trail, going to the right this time in a counterclockwise direction. A free permit is required before you take this trail. You also need a permit if you wish to camp at one of the six primitive campsites along the trail. You leave the interpretive center and hike down the 0.4-mile trail that has two switchbacks before reaching the canyon floor. (**Note:** The following narrative milepoints include the 0.4-mile descent with the Canyon Loop Trail.)

The red-blazed trail starts here with a right turn away from the steep canyon walls. The trail is on the right side of the stream, the beginning of Turner Creek. At 0.9 mile you pass the pioneer camps for Boy Scouts. Stay on the right side of the

Providence Canyon State Park Trails

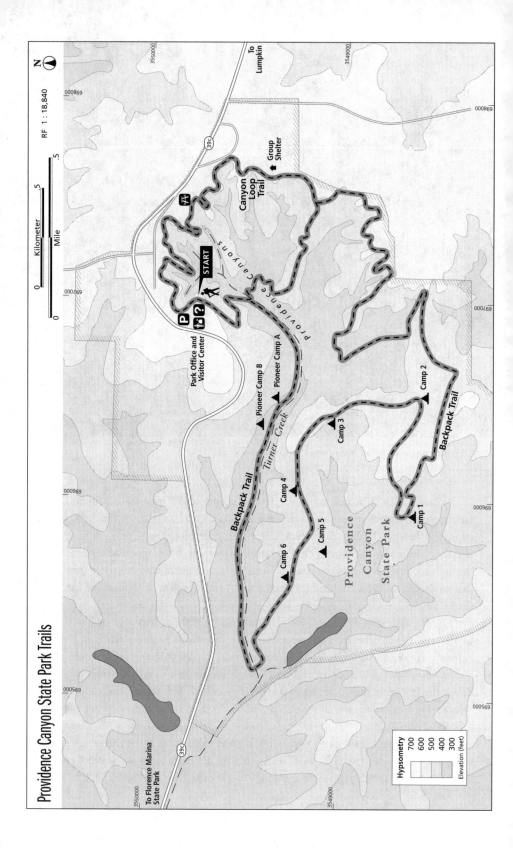

stream until you reach the left turn at the bridge crossing Turner Creek at 1.7 miles and start up out of the canyon. You are now in the forested area that surrounds the canyon, with large trees and more dense shrub thickets. The trail is eroded from foot travel as you climb about 100 feet and come to Campsite 6 on the left at 2.0 miles. You stay on more level ground now as you pass the spur trail to the right for Campsite 5 at 2.2 miles and continue past Campsite 4 at 2.3 miles. Look for the scratching and diggings of armadillos in the sandy soil along the trail. You pass Campsite 3 at 2.6 miles and begin a gentle climb to the highest site, Campsite 2, at 2.9 miles in a sharp turn to the right. Campsite 1, the last one on the trail, is at 3.4 miles.

You now leave the camping area and more heavily forested area for a more open plant community, remnants of former agriculture. At 3.9 miles you come to an old roadbed; turn left and follow it to an intermittent stream at Mile 4.2. Make a sharp turn to the left and begin the descent into a pleasant cove of more mature trees and spring flowers—a comfortable relief from the dry ridges and reforested farmland. At 4.6 miles, cross the stream; turn to the right, and begin the climb of about 130 feet to the level of the canyon rim at 5.0 miles. The undulating trail follows as close as possible to a contour with the steep, forested side on the left and the open level land on the right. At 5.6 miles you pick up the white-blazed Canyon Loop Trail, turn to the right, and follow the canyon rim. At 5.9 miles you pass the group shelter. From here you begin to see the first of the nine overlooks around the rim. They afford excellent views and photographic opportunities. Take the time to enjoy them. At Mile 6.4 arrive at the picnic area, restrooms, and the beginning of the wheelchair-accessible portion of the trail.

At 6.9 miles, the parking area is on the right, and at 7.0 miles you are back to the interpretive center and the close of the loop.

With overnight camping, this trail is an excellent practice hike to test camping equipment and prepare for longer hikes in the mountains or elsewhere.

Miles and Directions

The following loop trail combines the Backpacking Trail with the 0.4-mile descent to the canyon floor on the Canyon Loop Trail.

- **0.0** Start at the steps of the interpretive center. The Backpacking Trail coincides with the white-blazed Canyon Loop Trail for 0.4 mile to the canyon floor.
- **0.4** Turn right on the red-blazed Backpacking Trail and follow the beginning of Turner Creek.
- **0.9** Pass the Boy Scout Pioneer Camps on the right.
- **1.7** Cross Turner Creek on a footbridge, and begin to climb through a forest area.
- **2.0** Campsite 6 is on the left.
- **2.2** Pass the spur trail for Campsite 5 on right.
- **2.3** Campsite 4 is on the left.
- **2.6** Pass Campsite 3 on the right; begin a gentle climb.
- **2.9** Campsite 2 is on the right; make a right turn.
- **3.4** After a sharp turn to the left, you are at Campsite 1 on the right.

3.9 Intersect an old roadbed; turn left on the road and follow it to an intermittent stream.

4.2 Leave the roadbed; make a sharp left turn and descend into a forest cove.

4.6 Cross the stream; turn right and begin to climb back uphill.

5.0 After climbing 130 feet, you're at the canyon rim.

5.6 Rejoin the white-blazed Canyon Loop Trail; turn right.

5.9 Pass the group shelter on the right. Begin passing the nine viewpoints along the trail. Stop to enjoy, and perhaps photograph, the scenic canyon and its colorful walls.

6.4 The trail reaches the day-use area, with the picnic tables and restroom. The trail here is a wide, level wheelchair-accessible path. Follow on around with views of the canyon.

6.9 Pass the parking area on the right.

7.0 Arrive back at the interpretive center to close the loop.

57 Reed Bingham State Park Trails

Four loop trails totaling 4.0 miles allow easy walking through diverse habitats. The elevation of the Coastal Plain here is about 100 feet, and the trails vary only 3 or 4 feet. Two short loop trails, Turkey Oak and Upland, are designed to show specific land and habitat types. The Gopher Tortoise Trail demonstrates the habitat and habits of this rare turtle. A loop formed by the Little River and Bird Walk Trails includes long boardwalks that bring you especially close to open aquatic environments. Two short spurs on Little River Trail end in overlooks that afford views of the lake and river and in winter give you a closer view of the more than 2,000 vultures that winter here.

Start: Parking area trailhead for Upland Loop, Turkey Oak, and Little River/Bird Walk Trails; park road about 150 yards from campground entrance for Gopher Tortoise Trail

Distance: Upland Loop, 1.0-mile loop; Turkey Oak Trail, 0.5-mile loop; combined Little River and Bird Walk Trails, 2.2-mile loop; Gopher Tortoise Trail, 0.4-mile loop

Approximate hiking time: Upland Loop, 45 minutes; Turkey Oak Trail, 30 minutes; combined Little River and Bird Walk loop, 1 hour; Gopher Tortoise Trail, 30 minutes

Difficulty: Easy

Elevation gain/loss: Negligible

Trail surface: Hard sand; boardwalk

Lay of the land: Flat

Season: Year-round; summer months hot and humid; special activities in winter

Land status: Georgia State Parks Division

Nearest town: Adel

Fees and permits: Park Pass $3.00 per vehicle per day

Maps: USGS Adel quadrangle; page-size map showing trails, available in the park office; www.gastateparks.org for maps and photographs

Trail contacts: Reed Bingham State Park, Box 394B-1, Route 2, Adel, GA 31620; (229) 896–3551; www.gastateparks.org

Finding the trailhead: From Adel take exit 39 off Interstate 75; go 6.0 miles east on Highway 37 to Evergreen Church Road. Turn right and go 0.4 mile to Reed Bingham Road. Turn left and go

Green tree frogs are common in the wetland areas of the state.

0.6 mile to the park entrance; continue 0.1 mile and turn right on the park road. Go 0.5 mile to Gopher Tortoise Trail and another 1.3 miles to the parking area, the common trailhead for the Turkey Oak, Upland, and Little River and Bird Walk Trails.

The Hikes

Reed Bingham State Park is in south Georgia, about midway between the ocean and the Alabama line. This park on the Coastal Plain exhibits just about all the typical habitats of south-central Georgia, and the trails are designed to expose you to as many of these as possible. There are bay swamps, flat woods, river swamp, upland pinewoods, turkey oak–pinewoods on sand ridges, mixed Southern hardwoods, old fields, and more. The Little River flows through the park and has been impounded to form a 375-acre lake offering quality fishing. Boardwalks through the wetter habitats make it possible to view and experience a uniquely Southern swamp. Such varied habitats make birding exceptional.

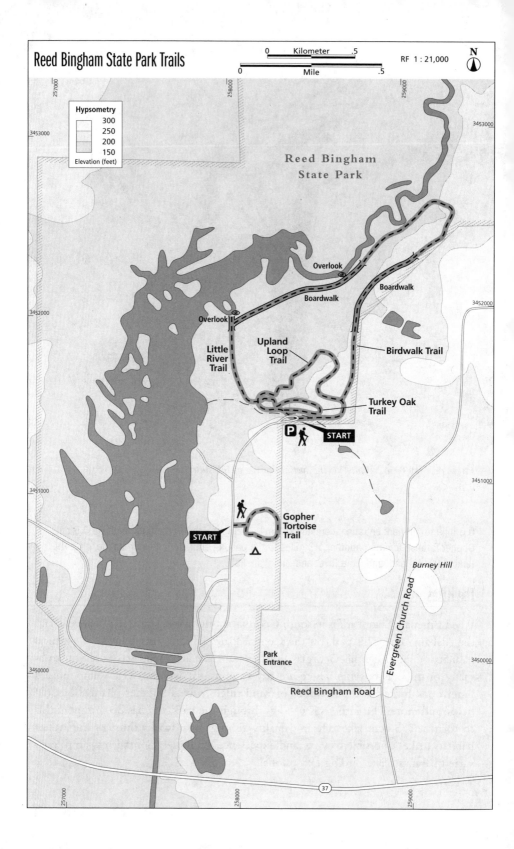

Reed Bingham State Park Trails

0   Kilometer   .5
0   Mile   .5

RF 1 : 21,000

N

Hypsometry

300
250
200
150

Elevation (feet)

Reed Bingham
State Park

Overlook

Boardwalk

Boardwalk

Overlook

Little
River
Trail

Upland
Loop
Trail

Birdwalk Trail

Turkey Oak
Trail

P

START

START

Gopher
Tortoise
Trail

Burney Hill

Evergreen Church Road

Park
Entrance

Reed Bingham Road

37

Both black and turkey vultures winter at this park. As many as 2,000 to 3,000 of these large, soaring birds can be seen at one time. The first Saturday in December is designated Buzzard Day, with boat rides up Little River to view the buzzard roosting areas, clogging, singing, and craft exhibits. Wildlife includes the rare gopher tortoise, alligators, deer, armadillos, raccoons, beavers, squirrels, bobcats, foxes, and rabbits. The lake provides good fishing for largemouth bass, crappie, bluegill, and redbreast sunfish. Boating and camping also are popular activities.

Three loops, Turkey Oak Trail (yellow blazed), Upland Loop (green blazed), and the combined Little River (red blazed) and Bird Walk (blue blazed) Trails, along with the Gopher Tortoise Trail, are referred to as the Coastal Plains Nature Trails. With the exception of the Gopher Tortoise Trail, all have a common trailhead and can be hiked in either direction or in any combination. It is best to pick up the color-coded brochures at the office and hike according to the numbered stations. They are especially useful if this is your first time hiking here. Two stone pillars mark the trailhead.

Turkey Oak Trail

The Turkey Oak loop takes you through pine flat woods and along a turkey oak–pinewoods sand ridge. This is the driest of the park's habitats; most of the trees, except for the pines, are quite small due to the lack of nutrients in the well-drained sandy soils. The seventeen stations along the trail are discussed in the yellow leaflet.

Upland Loop Trail

The Upland loop branches off the Turkey Oak Trail for a longer walk through upland pinewoods. Watch for evidence of digging and scratching marks left by armadillos searching for insects, their primary food source. You can identify gopher tortoise and armadillo holes by the low mound of sand and clay excavated from the holes. This trail leads through old fields. Fires that blackened trunks of the pine trees but did not kill them are a very important part of the Coastal Plain ecology, maintaining natural grasses, herbaceous plants, and shrubs. The nineteen stations along the trail are discussed in the green leaflet.

Little River and Bird Walk Trails

Hiked together, Little River and Bird Walk Trails make a 2.2-mile hike. Because of the boardwalks, these are the most interesting trails in the park. These trails take you into the fascinating wetland habitat of the river swamp, the floodplain, the creek swamp, and the Southern mixed hardwoods on low ridges, locally called "river bluffs." The recently completed boardwalks on the Little River side of the loop combine for 2,588 feet. Bird Walk Trail takes you through forested swamps, open pools, and shallow water areas. Between the boardwalks, the path goes through a pitcher plant savanna harboring insectivorous plants that grow in moist, sandy, and acid soil. Hooded and trumpet pitcher plants trap insects in their long leaves. The tiny sundews trap insects with sticky beads of plant juices on their leaves. The bladderwort, another insectivorous plant, grows in areas with shallow, standing water. The many species of frogs here are usually heard before you see them. In the wetland areas, chain, cinnamon, and royal ferns grow in abundance. On the river bluffs, large southern magnolias and many spring wildflowers add aroma and color to the hike. Seventeen stations are discussed in the blue Bird Walk Trail leaflet and twenty stations in the red Little River Trail leaflet.

Gopher Tortoise Trail

The Gopher Tortoise Trail, marked by a sign on the paved road near the campground, was developed through the Nongame Program of the Georgia Wildlife Resources Division. This well-marked and interpreted trail passes through wiregrass, turkey oaks, post oaks, and a few live oaks that grow in the sandy soil. The burrows of the large land turtles are obvious by the nearly white mounds of sandy clay at the entrance. The deep burrows are used by many other animals, including rattlesnakes, the large indigo snake, gopher frogs, and insects. As many as thirty-nine invertebrate and forty-two vertebrate animals are known to use the tortoise's burrow. The flat 0.4-mile trail is well worth the short walk. Twenty stations along the trail are discussed in the white leaflet.

58 George T. Bagby State Park Trails

An interconnected system of trails give visitors an appreciation of the diversity of the lower Coastal Plain. The hard-packed sandy-clay trail surface provides easy walking throughout 2.5 miles of interconnected trails. You walk through open and wooded areas and beside marsh and lake. The well-marked Chattahoochee Trail passes through several forest habitats. Numbered interpretive stations along the trail correspond with a leaflet, available in the lodge office, that helps identify the many plants and other features on the trail. A boardwalk crossing a pond and going along the lakeshore adds variety to the hike. The elevation of the lake is 180 feet; the trails are only a few feet above this, with only slight variation throughout their length.

Start: Lodge parking area trailhead
Distance: Total length of the four loops and connecting paths, 2.5 miles; Chattahoochee Trail, 1.1-mile lollipop
Approximate hiking time: Chattahoochee Trail, 1½ hours
Difficulty: Easy
Elevation gain/loss: Negligible
Trail surface: Hard sandy clay
Lay of the land: Flat flood plain
Season: Year-round

Land status: Georgia State Parks Division
Nearest town: Fort Gaines
Fees and permits: Park Pass $3.00 per vehicle per day
Maps: USGS Fort Gaines; page-size map, available at the lodge office and www.gastate parks.org
Trail contacts: George T. Bagby State Park and Lodge, Route 1, Box 201, Fort Gaines, GA 31571; (912) 768-2571; www.gastate parks.org

Finding the trailhead: The park entrance is 3.0 miles north of Fort Gaines on Highway 39. The trailhead for the Chattahoochee Trail is at the end of the parking area for the lodge. It provides connection with all other trails in the park.

The Hike

The park is on the shore of Lake Walter F. George, a 48,000 acre Army Corps of Engineers reservoir on the Chattahoochee River. The park features a sixty-room lodge, conference center, restaurant, an eighteen-hole golf course, a boat dock at the lodge, and a marina with ample docking on the lake. Because of the hard sandy clay trail surface, wheelchairs can navigate most of the trails and other features with minimum assistance.

You can begin at the lodge parking area trailhead. There are two other access points where the park road ends at the trail. The series of four small loops all start at the lodge.

Blue blazes mark the Chattahoochee Trail throughout. Thirty-three numbered interpretive stations begin at the outset. Number 1 identifies a large willow oak. Many trees and other plants are identified on the page-size map. At Station 19, you

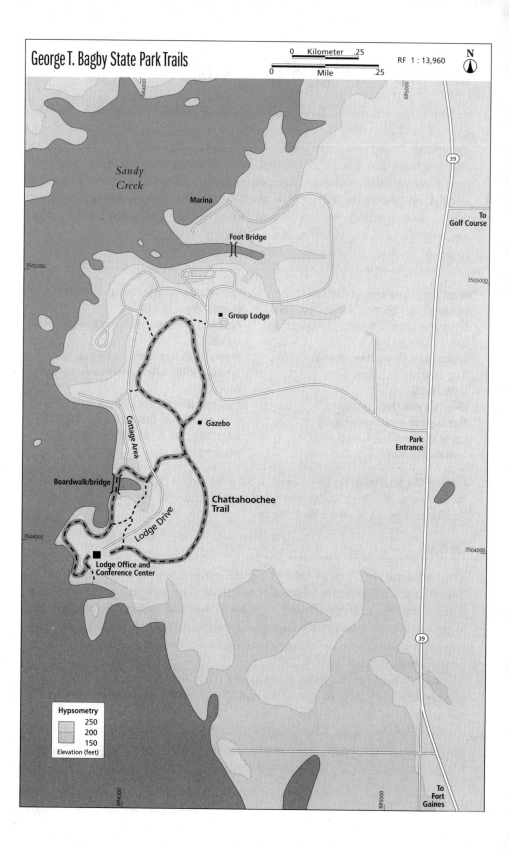

come to a fork in the trail. Take the right fork and go by the beautiful gazebo with a wheelchair ramp. Deer, turkeys, squirrels, and other mammals and birds are attracted to the area near the gazebo, making this a great place to just sit, watch, and listen. The trail goes through alternately dry and moist areas, with different plants and animals in each. The gopher tortoise holes are easy to spot by the mound of sand and clay at the burrow opening. Armadillo diggings also are quite evident along the path. Foxes will modify and use the abandoned tortoise holes; one such modified hole is at Station 33.

At Station 27, a spur trail on the right goes to the group lodge. Turning to the left, you complete the first loop at the last interpretive station, Number 33. Continue toward the lodge for 100 yards; turn right on the connector trail between the Chattahoochee Trail and East Lodge Loop and go 0.2 mile. Turn right and follow the Lodge Loop to the boardwalk. The small pond is trapped from the main lake and is an excellent place to see waterbirds, beavers, frogs, colorful dragonflies, and many other interesting aquatic animals. You may even see an alligator.

After the boardwalk, you continue another 0.2 mile to the lodge and close the loop.

Additional Trails
The other trails in the park are short destination trails to the lodge, boat dock, fishing pier, boardwalk, and other points of interest.

Honorable Mention

R Kolomoki Mounds State Historic Park

Located 6.0 miles north of Blakely, this unusual park is an important archaeological site as well as a scenic recreation area. The mounds here were built between 250 and 950 A.D. by the Swift Creek and Weeden Island Indians. Among the mounds is Georgia's oldest great temple mound. Along with the early American history and artifacts, the park offers other outdoor activities. Three miles of hiking trails in two loops take you along the edge of Lakes Kolomoki and Yohola, beside a wetland habitat with marsh grasses and shrubs. In the dryer areas look for armadillo diggings and gopher tortoise burrows. Another set of trails gives you a good feel and view of the seven mounds, with excellent explanations of the site. The museum is designed so that you are actually inside an excavated portion of a mound.

For more information: Kolomoki Mounds State Historic Park, 205 Indian Mounds Road, Blakely, GA 39823; (229) 724–2151; www.gastateparks.org.

DeLorme: Georgia Atlas and Gazetteer: Page 56 A2

Southeast Georgia:
Coastal Plain and Atlantic Coast

End of the Nannygoat Beach Nature Trail on Sapelo Island (Hike 64).

59 George L. Smith State Park Trails

George L. Smith State Park, with 6.0 miles of hiking trails and 7.2 miles of canoe trails, offers the visitor much to do and see in an area of unique ancient sand dunes. The park is located on the lower Coastal Plain in an area of old dunes that support a dwarf oak forest, characterized by longleaf pines and turkey oaks and wiregrass. The gopher tortoise and the several species of animals associated with the tortoise's burrows add great interest for the naturalist hiker. The featured 3-Mile Loop Trail is a flat hike alongside Fifteen Mile Creek and through a wiregrass/longleaf pine plant community. A short boardwalk takes you close to a small creek. Housed in the covered bridge, the historic Parrish Mill, once used for grinding corn and wheat and sawing lumber, is still grinding corn.

Start: At the historic mill house and covered bridge

Distance: 3-Mile Loop Trail, 3.0-mile loop; Upper Loop Trail, 2.3-mile loop; Cabin Loop Trail, 0.3-mile loop; Campground Trail, 0.4 mile one-way

Approximate hiking time: 3-Mile Loop Trail, 1½ hours; Upper Loop Trail, 1 hour; Cabin Loop and Campground Trails, 45 minutes each

Difficulty: Easy

Elevation gain/loss: Negligible

Trail surface: Sandy clay

Lay of the land: Flat; elevation between 200 and 260 feet

Season: Year-round

Land status: Georgia State Parks Division

Nearest town: Twin City

Fees and permits: Parking $3.00 per vehicle per day

Maps: USGS Twin City; map of the park with trails, available at the park office

Trail contacts: George L. Smith State Park, 371 George L. Smith State Park Road, Twin City, GA 30471; (912) 763-2759; www.ga stateparks.org

Finding the trailhead: From Twin City take Highway 23 south 3.0 miles to George L. Smith State Park Road. Turn left and go 1.8 miles to the park entrance and parking area near the office and covered bridge. To reach the 3-Mile Loop Trail, walk through the Mill House Covered Bridge.

The Hike

This park is best known now for the newly refurbished Parrish Mill, a combination gristmill, saw mill, covered bridge, and dam built in 1880 and now open for tours. There are 7.2 miles of canoe trails in the 412-acre lake and surrounding marsh habitat.

As you begin, take a few moments to enjoy the beauty of the lake with its picturesque cypress trees reflecting in the dark water. The 3-Mile Loop Trail begins after

The Mill House covered bridge is the trailhead for the 3-mile Loop Trail.

you walk through the mill house, which is a covered bridge that houses Parrish Mill, to the end of the earthen dam. At this point you will see the sandy road that bisects the loop trail. You can walk the road out and back or use it as a shortcut for only part of the trail. To walk the whole loop, take the path to the right past the large information board showing the trail. Blue blazes mark the designated path; however, the trail is so obvious, there is hardly a need for blazes.

On the right, the moist soil supports dense vegetation of titis, water oaks, maples, and magnolias; a wide variety of herbs, shrubs, and vines; and at least two species of tupelo—black and water. On the left are the well-drained, sandy soils of the ancient dunes, with turkey oaks, longleaf pines, sparkleberry bushes, reindeer lichens, bracken ferns, and other shrubs and herbs. At 0.25 mile a short spur trail leads to a small spring branch, a tributary of Fifteen Mile Creek. Beside the dense shrubs and cypress and tupelo trees, you can expect to find several ferns, including royal, cinnamon, and sensitive ferns. The pretty white Gordonia, or loblolly bay, a member of the tea family, blooms in July. Frogs and toads are numerous. This spur ends at a short footbridge over the branch.

Returning to the main path, look for the tracks of any of the several mammals living here but rarely seen. The tracks of white-tailed deer, rabbits, gray and fox

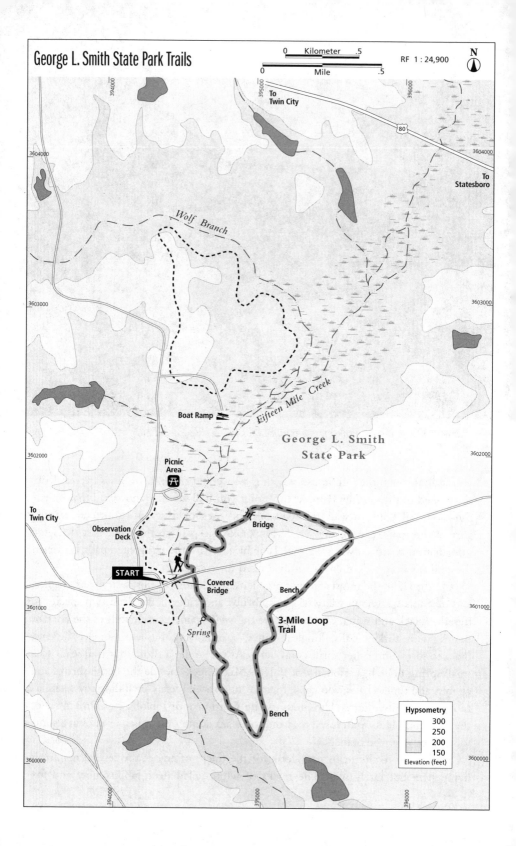

squirrels, raccoons, opossums, armadillos, bobcats, otters, and foxes may be seen in the sand. During the warm months you may see a number of different butterflies, including the giant swallowtail.

There is a bench just before the 1-mile marker. If time is not a factor, you can sit here and simply enjoy the surroundings. All along this part of the trail, you are following downstream with Fifteen Mile Creek on the right, even though it is rarely visible through the dense vegetation.

At 1.1 miles the trail comes to a sandy, two-track road. *Do not follow the road.* Continue on the trail, which turns slightly to the right, away from the road. The trail now leaves the dense vegetation and goes through the more open, sandy, drier habitat with dwarf turkey oaks and longleaf pines, an occasional yucca (Spanish bayonet), wiregrass, and a wide variety of flowering plants, including red mint, or scarlet wild basil, a favorite of hummingbirds. This is the typical home of the gopher tortoise, a species that is on the decline because of habitat loss. The tortoise is truly an anchor species—their burrows provide vital habitat for a great many other species, from insects, spiders, and toads to snakes, including the endangered indigo snake and the eastern diamondback rattlesnake. Researchers have identified more than 350 species of animals that find protection from heat, cold, and even fire in the burrows, which also furnish needed moisture.

From the first mile marker to the second, you are in the typical sandy ridge habitat of the tortoise, characterized by the open turkey oak and longleaf pine forest. You can easily identify the burrows by the large, sandy mound in front of each hole. When walking the trail, avoid disturbing the area around the burrows. If you are fortunate enough to see a tortoise, don't bother it; just let it be.

Birds you are apt to see include a number of warblers, cardinals, and other songbirds; kingbirds and other flycatchers; hawks; crows; and vultures. Herons, egrets, ibises, wood ducks, cormorants, and other waterbirds are associated with the lake and creeks here.

At 1.6 miles you come to another bench near an interesting stand of longleaf pines. The oaks are draped with Spanish moss. Large bracken ferns are present throughout this part of the trail. In summer you may also see a small white flower called the tread-softly, or spurge nettle. Don't try to pick it. The stiff sharp hairs can cause a painful irritation. Fortunately this flower is not very common on the path.

At 2.0 miles, you cross the wide unpaved road that is the extension of the road from the mill. A sign with a map shows where you are.

The path leads toward the lake and some of the more moist areas and eventually along the lake. You pass through a patch of switch cane and across a small footbridge at 2.3 miles. The dense vegetation gives a junglelike appearance. After the large sand bank on the left, the oaks are more heavily festooned with Spanish moss. The lake is now on the right; when it's full you can see it through the dense stand of cypress that borders most of the lake. If the lake level is low, you can actually walk among the large buttressed cypress trees.

From here to the end of the loop, you continue walking through a similar habitat to the beginning of the trail but at a much more attractive site. The walk ends at the road to the mill house.

Miles and Directions

0.0 Start at the end of the covered bridge.

0.25 Pass a short spur to the right that leads to a spring area.

0.9 Here's a rest bench if you're so inclined.

1.1 Pass an old, sandy road; stay on the trail.

1.6 Come to another bench. (**FYI:** You should have seen at least one gopher tortoise burrow by now.)

2.0 Cross a wide unpaved road to continue the loop. (**FYI:** A map on the sign here gives you your location.) (**Bailout:** Turn left on the road to return to the bridge in 0.8 mile.)

2.3 After a walk through a more moist bamboo area, cross a small bridge over an intermittent stream. (**FYI:** At times, this may just be a wet area.)

3.0 You are back to the road. Turn right; you are only a few yards from the mill house and covered bridge.

3.1 Continue through the bridge and arrive back at the parking area.

Additional Trails

The **Campground,** or **Squirrel Run, Trail** begins at the picnic area on the campground side of the office at a railing. It follows along the lake, the shoreline of which is a picturesque stand of cypress trees. This 0.5-mile path winds through a pleasant stand of pines, water and willow oaks, yellow poplars, maples, Gordonia, and other vines and shrubs. At 0.25 a boardwalk takes you through a cypress stand on the edge of the lake. A large platform and benches provide the opportunity to just sit and enjoy this unique, almost subtropical cove. The path ends at 0.4 mile at the camping area.

Cabin Loop, Upper Loop, and **Campground Trails** are well worth taking the time to enjoy. Each is unique in the plants and animals you will see.

60 Magnolia Springs State Park Trails

Crystal clear Magnolia Springs flows an estimated nine million gallons of water per day. The spring and stream that runs from it are home to a wide variety of fish and plant life and attract many species of wading and shorebirds and reptiles, including alligators. This area also supports nesting colonies of the endangered red-cockaded woodpecker and other wildlife, including gopher tortoises, deer, beavers, squirrels, and armadillos. The featured hike incorporates the Beaver Trail into a 1.8-mile lollipop.

Any visit to Magnolia Springs State Park should include a visit to the Bo Ginn Aquarium and Aquatic Education Center, located across the footbridge a short distance from the park side of the spring.

Start: Picnic Shelter 8 for the Beaver, Woodpecker, and Biking/Hiking Trails
Distance: Woodpecker Woods Nature Trail, 0.5 mile one-way; Beaver Trail, 2.3-mile lollipop; Biking/Hiking Trail, 1.7 miles, one-way
Approximate hiking time: Beaver Trail, 2 hours; Woodpecker Woods Nature Trail, 45 minutes; Biking/Hiking Trail, 1 hour
Difficulty: Easy
Elevation gain/loss: Negligible
Trail surface: Sandy loam

Lay of the land: Coastal Plain flat
Season: Year-round
Land status: Georgia State Parks Division
Nearest town: Millen
Fees and permits: Parking $3.00 per vehicle per day
Maps: USGS Millen; trail maps available from the park office
Trail contacts: Magnolia Springs State Park, 1051 Magnolia Springs Drive, Millen GA 30442; (912) 982-1660; www.gastateparks.org

Finding the trailhead: From Millen, start at the intersection of Highway 17 and U.S. Highway 25 North. Go 5.0 miles north on US 25, and turn right into the park entrance on Magnolia Spring Drive. Go 0.3 mile to the park office and 0.6 mile to the Picnic Shelter 8. This is the trailhead for Beaver, Woodpecker Woods Nature, and Biking/Hiking Trails.

The Hike

Beaver Trail begins with a boardwalk bordering the attractive Upper Magnolia Springs Lake and continues to the lake's headwater area. Stand or sit at the large raised deck for a fine view of the lake and wildlife. You continue on the turn through the drier, sandy area to experience the home of the gopher tortoise. Tall longleaf pines grow with small oak trees and wiregrass on the drier sites; sprawling water and live oaks and other hardwood trees thrive in the more moist areas.

Start at Picnic Shelter 8 on the connector trail to the Woodpecker and Beaver Trails. Turn right and continue toward the Beaver Trail. A section of the Woodpecker Trail coincides with the Beaver Trail, and you come to the access trail to the dam and amphitheater area. At the dam you begin the Beaver Trail in a dense shrub bay and into a longleaf pine and oak stand. Crossing the paved road, you walk along the

The Woodpecker Woods Nature Trail boardwalk leads to a viewing deck over the lake.

east side of the lake past the racks where rental boats are stored to a boardwalk crossing a small wooded swamp of tupelo, cypress, maple, titi, buttonbush, and other trees and shrubs.

As the trail hugs the edge of the lake, watch for great blue herons, little blue herons, egrets, anhingas, and other waterbirds, especially wood ducks anytime of the year and many other ducks during winter. Another boardwalk crosses a wet area and you remain in the woods where dead trees serve as dens for wildlife and attract birds like the large, showy pileated woodpecker. The large longleaf pines provide habitat needed by the endangered red-cockaded woodpecker. At 1.0 mile a short spur off the main trail turns to the left and to an observation platform standing well above the water level at the upper end of the lake. This provides an excellent view of the lake habitat and the great number of animals using the lake, including beavers, turtles and frogs of many kinds, ducks, herons, egrets, kingfishers, and an ample variety of other birds. Large fish can be seen splashing for food among patches of white water lilies. The overlook is especially interesting during winter when the migratory waterbirds are in residence.

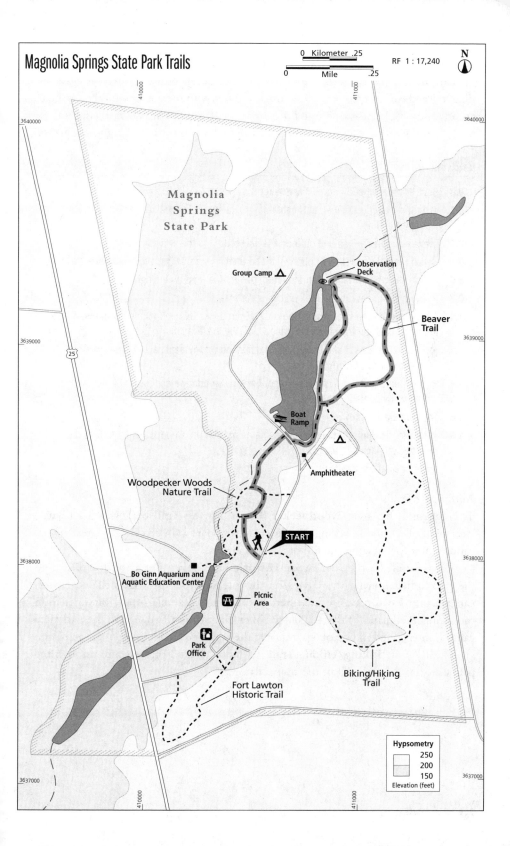

Magnolia Springs State Park Trails

0 Kilometer .25

0 Mile .25

RF 1 : 17,240

N

Magnolia
Springs
State Park

Group Camp ▲

Observation
Deck

**Beaver
Trail**

Boat
Ramp

▲

Amphitheater

Woodpecker Woods
Nature Trail

25

START

Bo Ginn Aquarium and
Aquatic Education Center

Picnic
Area

Park
Office

Biking/Hiking
Trail

Fort Lawton
Historic Trail

Hypsometry
250
200
150
Elevation (feet)

Return to the trail. The soil changes to the dry sandy ridge condition that is a remnant of the ancient sand dunes of a former ocean beach. Prickly pear cactus, small twisted turkey oaks, a few tall longleaf pines with their enormous cones, holes leading into gopher tortoise burrows, deer, and armadillos are characteristic of this sandy area. The trail loops back to the nature trail and returns to Magnolia Springs.

Miles and Directions

0.0 Start at the trailhead near Picnic Shelter 8.

0.15 Meet the Woodpecker Trail; turn right and walk a short distance with a section of the Woodpecker Trail.

0.25 Leave Woodpecker Trail and start on the access trail to the dam.

0.5 Reach the dam near the amphitheater and another starting point for the Beaver Trail.

0.6 After a short boardwalk, reach the return trail for the loop on the right.

0.7 Reach another short boardwalk across a wet area.

1.0 A short trail on the left leads to the observation deck. Be sure to spend some time here. Return to the loop trail; there's a gentle increase in elevation.

1.2 You are in the area of the ancient sand dune and prickly pear cactus, small twisted turkey oaks, and tall longleaf pines.

1.4 By this point, you should have seen gopher tortoise burrows and tracks of deer and armadillo in the sandy soil.

1.6 The loop closes; turn left.

1.8 Return to the dam. (**Option:** Follow the same trails to the Woodpecker Trail.) Take the road back to Picnic Shelter 8.

2.3 Arrive back at the trailhead.

Additional Trails

The delightful 0.5-mile **Woodpecker Woods Nature Trail** begins at the crystal-clear pool of Magnolia Springs. An interpretive boardwalk gives you a great observation point for viewing the life of the spring area.

The 0.6-mile loop **Fort Lawton Historic Trail** begins just across the road from the park office. During the Civil War, this site was used as a Confederate prison camp. Camp Lawton was located here because of the ample supply of water from the spring. Remnants of the 40,000-prisoner camp can still be seen in the park. The camp is interpreted in pamphlets available the park and also in the on-site museum.

The 1.7-mile **Biking/Hiking Trail** is a more "upland" habitat trail through the palmetto and oak area. All of the trail is flat.

61 General Coffee State Park Trails

Few trails provide the lower Coastal Plains river swamp experience with so little effort as do the 4 miles of easy trails in General Coffee State Park. The park is a fascinating area of sand ridges and river swamp. A boardwalk and several bridges provide access deeper into the swamp. The flora and fauna of the river swamp and sand ridge make this trail a most interesting experience. A variety of rare plants and animals may be seen from the trail as you walk through both the river swamp edge and into the sandy ridges. The featured hike combines the River Swamp and Gopher Tortoise Trails for a 3.5-mile lollipop trek.

Start: Near Picnic Shelter 4 at the large sign with the trail inscribed on it
Distance: River Swamp Trail, 3.0 miles one-way; Gopher Tortoise Trail 1.0-mile loop; East River Swamp Trail, 0.9 mile one-way
Approximate hiking time: River Swamp and Gopher Tortoise Trails combined, 3 hours; East River Swamp Trail, 1 hour
Difficulty: Easy
Trail surface: Sandy loam
Lay of the land: Mostly flat; gentle elevation changes in the sandy ridge

Season: Year-round
Land status: Georgia State Parks Division
Nearest town: Douglas
Fees and permits: Parking $3.00 per vehicle per day
Maps: USGS Douglas North; maps of park and trail, available from the park office and trading post
Trail contacts: General Coffee State Park, 46 John Coffee Road, Nicholls, GA 31554; (912) 384-7082; www.gastateparks.org

Finding the trailhead: At the intersection of U.S. Highway 441 and Highway 32 in Douglas, go east 5.9 miles on Highway 32 to the General Coffee State Park entrance on the left. Go 0.4 mile on the park access road. The trailhead is near the picnic shelters just off the main access road. A wooden sign at the trail entrance to the wooded area has an outline map of the trail.

The Hike

Trees in the swamp are much taller than those on the sandy ridge. This difference is so great that from a distance the "ridge" does not stand out above the swamp.

Orange blazes mark the way as the **River Swamp Trail** penetrates the thick vegetation. The river swamp habitat is best seen from a short spur trail that takes off to the right about 0.25-mile along the trail. This boardwalk and bridge, the beginning of the East River Swamp Trail, provide a vista of a relatively undisturbed swamp. Such swamps are a crucial part of the Coastal Plain river system. This is Seventeen Mile River, which continues on to join the Satilla River and on to the Atlantic Ocean. Trees in this moist-soil area include the large buttressed tupelo and cypress, red maple, yellow poplar, live and water oaks, and slash and longleaf pines. Sphagnum moss and chain and royal ferns grow in the very wet areas. Titi and wax myrtle make up most

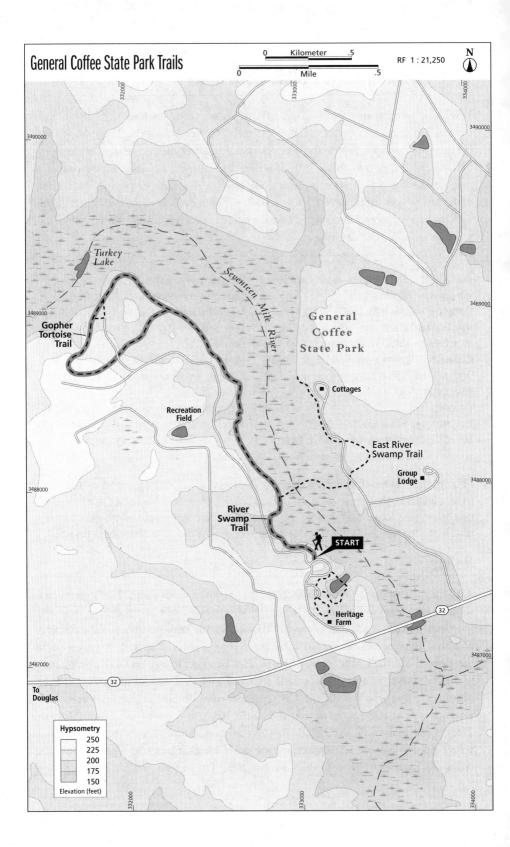

General Coffee State Park Trails

RF 1 : 21,250

N

Turkey Lake

Seventeen Mile River

General Coffee State Park

Gopher Tortoise Trail

Cottages

Recreation Field

East River Swamp Trail

Group Lodge

River Swamp Trail

START

Heritage Farm

32

To Douglas

32

Hypsometry
250
225
200
175
150
Elevation (feet)

of the shrub vegetation, along with an occasional dense thicket of privet hedge that has escaped cultivation.

You continue on the main trail. As the habitat changes from the river swamp on the right to the sandy ridge, palmetto and wax myrtle bushes are more evident, along with larger water and live oaks on the left. This is where the rare greenfly orchid lives as an epiphyte on the limbs and trunks of the larger oaks.

Leaving the river swamp, the path moves into the sandy ridge plant and animal community where gopher tortoises and armadillos burrow into the soft, sandy soil. Burrows created by the tortoise to escape heat and cold are used by the endangered indigo snake, frogs, diamondback rattlesnakes, insects, spiders, and a host of other animal. The tortoise is a native that has been here for many thousands of years, while the armadillo has lived here less than one hundred years, having extended its range only recently eastward from west of the Mississippi River. At 1.2 miles the trail joins the **Gopher Tortoise Trail.** Other paths and jeep trails cross the yellow-blazed trail. Watch for the blazes to stay on the loop, which returns to the main trail back to the trailhead. Side trails lead to various campgrounds in the park and to the small lakes on Seventeen Mile River. Park personnel have marked the trails carefully to help hikers avoid getting lost. Just look for and follow the yellow blazes.

On the ridge, the trees are more stunted, and the soil so well drained that it is dry most of the time. Turkey oaks, scrubby post oaks, and longleaf pine are the common trees along the loop. One of the more common shrubs is the sparkleberry, with its silver-underside leaves that seem to sparkle when moved by the wind. At the end of the loop, backtrack on the River Swamp Trail 1.2 miles to the trailhead.

Caution: Avoid hiking at night without a good light because of the nocturnal habits of the rattlesnake and cottonmouth.

Miles and Directions

0.0 Start near Picnic Shelter 4 at the wooden sign showing the trail.

0.4 The trail on the right is the beginning of the 0.9-mile East River Swamp Trail. (**FYI:** The raised platform provides a good view of the swamp without having to walk in it.) Stay on the orange-blazed trail.

0.7 Move away from the river swamp into the drier ridge area with palmetto and wax myrtle bushes and larger water oak trees. (**FYI:** Greenfly orchids grow on the oak limbs and trunks.)

1.2 Begin the Gopher Tortoise loop.

1.6 A turnoff to the left intersects the end of road that bisects the loop.

1.8 You are now near the crest of the sandy ridge and the pioneer camping area. Small, twisted oaks demonstrate well-drained sandy soil that is dry shortly after even the hardest rains.

2.0 Cross the spur road into the tortoise area.

2.3 Close the Gopher Tortoise loop. Turn right to return to the trailhead on the River Swamp Trail.

3.5 Arrive back at the trailhead.

Additional Trails

The **East River Swamp Trail** is a must-do trail. The two boardwalk sections alone make it worth the 1.8-mile out-and-back hike.

The **Lake Trail** and **Heritage Trail** are good options if you have the time. On the Heritage Trail, a pioneer homestead of typical buildings depicts early life in this part of the Georgia.

62 Little Ocmulgee State Park Trails

This park is an excellent example of a Coastal Plain sandy ridge habitat with the added interest of a lake. The loop trails pass through towering longleaf pines and stunted scrub oaks. There is very little elevation change here—the lake elevation is 159 feet and the sand ridge is 240 feet. The park's Pete Phillips Lodge has sixty rooms and a restaurant.

Start: The outer end of the tennis court parking area

Distance: Oak Ridge Trail, 1.8-mile lollipop

Approximate hiking time: 1½ hours

Difficulty: Easy

Elevation gain/loss: About 80 feet

Trail surface: Sandy loam

Lay of the land: Relatively flat

Season: Year-round; early spring, late fall, and winter to avoid biting and other annoying insects

Land status: Georgia State Parks Division

Nearest town: McRea

Fees and permits: Parking $3.00 per vehicle per day

Maps: USGS McRae; detailed trail map, available at the Pete Phillips Lodge and park office

Trail contacts: Little Ocmulgee State Park, P.O. Drawer 149, McRae, GA 31055; (912) 868-7474; www.gastateparks.org

Finding the trailhead: From McRae travel 2.0 miles north on U.S. Highway 319/441. The park entrance is on the left. The trailhead is at the end of the tennis court parking area.

The Hike

The park's sand ridge habitat supports such wildlife as gopher tortoises, indigo snakes, white-tailed deer, gray and fox squirrels, and both land and waterbirds. There's a lake with good warm-water fishing. Flora spans from a canopy of picturesque trees festooned with Spanish moss to the insectivorous pitcher plant at the swamp's edge.

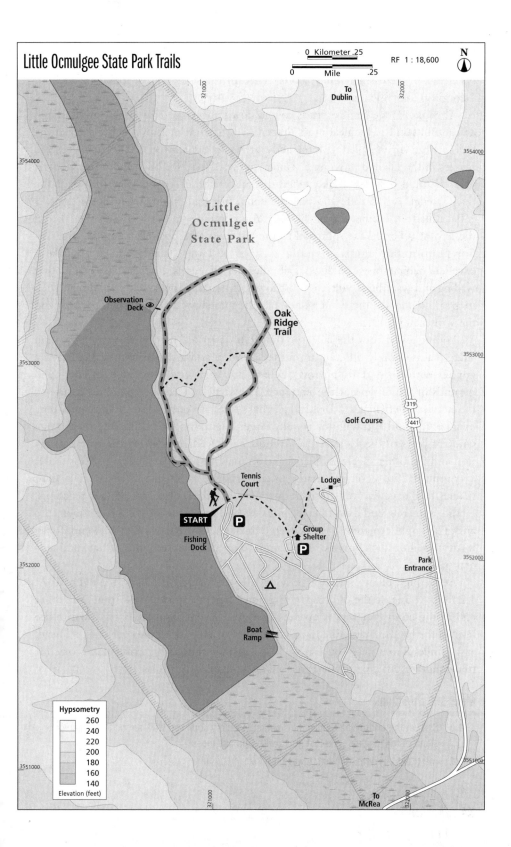

At one time this area was at the edge of the ocean. As the ocean receded, the beach dunes were left behind and today form the sandy ridges found throughout Georgia's Coastal Plain.

The Oak Ridge Trail begins as you go down into a small bay swamp and through a beautiful stand of longleaf pines draped with Spanish moss. Along the sides of the trail, a large shrub called yaupon holly grows in tight thickets. This holly has red berries in the fall and provides a winter supply of food for birds and other wildlife. You continue beside the lake, where the insectivorous pitcher plant grows at the shallow edge. At 0.5 mile you pass the connector trail that makes a shorter loop. It is 0.4 mile to the other leg of the loop. You continue up the trail with the lake on the left. At 0.7 mile, the spur trail to the left leads to a boardwalk and an observation platform that affords a beautiful view of the Little Ocmulgee Lake. The lake is excellent habitat for wood ducks, gallinules, herons, egrets, anhingas, and many other wading and waterbirds. Vultures roost in the trees along the lakeshore and may flock in great numbers in the winter. They, like the migratory ducks and moorhens, spend the winter here.

Hiking away from the lake, the trail follows an old road as you enter the sand ridge that is entirely different from the lakeshore and loamy swamp soils. Here the gopher tortoise digs its burrows, which are very visible because of the small mounds of white sand at the entrance. The scrubby oaks are dwarfed because of the nutrient-deficient sand. Although these trees are only 10 to 20 feet high, they may be very old and will not get any larger. Lightning fires occurring over thousands of years in the Coastal Plain produced the wiregrass–longleaf pine association and the other species of plants and animals found here. This trail area is under a continual "fire ecology" management program to maintain the native plant species that have evolved from frequent natural fires. Deer, armadillos, raccoons, rabbits, squirrels, and a number of birds and other species of wildlife frequent the area. The gopher tortoise once occurred throughout the lower Coastal Plain. Today it survives almost exclusively on the undeveloped, protected lands of state and federal parks.

At the high point on the ridge, Mile 1.0, you turn right, still on the old road. At 1.2 miles you leave the old road, going down a gentle grade. At 1.3 miles the other end of the connector trail is on the right. At 1.7 miles you are back down to the level of the lake and close the loop. The trailhead and parking area are straight ahead, at 1.8 miles. From here you can walk a 0.25-mile trail to the group camp or continue another 0.2 mile to the Pete Phillips Lodge.

Miles and Directions

0.0   Start at the end of the tennis court parking lot. Very soon you walk through a magnificent stand of tall longleaf pine festooned with Spanish moss.

0.1   The trail forks here. Turn left, toward the lake.

0.2 Walk along the edge of the lake on a short spur to view the insectivorous pitcher plant at the water's edge.

0.3 Back on the main trail, continue along the shore.

0.5 The trail to the right is a short loop connector. Continue along the lake. (**Option:** Go 0.4 mile to the return portion of the Oak Ridge Trail for a shorter return to the trailhead.)

0.7 On the left is the 261-foot boardwalk that takes you over the open water/marsh end of the lake to the observation platform, an excellent vantage for viewing a wide variety of fish, birds, and mammals. Returning to the trail, you will be following an old road up the gentle slope of the sandy ridge.

1.0 You are near the highest point of the trail. (**FYI:** Look for gopher tortoise burrows—mounds of white sand and clay in front of a large hole, and diggings of armadillos. Wiregrass, longleaf pines, and the short twisted oaks are key plants in this soil type.)

1.2 Leave the old road; turn to the right and begin the descent from the "ridge."

1.3 The other end of the connector trail is on the right. (**FYI:** You should see tracks of deer, raccoons, armadillos and other animals in the sandy path.)

1.7 Return to the lake level and close the loop.

1.8 Arrive back at the trailhead parking area. (**Option:** Continue 0.25 mile to the group camp or 0.2 mile to the lodge.)

More Information

Food/Lodging
Pete Phillips Lodge, located within the park (229–868–7474; www.gastateparks.org/lodges/ocmulgee), has sixty rooms and a restaurant.

63 Skidaway Island State Park Trails

Skidaway is a barrier island south of historic Savannah. The estuaries and salt marshes bring both salt and fresh water to the area. The interconnected loops of the featured Big Ferry Nature Trail take you past a Prohibition-era moonshine still, shell middens left by early American Indians, and Civil War earthworks. Spanish moss–draped live oaks and stately longleaf pines with cabbage palms and palmettos give the trails a subtropical atmosphere and provide excellent birding and wildlife-viewing opportunities. These trails are at the tidal river level.

Start: Sandpiper Trail, at the visitor center; alternate trailhead for the Big Ferry Nature Trail, on the road to the pioneer campground at a large sign for the trail
Distance: Big Ferry Nature Trail, 2.5-mile lollipop; Sandpiper Trail, 0.8-mile loop; Skidaway Narrows Trail, 0.7-mile loop; connector trail between Skidaway Narrows and Big Ferry Trails, 0.6 mile one-way, for a total of 4.6 miles of interconnected loops
Approximate hiking time: Big Ferry Nature Trail, 2½ hours
Difficulty: Easy
Elevation gain/loss: Negligible

Trail surface: Sandy clay and sandy loam; some gravel roads, wooden bridges and boardwalks
Lay of the land: Flat
Season: Year-round
Land status: Georgia State Parks Division
Nearest town: Savannah
Fees and permits: Parking $3.00 per vehicle per day
Maps: USGS Isle of Hope; trail maps and interpretive leaflets, available at park office
Trail contacts: Skidaway Island State Park, 52 Diamond Causeway, Savannah, GA 31411-1102; (912) 598-2300; www.gastateparks.org

Finding the trailhead: From Savannah take Interstate 16 east about 6.0 miles to exit 34, which runs into DeRenne Avenue. Turn right on Waters Avenue and go straight ahead to Diamond Causeway. The park entrance is on the left at the Skidaway State Park entrance sign. The trailhead for the Sandpiper Trail is at the visitor center. The trailhead for the Big Ferry Nature Trail, marked by a large wooden sign, is on the park road to the pioneer campground

The Hike

Skidaway Island is home to such wildlife as deer, wild hogs, alligators, other reptiles and amphibians, and gray and fox squirrels. Flowers peculiar to the salt marsh include the sea ox-eye, a yellow daisylike flower that blooms late spring to summer.

The Big Ferry Nature Trail starts at the park road for the pioneer campground, also the connector trail to Skidaway Narrows Trail. A sign designates the trailhead. The trail begins along the old road to the abandoned Big Ferry landing. Before the bridges were built, all access to the barrier islands was by private boat or, like Skidaway, by ferry.

Tall longleaf pines and spreading live oaks draped with Spanish moss give the trail a cathedral-like feeling. Cabbage palm, wax myrtle, and bay trees add to the sub-

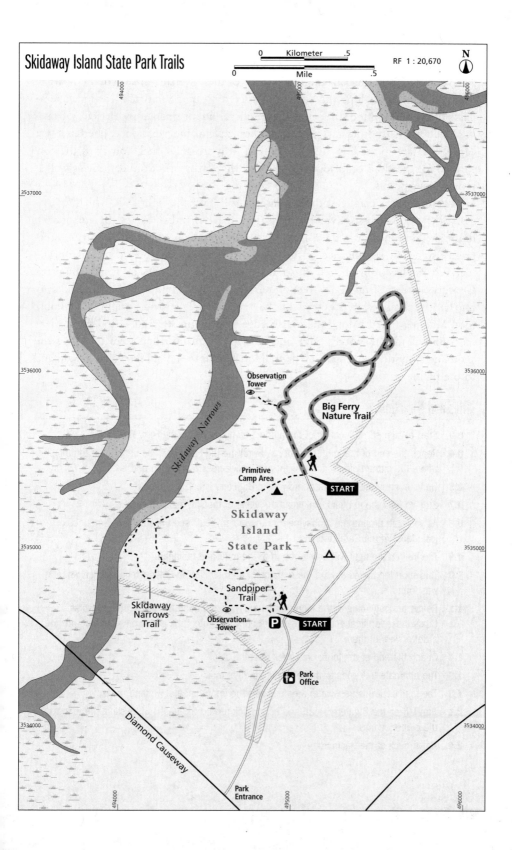

Skidaway Island State Park Trails

Kilometer .5

Mile

RF 1 : 20,670

N

Observation Tower

Big Ferry Nature Trail

Skidaway Narrows

Primitive Camp Area

START

Skidaway Island State Park

Sandpiper Trail

Skidaway Narrows Trail

Observation Tower

START

Park Office

Diamond Causeway

Park Entrance

tropical atmosphere. The well-marked path crosses a freshwater slough with an interpretive marker pointing out the importance of these wetland areas. The first part of the trail loops back along the salt marsh edge for a quick return. Near-intact remnants of old moonshine stills are from the illegal liquor operations carried out during Prohibition. Another interpretive marker explains their existence. The Civil War earthworks are located at the end loop of a figure-eight trail. You cross the low earthen fortifications on bridges that protect the earthworks from damage as well as provide viewpoints.

The trail loops back past the moonshine still. Take the right fork, which follows along the coastal marsh. Evidence of early American Indian use of the area is seen in the shell mounds, or middens, left by the Gaulli Indians and discussed on an interpretive sign. The significance of the salt marshes is also interpreted by appropriate markers. Patches of bright red on some of the trees is a species of lichen unique to Georgia's barrier islands. Resurrection ferns grow on the limbs of live oaks, and during fall the attractive red berries of the yaupon holly provide important wildlife food. Walking quietly along the marsh edge, you might see fiddler and ghost crabs scurrying along the water's edge and among the many fallen trees that give the shoreline a mystical appearance. The trail loops back to the old ferry access road and to the trailhead.

Miles and Directions

0.0 Start at sign at the junction of the pioneer camp road and Big Ferry Road.

0.4 Reach the end of the long, straight road with the Big Ferry Trail. You come near the marsh where the old ferry landed. Turn right and walk across a short footbridge.

0.5 On your left is the 390-foot boardwalk to Big Ferry Island hammock.

0.7 Stop to read the markers explaining the value of the salt marsh habitat.

0.8 As you start around the embayment of the marsh, you'll see the small shell mounds (middens) of the Gaulli Indians.

0.9 The trail on the right will be the return to the road and trailhead.

1.0 This short loop goes around the remains of a Prohibition-era moonshine still, left where it was found.

1.1 Reach the beginning of the loop that carefully goes around the Civil War earthworks. Cross these fortifications on bridges that not only protect the earthworks but also provide a better view of them.

1.4 Reach the end of the loop; backtrack past the still.

1.6 The alternate trail goes to the left. Take the right fork.

1.8 The marker at this freshwater area explains the importance of wetland areas.

2.1 Turn left on the Big Ferry Road and head back toward the trailhead, passing the road to the pioneer camp.

2.5 Arrive back at the trailhead.

Skidaway State Park trails are excellent for family hiking.

Additional Trails

These two shorter loop trails are wheelchair accessible and are ideal for off-road baby strollers.

Sandpiper Trail

The Sandpiper Trail begins behind the visitor center and meanders for about 1.0 mile along the edge of the salt marsh. Fiddler crabs can be seen scurrying among the clumps of black needle rush and cordgrass. After the trail crosses the first bridge, it leads to an island hammock of drier, higher land that supports animals and plants that cannot live in the salty, wet marsh. Deer, raccoons, opossums, gray and fox squirrels, wild hogs, mice, and a number of different birds use the higher land. Cabbage palms, saw palmettos, large live oaks, and longleaf pines are the dominant plants. Crossing the next bridge, the path leads to one of several Confederate earthworks on Skidaway Island. To the right of the trail is the great expanse of the tidal marsh that serves as an important nursery area for fish, shrimp, oysters, and crabs. Salt flats form on the shallower part of the marsh that is covered only during the highest tides. Evaporation leaves the white salt behind on the mudflats. The trail ends near a swimming pool at the visitor center.

Skidaway Narrows Trail

At the back side of the Sandpiper Trail you come to a T junction with the Skidaway Narrows Trail. Turn right to follow the new portion of the trail into a forested area and then along the edge of the waterway called Skidaway Narrows. It is not unusual to see large pleasure boats on this waterway, part of the Intracoastal Waterway from New York to Miami. This part of the trail adds more high ground and a boardwalk over a section that floods during exceptional tides. From the tidal area, the trail continues to the road with the pioneer campground. At the other end of the campground road, the trail connects with the Big Ferry Nature Trail, which you can follow back to the trailhead.

64 Sapelo Island Trails

Sapelo Island is a 16,500-acre barrier island with grand maritime forests of live oaks festooned with Spanish moss; longleaf and slash pines hold the higher ground. Nanny Goat Beach Nature Trail begins a short distance from the Reynolds Mansion (Big House) and offers the opportunity to hike in the tidal zone with salt marsh, ancient and active dunes, and a walk along the beach. Key points along the trail are interpreted with descriptive markers and with a leaflet available from the Sapelo Visitor Center on the mainland. The mansion can be reserved for groups and conferences.

Start: On Beach Road, 0.1 mile from the Reynolds Mansion at information sign
Distance: Nanny Goat Beach Nature Trail, 2.5 miles out and back
Approximate hiking time: 2 hours
Difficulty: Easy
Elevation gain/loss: Negligible
Trail surface: Sandy and sandy loam
Lay of the land: A series of ancient and active sand dunes in succession before the beach
Season: Year-round
Land status: Georgia Department of Natural Resources, Wildlife Resources Division
Nearest town: Darien
Fees and permits: Round-trip ferry, $10.00 per adult, $6.00 per child
Maps: USGS Doboy Sound; University of Georgia Marine Extension Service, *Guide to*

Coastal Fishing (includes Sapelo Island under "McIntosh County")
Trail contacts: Sapelo Island Visitor Center, Route 1, Box 1500, Darien, GA 31305; (912) 437-3224. Visitor center hours: Tuesday through Friday 7:30 A.M. to 5:30 P.M., Saturday 8:00 A.M. to 5:30 P.M., Sunday 1:30 to 5:00 P.M.; closed Monday. Required reservations for transportation to the island on the state ferry are made through the visitor center, which can also provide information on island tours and overnight accommodations and other services operated by residents of Hog Hammock. Sapelo Island Visitor Center: www.sapelonerr.org; Georgia Department of Natural Resources: www.gadnr.org or www.gastateparks.org; Georgia Wildlife Resources Division: www.georgiawildlife.com

Finding the trailhead: From Darien take Highway 99 east 8.0 miles to Meridian. Turn right on Landing Road and go 0.8 mile to the Sapelo Island Visitor Center. The ferry landing is 0.1 mile farther.

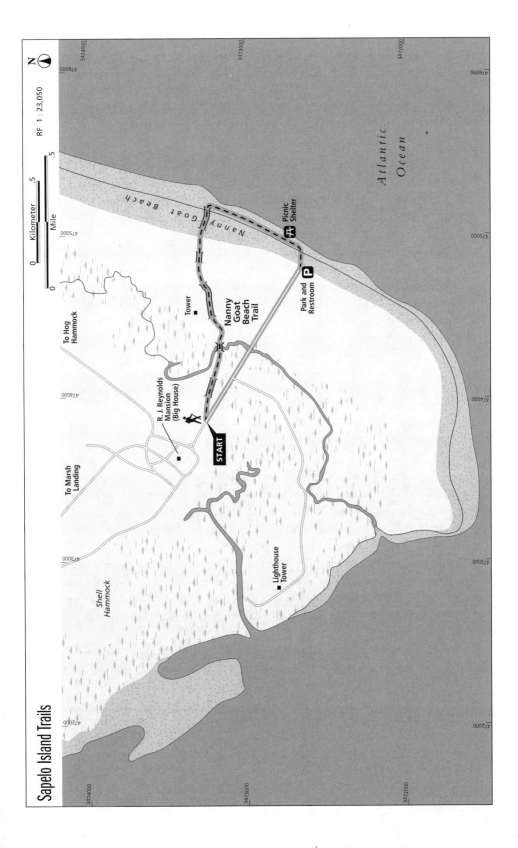

Sapelo Island Trails

The Nanny Goat Beach Trail begins on the one-lane paved road from the Reynolds Mansion to Nanny Goat Beach. The parking area at the trailhead has a large sign with information about the trail.

From exit 58 off Interstate 95, turn left (east) on Highway 57 and go 1.0 mile to the flashing light. Continue straight on Highway 99 and go 9.1 miles to Meridian. Turn left on Landing Road and proceed as above.

The Hike

Sapelo Island is a designated Limited Access Island. The only access to the island for hiking or staying overnight is on the ferry operated by the Department of Natural Resources, Wildlife Resources Division, which leaves the mainland from the dock at the Sapelo Island Visitor Center for Marsh Landing on the island. Reservations must be made in advance. The round-trip is $10.00 per adult and $6.00 per child. There is no docking space assigned for private boats at Marsh Landing.

The best way to visit Sapelo Island is to arrange a personal tour, lodging, or other services with one of the concessionaires in Hog Hammock. Many of the residents of this private African-American community are descendants of slaves of Thomas Spalding, who owned the island prior to the Civil War. Several families in Hog Hammock provide overnight accommodations such as bed-and-breakfasts and other lodging and services. Some also provide guided tours, including one in a mule-drawn wagon. Specific information and a list of island residents who provide these services are available from the visitor center.

Nanny Goat Beach Nature Trail begins in an upland area near the Reynolds Mansion and goes across intertidal marsh, dunes, and interdune areas to Nanny Goat Beach. Interpretive signs along the way help you identify some of the plants and points of interest. The boardwalks and bridges are more than just a way to get across the wet areas. They make it possible to stop and get a closer look at the various aquatic environments. Fresh or brackish wet areas support alligators, turtles, small fishes, birds, and myriad insects and other invertebrates. This hike is an easy way to see some of the tidal influence on the salt marsh.

The boardwalks over both the "ancient" and active dunes protect them from damage by foot traffic and give visitors the opportunity to see these highly sensitive areas up close without damaging them beyond repair. Walking on the dunes breaks them down and makes them vulnerable to intrusion by the ocean during storms, causing even greater damage.

Native mammals you are likely to see on the island include white-tailed deer, raccoons, opossums, armadillos, gray squirrels, marsh rabbits, and otters. Feral cattle on the island are the descendants of dairy and other cattle once maintained by R. J. Reynolds. The true source of the island's feral pigs is unknown.

More than 200 species of birds are known to use the island either as residents or while migrating north or south. One of the most colorful of the birds that nest on Sapelo is the painted bunting. The seldom-seen chachalaca is a relative of the wild turkey that is seen much more often.

From the parking area trailhead, shaded by live oaks, you can look out onto a meadow where you might see a painted bunting during nesting season. The first boardwalk is over a freshwater area and then along the old beach road to the walkway and pavilion out on a salt flat. This highly saline area is only occasionally bathed with tidal water. An interpretive sign tells about the plants in this unique place. Take advantage of the blind placed here to watch or photograph birds and other animals. It is an excellent birding area for wading and shorebirds, especially during migration. Along the bank of the salt flat, the daisylike sea ox-eye blooms with yellow flowers during summer.

You now reach the salt marsh—a sea of green or gold, depending on the season. The plants here are black rush and cordgrass. The cordgrass on these great expanses of tidal flats provides cover for marsh animals and holds the soft marsh soils from erosion. Here are the nursery grounds for many species of saltwater fish and other aquatic animals. The marshes dampen the surge of storms on the coast and filter the entire water cycle of tides and incoming fresh water.

A footbridge crosses tidal Dean Creek, whose flow changes direction with the incoming or outgoing tide. After the bridge you will see a grand southern magnolia with its large evergreen leaves and fragrant white blossoms that bloom midspring. You'll also see live oaks and wax myrtles in this pleasant oak hammock. Benches here in the shade invite one to stop and rest awhile. Resurrection ferns grow in green patches along with Spanish moss on the limbs of live oaks.

You are now getting closer to the beach. First are the old, less-active dunes. The boardwalk makes it possible to walk over and experience the dune habitat without destroying the fragile plant and animal communities. A low observation tower and platform affords a unique viewpoint. From here the walkway passes through the interdune area, or savanna, with its wide variety of plants and animals. This is a favorite place for deer, rabbits, and rodents—and for their predators, including bobcats and snakes.

Finally the boardwalk climbs the active dune. Here the graceful sea oats and other salt-tolerant plants provide a picture-postcard scene. Across the dune is the Atlantic Ocean and Nanny Goat Beach. You go right down to the beach on the walkway. Loggerhead turtles come ashore here to lay their eggs, pelicans glide with wingtips almost touching the waves, and shorebirds run up and down the surf in search of food.

The beach pavilion with picnic tables and a comfort station is down the beach about 200 yards. The return to the parking area can be back along the trail or down to the pavilion and back by way of the beach road to the parking area and the Reynolds Mansion.

The beautifully restored Sapelo Island lighthouse is located on a road off the Beach Road, heading south. The road to the lighthouse is 1.0 mile one-way from Beach Road, an excellent optional hike.

Miles and Directions

0.0 Begin at the sign on the Beach Road, 0.15 mile from the Reynolds Mansion. Live oaks shade the area, with a large meadow off to the left.

0.1 Come to a boardwalk over a freshwater wetland area.

0.2 The trail now follows an old beach road. In a short distance you have a salt flat on the right.

0.3 Cross tidal Dean Creek on a bridge. (**FYI:** The water may be still or flowing in either direction, depending on the tide.)

0.4 Come to a bench in the shade under a large magnolia tree. Take the time to sit and enjoy this pleasant, picturesque spot.

0.5 Cross an ancient dune on a well-designed boardwalk.

0.6 You are now in a pine-oak forest, extremely important in this coastal environment. (**FYI:** If you have not already noticed, the habitat types change with only a few yards distance. Just like the marsh grasses, these sturdy forest areas dampen the frequent storms of the coast.)

0.7 Another boardwalk helps you across a secondary dune. A low tower provides an exceptional view of the area you have just walked through.

0.8 Cross another dune on a boardwalk, this time over the active primary dune.

0.9 The expanse of an undeveloped beach is a welcome sight. Turn right.

1.2 Reach a covered picnic shelter with benches and tables, where you can enjoy a picnic lunch or dinner.

1.3 Reach the end of the Beach Road. Use the wooden walkway to the parking area and restroom.

2.0 Begin the long straight road return to the trailhead.

2.5 Arrive back at the trailhead.

More Information

Organizations

Friends of Sapelo (www.sapelonerr.org/friends) is a private nonprofit group devoted to preserving the culture and natural history of the island.

65 Laura S. Walker State Park Trails

The featured Big Creek Nature Trail passes through native pinewoods of the Coastal Plain habitat, a planted pine plantation, and a large Carolina bay. Small boardwalks cross wet areas. The Lake Trail, on the west side of the lake, follows the lakeshore from the picnic shelter parking area to an observation deck on the upper end of the lake.

Start: Across the park entrance for the Big Creek Nature Trail; on the opposite side of the lake for the Lake Trail
Distance: Big Creek Nature Trail, 1.3-mile loop; Lake Trail, 1.2 miles out and back
Approximate hiking time: 1 hour for both trails
Difficulty: Easy.
Elevation gain/loss: Negligible
Trail surface: Sandy loam and sand; bridge and boardwalk
Lay of the land: Flat and gently rolling ancient sand dunes
Season: Year-round; best in winter, spring, and fall; hot and sticky in summer, with an abundance of annoying biting flies, mosquitoes, and gnats
Land status: Georgia State Parks Division
Nearest town: Waycross
Fees and permits: Parking $3.00 per vehicle per day
Maps: USGS Hoboken West; map of the nature trail, available at park office
Trail contacts: Laura S. Walker State Park, 5653 Laura S. Walker Road, Waycross, GA 31501; (912) 287-4900; www.gastate parks.org

Finding the trailhead: From Waycross take U.S. Highway 1/23 south 6.8 miles to Highway 177; turn left. The trailhead for the Lake Trail is 3.5 miles on the left. Continue 1.1 miles around the lake, across the dam, and to the trailhead for the Big Creek Nature Trail; park here for the trail. The entrance to Laura S. Walker State Park is 0.1 mile farther. Since the trailhead is across Highway 177 from the park entrance, you can park near the office and visitor center and walk to the trailhead.

The Hike

Laura S. Walker State Park is located southeast of Waycross on Highway 177—only a few miles as the egret flies from Okefenokee Swamp. The park was a Civilian Conservation Corps camp during the mid-1930s, and some of the earliest history has been preserved. The uniqueness of this corner of the Coastal Plain is seen in the plants and animals along the trail. Gopher tortoises, indigo snakes, alligators, and white-tailed deer are some of the more dramatic species found here along with an abundance of forest and wading birds. The perfoliate rattleweed (listed as an endangered plant in Georgia) is one of the interesting plants found along the trail. The trail and its characteristic plants and animals are described in a leaflet, available in the visitor center.

Big Creek Nature Trail starts out through a new longleaf pine planting, which is only about fifteen years old. Leave the cleared area and enter a typical Coastal

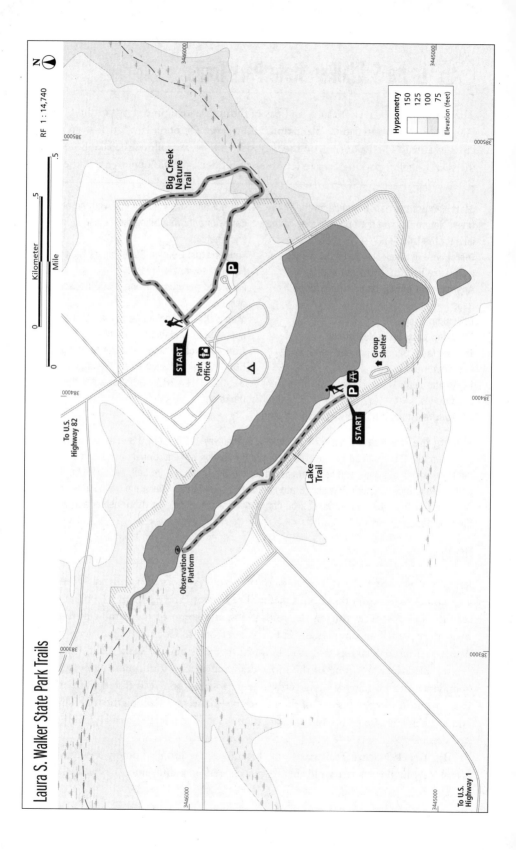

Laura S. Walker State Park Trails

Plain pinewoods—parklike forest of longleaf pines, palmetto, oaks, and dense shrubs and laurel oaks, sparkleberry, and honeysuckle and other vines. Rest benches have been placed along the trail, making it a great place for early morning birding. The older longleaf pines have large cuts in their trunks where pine resin was harvested to make turpentine; this was a major local industry until the mid-1950s. In this area, only a few yards from the trail, white mounds of sand betray the oval-shaped hole of the gopher tortoise. These large land turtles excavate burrows several feet long ending in an underground chamber that is shared with a surprising number of other animals, including the eastern diamondback rattlesnake, the indigo snake, a species of frog, and insects that are endemic to the tortoise's burrow.

As the trail enters the wetland area, called a "Carolina bay," a boardwalk stays above the water level and makes it possible to penetrate this fascinating habitat. The stream of dark, tea-colored water is called Big Creek. Sweet gums, tupelos, and live and laurel oaks make up most of the tall forest cover. Shrubs include titi and wax myrtle. The aquatic golden-club (locally called poorman's soap), cinnamon fern, sphagnum moss, and a variety of other plants grow under the larger trees and give the area a tropical, junglelike atmosphere. Short bridges cross the wet areas. The trail leaves the swamp area and returns to the pinewoods, where clay was dug to build the dam for Laura S. Walker Lake. One of the pits is now a small pond surrounded by dense vegetation. The trail returns to the trailhead through cut-over pinewoods with dogwood, sassafras, and other deciduous trees festooned with yellow jasmine vines. The ground cover is very dense along this part of the trail, but the path is wide and easy to follow. The bluejack oak, a small oak endemic to these well-drained sandy soils, honeysuckle, bracken ferns, and rattleweed add variety to this pleasant 1.3-mile walk.

The **Lake Trail,** on the opposite side of the lake from the nature trail, is a 1.2-mile out-and-back trail with an observation platform overlooking the lake. This short walk is through the slash-longleaf pine open area with scattered small oaks and palmetto. The observation deck provides a fine up-close view of the relatively shallow lake and aquatic plant and animal life.

66 Crooked River State Park Trails

The park's three trails provide 2.9 miles of easy hiking. The park and trails are on an 8-foot "bluff," with no more than a 10-foot change in elevation throughout. The featured Semper Virens Nature Trail loop takes you to the marsh, then into a maritime-forested area and the open palmetto. The Palmetto Hiking Trail is 1.4 miles through a more open longleaf pine–live oak wooded area with palmetto under the trees and in the open. The 0.4-mile Bay Boardwalk Trail, a very pleasant close-up look at a freshwater bay, takes off from the Palmetto Trail close to the Nature Center.

Start: Semper Virens Nature Trail, just beyond Cabin 11 at the end of the road at the large sign; Palmetto Hiking Trail, between cabin group 1–5 and 6–11; Bay Boardwalk Trail, off the Palmetto Hiking Trail
Distance: Semper Virens Nature Trail, 1.0-mile lollipop; Palmetto Hiking Trail, 1.4-mile loop; Bay Boardwalk Trail, 0.4-mile lollipop; the three trails combined, 2.9 miles
Approximate hiking time: Semper Virens Trail, 1 hour; Palmetto Trail with Bay Boardwalk Trail, 1 hour
Difficulty: Easy
Elevation gain/loss: Negligible

Trail surface: Sand and sandy loam
Lay of the land: A low "bluff" above the Crooked River
Season: Year-round
Land status: Georgia State Parks Division
Nearest town: St. Marys
Fees and permits: Parking $3.00 per vehicle per day
Maps: USGS Harrietts Bluff; Crooked River State Park map
Trail contacts: Crooked River State Park, 6222 Charlie Smith Sr. Highway, St. Marys, GA 31558; (912) 882-5256; www.gastate parks.org

Finding the trailhead: From Kingsland (on U.S. Highway 17) go east 2.0 miles on Highway 40 to Interstate 95. Continue on Highway 40 for 2.2 miles to Kings Bay Road. Turn left onto Charlie Smith Sr. Highway and go 2.9 miles to the Crooked Creek Park entrance. Continue 0.6 mile to the park office and 0.8 mile to the road's end at a parking area and information sign. This is at the trailhead for the Semper Virens Nature Trail.

The Hike

Crooked River State Park is one of only a few places along Georgia's coastal marshes and live oak forests where you can hike. The trails in this small park are short but provide a good cross section of the varied habitat of the Atlantic Coast area. Three interlocking trails provide exposure to the mystical maritime forest of live oaks and Spanish moss and a walk through more open palmetto-pine land.

This park is in the extreme southeast corner of the state near the towns of St. Marys and Kingsland. It is also close to the Kings Bay Naval Submarine Base and Cumberland Island National Seashore.

Barred owls may be heard throughout the state. ▶

Crooked River State Park Trails

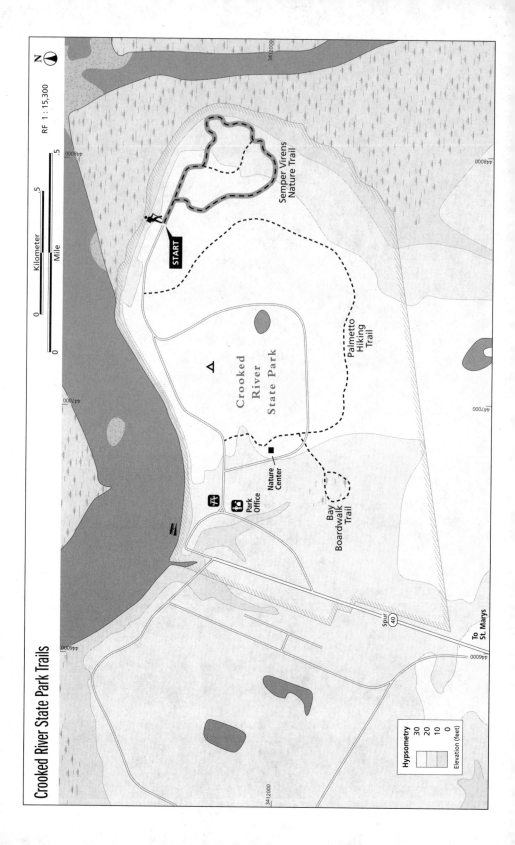

RF 1 : 15,300

Semper Virens Nature Trail

START

Crooked River State Park

Palmetto Hiking Trail

Nature Center

Park Office

Bay Boardwalk Trail

Spur 40

To St. Marys

Hypsometry
30
20
10
0
Elevation (feet)

During the warm months, prepare for various biting flies, mosquitoes, no-see-ums, and ticks when hiking these trails. Be sure to bring a good repellent. There are fewer annoying insects in the cooler months, and ticks are much less of a problem if you stay on the trail.

Start the nature trail at an interpretive sign designed and made by an Eagle Scout that tells about providing and protecting bat habitat. Bat boxes have been placed on trees along this roadway. Go down a rather straight and sandy old road with palmettos on one side and young live oaks, wax myrtles, and bracken ferns on the other. The white sand, pine needles, and oak leaves make the roadway easy to walk on. A shortcut trail on the right at 0.2 mile allows for an 0.8-mile loop. For this hike, you continue on the main path. Large southern magnolias are visible from the path. As you enter a mature live oak hammock, a narrow path turns into a scenic and interesting live oak forest where a sign reads SEMPERVIRENS—THE LIVING TRAIL with an arrow pointing to the left. Spanish moss, large grapevines, a smattering of palmettos, smaller hollies, wax myrtles, and many other vines and shrubs give the area a tropical atmosphere. Short boardwalks cross the wet areas. Large sweet gum, wild cherry, and hickory trees add to the forest canopy. This maritime forest is characteristic of the land along the tidal rivers and the barrier islands of Georgia.

At 0.4 mile a spur trail leads off the main path, and a sign points to the forest edge and the salt marsh. It is possible to walk a short distance into the marsh depending on the tidal level at the time. This point offers a good view of the sharp line separating the trees from the marsh, the great expanse of marsh grass, and an opportunity to listen and look for such birds as the clapper rail, gallinules, herons, and egrets. Gulls and terns are usually flying over the marsh and river.

Return to the path and continue the loop. At one point you go through a small opening that has gopher tortoise burrows and much evidence of armadillo digging. All along the trail you'll see the scratching marks made by this hard-shelled mammal, a recent invader into Georgia from west of the Mississippi River.

The loop continues along the marsh, even though it is not always visible. Turning away from the marsh, you come to the other end of the shortcut trail at 0.5 mile. You are now in an area of thick palmetto and tall pines. This variation in habitat gives you an entirely different perspective on the Coastal Plain vegetation. Here the palmetto is very thick, and the scattered slash and longleaf pines give more of a park-like appearance. For the birder, this is where you might spot the beautiful painted bunting during late spring and summer, as well as king birds, mockingbirds, cardinals, thrashers, catbirds, warblers, flycatchers, and other shrub- and open-woods-inhabiting birds. Butterflies abound along this loop. Look for deer, squirrels, and lizards as wells as the armadillos and gopher tortoises. Return to the trailhead for a 1.0-mile hike.

Miles and Directions

A leaflet identifying numbered features along the Semper Virens Nature Trail is available at the park office.

0.0 Start at the information sign in the parking area.

0.2 An optional shortcut trail goes off to the right.

0.4 A spur trail leads off the main path.

0.5 Meet up with the other end of the shortcut trail.

1.0 Arrive back at the trailhead.

Additional Trails

The **Palmetto Hiking Trail** can be hiked as a loop of 1.4 miles by returning to the trailhead via the park road. The Palmetto Trail and its **Bay Boardwalk Trail** spur (0.4-mile lollipop) add variety to your hiking experience and the opportunity to see more wildlife.

67 Harris Neck National Wildlife Refuge and Savannah Coastal Refuge Complex

Fifteen miles of interconnected roads and trails provide easy access to a variety of habitats, including mixed pine-hardwood forest, open fields, thickets, freshwater impoundments, salt marsh, and mudflats. The terrain here is such that a brisk walk or hike for exercise is just as appropriate as a slow, deliberate wildlife- or bird-watching walk. With the variety of habitat types and trails, the park offers many choices for trail length or type.

Start: Parking area and kiosk a short distance from the entrance; parking areas where foot trails leave the wildlife drive
Distance: More than 15 miles of paved roads and walking trails, all accessible to hiking, including: Bluebill Pond Trail, 0.5 mile; Field Trail, 0.35 mile; Runway Trail, 2.3 miles; Woods Trail, 0.6 mile; Gould's Cemetery Trail, 1.1 miles; Lorillard Mansion Trail, 1.1 miles
Approximate hiking time: 2 to 4 hours
Difficulty: Easy
Elevation gain/loss: Negligible
Trail surface: Dirt, paved, and paved roads; sandy loam
Lay of the land: Flat; sea level to 20 feet above
Season: Year-round

Land status: U.S. Fish and Wildlife Service
Nearest towns: Eulonia, Riceboro
Fees and permits: No fees or permits required
Maps: USGS Shellmans Bluff, Seabrook, St. Catherines Sound, and Sapelo Sound; page-size map of the refuge, available at the refuge office; University of Georgia Marine Extension Service, *Guide to Coastal Fishing* maps by county (Harris Neck and Blackbeard Island on the McIntosh County map)
Trail contacts: Savannah Coastal Refuges, Parkway Business Center, Suite 10, 1000 Business Center Drive, Savannah, GA 31405; (912) 652-4415; www.fws.gov/southeast/; for Harris Neck: (912) 832-4608

Finding the trailhead: From Interstate 95 take exit 67 (South Newport) and go south on U.S. Highway 17 for 1.1 miles to Harris Neck Road (Highway 131). Turn left on Harris Neck Road and go 6.5 miles to the entrance of the Harris Neck National Wildlife Refuge on the left. Turn left and drive to the parking area with large board and kiosk with information about the wildlife drive and box with maps and refuge brochures. Walking trails from the wildlife drive are marked no motorized vehicles. Hiking along the roadway is permitted.

The Hikes

The Savannah Coastal Refuge Complex is a series of seven national wildlife refuges strung along the entire Georgia coast. Although most of the refuges are barrier

islands and require personal or chartered boats to get to them, Harris Neck and Savannah Refuges are easily accessible by car. At Savannah NWR, you can walk the dikes that remain from the days of the old rice plantations. There are no designated trails, but the area offers unparalleled opportunity to view wildlife. Take care to protect yourself from biting insects and ticks. Mosquitoes, deerflies, and gnats can be bad late spring through early fall.

In the late 1930s the Federal Aviation Administration constructed an emergency-landing runway for commercial air traffic from Miami to New York. Later the island became a World War II military air base for patrolling the mid-Atlantic coastline. The runways remain today, although they are almost obliterated by vegetation, providing some of the best wildlife watching and birding in the area. The fields and shrubby areas are especially good habitat for painted buntings and other songbirds. Waterfowl, wading birds, and other species associated with the aquatic habitat use the four ponds named Snipe, Goose, Greenhead, and Teal. Alligators and otters use these and the other ponds and may be seen almost any time of the year. These freshwater ponds are an added bonus to the salt marsh habitat, with the many species living there.

The off-road trails are over firm, sandy loam or sand. You will be able to see many kinds of wetland and upland birds, as well as deer, armadillos, squirrels, rabbits, feral pigs, and other mammals. Reptiles and amphibians, including frogs, toads, lizards, turtles, snakes, and alligators, are active and may be seen or heard except during two or three cold weather months. Hiking is permitted on designated trails and roads daily from sunrise to sunset.

All trails can be hiked from the beginning of the wildlife drive. Most roads other than the old runways are relatively narrow, one-lane, one-way paved roads.

The first 0.5-mile section is under a closed canopy of live oaks and other oaks and hardwoods, all festooned with Spanish moss. This roadway leads to the first two of six freshwater impoundments constructed to provide habitat for migratory waterfowl, the primary purpose for the federal refuge. Bluebill Pond is on the south (right) side of the 0.2-mile dike. On the other side is Woody Pond, where most of the nesting activity of the endangered wood stork takes place. There are more than one hundred active nests on the upper end of this pond. The Bluebill Pond Trail follows over the dike and to the right around Bluebill Pond and back to the roadway, then along the road back to the dike. You are in the woods for all but the dike and short roadway on this trail.

Drive or walk 0.5 mile farther along the wildlife drive to an unmarked, unpaved lane that leads off to the right to a runway and the dike for Snipe Pond. This trail passes through mostly old-field habitat. You can continue on to the left along the runway and return to the wildlife drive where it passes through the middle of the

Live oak forests on Harris Neck National Wildlife Refuge are great birding areas.

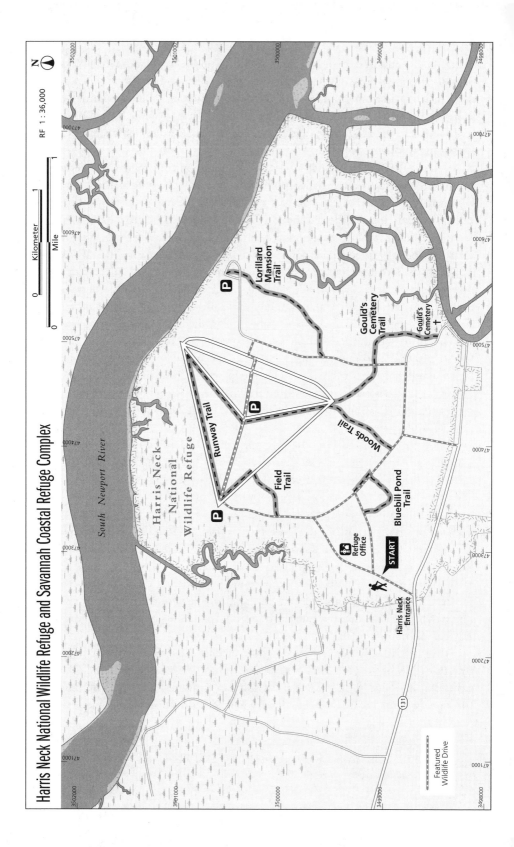

Harris Neck National Wildlife Refuge and Savannah Coastal Refuge Complex

RF 1 : 36,000

N

South Newport River

Harris Neck National Wildlife Refuge

Runway Trail

Field Trail

Woods Trail

Bluebill Pond Trail

Lorillard Mansion Trail

Gould's Cemetery Trail

Gould's Cemetery

Refuge Office

START

Harris Neck Entrance

131

Featured Wildlife Drive

abandoned airfield. Excluding the center runway, the remaining abandoned runways make up more than 4 miles of ideal hiking and wildlife viewing.

The wildlife drive leads through the runway system and enters a beautiful wooded area of live oaks draped with Spanish moss, palmettos, and many other tree and shrub species. At the T intersection the wildlife drive goes to the right. This is a good place to park and walk the wooded loop that once contained the barracks and other housing during World War II. It is almost completely covered by an old, impressive live oak canopy. This is also an excellent area for migrating warblers in early spring.

The road to the left from the T intersection goes to the site of the Lorillard Mansion. The grand mansion and other buildings were razed because of their unsalvageable condition by the time Harris Neck was obtained by the U.S. Fish and Wildlife Service. The only thing that remains of the mansion's original glory is the elaborate fountain that's almost completely hidden in the lush vegetation. Several ornamental plants from the mansion's gardens have continued to reproduce along with the native plants.

The next trail leaving the wildlife drive is about 0.25 mile south from the T intersection and turns off to the left. This can be hiked as a 2.1-mile loop out to the mansion site, with the return along the paved road. It passes through both old fields and wooded areas that offer a pleasant variety of habitats for birding and wildlife watching.

The last of the walking trails is only about 200 yards beyond on the wildlife drive. The walking trails go off either side of the roadway. Both are 0.5 mile one-way. The trail to the east leads to Gould's Cemetery; the trail on the other side leads to the runway complex. Both trails pass through old fields and woods; the path to the cemetery comes to the edge of the salt marsh.

The wildlife drive ends at Harris Neck Road. A turn to the right takes you back to the refuge entrance in 1.0 mile.

Miles and Directions

Refuge trails are both drives and walking trails. Many variations of hikes are possible on Harris Neck. Simply study the map for a few minutes and choose a place to walk or drive. Many visitors drive to certain points of interest, park, and then hike. Most of the roads and trails are wheelchair accessible, especially chairs with wide tires. These roads and trails are ideal for taking children in off-road strollers.

68 Okefenokee National Wildlife Refuge Trails

The Okefenokee Swamp, more than 400,000 acres, is one of the oldest and best-preserved freshwater areas in the United States. Although the swamp may be best seen from a canoe, there are several interesting walking trails, including a boardwalk that penetrates the swamp for almost a mile.

Start: All trails, from Swamp Island Drive; Canal Digger's Trail also from the visitor center
Distance: Canal Digger's Trail, 1.1-mile lollipop; Woodpecker Trail, 0.3-mile loop; Chesser Island Homestead Trail, 0.3-mile loop; Deer Stand Trail, 1.2 miles out and back; and the Boardwalk, slightly less than 2.0 miles out and back into the swamp to the observation tower
Approximate hiking time: Boardwalk, 1 hour; other trails, less than 1 hour each
Difficulty: Easy; boardwalk and parts of dirt trails wheelchair accessible
Elevation gain/loss: Negligible
Trail surface: Sandy soil, boardwalk, some paved road
Lay of the land: generally flat
Season: Year-round. The Main Gate is open November through February one-half hour before sunrise until 5:30 P.M. (Swamp Island Drive gate closes at 4:00 P.M.). March through October the gate is open one-half hour before sunrise until 7:30 P.M. (Swamp Island Drive gate closes at 6:00 P.M.). Visitor Center is open 9:00 A.M. to 5:00 P.M. The Refuge is open daily except Christmas Day.
Land status: U.S. Fish and Wildlife Service
Nearest town: Folkston
Fees and permits: Private vehicle, $5.00 (seven-day pass); Golden Age and Golden Eagle Passports apply
Maps: USGS Chesser Island and Chase Prairie; maps of trails and other features of the swamp, available at the visitor center; map of refuge and swamp: http://okefenokee.fws.gov
Trail contacts: Refuge Manager, U.S. Fish and Wildlife Service, Okefenokee National Wildlife Refuge, Route 2, Box 3330, Folkston, GA 31537; (912) 496–7836; www.fws.gov/southeast/; canoe reservations: (912) 496–3331

Finding the trailhead: From Folkston start at U.S. Highway 1/23. Go west on West Main Street 0.25 mile to South Okefenokee Drive, which becomes Okefenokee Parkway. Turn left (south) and go 7.8 miles to THE OKEFENOKEE REFUGE sign. Turn right and go 2.7 miles to the gated entrance with tollbooth; continue 1.5 miles to the visitor center. The Swamp Island Drive is 0.15 mile from the visitor center. All trails lead off this road. Canal Digger Trail crosses Swamp Island Road at 0.2 mile. (The trail also can be started from the visitor center.) The Woodpecker Trail is at 1.2 miles, Chesser Homestead Trail is at 3.3 miles, and the Deer Stand Trail takes off from the Homestead Trail. The Boardwalk is 0.5 mile farther, or 3.8 miles from the beginning of the drive.

The Hikes

Okefenokee Swamp and National Wildlife Refuge provides interpretive displays describing human and natural history; botanical diversity; and unparalleled wildlife watching, including alligators, other reptiles and amphibians, and birds. The topog-

An alligator nest in Okefenokee Swamp.

raphy is very flat, with a total elevation change from 120 feet at the swamp edge to 150 feet above sea level on Trail Ridge east of the swamp.

Winter is the best time for migratory waterfowl, including sandhill cranes, the beginning of osprey nesting, and many wading birds. Spring is prime season for wildflowers, wading bird rookeries, and great numbers of migrating warblers. Spring is also when alligators begin sunning. In summer listen for the fascinating sounds of more than a dozen species of frogs, including green tree, pig, carpenter, and cricket frogs. Wildflowers and wildlife also abound. Fall brings beautiful leaf colors and migratory birds to and through the swamp.

The 1.1-mile **Canal Digger's Trail** leaves the visitor center and follows the upland portion of the Suwannee Canal. A pamphlet available at the center describes the history of the aborted attempt many years ago to drain the swamp. The trail parallels the remnant canal on a sandy trail, crosses the Swamp Island Road, and continues east for another 0.5 mile. This is a good trail for viewing some of the interesting upland wildlife living at the swamp edge, including gopher tortoises, lizards, and other reptiles; birds; and mammals, including armadillos.

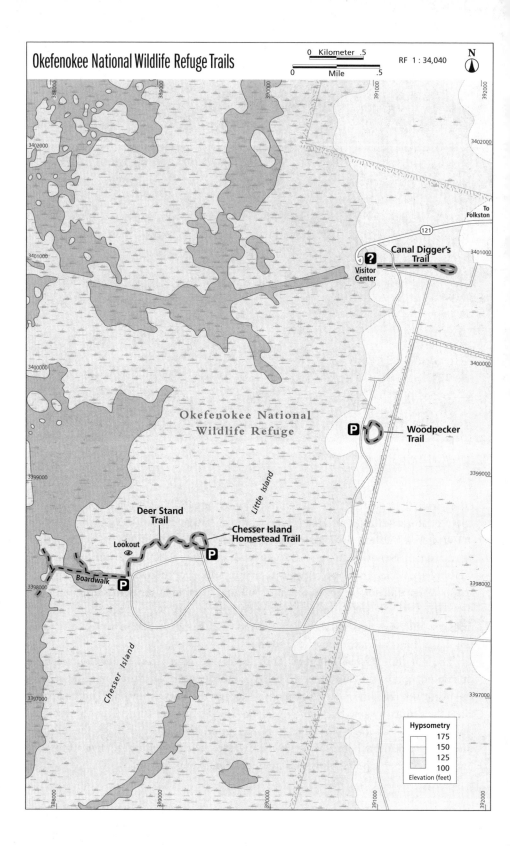

Okefenokee National Wildlife Refuge Trails

0   Kilometer   .5

0   Mile   .5

RF 1 : 34,040

N

To Folkston

121

Canal Digger's Trail

Visitor Center

Woodpecker Trail

Okefenokee National Wildlife Refuge

Little Island

Deer Stand Trail

Lookout

Chesser Island Homestead Trail

Boardwalk

Chesser Island

Hypsometry

175
150
125
100

Elevation (feet)

The 3.8-mile Swamp Island Drive from the visitor center to Chesser Island provides access to the other trails, crossing the Canal Diggers Trail at 0.2 mile. **Woodpecker Trail,** at 1.2 miles, is designed to show the habitat and offer possible sightings of the endangered red-cockaded woodpecker. This 0.3-mile trail is packed with observation opportunities for birders wishing to add this rare woodpecker to their Life List. The trail circles through a mature stand of longleaf pines supporting an active colony of this small woodpecker, which nests in the cavity of a live tree. Whitish pine resin flowing from the area around the cavity is very visible. Trees with nest cavities have been marked with a band of white paint, making them easy to locate. Deer, squirrels, and other species of birds are seen frequently on this trail.

The **Chesser Island Homestead Trail,** at 3.3 miles on the drive, is a pleasant 0.3-mile walk through a typical Okefenokee homestead farm of the 1930s and earlier. The well-preserved house, outbuildings, and other artifacts of farm life are quite picturesque.

The 0.6-mile **Deer Stand Trail** from the homestead area takes you through swamp-edge trees and shrubs to an observation tower. The observation tower is an ideal place to sit quietly and watch for deer and other wildlife in the clearings nearby. From the tower, the trail continues on to the parking area restroom and beginning of the Boardwalk.

The **Boardwalk** allows you to experience the swamp habitat from within 2.5 feet of the surface. Alligators, sandhill cranes, herons, egrets, ibises, anhingas, warblers, red-winged blackbirds, raccoons, otters, frogs, turtles, insects, and other aquatic and tree-dwelling animals may be seen along the way. The Boardwalk penetrates slightly less than 1 mile into the Okefenokee. It goes from the dense vegetation of the swamp's edge to the open swamp, called a prairie in the Okefenokee, and finally to the observation tower tucked among the cypress trees with a good view of Seagrove Lake. From this height, the swamp presents a primal view with nothing but undisturbed swamp to the horizon in all directions.

On the way to the tower you pass two spur walkways on the right leading to photo blinds, completely enclosed with portals for observation or photography. The first one is at 0.25 mile; the other at 0.5 mile before the tower. Both photo blinds can serve as a place to rest and absorb the beauty, get out of the rain, or sit and quietly watch for wildlife. The boardwalk is completely wheelchair accessible except for the tower steps.

Additional trails are planned, including a 4-mile one-way trail that will be an extension of the Canal Digger's Trail. At least two other trails should be ready for hiking soon.

Honorable Mentions

S Big Hammock Natural Area

The sandy ridges of Georgia's Coastal Plain are a pleasant relief to the otherwise flat topography. Big Hammock is one of the largest and least disturbed of these unique areas. A number of plant and animal species are endemic to these sandy soils. Two loop trails, 1.5 miles and 6.0 miles, lead you through the most impressive parts of this distinctive habitat. Entering the woods from the road, the trail leads to the right through the moist base of the sand ridge, where bracken ferns, titi, and other moisture-tolerant plants occur. A boardwalk spur trail leads into and through a cypress head before making the short climb up the ridge. Turkey oaks and clumps of wiregrass are indicative of the sandy soils of the ancient dunes. The gopher tortoise is a primary inhabitant of the sand hills along with the armadillo, a more recent arrival. The trees on the ridge crest—turkey oaks, sand pines, and others—are twisted and stunted. There is little herbaceous growth here, although prickly pear cactus, Georgia plume, sand spike-moss, and other plants tolerant of the dry, sandy soil are abundant.

You cross the crest of the sand dune where it becomes obvious that this sandy ridge is a high point and the only change in elevation in otherwise very flat topography. The path leads down the slope of the dune into another valley between successive dunes or ridges. In the valley, the forest type changes abruptly to tall longleaf pines, white oaks, live oaks with resurrection ferns on their limbs, ironwood, maples, and other plants requiring more moisture.

For more information: Wildlife Resources Division, Game Management Section, Fitzgerald, GA 31750; (229) 426–5267;. www.gohuntgeorgia.com.

DeLorme: Georgia Atlas and Gazetteer: Page 54 D1

T Hofwyl-Broadfield Plantation Historic Site

This site is a must if you are visiting the Coastal Golden Isles: Sapelo, St. Simons, Jekyll, and Cumberland Islands. The plantation was preserved by the efforts of Ophelia Dent, the last heir of the site, who left it to the state of Georgia for use as a state park. The land was developed for rice culture in the early 1800s, and rice continued to be grown here until 1913. Because of the canals and flooded fields, rice plantations attract both resident and migratory waterbirds. In fact, the bobolink was once known as the rice-bird because of the great numbers that stopped to eat the rice before harvest. Many migrating passerine birds stop on their flights up and down the Atlantic Coast. The bird populations make this one of the stops on the Colonial Coast Birding Trail.

There are 4.0 miles of walking trails at the site, including the 0.6-mile Rice Field Nature Trail, 0.4-mile Plantation House Trail, and a 2.7-mile hiking trail with a 0.3-mile Lake Loop connector. The old rice fields support a remarkable number of different animals, which are usually very visible as you walk the trails.

For more information: Hofwyl-Broadfield Plantation State Historic Site, 5556 U.S. Highway 17 North, Brunswick, GA 31525; (912) 264–7333; www.gastateparks.org.

DeLorme: Georgia Atlas and Gazetteer: Page 63 C7

∪ Cumberland Island National Seashore

Cumberland Island National Seashore is located on the largest and southernmost of Georgia's barrier islands. With its maritime forests, dunes, beaches, marshes, and island atmosphere, it provides an unparalleled escape from the mainland. Although inhabited by humans for thousands of years, Cumberland Island is still in a near-wilderness state. The island is 16 miles long and 3 miles wide at its widest point. One unpaved road, Main Road, runs from the Dungeness Ruins on the south end to Cumberland Wharf at the north end.

A system of trails with connecting paths provides hikers and campers with many miles of walking trails. All trails are flat, and walking is easy; sand dunes can only be crossed at specified places. Sea Camp Beach is the only developed campground, with restrooms, cold showers, and drinking water. Four primitive campgrounds are located in backcountry sites. If attempted in one day carrying the necessary hiking equipment, the 10.6-mile one-way hike to Brickhill Bluff, the longest hike to any of the primitive campsites, can be considered strenuous in hot weather. Permits and reservations are required for all overnight camping on the island.

Access to the Cumberland Island National Seashore is by ferry. Private boats are permitted to dock at the two docks for day-use only; no overnight docking is permitted. The Cumberland Island Ferry Landing is in St. Marys at the end of Osborne Street. Excellent maps of the island can be purchased at the ferry dock.

For more information: Superintendent, Cumberland Island National Seashore, P.O. Box 806, St. Marys, GA 31558; (912) 882–4335; www.nps.gov.

DeLorme: Georgia Atlas and Gazetteer: Page 71 ABCD7

Long Trails

The popular Amicalola Falls State Park approach to the Appalachian Trail (Hike 69).

69 Appalachian Trail in Georgia

The Appalachian Trail (AT), said to be the longest continually marked trail in the world, begins at Springer Mountain in Georgia and ends 2,100 miles north at Mount Katahdin in Maine. Because of the many approach trails on public land, this trail presents a many-faceted hiking opportunity for thousands of hikers each year. Congress authorized the Appalachian Trail as the first National Scenic Trail in 1968. The Appalachian Trail Conference now has responsibility for the trail.

Start: If you are a "through-hiker" planning to hike the entire trail, your starting point is either Springer Mountain in Georgia or Mount Katahdin in Maine. The preferred start, whether you plan to hike only the Georgia section of the AT or go on to Mount Katahdin, is at the visitor center at Amicalola State Park. From the park, take the 7.4-mile approach trail to Springer Mountain, the official southern terminus. If you want to hike only part of the trail in Georgia, you can begin your hike at numerous points along the trail. Five shorter hikes are discussed below.

Distance: The total Appalachian Trail is 2,100 miles long. The Georgia section is 75.6 miles. Some of the shelters are well off the main trail. Whitly Gap shelter at Wildcat Mountain is 1.1 miles off the AT on a well-marked, blue-blazed trail. Other shelters are as much as 0.3 mile off the AT on side trails. Trail relocation to prevent overuse causes variations in mileage from year to year. Anyone planning to hike long sections of the trail should first contact the Georgia Appalachian Trail Club (www.georgia-atclub .org) or the Appalachian Trail Conference for current information (see Appendixes A and D).

Difficulty: Moderate to strenuous

Elevation gain: The trail begins at 3,872 feet on Springer Mountain and drops to about 2,500 feet at Three Forks, the lowest point on the hike in Georgia. The highest mountain crossed by the trail is Blood Mountain (4,458 feet). Tray Mountain is 4,430 feet. Most of the ridges crossed on the trail are at about 3,000 feet.

Season: This trail is hiked in all seasons, but sudden and extreme weather changes are the rule. Heavy rainstorms can be expected from late winter through summer. From late fall through early spring, be prepared for sudden cold, wet weather with freezing rain and snow. If you plan to hike the entire Appalachian Trail to Maine from Georgia, a March or April start is strongly advised. The Georgia section can be hiked at any time of year, with spring and fall the most popular.

Nearest towns: There are five paved highway crossings leading to Dahlonega, Cleveland, Blairsville, Helen, and Clayton.

Fees and permits: Both the national forest and state parks have day-use parking fees at some trailheads. Parking at Amicalola State Park, the main approach trailhead, is $3.00 per vehicle per day. Arrangements can be made for longer term parking at the visitor center.

Maps: USGS Amicalola, Nimblewill, Noontootla, Suches, Neels Gap, Cowrock, Jacks Gap, Tray Mountain, Macedonia, and Hightower Bald; *The Appalachian Trail in Georgia* (map and brochure), Georgia Appalachian Trail Club, Inc.; *The Guide to the Appalachian Trail in North Carolina and Georgia,* the Appalachian Trail Conference; Appalachian Trail–Chattahoochee National Forest Georgia, USDA Forest Service

Trail contacts: Georgia Appalachian Trail Club, Inc., P.O. Box 654, Atlanta, GA 30301; www.georgia-atclub.org
Appalachian Trail Conference, P.O. Box 807, Harpers Ferry, WV 25425-0807

Through-hikers on Blood Mountain, the highest point on the Appalachian Trail.

USDA Forest Service, Forest Supervisor, 1755 Cleveland Hwy., Gainesville, GA 30501; (770) 297-3000; www.fs.fed.us/conf; for specific Ranger Districts, see Appendix D

Georgia Department of Natural Resources; www.gadnr.org

State Parks and Historic Sites Division; www.gastateparks.org

Georgia Wildlife Resources Division, Game Management Section, 2150 Dawsonville Highway, Gainesville, GA 30501; (770) 535-5700; www.gohunt.georgia.com for hunting, fishing seasons, and general wildlife information

Finding the trailhead: The southern terminus for the trail is remote Springer Mountain near Forest Service Road 42. Since this area is difficult to reach by automobile, the recommended approach to Springer Mountain is via the access trail from Amicalola Falls State Park. This is a preferred starting point for all long-hikers because of the special parking area and the information available at the visitor center. There are scales available to weigh your pack and a register to record your hike with time, date, and destination. This trailhead is described below under The Amicalola Falls State Park Approach Trail.

There are a number of ways to get to the trail, including five major paved-road crossings. From south to north: Highway 60 (Woody Gap), U.S. Highway 19/129 (Neels Gap), Highway 348 (Richard B. Russell Scenic Highway at Hog Pen and Tesnatee Gaps), Highway 17/75 (Unicoi Gap), and U.S. Highway 76 (Dick's Creek Gap). A number of Forest Roads cross or end at the Appalachian Trail, and several Forest Service trails reach the AT. These approaches will be discussed here or have been discussed in other hikes.

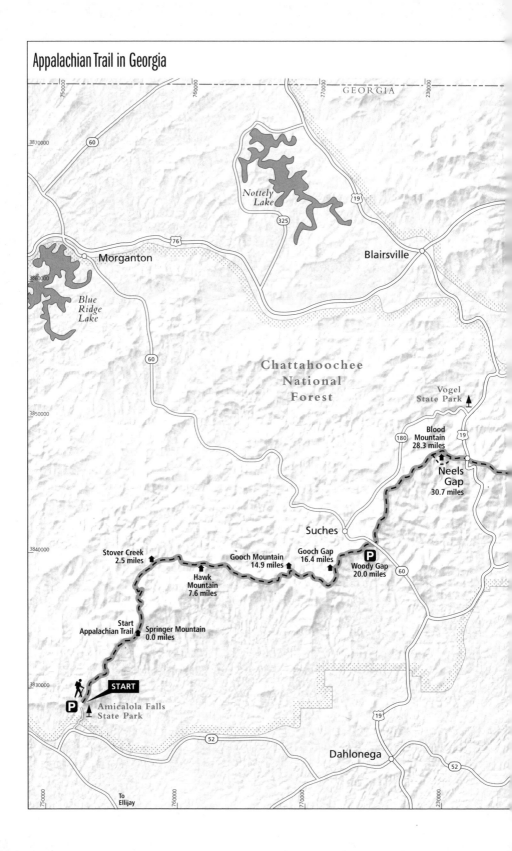

Appalachian Trail in Georgia

GEORGIA

Nottely Lake

Morganton

Blairsville

Blue Ridge Lake

Chattahoochee National Forest

Vogel State Park

Blood Mountain
28.3 miles

Neels Gap
30.7 miles

Suches

Stover Creek
2.5 miles

Gooch Mountain
14.9 miles

Gooch Gap
16.4 miles

Woody Gap
20.0 miles

Hawk Mountain
7.6 miles

Start Appalachian Trail

Springer Mountain
0.0 miles

START

Amicalola Falls State Park

Dahlonega

To Ellijay

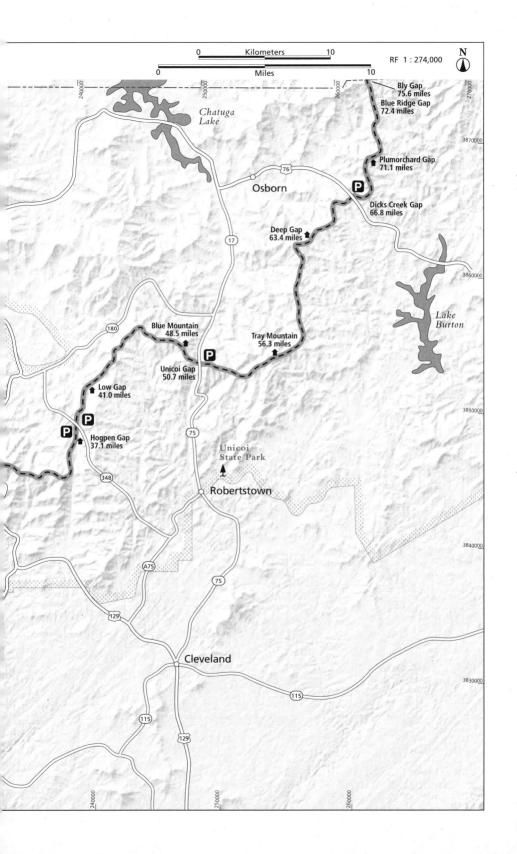

RF 1 : 274,000

N

Kilometers 10
0
Miles 10
0

Bly Gap
75.6 miles
Blue Ridge Gap
72.4 miles

Plumorchard Gap
71.1 miles

Osborn

Dicks Creek Gap
66.8 miles

Deep Gap
63.4 miles

*Chatuga
Lake*

*Lake
Burton*

Blue Mountain
48.5 miles

Tray Mountain
56.3 miles

Unicoi Gap
50.7 miles

Low Gap
41.0 miles

Hogpen Gap
37.1 miles

*Unicoi
State Park*

Robertstown

Cleveland

The Hike

A long trail concept along the Appalachian Mountains grew out of a 1921 proposal by forester and land-use planner Benton MacKaye. For sixteen years, hiking clubs, Civilian Conservation Corps (CCC) members, and many other volunteers worked to see MacKaye's dream come true. On August 14, 1937, the final two miles were opened in Maine, completing the 2,054-mile trail from Georgia to Maine. The trail has undergone many changes since 1937. Storms, changes in land use, and other factors have made it necessary to reroute sections of the trail. This is an ongoing process. The original terminus in Georgia was Mount Oglethorpe, 20 miles farther south than today's Springer Mountain.

A wilderness hike in rugged terrain along a clearly marked trail for many miles with appropriately spaced shelters, scenic vistas, wildlife, and a variety of hiking adventures and challenges on a world-famous trail make the Appalachian one of the most popular of all hiking trails. Spring and early summer offers displays of azalea, mountain laurel, rhododendron, and many other wildflowers. October brings spectacular leaf color. Mountain scenery that is hidden from view by summer foliage is open in winter, with many eye-catching vistas. The Georgia section of the trail is 76 miles long from Springer Mountain to Bly Gap on the North Carolina state line.

There are fourteen primitive shelters spaced about a day's hike apart on the trail. Most are three-sided and are close to water. The oldest shelter, located atop Blood Mountain, was built by the CCC in the 1930s. This four-sided stone structure has a fireplace and a sleeping platform.

Hikers use the Appalachian Trail in many ways. Through-hikers start at Springer Mountain or the Amicalola Falls State Park approach and plan to hike the entire 2,100 miles to Mount Katahdin in Maine. It is estimated that about 10 percent of them actually hike all the way, taking four to six months. The rest discontinue the hike at varying distances up the Blue Ridge. Many others hike only portions of the trail; still others hike only a few miles to some interesting point, usually using any one of the approach trails, or start at one road crossing and end at another. The beauty of the Appalachian Trail is that it seems to accommodate all. This concept is best described by the plaque on Springer Mountain that reads: GEORGIA TO MAINE—A FOOTPATH FOR THOSE WHO SEEK FELLOWSHIP WITH THE WILDERNESS.

AT Approaches

The Amicalola Falls State Park Approach Trail is the most popular trailhead for south-to-north through-hikers or for those who want to hike up to Springer Mountain, spend a night in the shelter, and return. This is a moderate to strenuous 7.4-mile one-way hike. To reach the park from Dahlonega, go 14 miles west on Highway 52. From Ellijay go 20 miles east on Highway 52. The trailhead is at the visitor center. The park has a special parking area for Appalachian Trail users. There is now an Appalachian shelter close to the visitor center for those who want to spend the night for an early start the next morning.

From the visitor center (elevation about 1,800 feet) hike the blue-blazed trail past the falls (2,600 feet) and into the woods beyond the lodge. Continue to climb along old roads for about 4.0 miles to Frosty Mountain (3,382 feet). Go through Nimblewill Gap (3,049 feet) and up to Black Mountain (3,600 feet), through another 3,200-foot-high gap where Gilmer, Fannin, and Dawson Counties join. The final climb to Springer Mountain (3,782 feet) is 580 feet uphill to the beginning of the Appalachian Trail. The trail then passes through a forest of the stunted oaks that will be seen at most of the higher mountain crossings on the way to Bly Gap at the North Carolina line, 76 miles away.

Jarrard Gap and Slaughter Gap Approach Trails begin at Lake Winfield Scott, 4.5 miles east of Suches on Highway 180.

Byron Reece Picnic and Parking Area is about 0.4 mile north on U.S. Highway 19/129 from Neels Gap. The trailhead for this spur trail at the parking area is about 0.7 mile from the Appalachian Trail, a moderate climb from 3,040 feet to Flatrock Gap at about 3,460 feet. To the right is a stiff climb to the top of Blood Mountain. To the left the trail drops down 1.0 mile to Neels Gap. Another trail, the Freeman Trail, takes off from the Flatrock Gap junction. It is discussed in the following day hikes section. The spur trail and parking area were designed to take pressure away from Neels Gap and the Walasi-Yi Center, where hiking and backpacking supplies are available.

Jacks Knob Trail provides access to the Appalachian Trail at Chattahoochee Gap.

Dockery Lake Trail is a 3.4-mile trail from the Dockery Lake Recreation Area. The recreation area is on Highway 60, 12 miles north of Dahlonega. The trailhead is at the parking lot for the picnic area. This trail climbs about 400 feet to Millers Gap on the Appalachian Trail. This hike goes up Pigeon Roost Creek, a tributary of Waters Creek. The trail is moderate along the creek and becomes strenuous in the last climb to the gap.

Miles and Directions

The following information will help you plan shorter hikes and orient you to trail and road crossings, with distances between roads and location of shelters. It is not intended to be a complete trail description.

The Appalachian Trail from Amicalola Falls State Park Approach Trail to Bly Gap, with checkpoint distances and elevations

Amicalola Falls State Park Approach Trail: parking area, food, and lodging at the lodge. From visitor center, 1.05 miles to top of falls; 5.4 miles to Nimblewill Gap; 6.0 miles to Black Mountain; 7.5 miles to Springer Mountain.

> **0.0 Springer Mountain.** Southern terminus of Appalachian Trail. Begins on white-blazed trail to Bly Gap, North Carolina. Elevation 3,782 feet; trail shelter; water; plaque and registration box.

2.5   **Stover Creek Shelter.** Water.

4.1   **Three Forks.** Elevation 2,500 feet; water; Forest Road 58; limited parking.

7.6   **Hawk Mountain trail shelter.** Elevation 3,380 feet; water.

8.1   **Hightower Gap.** Elevation 2,854 feet; Forest Roads 69 and 42.

11.6   **Cooper Gap.** Elevation 2,820 feet; Forest Roads 80, 42, and 15.

14.9   **Gooch Mountain Shelter.** On a short side trail on left; good spring.

16.4   **Gooch Gap Shelter.** Elevation 2,784 feet; water; FR 42.

20.0   **Woody Gap.** Elevation 3,160 feet; Highway 60; first paved road, parking area, and trail information sign.

21.0   **Big Cedar Mountain.** Good view from rock ledges.

22.9   **Miller Gap.** Elevation 2,980 feet; Dockery Lake Trail on right.

25.3   **Jarrard Gap.** Elevation 3,310 feet; water; Jarrard Gap Trail to Lake Winfield Scott.

27.4   **Slaughter Gap.** Elevation 3,850 feet; end of Duncan Ridge Trail; Coosa Backcountry Trail to Vogel State Park; information board with detailed discussion of hypothermia; water nearby.

28.3   **Blood Mountain.** Elevation 4,458 feet; no water; stone trail shelter; highest point on Appalachian Trail in Georgia.

29.3   **Flatrock Gap.** Elevation 3,460 feet; spur trail to Byron Reece Memorial parking area; Freeman Trail.

30.7   **Neels Gap.** Elevation 3,125 feet; Walasi-Yi Center with hostel for through-hikers only from March to Memorial Day. The center also has a hiking and camping outfitting store with books, maps, and snacks.

34.1   **Wolf Laurel Top.** Campsite and views.

35.3   **Cowrock Mountain.** Elevation 3,852 feet; vistas from rock outcrops.

36.2   **Tesnatee Gap.** Elevation 3,120 feet; Highway 348 (Russell Scenic Highway); Logan Turnpike Trail, parking.

36.9   **Wildcat Mountain.** Elevation 3,730 feet; Whitly Gap trail shelter is about a mile south on a blue-blazed trail; water; good views; Ravens Cliff Wilderness.

37.1   **Hog Pen Gap.** Elevation 3,480 feet; Highway 348; parking, interpretive signs and markers.

41.0   **Low Gap.** Elevation 3,032 feet; trail shelter; water.

46.3   **Chattahoochee Gap.** Elevation 3,520 feet; water; beginning of the Chattahoochee River; Jacks Knob Trail to Highway 180 and Brasstown Bald.

48.5   **Blue Mountain.** Elevation 4,020 feet; trail shelter; water.

50.7   **Unicoi Gap.** Elevation 2,949 feet; Highway 17/75; parking.

53.3   **Indian Grave Gap.** Elevation 3,120; Forest Road 283; Andrews Cove Trail to Andrews Cove Recreation Area.

54.0   **Forest Road 79.** Elevation 3,400 feet; Forest Road 79 leads down to Robertstown and Helen.

55.1   **Tray Gap.** Elevation 3,841 feet; FR 79.

56.2 **Tray Mountain.** Elevation 4,430 feet; trail shelter; water; rock outcrops and scenic views; only a few feet lower than Blood Mountain; Tray Mountain Wilderness.

61.5 **Addis Gap.** Elevation 3,300 feet; Forest Road 26; campsite; water.

63.4 **Deep Gap Shelter.** To right of trail 0.3 mile; water in piped spring.

66.8 **Dicks Creek Gap.** Elevation 2,675 feet, U.S. Highway 76; parking; picnic area.

71.1 **Plumorchard Gap.** Elevation 3,100 feet; unique trail shelter put in place by helicopter; water.

72.4 **Blue Ridge Gap.** Elevation 3,020 feet; Forest Road 72.

75.6 **Bly Gap.** Elevation 3,840 feet; North Carolina line; no road to this gap as you leave Georgia.

Day Hikes

There are several excellent day hikes associated with the Appalachian Trail.

The **Springer Mountain** area has two loops. The shorter loop is the Benton MacKaye Trail, with white diamond blazes from Springer Mountain to Big Stamp Gap and then to Appalachian Trail. Turn left and go back along the Appalachian Trail to Springer Mountain for a 4.3-mile loop. For a 10.0-mile loop, hike to Three Forks on either the Benton MacKaye or Appalachian Trail and return to Springer Mountain on the other. This trail system is reached on FR 42.

Woody Gap to Big Cedar Mountain is a short 2.4-mile out-and-back hike to excellent views from the top of Big Cedar. Woody Gap is at 3,160 feet elevation. The rocky overlook at Big Cedar Mountain is at 3,721 feet.

Blood Mountain is the destination from several points along the AT. It can be reached in a strenuous hike from Vogel State Park, using the Coosa Backcountry Trail to Slaughter Gap and up to Blood Mountain. From Lake Winfield Scott, hike up Jarrard Gap Trail to the Appalachian Trail, north on the Appalachian Trail to Slaughter Gap, 1.0 mile to Blood Mountain, and back to Slaughter Gap and down Slaughter Creek Trail to Lake Winfield Scott.

Hog Pen Gap to Wildcat Mountain takes you into the Raven Cliffs Wilderness Area on a 1.2-mile one-way easy to moderate hike. From the parking area at Hogpen Gap (Highway 346) go south on the Appalachian Trail to the blue-blazed Whitly Gap Trail. Turn south for 1.0 mile along the ridge to the overlook and to Whitly Gap shelter.

Tray Mountain is unique in both vegetation and geology. FR 79 reaches the Appalachian Trail east of Indian Grave Gap. Park here and hike 1.7 miles to Tray Gap and up the trail to the rocky summit of Tray Mountain, another steep 0.5 mile. Or drive on FR 79 to Tray Gap and hike the 1.0-mile round trip to the top of Tray Mountain. A much longer 8.0-mile out-and-back hike can be made from Unicoi Gap on Highway 17/75 along the Appalachian Trail.

More Information

Additional Resources

The Georgia section of the Appalachian Trail is described in detail in *The Guide to the Appalachian Trail in North Carolina and Georgia*. This book and maps contain trail mileages, water and shelter locations, side trails, and other pertinent information necessary to hike in the two states. It can be purchased from many local hiking and backpacking stores or from the Appalachian Trail Conference, P.O. Box 807, Harpers Ferry, WV 25425-0807.

Special Considerations

Because the route of the Appalachian Trail in Georgia is excellent black bear habitat, it is necessary to take the usual precautions with food at campsites. Hang food from a tree limb at least 10 feet off the ground, and do not leave food in your tent if you are away from it

for several hours. There is little physical danger from bears, which are usually only a nuisance at heavily used campsites.

Organizations

Georgia Appalachian Trail Club (P.O. Box 654, Atlanta, GA 30310; www.georgia-atclub.org) is a very active organization. They manage the trail through a cooperative agreement with the USDA Forest Service, Chattahoochee National Forest.

Benton MacKaye Trail Association (P.O. Box 53271, Atlanta, GA 30355-1271; www.bmta.org) has developed a great Benton MacKaye Trail with the same Springer Mountain trailhead but going north into Tennessee, eventually tying into the Appalachian Trail for a return loop. It is hoped that this trail will take some of the pressure off the AT.

70 Bartram National Heritage Trail

The 33.2-mile Georgia section of this long trail goes through a variety of habitat types, from high mountain ridges to the banks of the National Wild and Scenic Chattooga River. The Bartram Trail enters Georgia from North Carolina near Commissioner's Rock and follows the ridge crest that forms the Tennessee Valley Divide down to Warwoman Dell. It crosses the second highest mountain in the state, Rabun Bald, at 4,696 feet. From there it drops down to the Chattooga River and joins the Chattooga River Trail for 8.1 miles. You pass through one gap and around one ridge crest to the next until you reach the lower elevations at Martin Creek Falls and end this first segment at Warwoman Road and Warwoman Dell Day-Use Area.

Start: There are several ways to hike this trail. If you plan to hike the entire length, start at the crossing on Hale Ridge Road (Forest Road 7) rather than hiking up 2,600 feet to Rabun Bald from the Chattooga River. You can start hiking from Warwoman Dell near the middle of the long trail and go either east to the Chattooga River or north up to Rabun Bald.

Distance: Total length in Rabun County, 37.0 miles; 17.5 miles one-way from Hales Ridge Road to Warwoman Dell; 8.6 miles to Sandy Ford Road at Chattooga River; and 8.1 miles with the Chattooga River Trail to Highway 28 at Russell Bridge.

Approximate hiking time: A minimum of 3 days from Commissioner's Rock to Highway 28 on the Chattooga River; 4 days would be more comfortable. From Rabun Bald to Warwoman Dell, a long day, preferably 2 days. Warwoman Dell to Chattooga River, 4 or 5 hours; from Sandy Ford to Highway 28, 3 or 4 hours. All hikes require a vehicle shuttle with drop-off and pickup.

Difficulty: Moderate to strenuous in the northern section; moderate to easy the rest of the way

Elevation gain: Highest point, Rabun Bald (4,696 feet); Hales Ridge Road crossing, 3,280 feet; Warwoman Road crossing, 1,920 feet; Chattooga River at Sandy Ford, 1,400 feet

Trail surface: Dirt, rocky; rutted in places; some paved and unpaved road

Lay of the land: Mountainous in northern section; ridge and valleys in the section from Warwoman Dell to the river

Season: Year-round. The northern section of the trail is best spring through fall. Winter hiking along the ridge crests can be very windy and cold. The trail is open all winter except during periods of heavy snowfall. Rabun Bald is especially beautiful during the fall leaf change and in early spring when the leaves of the many species of trees are just beginning to show myriad shades of green. Masses of rhododendron bloom in early summer. The section of the trail below Warwoman is year-round. The Chattooga River is open to year-round fishing, including winter trout fishing.

Land status: Chattahoochee National Forest

Nearest town: Clayton

Fees and permits: No fees or permits required at Rabun Bald, Warwoman Dell, Sandy Ford, and Highway 28 at Russell Bridge

Maps: USGS Rabun Bald, Rainy Mountain, Whetstone, and Satolah; Chattahoochee National Forest map; page-size map available at the Tallulah Ranger District office in Clayton

Trail contacts: USDA Forest Service, Tallulah Ranger District, 809 Highway 441 South, Clayton, GA 30525; (706) 782-3320; www.fs.fed.us/conf
Bartram Trail Society; www.bartramtrail.org

Finding the trailhead: From Clayton go 6.5 miles north on U.S. Highway 441 to Dillard. Continue 0.8 mile to Highway 246; turn right (east) to North Carolina, where the road becomes North Carolina Highway 106. Go 7.0 miles to Hale Ridge Road in the Scaly Mountain community. Go 2.0 miles to the forks, and stay on paved Hale Ridge Road. The pavement ends; continue to the Georgia state line. The north end of the Bartram Trail crosses Hale Ridge Road (FR 7), about 400 yards from the North Carolina line. Limited parking space is available at this crossing. Because it is downhill most of the way, this is the best trailhead to use if you plan to hike the whole 31.9 miles to Highway 28.

Another access point with good parking is Warwoman Dell Day Use Area on Warwoman Road, 3.0 miles east of Clayton. From Warwoman Road at Antioch Church, 3.0 miles east of Warwoman Dell, take Pool Creek Road 0.6 mile to Dicks Creek Road. Go 3.3 miles to forks in the road; take right fork to the junction of the Bartram and Chattooga River Trails. This is Sandy Ford at the river. You join the Chattooga River Trail at this point and go northeast together 8.1 miles to West Fork and the Highway 28 bridge (Russell Bridge), where both trails cross the bridge into South Carolina. The trailhead for both trails is here as described above.

The Hike

William Bartram, for whom this trail is named, collected seeds and plants in northeast Georgia in spring 1776. He was traveling alone, after his Indian guide failed to return, on a trip across the Blue Ridge Mountains to the Overhill towns, where he

Bartram National Heritage Trail

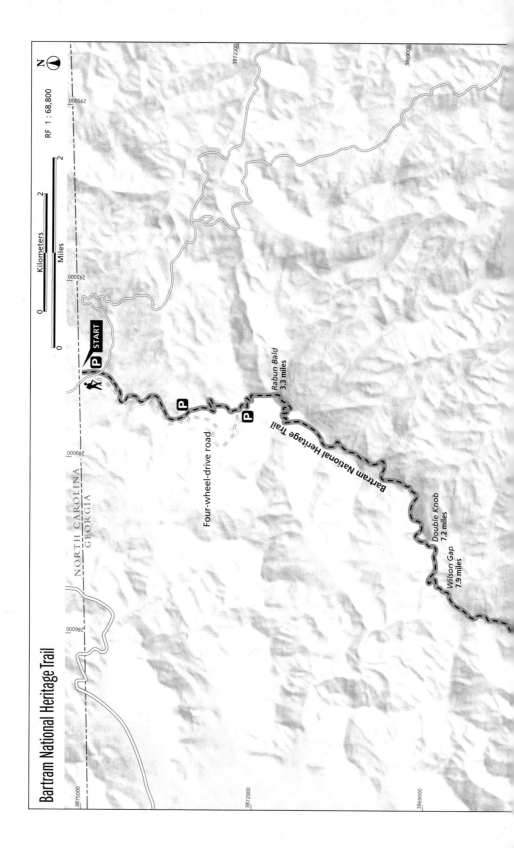

RF 1 : 68,800

Kilometers

0   2

Miles

0

START

P

NORTH CAROLINA
GEORGIA

Four-wheel-drive road

P

P

Rabun Bald
3.3 miles

Bartram National Heritage Trail

Double Knob
7.2 miles

Wilson Gap
7.9 miles

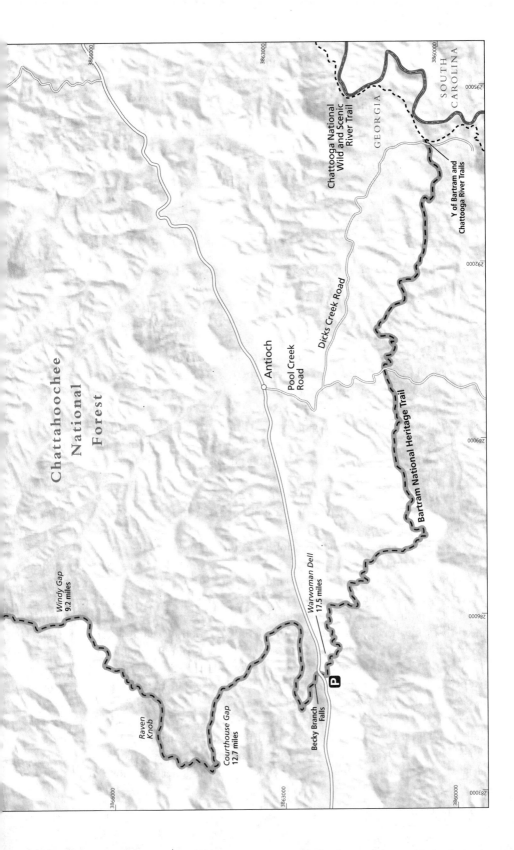

Chattahoochee
National
Forest

Windy Gap
9.2 miles

Raven
Knob

Courthouse Gap
12.7 miles

Becky Branch
Falls

Warwoman Dell
17.5 miles

P

Bartram National Heritage Trail

Antioch

Pool Creek
Road

Dicks Creek Road

GEORGIA

Chattooga National
Wild and Scenic
River Trail

SOUTH
CAROLINA

Y of Bartram and
Chattooga River Trails

visited the heart of the Cherokee Nation in Tennessee on the Little Tennessee River, now covered by the lake behind the infamous Tellico Dam.

Today very little of the actual path that Bartram followed is on public land. But the great expanse of the Chattahoochee National Forest has made it possible to preserve this 33-mile section of his travels. The trail continues in the Nantahala National Forest in North Carolina. Virtually all the forests that Bartram saw have been logged over time and again in the nearly 225 years since he rode his horse through the mountains. Although the great cove hardwood forests of yesteryear are gone, the high ridges that separate the Tennessee River Valley from the Savannah River Valley, supporting only stunted oaks and rhododendron thickets, may still look much the same. With the recovery of the forests under management of the USDA Forest Service, it is easy to imagine the magnificence of the original southern Blue Ridge Mountains as you look out from the truncated tower on Rabun Bald or over the valleys down to Martin Creek toward Warwoman Dell.

The Bartram trail was dedicated a National Recreation Trail on April 22, 1978. This Georgia mountain section is only a short part of a much longer proposed trail.

Begin the hike where the trail crosses Hale Ridge Road (FR 7), 0.15 mile from Commissioner's Rock at the North Carolina state line. This trail is marked by a rectangular yellow paint blaze. The elevation here is 3,280 feet, and the trail remains very near the same elevation to the crossing of Holcomb Creek before the climb to Beegum Gap and the top of Rabun Bald (4,696 feet). The last 1.5 miles of this climb is through a rhododendron thicket on a well-used rocky trail. The old Forest Service fire lookout was converted into a large observation deck by the Youth Conservation Corps. The 360-degree view from the stone-based deck offers a full, spectacular panorama of the many rounded knobs of these ancient mountains.

From Rabun Bald, the trail leads to the southwest, dropping rapidly to Flint Gap and to Saltrock Gap. Go to the east and south of 4,142-foot Flat Top. The trail drops quickly through a gap and up again to Wilson Knob and then in more moderate ascents and descents past Double Knob and Wilson Gap. Here the trail intersects a jeep road. The trail stays on the road for about a 0.5 mile and turns to the left and down to Windy Gap. After going around the east of Raven Knob, the path reaches Courthouse Gap, which is 12.7 miles from the beginning of the hike. For the next 3.5 miles, the trail turns to the southeast into the Martin Creek drainage. The trail heads back into thick rhododendron tunnels. The sound of falling water leads you to Martin Creek Falls, which cascades about 50 feet beside the trail before turning back to the west and to Becky Branch. Becky Branch Falls are described in Warwoman Dell Nature Trail and Becky Branch Falls Trail. The trail crosses Warwoman Road and enters the Warwoman Dell Recreation Area at 17.5 miles.

You now leave the higher mountains and meander over lower and more gentle hills and dells for 8.6 miles to Sandy Ford Road at the Chattooga River at Sandy Ford. This is an area of more open mixed hardwoods and pines along the higher, drier ridges and yellow poplar, beech, hemlock, and rhododendron along the shaded streams. This is a fine wildflower area in spring and, like the mountainous section, makes an interesting birding hike. Wildlife you might see includes deer, turkeys, gray squirrels and the less common fox squirrel, ruffed grouse, woodchucks, and chipmunks. Black bears, foxes, raccoons, and skunks are present but will seldom be seen.

At Sandy Ford the Bartram Trail joins the Chattooga River Trail about 100 yards beyond Sandy Ford Road. At this junction, look for the 2-foot-diameter rock with trail names and direction arrows carved in the stone. The trail from here to Highway 28 is described in the Chattooga National Wild and Scenic River Trail. Take the time to enjoy the wide expanse of the river here. Take the side trail and go down Dicks Creek to Dicks Creek Falls for a great view of the river.

The section of the Bartram Trail from Sandy Ford will be discussed with the Chattooga National Wild and Scenic River Trail. They join each other until both leave Georgia by crossing the Chattooga River at Russell Bridge on Highway 28.

If you have not already done so, read at least chapters three and four of Part III in *Travels of William Bartram* before hiking the Bartram Trail. Keep in mind that Bartram made his trip alone, with no previous knowledge of the southern Blue Ridge Mountain and only the barest verbal description of the topography to go on.

Miles and Directions

0.0 Start where the Bartram Trail enters Georgia at the North Carolina line.

0.1 Cross Hale Ridge Road (FR 7).

1.4 Pass through Webster Gap.

1.8 At Beegum Gap, pay close attention to the yellow blaze markers. A four-wheel-drive road leaves here that you will meet again.

2.2 Begin the ascent to Rabun Bald.

2.6 You are in the switchback path, with dense rhododendron on either side. The four-wheel-drive road from Beegum Gap ends here at a limited parking area.

3.3 Reach Rabun Bald and the sturdy observation deck. The elevation here is 4,696 feet.

3.6 At the edge of the Rabun Bald crest, a trail turns off to the left as you begin rapidly descending down the switchbacks.

5.1 At Saltrock Gap, you are on the Tennessee Valley Divide, which crosses Rabun Bald. You will follow on one side and then the other for about 6 more miles.

5.3 Skirt to the east of Flat Top without going to its 4,114-foot elevation.

5.8 Switchbacks begin your descent down to Wilson Gap.

6.4 Reach Wilson Knob (3,480 feet) and a beautiful view down the southeast over Indian Grave Hill and all the way to Warwoman Road.

7.2 You are east of and going around the two domes of Double Knob on a 3,470-foot contour.

7.9 Pass through Wilson Gap.

9.2 Pass through Windy Gap.

9.5 The trail on the left down Beck Ridge ends at Antioch on Warwoman Road.

10.6 Switchbacks head down toward Raven Knob on the right, after which you will leave the Tennessee Valley Divide.

12.7 Reach Courthouse Gap, and begin hiking east and southeast down Martin Creek watershed.

14.0 Listen for Martin Creek Falls on the left.

14.8 Turn toward the west now, almost paralleling Warwoman Road just below the trail.

15.5 Cross Becky Branch; turn hard left and go down Becky Branch Falls Trail.

16.2 Arrive at the end of the north, mountainous section of Bartram Trail at Warwoman Road.

17.5 Enter Warwoman Dell Day-Use Area.

Begin the following 16.7-mile section of Bartram Trail from Warwoman Road to Chattooga River by stepping down the shoulder of the road into the Warwoman Dell Day-Use Area.

0.0 Start at Warwoman Dell Day-Use Area.

0.1 Leave Warwoman Dell and continue on the yellow-blazed trail, heading east-southeast.

1.4 Hike up to Green Gap and turn left. Keep your eye on the yellow blazes. Avoid the several branching, unmarked trails on either side as you go toward the Chattooga River.

3.5 You have turned toward the east and are north of Rainey Mountain.

5.2 Reach Pool Creek Road after hiking almost due east. Cross the road, but stay on the right at the forks, following the yellow blazes.

6.8 Cross an unnamed old road. The trail turns to the left off the road, and work your way mostly downhill toward the river.

8.6 The Bartram Trail crosses Sandy Ford Road. About 100 yards beyond is the junction of Bartram and Chattooga River Trails. Look for the 2-foot-diameter rock with the trail names and direction arrows carved in the stone. The Bartram Trail from here to Highway 28, 8.1 miles, is described in the Chattooga National Wild and Scenic River Trail.

More Information

Food/Lodging

Dillard House, 1158 Franklin Street, Dillard, GA 30537; (800) 541–0671 or (706) 746–5348; www.dillardhouse.com/dining.html. This old family-style restaurant with mountain atmosphere and fine lodging accommodations provides a nationally famous dining experience.

Organizations

The **Bartram Trail Society** (www.bartramtrail.org) is active in preserving the history of Bartram's travels in Georgia and throughout the Southeast.

71 Chattooga National Wild and Scenic River Trail

This 16.7-mile trail follows the Chattooga River, which forms the state boundary between Georgia and South Carolina. Originating in North Carolina's Nantahala National Forest, the river flows through the Ellicott Wilderness and ends in Tugaloo Lake 50 miles downstream after dropping more than 2,000 feet. In May 1974, the river corridor was designated a National Wild and Scenic River. It is truly a wild and scenic area of mountainous terrain and beautiful streams.

The Georgia portion of the trail coincides with the Bartram Trail for 8.1 miles. The USDA Forest Service has standardized the blazes on both the Bartram and Chattooga River Trails. The Bartram Trail is marked throughout with a yellow paint blaze; the Chattooga River Trail is marked with a white metal diamond blaze. Where the trails travel together, both blaze marks are used.

Start: At either end of the trail; downstream trailhead, U.S. Highway 76 at the bridge; upstream trailhead, Highway 28 at Russell Bridge

Distance: Georgia section of the trail from US 76 to Highway 28, 16.7 miles one-way

Approximate hiking time: An ideal 3-day hike, with good primitive campsites and water; using alternate trailheads at either Earls or Sandy Ford in the middle of the hike, a pleasant one-day hike

Difficulty: Easy to moderate

Elevation gain: From 1,582 feet at the Highway 28 bridge to 1,208 feet at the US 76 bridge; numerous ridge spurs along the river, none of which vary significantly in elevation

Trail surface: Mostly sandy loam, with some wet areas; small stream crossings with and without bridges

Lay of the land: Mountainous stream corridor

Season: Year-round; spring and fall best with wildflowers, leaf colors, and bird migration; winter conditions, very cold to pleasant walking weather; year-round fishing in the Chattooga River

Land status: Chattahoochee National Forest in Georgia; Sumter National Forest in South Carolina

Nearest town: Clayton, Georgia; Westminster, South Carolina

Fees and permits: No fees or permits required

Maps: USGS Satolah, Whetstone, and Rainy Mountain; excellent large-scale detailed map of the Chattooga National Wild and Scenic River with trails available from the Forest Service

Trail contacts: Chattahoochee National Forest, Tallulah Ranger District, 804 Highway 441 South, Clayton, GA 30525; (706) 782-3320; www.fs.fed.us/conf and www.gamountains.com for general information; www.gohuntgeorgia.com for fishing and hunting seasons and other wildlife information

Finding the trailhead: Three roads provide access to the trail. East of Clayton, go 8.1 miles on US 76 to the Chattooga River for the lower trailhead (featured hike). For the upstream trailhead, go east of Clayton for 13.6 miles on the Warwoman Road to Highway 28; turn right and go 2.2 miles to the river at Russell Bridge.

The trail is accessible by two other roads that come to the Chattooga River about halfway from either end. Both are from Warwoman Road. To reach Dicks Creek and Sandy Ford at Antioch, take Pool Creek Road 0.6 mile to Dicks Creek Road. Turn left and go 3.3 miles to forks; take the right fork and go an additional 0.3 to junction of Bartram and Chattooga River Trails. For Earls Ford at the mouth of Warwoman Creek, go 2.2 miles farther east on Warwoman Road to Earls Ford Road. Turn right and go 3.1 miles to Bartram and Chattooga River Trails. Go an additional 0.5 mile, crossing the Warwoman Creek bridge to the river. These accesses are frequently used for fishing, boating, and other recreation.

The Hike

There are more than 50 miles of trails in the Chattooga National Wild and Scenic River corridor in Georgia and North and South Carolina. This hike covers only the Georgia section of the Chattooga River Trail, accessed from the US 76 bridge.

The Chattooga Wild and Scenic River Trail lives up to its name as a great rafting and kayaking stream, but there is so much more to enjoy in the river corridor, including good primitive campsites and excellent fishing. The area supports excellent wildflower displays in spring and summer. Wildlife includes wild turkeys, deer, raccoons, squirrels, and other small mammals. A variety of forest types—from old forest habitat to second-growth hardwoods and evergreens—make this a fine birding area.

This hike can be covered in a leisurely three-day, two-night trek and is ideal for a weekend. Since this trail is most often hiked in one direction and there is no public transportation, it is necessary to arrange for transportation at both ends of the hike.

Water is available all along the trail; however, you should drink it only after careful boiling, filtering, or chemical purification. The streams are highly vulnerable to *Giardia* and other bacteria causing intestinal diseases.

From the US 76 bridge, you follow up a blocked jeep road and cross the first of a number of small streams. This is in a good example of regenerated forest. Because the river was used to float logs to points to be transferred to land travel, the Chattooga River corridor was extensively logged during the late 1800s to early 1900s. There has been a remarkable recovery of the mixed-hardwood forest since it has become a national forest. Today you are able to see a wide variety of trees and other plants on this hike, including great yellow poplars as straight as a flagpole, hemlocks, the deciduous Fraser magnolia, bigleaf magnolia, hickories, oaks, maples, green and white ash, buckeyes, bass wood, and Carolina silverbells. The coves away from the river are resplendent with many spring flowers that bloom before the leaves are on the trees.

When the trail is close to the river, you have great views of this renowned world-class rafting, kayaking, and canoeing river. This is especially true at 2.9 miles, with your first good view of the river at the Paint Rock Class IV rapids. You leave the river for a while until at 4.8 miles you are again looking through the trees at the constricted river for about a mile. Then, after turning with the river, you are looking down at the Class III Eye of the Needle rapids.

Crossing Rock Creek at 8.0 miles, you are at the first road, unpaved Sandy Ford Road. Sandy Ford is popular because of the view of the river and because the shallowness and width of the river here make it great for wade fishing. Coming back to

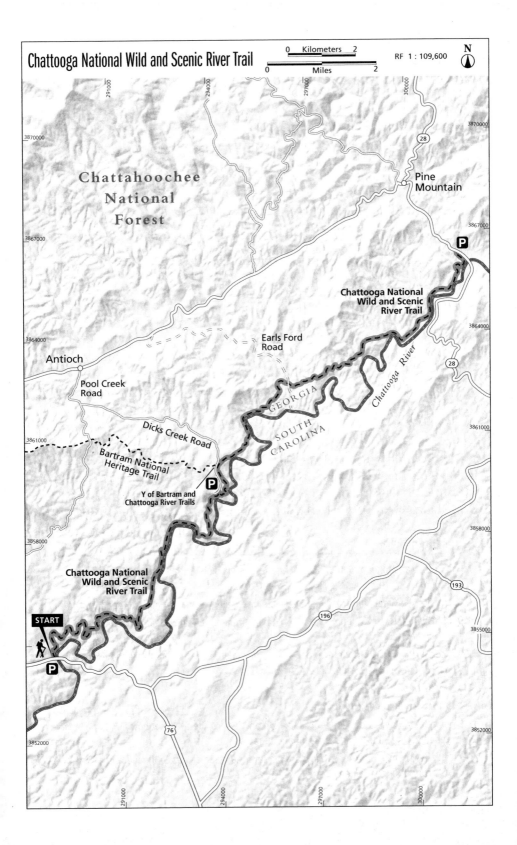

the road, you have the Bartram Trail on the left. It joins the river trail for the next 8.1 miles until they both cross into South Carolina at Russell Bridge on Highway 28.

Sandy Ford is an excellent primitive camping area. Stop here; take the time to walk the 100 or so yards down to the river and enjoy 60-foot Dicks Creek Falls and the grand view of the Chattooga. A submerged ledge across the river called Dicks Creek ledge creates a Class IV rapids as well as a great place to wade fish for redeye bass, a sunfish, or a stray rainbow or brown trout. There is a smooth sandy shore here. During summer, the river loses some of its trout water coolness and is warm enough for swimming and wading.

Bartram Trail joins here from Warwoman Dell to the west. A large, round river stone at this junction is engraved with direction arrows for both trails. The river trail continues upstream with the Bartram Trail and crosses Sandy Ford Road about a 0.5 mile from the forks in the trail.

At 10.2 miles you are at Warwoman Creek. Follow its meander around to Earls Ford Road and to the bridge over Warwoman Creek at 11.4 miles. This next section to Laurel Branch goes into one cove and over one ridge after another and is an outstanding wildflower path. Cross Laurel Branch at 12.9 miles. When you cross Bynum Branch at 13.6 miles, you should see several paths off to the left. Keep a sharp eye out for the yellow and white blazes. Very shortly you cross Adline Branch and walk beside Long Bottom, the only large, flat area suitable for farming. This area was in agriculture about twenty-five years ago. It is a pine plantation now. After you cross Holden Branch at 15.2 miles, you have only about a mile before West Fork and its bridge.

Cross the bridge at 16.2 miles. Stay close to the channel of the two rivers and climb up the bank to Highway 28. The parking area on the other side of the road at 16.7 miles is the Georgia end of the Chattooga River and Bartram Trails. If you arranged for a shuttle, a vehicle should be waiting.

Miles and Directions

0.0 Start at an old jeep road off US 76 on the Georgia side of the Chattooga River Bridge, where two large stones block access to motor vehicles.

0.6 Cross Pole Creek; turn right and begin the hike, going in and out of hardwood coves.

1.0 Cross the next small tributary and go through more coves and ridge points for the next 2.0 miles.

2.9 Come down closer to the river under a steep slope on the left, and leave the river again. (**FYI:** Enjoy a good view of a Class IV rapids.)

3.3 Cross one brook.

3.4 Cross another brook, hiking south.

3.6 Turn left and go north along this same stream, leaving the river that now flows in a steep-sided valley with falls and Class III and IV rapids.

4.8 The river comes back to you now as you have the steep slopes to the left and a view of the river through the trees.

5.3 Cross Licklog Creek on a bridge only about 150 yards from the river.

6.0 Turn right after crossing Buckeye Branch, walking close to the river with a steep, south-facing slope on the left.

6.5 Go up a steep slope and away from the river.

6.8 A path turns off to the right down to a sharp bend in the river, a popular place to fish or swim. You stay about 250 feet above the river.

7.6 Come back to an overlook close to the river and move away again.

8.0 Cross Rock Creek and the end of Dicks Creek Road at the place called Sandy Ford. (**FYI:** This is one of only two places on the Georgia side where you can drive to the river.)

8.5 Reach Dicks Creek Road.

8.6 The Bartram National Historic Trail comes in from the left. (**Note:** This is an alternate trail-head for both the Bartram and Chattooga River Trails. It is the halfway point between US 76 and Highway 28.) The trail will have both yellow and white blazes for the next 8.1 miles. (**FYI:** There are several good primitive camping areas along the river.)

9.3 The trail is a level walk to Dicks Creek; cross it by bridge.

9.8 Return to the river under a steep bluff on the left as you follow around a bend with the river in sight.

10.2 Leave the river along an old jeep road, with Warwoman Creek on the right.

11.2 Arrive at Earls Ford and cross Earls Ford Road.

11.4 After crossing a low knoll, cross Warwoman Creek on a bridge.

12.9 Cross Laurel Branch on a bridge. (**FYI:** The rolling path from Warwoman Bridge to Laurel Branch is a great area in spring for early wildflowers.)

13.6 Cross Bynum Branch. There are several paths off the trail; keep you eyes on the white and yellow blazes.

13.9 Cross Adline Branch on a bridge as you turn with the river and walk 0.8 mile on the ridge side of Long Bottom. (**FYI:** This floodplain is 200 yards wide, an exceptional floodplain for a mountain river. This plot of land was prime corn land as late as 1965.)

15.2 Cross Holden Branch and continue on up the river.

16.2 Cross West Fork, a major tributary of Chattooga River, on a nice bridge. The trail comes back down West Fork before you turn up to Highway 28.

16.7 Cross the highway to the parking area, the northern trailhead of Chattooga National Wild and Scenic River and the Georgia section of the Bartram National Heritage Trails.

More Information

Local Information

Visit www.gohuntgeorgia.com for hunting and fishing regulations and other wildlife information.

The site for the Rabun County Chamber of Commerce (www.gamountains.com) lists information on area recreation and dining, hiking and fishing, and other outdoor services.

Food/Lodging

Dillard House, 1158 Franklin Street, Dillard, GA 30537; (800) 541-0671 or (706) 746-5348; www.dillardhouse.com/dining .html. This old family-style restaurant with mountain atmosphere and fine lodging accommodations provides a nationally famous dining experience.

72 F. D. Roosevelt State Park: Pine Mountain and Mountain Creek Nature Trails

F. D. Roosevelt State Park is located on Pine Mountain. The long, narrow ridge composed of quartzite rock formations is the southernmost mountain in Georgia. The Pine Mountain Trail goes through all the habitat types associated with this unique and beautiful mountain. The Pine Mountain Trail system totals 37.6 miles of easy to moderate trails and has something for every level of hiking ability. The casual walker can find a quiet 1- or 2-mile walk in a forested area with grand views. The serious backpacker can test gear and physical ability and spend several days on the trail and never backtrack.

The Mountain Creek Nature Trail at the foot of the mountain around the developed campgrounds and Lake Delano offers an entirely different experience along meandering streams in mature forests on relatively level land.

Start: Mountain Creek Nature Trail, at the trading post in the RV campground; Pine Mountain Trail (west end), at U.S. Highway 27 and Highway 190; Pine Mountain Trail (east end), at U.S. Highway 85W and Highway 190; four connector trails that form loops off the main trail; at any of the six places Highway 190 crosses the trail

Distance: Mountain Creek Nature Trail, 2.8-mile loop; Pine Mountain Trail, 24.5 miles one-way; four connector trails that provide for pleasant day-hike loops, an additional 9.0 miles

Approximate hiking time: Mountain Creek Nature Trail, 1½ hours; full Pine Mountain Trail, 3 days; many variations of loop trails and alternate starting points, figure on hiking comfortably 2 to 2.5 miles per hour

Difficulty: Pine Mountain Trail, moderate thanks to numerous switchbacks that have eliminated many of the steep climbs; Mountain Creek Nature Trail, easy with two short moderate sections

Elevation gain: Lowest point on Mountain Creek Nature Trail, about 820 feet; highest point on Pine Mountain, Dowdell Knob at about 1,420 feet; west trailhead, about 1,000 feet; east trailhead, about 1,300 feet

Trail surface: Dirt and rocky in places; some short sections on paved road

Lay of the land: Low mountainous and hilly

Season: Year-round; spring and fall best for weather, wildflowers, birding, and scenery; hot in summer; rare snows for interesting winter hikes

Land status: Georgia State Parks Division

Nearest town: Pine Mountain

Fees and permits: $3.00 per vehicle per day

Maps: USGS Pine Mountain and Warm Springs; detailed map of the trails for sale by the Pine Mountain Trail Association (all funds from map sales used to maintain the Pine Mountain Trail); page-size map of the park including the trail, available from the park office

Trail contacts: F. D. Roosevelt State Park, 2970 Highway 190, Pine Mountain, GA 31822; (706) 663-4858
Pine Mountain Trail Association, Inc., P.O. Box 5, Columbus, GA 31902; www.pinemountain trail.org

Finding the trailhead: The park is in the west central part of the state about 25 miles north of Columbus.

The western trailhead for the Pine Mountain Trail is just off US 27 on Highway 190 near the Gardens Country Store. The eastern trailhead leads away from the paved parking lot and picnic area at the WJSP-TV tower, just north of Highway 190 on U.S. Highway 85W. The trail can also be accessed where it crosses Highway 190, which runs along the top of Pine Mountain. Three of the five crossings have named off-road parking lots. Paved parking and trail access is available at Dowdell Knob.

For the Mountain Creek Nature trailhead, take the park road across Highway 190 from the park office. Go 1.5 miles to the trading post in the RV campground on the north side of Lake Delano. The trailhead is beside the trading post.

The Hikes

Although the trails on Pine Mountain are very much like many of the trails in the mountains of north Georgia, the views seem to be much more panoramic because everything surrounding Pine Mountain is flat. The forest is composed of shortleaf pine, hickory, blackjack oak, chestnut oak, and black oak on the drier ridge tops. The undergrowth includes red buckeye, pawpaw, Piedmont azalea, sparkleberry, blueberry, and huckleberry. In the coves and moister sites, you can find sweet gum, yellow poplar, beech, and maple along with loblolly pines.

There are thirteen primitive campsites for backpacking hikers along the Pine Mountain Trail. Campers must use designated campsites, and campfires are permitted unless otherwise noted. Overnight campers must obtain a permit at the park office before camping.

Pine Mountain Trail

The Pine Mountain Trail can be started from either end or from several points along Highway 190. Starting from the television tower on the east end is a good choice.

Enter the picnic area from US 85W, which has space for several vehicles; a $3.00 per vehicle per day Georgia Park Pass is required. The trail is well marked with blue blazes. About 100 yards on the trail, there is a green metal box on a post that houses the trail register sheets. It is always a good idea to register when starting the hike. A register is also located at park headquarters. These registers give park personnel and the Pine Mountain Trail Association a tally of the number of people who use the trail. It is estimated that more than 50,000 hikers use some parts of the trail annually, coming from many states and foreign countries.

The trail is measured from west to east with stone cairns and signs at each mile. The trail crosses Highway 190 at five places, which makes it possible to park and walk sections of the trail from one crossing to another and return by road to the parking point. With the approval of the Department of Natural Resources, Pine Mountain Trail Association members have scouted out and marked the connector trails with white blazes. These connectors have added greatly to the variety of the

F. D. Roosevelt State Park: Pine Mountain and Mountain Creek Nature Trails

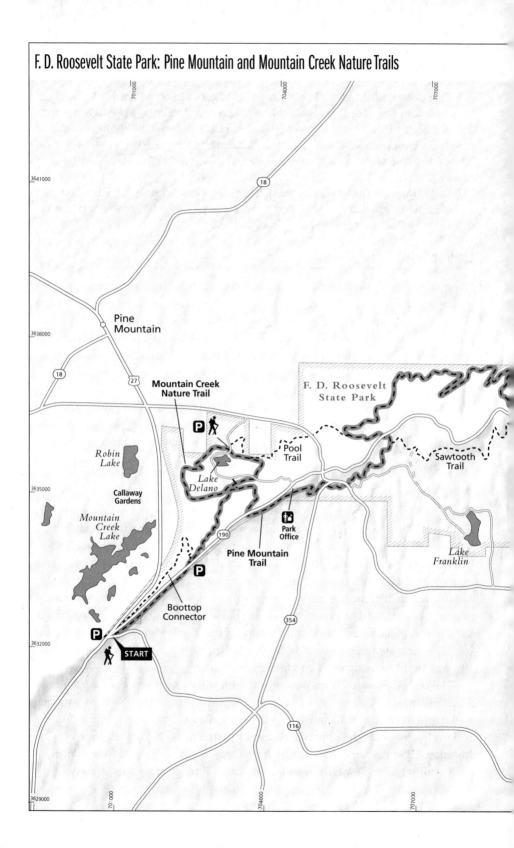

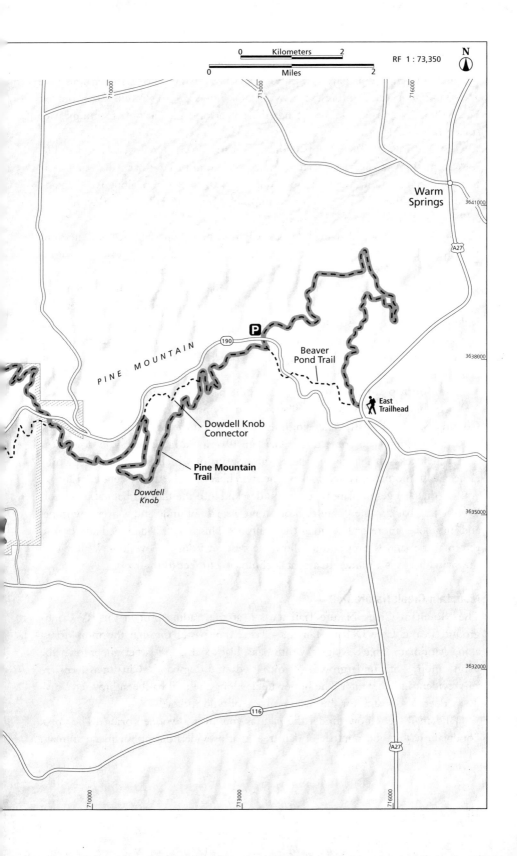

RF 1 : 73,350

N

Kilometers
Miles

Warm
Springs

A27

PINE MOUNTAIN

P 190

Beaver
Pond Trail

East
Trailhead

Dowdell Knob
Connector

Pine Mountain
Trail

Dowdell
Knob

116

A27

long trail and have added 9.0 miles to its total length. These loop sections make nice day hikes. All the loops have campsites, providing flexibility for an overnight hike and camping in secluded forest areas. Most of the sites are near ample water sources; however, it is necessary to use standard backpacking purification techniques for stream or standing water.

The 7.3-mile **Wolfden Loop Trail** starts at the WJSP–TV tower. The plant life, rock formations, streams, and waterfalls along the trail make it particularly interesting. Some of the most interesting rock outcrops and cascades are along Wolfden and Cascade Branches. Three primitive campsites—Sassafras Hill, Old Sawmill, and Bumblebee Ridge—are on this loop.

The 4.3-mile loop that includes **Dowdell Knob** is especially scenic. The view from the Dowdell Knob overlook is an impressive panorama. This was one of President Roosevelt's favorite places to go for a cookout. Information plaques tell of his visits. There is one campsite, Brown Dog, near Mile 16.0 and Brown Dog Bluff.

The longest of the connector trails, the 2.7-mile **Sawtooth Trail,** is between Mile Markers 6 and 11 south of Highway 190. This connector forms the 7.8-mile Big Poplar Loop and sports such interesting names as Rattlesnake Bluff, Indian Mountain, and Fox Den Cove. Big Knot, Beech Bottom, and Grindstone Gap campsites are located on this loop.

The **Boottop Connector** forms a 3.4-mile path on the north side of Highway 190 beginning or ending at the Callaway Country Store. To hike the loop from the Country Store, hike east, paralleling Highway 190 on the south side for 1.3 miles; cross the road and you come to the Gardens Overlook. Here you drop down several switchbacks on the steep slope, at the bottom of which is a spring seep and a rather dense mountain laurel thicket. The switchbacks make the descent easy and let you see the changes in plant types as you descend into the moister habitat. Then follow the trail back to the Country Store along a series of undulations over low ridges and into coves more or less along the contours. This is a well-designed addition to the total trail and is easy if you follow the descent from the overlook. Walking up the switchbacks is a moderate ascent, a climb of 240 feet to the road.

Mountain Creek Nature Trail

The Mountain Creek Nature Trail starts near the trading post in the RV campground area at Lake Delano. This red-blazed trail passes through the moist forest along Mountain Creek. Maples, white oaks, black oaks, and sweet gums form the main canopy, with undergrowth of sourwoods and dogwoods. Christmas ferns are very evident in late winter. The honeysuckle along the trail has been browsed heavily by deer. Also watch for the scratch marks of wild turkeys.

This small creek flows under the path as you cross a wooden bridge. The creek floodplain has a good number of den trees that provide housing for many animals, including squirrels, raccoons, opossums, and wood ducks. Look for tracks of raccoons in the wet areas beside the stream.

Alternate hiking trails make it possible to return to the trading post after about a 1.0-mile walk. You cross the creek on a footbridge and follow close to the bank of the deep-sided stream. Mountain laurel and large southern magnolias and loblolly pines grow close to the creek. Leave the creek and pass through an open forest of yellow poplars, maples, and oaks. A spring flows from the remains of the old Civilian Conservation Corps fish hatchery. The earthwork dams and stone spillway are still very evident. From here the trail crosses a service road that will lead to the Pine Mountain Trail not far from the Dead Pine Campground. The path climbs through a dry hillside to the paved road from the campground to Highway 190 and the park office. Cross the road and descend into another small stream watershed. The exposed stones under the power line right-of-way show the quartz crystals typical of the geology of Pine Mountain. The bottom of this north-facing cove is dense with mountain laurel. You cross a footbridge just before the 1.8-mile Pool Trail branches off. From here you pass the short Delano Trail on the right that goes around Camp Areas 1, 2, and 3. The last part of your hike is through parts of the camping and picnic area before you return to the trading post.

Miles and Directions

0.0 Start at the trading post in the RV campground.

0.2 Cross the first bridge over Mountain Creek.

0.3 With the creek on your left, pass thick brushy patches of bamboo and privet hedge that has escaped cultivation.

0.5 Turn sharply left as you follow the creek.

0.6 Turn left; cross Mountain Creek on the second bridge and then quickly turn right up the stream.

1.0 You are following the creek on your right in a more open woods of large yellow poplar, maple, and oak trees.

1.4 Come to the old earthworks and remains of the Civilian Conservation Corp fish hatchery. A spring flows from this site.

1.8 Cross the connector trail to the longer Pine Mountain Trail, with the parking area to the left.

2.1 Cross the paved park road that leads to Highway 190 and the park office.

2.3 From the road, descend into a small stream watershed. (**FYI:** Look for the exposed stones in the path that show the quartz crystals typical of Pine Mountain rock.)

2.5 The Pool Trail turns to the right and goes for 1.5 miles to the Pine Mountain Trail.

2.6 The short Delano Trail takes off to the right and circles Campground 3.

2.8 After walking on the park roads through upper and lower Campground 4, arrive back at the trading post.

More Information

Local Events/Attractions

Warm Springs, GA, www.warmspringsga.com. **Little White House Historic Site;** 401 Little White Road, Warm Springs, GA 31830; (706) 655-5870 or (800) 864-7275; www.gastate parks.org/info/littlewhite/.

Food and Lodging

Callaway Gardens, Highway 18/354, Pine Mountain, GA 31822; (800) 225-5292; www.callawaygardens.com. The Gardens is a 13,000-acre resort and gardens with dramatic azalea and other plantings along with Sibley Gardens Center, Day Butterfly Center, and Pine Mountain Birding Area.

Organizations

The Pine Mountain Trail Association is a dynamic group devoting thousands of volunteer hours to trail maintenance and planning. Their excellent Web site (www.pinemountain trail.org) is very informative.

Appendix A: Local Hiking Clubs and Conservation Organizations

There is a strong awareness in Georgia of the need to take care of the pristine environment suitable for a quiet walk in the woods or an extended backpacking hike into wilderness areas and the need to protect significant historical sites. This has come about in great measure by members of hiking clubs, conservation organizations, and concerned private citizens who are willing to spend time to work on trails and speak out for good land management. The trail clubs have spent countless hours of volunteer work to maintain the Appalachian, Benton MacKaye, Bartram, and Pine Mountain Trails as well as many miles of other trails. Most of these groups have monthly outings. In addition, organizations not specifically involved in hiking trail activities devote many hours working on forest and stream habitat protection. Following is a list of some of these organizations.

Atlanta Audubon Society, P.O. Box 29217, Atlanta, GA 30359; (770) 955–4111; www.atlantaaudubon.org

Augusta Canal Authority, 801 Broad Street, Room 507, Augusta, GA 30901; www.augustacanal.com

Benton MacKaye Trail Association, P.O. Box 53271, Atlanta, GA 30355-1271; www.bmta.org

Georgia Appalachian Trail Club, P.O. Box 654, Atlanta, GA 30301; www.georgia-at club.org

Georgia Conservancy Inc., 781 Marietta Street NW, Suite B100, Atlanta GA 31410; (404) 876–2900; www.georgiaconservancy.org

Georgia Wildlife Federation, 11600 Hazelbrand Road, Covington, GA 30014; (770) 929–3350; www.gwf.org

The Nature Conservancy, 1401 Peachtree Street NE, Suite 136, Atlanta, GA 30309; (404) 873–6946

Pine Mountain Trail Association, Inc, P.O. Box 5, Columbus, GA 31902; www.pinemountaintrail.org

The Sierra Club, Georgia Chapter, P.O. Box 46751, Atlanta, GA 30346; (404) 888–9778; www.georgia.sierraclub.org; www.sierraclub.org

Appendix B: Federal and State Land Management Agencies

State Agencies

Georgia Department of Natural Resources; www.gadnr.org.

Georgia Parks and Historic Sites, 2 Martin Luther King Jr. Drive, Suite 1352, Atlanta, GA 30334; (404) 656–2770; www.gastateparks.org. Information on trails, overnight accommodations, and special events in state parks and historic sites. A $3.00 daily or $30.00 annual parking pass, called a ParkPass, is required of visitors using state park facilities, including trails. Daily parking passes may be obtained at collection boxes in each park or at the park offices. Senior citizen discounts are available for the annual ParkPass.

Georgia Department of Natural Resources, Wildlife Resources Division, 2070 U.S. Highway 278 SE, Social Circle, GA 30279; (770) 918–6416; www.gawildlife.com or www.gohuntgeorgia.org. For information about trails, fishing, and hunting seasons and regulations on Wildlife Management Areas, contact the Wildlife Resources Division office in Social Circle or any of the regional offices throughout the state.

Federal Agencies

USDA Forest Service

The Chattahoochee and Oconee National Forests contain a number of recreation areas. Most of the developed areas are open from late spring to early fall; some are open year-round. These areas are developed for many different types of outdoor activities. A fee is charged for use of some of the areas. Information about trails, recreation areas, wilderness areas, and other features of the forests is available from the Forest Supervisor's office in Gainesville or from any of the District Ranger offices.

USDA Forest Service Southern Regional Office, 1720 Peachtree Road NW, Atlanta, GA 30367; (404) 347–4191; www.fs.fed,us/.

USDA Forest Service, Chattahoochee-Oconee National Forests, Forest Supervisor, 1755 Cleveland Highway, Gainesville, GA 30501; (770) 536–0541. Trail and Recreation Information: www.fs.fed.us/conf/; click on individual districts.

National Park Service

Southeast Regional Office, National Park Service, 75 Spring Street SW, Atlanta, GA 30303; (404) 331–5187; www.nps.gov.

National Parks in Georgia with trails:

Superintendent, Chickamauga and Chattanooga National Military Park, P.O. Box 2128, Fort Oglethorpe, GA 30742; (706) 866–2512; www.nps.gov/chch.

Superintendent, Chattahoochee River National Recreation Area, 1978 Island Ford Parkway, Atlanta, GA 30350; (770) 399–8070; www.nps.gov/chat.

Superintendent, Kennesaw Mountain National Battlefield Park, 900 Kennesaw Drive, Kennesaw, GA 30144; (770) 427–4686; www.nps.gov/kemo.

Superintendent, Ocmulgee National Monument, 1207 Emery Highway, Macon, GA 31217; (912) 752–8257; www.nps.gov/ocmulgeenm.

Superintendent, Cumberland Island National Seashore, P.O. Box 806, St. Marys, GA 31558; (912) 882–4335; www.nps.gov/.

U.S. Fish and Wildlife Service:

1875 Century Boulevard SW, Atlanta, GA 30303; (404) 679–7287. For trail and recreation information: www.fws.gov/southeast.

National Wildlife Refuges in Georgia:

Piedmont National Wildlife Refuge, Route 1, Box 670, Round Oak, GA 31038; (912) 986-5441.

OKefenokee National Wildlife Refuge, Route 2, Box 3330, Folkston, GA 31537; (912) 496-7366.

Savannah Coastal Refuges, P.O. Box 8487, Savannah, GA 31088; (912) 944-4415.

Appendix C: Additional Resources

Natural history and geographic guides are included in the following list, but it is by no means exhaustive. Many other books are available that deal with Georgia geography, natural history, and cultural history.

General

Appalachian Trail Guide to North Carolina and Georgia, Ninth Edition; Appalachian Trail Conference and Georgia Appalachian Trail Club, Inc.

Camping and Woodcraft by Horace Kephart; The University of Tennessee Press.

The Chattooga Wild and Scenic River by Brian Boyd; Ferncreek Press.

A Child's Introduction to the Outdoors by David Richey; Pagurian Press Limited.

The Complete Walker III by Colin Fletcher; Alfred A. Knopf.

Finding Your Way in the Outdoors by Robert L. Mooers Jr.; E. P. Hutton Co. Inc.

The Georgia Conservancy's Guide to the North Georgia Mountains, edited by Fred Brown and Nell Jones with preface by Jimmy Carter.

Georgia Rivers, edited by George Hatcher; University of Georgia Press.

Hiking Guide to Georgia's Rabun County by Brian Boyd; Ferncreek Press.

The Hiking Trails of North Georgia by Tim Homan; Peachtree Publishers, LTD.

The Natural Environments of Georgia by Charles H. Whorton; Georgia Department of Natural Resources, Bulletin 114.

The Thru-Hikers Handbook, 1993: A Guide for End-to-End Hikers of the Appalachian Trail by Dan "Wing Foot" Bruce; Appalachian Trail Conference.

Travel Light Handbook by Judy Keene; Contemporary Books Inc.

The Travels of William Bartram, edited by Mark Van Doren; Dover.

Waterfalls of the Southern Appalachians, A Guide to 40 Waterfalls of North Georgia, Western North Carolina & Western South Carolina by Brian Boyd; Ferncreek Press.

Wild Places of the South by Steve Price; The East Woods Press.

Flora

The Ferns of Georgia by Rogers McVaugh and Joseph H. Pyron; University of Georgia Press.

Native Trees of Georgia by G. Norman Bishop; Georgia Forestry Commission.

Trees of the Southern United States by Wilbur Duncan and Marion B. Duncan; University of Georgia Press.

Wildflowers of the Southeastern United States by Wilbur H. Duncan and Leonard E. Foote; University of Georgia Press.

Fauna

Butterflies of Georgia by Lucien Harris Jr.; University of Oklahoma Press.

Snakes of the Southeastern United States by Jeffrey J. Jackson; Cooperative Extension Service University of Georgia and U.S. Fish and Wildlife Service.

Appalachian Trail Videos

Amazing Grace, The Story of the Blind Appalachian Trail Thru-Hiker by Bill Irwin; Lynne Welden Productions.

Five Million Steps, The Thru-Hikers Story by Lynne Welden; Lynne Welden Productions.

Appendix D: Other Georgia State Parks with Hiking Trails

State Park Nearest City Phone Number	Trail Name(s)	Miles	Rating*	Blaze	Map	Features
Elijah Clark Lincolnton (706) 359–3458	Hannah Clark	3.5	E	White	No	Forest/stream
Hart Hartwell (706) 376–8756	Hart S.P.	1.5	E	None	No	History, scenic lake
John Tanner Carrolton (706) 832–7545	Nature	1.3	E	None	No	Mixed forest
A. H. Stephens Crawfordville (706) 456–2602	Beaver Lodge Buncombe ADA	3.0 1.5 1.0	E M E	White White White	Yes No Yes	Beaver lodge Lake/forest Wading pool
Hamburg Mitchell (912) 552–2393	Nature	2.3	E	White	Yes	Alligator, beaver habitat
Seminole Donalsonville (912) 861–3137	Wiregrass Loop	2.2	E	None	No	Wiregrass–longleaf pine habitat
Stephen C. Foster Fargo (912) 637–5274	Nature	1.5	E	None	No	Okefenokee Swamp, boardwalk
Fort McAllister Richmond Hill (912) 727–2339	Savage Island	4.36	E	None	Yes	Coastal forest, marsh views
Fort Morris Midway (912) 884–5999	Historical	1.5	E	None	No	Historic site, salt marsh, river

*Rating: E=Easy; M=Moderate

Index

Amicalola Falls State Park Trails 124

Andrews Cove Recreation Area
Trail 103

Angel Falls Trail 89

Anna Ruby Falls Trail 98

Appalachian Trail in Georgia 306

Arabia Mountain Trail 216

Arkaquah Trail 65

Arrowhead Wildlife Interpretive Trail 46

Aska Area Trails 167

Augusta Canal National Heritage Area
Trail 237

Bartram National Heritage Trail 314

Becky Branch Falls Trail 92

Benton MacKaye Trail 170

Big Hammock Natural Area 302

Black Rock Mountain State Park
Trails 149

Bobby Brown State Park 206

Brasstown Bald Trail 65

Brasstown Valley and Mountain
Park 169

Broad River Trail 163

Charlie Elliott Wildlife Center 205

Chattahoochee River National
Recreation Area 222–35

Chattooga National Wild and Scenic
River Trail 321

Chickamauga Battlefield National
Military Park 49

Chickamauga Creek Trail 24

Cloudland Canyon State Park Trails 35

Cochran Shoals 235

Cohutta Wilderness Area   170

Cooper Creek Wildlife Management
Area Trails 60

Crockford–Pigeon Mountain Wildlife
Management Area Trails 40

Crooked River State Park Trails 288

Cumberland Island National
Seashore 303

Davidson–Arabia Mountain Nature
Preserve Trails 216

DeSoto Falls Trail 57

Dukes Creek Trail 106

Duncan Ridge National Recreation
Trail 168

East Palisades Trail 223

Ellicott Rock Wilderness Trail 86

F. D. Roosevelt State Park 326

Fort Mountain State Park Trails 119

General Coffee State Park Trails 269

George L. Smith State Park Trails 260

George T. Bagby State Park Trails 255

Hard Labor Creek State Park Trails 186

Harris Neck National Wildlife Refuge
and Savannah Coastal Refuge
Complex 293

Hemlock Falls Trail 145

High Falls State Park Trails 193

High Shoals Scenic Area and Falls
Trail 82

Hofwyl-Broadfield Plantation Historic
Site   302

Holcomb Creek Trail 167

Island Ford Trail 232

Jacks Knob Trail 73
James H. (Sloppy) Floyd State Park 49
Johns Moutain Trail 27
Johnson Ferry North Trail 229

Kennesaw Mountain National Battlefield
   Park 235
Keown Falls Trail 27
Kolomoki Mounds State Historic
   Park 258

Ladyslipper Trail 168
Lake Conasauga Recreation Area
   Trails 52
Lake Russell Recreation Area 111, 168
Lake Russell Wildlife Management
   Area 163
Lake Winfield Scott Recreation Area
   Trails 76
Laura S. Walker State Park Trails 285
Leonard E. Foote Hike Inn Trail 127
Lion's Eye Nature Trail 98
Little Ocmulgee State Park Trails 272

Magnolia Springs State Park Trails 265
Mistletoe State Park Trails 196
Moccasin Creek Wildlife Trail 145
Mountain Creek Nature Trail 326

Ocmulgee National Monument 207
Ocmulgee River Trail 206
Oconee River Recreation Area
   Trails 172
Okefenokee National Wildlife Refuge
   Trails 298

Panola Mountain State Conservation
   Park Trails 213

Panther Creek Trail 114
Piedmont National Wildlife Refuge
   Trails 201
Pine Mountain Trail 326
Pocket Recreation Area Trail 33
Providence Canyon State Park Trails 245

Rabun Beach Recreation Area 89
Raven Cliff Falls Trail 108
Red Top Mountain State Park Trails 179
Reed Bingham State Park Trails 250
Richard B. Russell State Park Trails 183
Rum Creek Wildlife Management Area
   Nature Trail 205

Sapelo Island Trails 280
Skidaway Island State Park Trails 276
Smith Creek Trail 99
Smithgall Woods and Dukes Creek
   Conservation Area Trails 141
Sosebee Cove Trail 80
Sourwood Trail 111
Sprewell Bluff State Park Trails 242
Sweetwater Creek State Conservation
   Park Trails 208

Tallulah Gorge State Park Trails 154
Three Forks Trail 95
Tugaloo State Park 169
Twin Bridges Trail 176

Unicoi State Park Trails 138

Victoria Bryant State Park Trails 159
Vogel State Park Trails 132

Wagon Train Trail 69
Warwoman Dell Nature Trail 92
Watson Mill Bridge State Park Trails 189
West Palisades Trail 226

About the Author

A native of Chattanooga, Tennessee, Donald W. Pfitzer retired from the U.S. Fish and Wildlife Service as an assistant regional director of the Southeast Region after thirty-three years as a fish and wildlife biologist and public affairs officer. He has a master's degree in entomology and botany and has produced thirteen wildlife movies for television for the Tennessee Game and Fish Commission. In 1955 he originated and hosted the first outdoor television program in the Southeast, *Woods and Waters,* and has written many technical and popular articles on fish, wildlife, and nature in general.

Don is a member and past president of the Southeastern Outdoor Press Association and the Georgia Outdoor Writers Association. He also is a member of the Outdoor Writers Association of America, charter member of the Georgia Conservancy, and a member of a number of other conservation organizations. He continues to be active in environmental education, writing, and photography.